THE
FOOD

OF
FRANCE

THE FOOD

WAVERLEY ROOT

OF FRANCE

WITH AN INTRODUCTION BY
SAMUEL CHAMBERLAIN

Illustrated by Warren Chappell

VINTAGE BOOKS
A DIVISION OF RANDOM HOUSE
NEW YORK

Everyone who has visited France knows that it is a nation of hardy, persistent individualists. The French simply refuse to conform to type, whether it be a question of dress, of manners, or of politics, particularly the last. This quality of independence manifests itself with unusual emphasis in the matter of food and wine. This may seem surprising to those who have formed a conception of typical French fare. The genuine French cuisine, however, is an absolute tapestry of individualism, varying abruptly from one province to another, to the fascination of food-minded travelers. There is nothing "typical" about it.

Not that it is always easy to encounter regional dishes in France. A smoke screen of "international" cooking, prevalent in many of the larger hotels, often hides the local specialties from the exploring epicure. Such delicious standbys of French cookery as *blanquette de veau, pot-au-feu,* and *bœuf bourguignon* are usually considered too humble for inclusion in a sophisticated menu. Many hotels find it safer to cling to the easy expedient of beef, chicken, or veal, thus avoiding the risk of offending a clientele that might be distressed by snails, pigs' feet, *gras double,* or *tripes à la mode de Caen.* The adventurous diner in France needs the company of a guide, philosopher, and talented epicure to be informed of the treasury of noble dishes which awaits him in his travels. This is precisely what Waverley Root has provided in this closely packed lexicon of the bounty of France.

One can't help but marvel at the patience, the erudition, and the study that have gone into the preparation of this book, not to speak of the countless kilometers on the road and the convivial meals that Waverley Root has enjoyed in the process. It takes about thirty years of traveling to compile a work as complete and scholarly as this, and the author's reminiscences appropriately reach back to 1927. His long career as a much-traveled newspaper correspondent has made possible this revealing by-product. He knows France intimately, thoroughly, and affectionately, not only her cooking, but her history and geography as well. As a result, the attentive reader of *The Food of France* will be enriched by a wealth of background information to his gastronomic adventures. This is indeed basic reading on the good things of France, and how they came about.

This is not a book of French regional recipes, although the author writes of some specialties so graphically that a good cook could make the dish from his appetizing description alone. He delves deeply into the history of famous French specialties, however. The mystery of the naming of *homard à l'américaine*, the difference between *andouille* and *andouillette*, the patient preliminaries to a perfect *foie gras*, the care and feeding of Belon and Marennes oysters, and the subtleties of the three different *cassoulets* of Languedoc—all these remain mysteries no more. As for the controversial *bouillabaisse* and the moot question of populating it with lobster, many pages are devoted to a detailed account of its picturesque ingredients and the little-known *rouille* that provides the crowning touch.

The absorbing subject of French wines, the great Bordeaux and Burgundies as well as the unpretentious *vins du pays*, is treated with the skill of a veteran sommelier. The story of Champagne and the discovery of the venerable Dom Perignon is told in detail. An invaluable list of the good years in each wine region is given. Cognac and Armagnac, the two great French brandies, are no longer a mystery after reading this book. The story of distilling a thin white wine and aging it in casks of Limousin oak, and the meaning of such perplexing labels as V.S.O.P. and Extra are covered in admirable detail.

Introduction

Before conducting you through the French provinces, the author launches into an enlightening study of food in Europe. Why do poor countries raise potatoes and turnips, pigs, goats, and geese? Why do the British indulge in a big breakfast? Why do the French employ their essential fats—butter and oil—more wisely than their neighbors? The answer is found in the early pages.

Surprisingly enough, this gastronomic exploration begins in the Touraine, where the cooking has no decided regional character. But it is pure French cooking, in keeping with the pure spoken accent of the "Garden of France." All sorts of historical side lights unfold with this narrative on food. There are glimpses of Rabelais, Clouet, and Leonardo da Vinci, whose tomb is in Amboise. You learn how the art of pruning vines was accidentally developed in the wake of vagrant, munching donkeys. With restrained humor the author tells of Diane de Poitiers's hardy bathing habits, of Parmentier's popularizing of the potato, of the origin of the word *soupe*. On reading this chapter, one feels an overwhelming urge to head straight for the château country, to see Chenonceau and Azay-le-Rideau and Chinon, and to order a fragrant *friture de la Loire* accompanied by a cool Château Moncontour. It is a sensation repeated after reading almost every chapter, except a few about regions where the epicurean rewards are admittedly meager.

The author has his own excellent way of grouping the French provinces, placing the Poitou, Anjou, Berry, Orléanais, and Ile-de-France in a "golden crescent" of gastronomy. In this unhurried narrative he sometimes wanders far afield to the painters of the Ile-de-France—Corot, Daubigny, Monet, and Sisley—and to the Barbizon School and its enthusiasts. You learn that Lutetia, the Roman name for the settlement that became Paris, is not all complimentary, and that lark *pâté* has been made in the same pastry shop in Pithiviers for the past two centuries. Did you know that the name of the Plantagenet kings was derived from the fact that a nobleman of the Foulques family of Angers had the habit of wearing a sprig of heather in his hat? This book is full of surprising fragments such as this.

The flatlands of northern France are less rewarding to the epicure, and the author spends little time exploring them, except to tell of Champagne, "the most famous single wine in the world." But Normandy, rich in cream, butter, cheese, apples, and the fruit of the sea, is something else again. It takes pages to tell of this Viking outpost and the circus of characters who ruled it before it finally became French, and more pages to tell of Camembert, Calvados, and *sole normande.*

Brittany, the land of robust fishermen, hard cider, shellfish, tough pancakes, and mutton fed in the salt marshes, is a more austere land. You learn of the sweet plums that were named for the frail wife of Francis I, that the word "ostracism" has a gastronomic ancestry, and why Breton fruit-growers need no interpreter when they sell their produce in Wales.

Bordeaux, of course, opens up a vista of incomparable wines. The outgrown Classification of 1855 is discussed at length, and you discover why the label on Château Mouton-Rothschild reads *"Second ne daigne, Mouton suis."* There is an outline of the great vineyards and years, the subtle Médocs, the husky Saint-Emilions, and the golden Sauternes. Several paragraphs are devoted to the carefully regulated boundaries of the Charente region, which produces Cognac.

In the mighty dukedom of Burgundy you are given glimpses of history as far back as the ill-fated Vercingetorix and the Romans. Romanesque architecture comes into its own here, and this diversified account pays tribute to Cluny, Vézelay, La Charité-sur-Loire, and the cooking skills of the Benedictine monks. This is the land of *escargots de Bourgogne,* Charolais beef, Dijon mustard, and the *saupiquet,* an inspired method of serving ham. And, as everyone knows, Burgundy produces wines of unparalleled splendor. The author conducts a leisurely tour down the Golden Slope of wine, from Dijon southward through the Beaujolais, uttering only one unkind word along the way—to slap down red sparkling Burgundy as a monstrosity.

Next you are taken to the mountains where, it is said, a native would prefer a homely wife who is a good cook to a pretty one who is not. The Franche-Comté, noted for its crayfish, morels, *quenelles*, and *pocheuse*, produces a wine the color of red onion skin called *pelure d'oignon*. It is also the home of Pasteur, who had kind things to say about the healthy properties of wine, and of the *fondue*, the most friendly way of serving cheese. Here you learn, with surprise, how the crown prince of France came to be called the dauphin. In the neighboring Alps you encounter *gratin dauphinois*, a famous way of preparing potatoes, and superlative lake fish named *fera*, *lavaret*, and *omble chevalier*.

All this time you have been in the realm where butter serves as the basis for cooking. Crossing into Alsace and Lorraine, you suddenly enter into the domain of fat, provided by those two stalwarts of the barnyard, the pig and the goose. Here, for the first time, a foreign cookery makes itself felt. The German cuisine has long since crossed the Rhine, and you are in the land of sausage and sauerkraut, rolled tongue, and stuffed suckling pig. But there are subtler dishes too, including *truite au bleu* and the divine *foie gras*, most prized of French delicacies. You learn how Alsatian geese are fattened to develop their oversized livers, and how Alsace derived its name from a river call Ill. Neighboring Lorraine has less to offer in the way of gastronomic novelty, although its *quiche lorraine* is an accepted classic.

The pig still reigns supreme in the central plateau of France, but the epicurean outlook is not so rosy. In austere Auvergne the food is hearty but undistinguished, with cabbage, mutton, and garlic playing major roles. Limousin is a dreary place for the gastronome, but nearby Périgord, by contrast, is one of the choicest spots in all France, and a name synonymous with fine food. This is the setting of the beautiful black truffle and the home of the giant Toulouse goose, whose liver is as prized as that of his Alsatian cousin. The nearby region of Rouergue produces one of the world's most widely known cheeses: Roquefort. This chapter tells how ewe's milk is transformed into cheese in drafty mountain caves.

The tireless author next conducts his readers to Languedoc, telling how it derived its name and pointing out the beauties of its cities: Albi, Carcassonne, Toulouse, and Montpellier. One dish dominates all others here, the celebrated *cassoulet*. Its three classic variations are described in such detail that they cannot be forgotten.

It is in Provence that Waverley Root apparently feels happiest. Here is the stronghold of olive oil, garlic, eggplant, tomatoes, Mediterranean fish, and rich spices. The most poetic passages of this book are reserved for the olive groves of Provence and the thick, fragrant oil that they produce. The reader learns much about the "truffle of Provence" (garlic) and about the painters who have thrived here, among them Cézanne, Van Gogh, Renoir, Matisse, and Picasso. It is impossible even to sketch the highlights of this long, enthusiastic chapter. You learn about *ratatouille* and *aïoli*, *brandade* and *bourride*, and the difference between *soupe de poissons* and *soupe aux poissons*, which is considerable. The *loup*, cooked over vine cuttings, and the red mullet are two Mediterranean fish to remember. But one famous dish overshadows everything else in Provence: the immortal *bouillabaisse*. It receives a masterful essay of many pages before the author conducts you through an epicurean tour of the Riviera, ending in the ancient market in Nice. Here another foreign influence enters the picture, this time Italian.

x

Introduction

Pizza, cannelloni, and *gnocchi* from across the border find ready acceptance in the Comté de Nice.

Nothing essential is omitted from this remarkably complete book, not even much-neglected Corsica. You are transported to this verdant, mountainous island, where the food, except for native lobsters, is not exceptional, but where the scenery and seaports are unforgettable. They eat black crows in Corsica, and like them, and they have a frank enthusiasm for wild boar.

One more region in France remains to be covered, the Pyrenees. Here the Spanish influence makes itself apparent, as well as that of a black-haired people with a mysterious language, the Basques. This mountain tour begins in the Basque country, famed for its ham, chocolate, and a local fish soup called *ttoro.* You learn the derivation of the word "bayonet" and how to make the celebrated *piperade,* perhaps the forerunner of the Spanish omelette.

In the adjoining Béarn you are deep in the land of Henry IV, *bon vivant* and *vert galant.* You find why the gay monarch tossed a roast chicken under the bed of his mistress, Gabrielle d'Estrées, and read the story of his politically valuable *poule-au-pot.* The *garbure* of Béarn, a whole meal in a soup, is described in tempting detail. Finally, in the seldom visited Roussillon, the author of this scholarly volume tells of the influence of Catalan cooking, fragrant with garlic and herbs.

This is a work for posterity. It will be entirely reliable decades from now. Present and future generations will rejoice in this definitive treatise, the first written in English on an absorbing and heart-warming subject.

SAMUEL CHAMBERLAIN

✲✲✲✲✲✲✲✲✲✲✲✲✲✲✲✲✲✲ *Contents* ✲✲✲✲

Contents

Maps prepared by GUY FLEMING *from sketches by the author*

THE
FOOD

OF
FRANCE

Butter, Lard, and Oil

As far back as the records go, the people of the land now known as France have thought of food in terms of its taste more often than in terms of its nutritive qualities. Like the people, the sense of taste may have been somewhat crude in early times, but still it was pampered. The Celts were great users of caraway seeds. The Gauls seemed determined to shock the taste buds by mingling such ingredients as resin, mint, pepper, and honey in a single pungent sauce—which was natural considering some of the dishes then on the menu: heron and dormouse. When the Franks entered Gaul, they adopted the cooking they found there—perhaps because they were a ruder race with no culinary tradition of their own to oppose to the one they found, but more probably because food is a function of the soil, for which reason every country has the food naturally fit for it.

There is a harmony among all things and the places where they are found. Would you need to know the name of the Pekinese to realize that it was originally a dog from China? The peacock, and for that matter the common hen, are obviously natives of India. Where could the eucalyptus have come from except Australia? Food is a part of this general harmony. It could hardly be otherwise, for food, with the exception of a very few minerals, is made up of the living things, vegetable or animal, which spring from the soil of a region, the people of which are made, in the most literal sense, of the food they eat. A cuisine is not shaped so much by its consumers as they, again in the most literal sense, are shaped by it.

It is true that after the land has imposed upon its inhabitants the sort of food its soil is able to produce, and has persuaded them by its climate to absorb it in the forms and quantities that the weather demands, the inhabitants may then impose upon the preparation of their food some of their own more subtle qualities, which it may please them to consider as having developed independently of such gross functions as digestion. Although the sort of food which France ate in the days of the Celts and the Gauls and the Franks was determined by the nature of the country as much as by borrowings from Roman cooking, it might not have developed by itself, as a result of natural forces, during the Dark Ages, when all perceptions, including sensory ones, seem to have been dulled, if the human contribution had not been added to the natural one. Toward the end of the Merovingian era, say about A.D. 750, cooking, like learning, took refuge in the convents and monasteries, the only places where you could find a book or a decent meal, a fact that accounts for the stock characters of the jolly friars and the rollicking abbesses. The monasteries raised their own grapes and made their own wine. They brewed their own beer; many of them still do. We of the Lighter Ages still follow a meal with Benedictine or Chartreuse without stopping to consider the meaning of those names. When the fallow period was over, literature emerged from the monasteries, and so did cooking. No international ecclesiastical flavor had been added. From the cloisters of each country the cuisine proper to that country came forth. The land continued to form the food. The food continued to be intimately and inextricably involved with the geography and the climate and the history and the habits and the culture—in short with the entire environment —of the land.

The most obvious of the interrelationships between a country and its cooking is the construction of its menu in accord with the sort of food the land naturally provides. One of the most fundamental divisions in types of cooking is between that of countries where the basic cereal is rice and those where it is some grain like wheat or maize, most readily usable in the form of flour. The building up of a cuisine about one or the other was originally, of course, a matter not of choice, but of what nature could best furnish. The presence or absence of fish or game, of certain fruits or specific vegetables, is too patent an influence to need mentioning. Sometimes the influences are less apparent. For instance, is the fact that American cooking tends to be sweet a partial result of the use by American Indians of maple sugar instead of salt to season their food?

The effect of the soil and the climate on foods which bear the same name in different places, but may produce quite diverse effects on the palate, is a rather more subtle example of the kinship between place and kitchen—the ecological relationship, I suppose you might call it, between geography

5

and cuisine. Winegrowers are extremely careful about the variety of grapes they plant, but it seems to be the fact nevertheless that the nature of the soil, the exposure of the vineyards, the amount of sun, and the dosage of rain, have much more to do with the taste of the finished product than has the parentage of the grape. When phylloxera devastated the vineyards of France, immune vines from California were brought in to replace them. The wine from the grapes which stayed at home and that from those which emigrated are far apart now. In France, the Californian vines became Gallicized.

There is a theory that some regions make fine beer and other produce only an execrable brew because of differences in the local water. The water that cattle drink is also sometimes held to affect the quality of cheese made from their milk. Everyone knows the effect on the taste of meat of the sort of pasture available. Some of the most prized mutton in France is obtained from sheep that graze on the salt tidal marches along the seashore—the *prés salés*, which is the name you will find on the restaurant menu when meat from these animals is served. I once raised myself, on a farm in Vermont, a pair of pigs each of which consumed two twelve-quart pails of apples twice daily for the last two months of its life. I have never tasted better pork. It had a faint flavor of the fruit—built-in applesauce.

When the land gives its savor to the food it often also gives it its name. The most basic foods tend to be known by the names of the regions they come from. Everywhere in Europe the workman or the peasant fills his lunchbox with bread, cheese, sausage, and wine. Bread, probably because its (sometimes) simple and undiversified nature causes it to spread over a wide area, is less likely to bear a place name than the other components of the worker's lunch, though we do speak of French bread and Vienna bread. But for wine, cheese, and sausage, it is the rule that the name of the food is the name of the place that gave it birth.

This was almost inevitable for wine, the flavor of which depends so closely upon the place where it is grown that to name the place is to describe the wine. Anyone who drinks wine regularly can tell a Burgundy from a Bordeaux. Connoisseurs can tell you from what community an unknown wine comes. Expert sommeliers will locate the particular plot of ground within the community which produced a given bottle.

Most cheese names are place names: Limburger, Cheddar, Gruyère, Parmesan, and Roquefort, products of five different countries, all point to the localities where they originated. Sausage usually carries the label of its birthplace even when it is imitated in foreign countries which have forgotten that the frankfurter was invented in Frankfort and boloney in Bologna. The cousin of the sausage, ham, is also apt to be tagged with the name of the place it comes from—Virginia, Parma, York, Westphalia. These are all place names, owing in large degree to the local variations nature has imposed upon universally known foods, rather than to the particular type of processing the food has undergone. More artificial are the place names that identify an elaborate dish with the locality that applied a special treatment to it—on French menus, for instance, you will find duck offered in the style of Nantes, of Alsace, of Bordeaux, of Nîmes, and, above all, of Rouen (I have a cookbook that lists twenty-four ways of preparing duck, all ascribed to Rouen).

There is a point at which a geographical and an economic factor come together to determine the type of food of a region—a poor country, whether poor in money or in soil, will tend to eat the foods that produce the greatest output for the least input. The favorite vegetable in poor regions is likely to be the bulky potato, with which a good chef can perform miracles, but which in general does not encourage refinement in cooking, or the turnip, sometimes in very lowly forms indeed. The goat, which can live on pasture which would starve a sheep, tends to replace that animal. Instead of cattle, you find the hog, a most efficient machine for making the most meat out of the least and most unpromising material. And in poor country, poultry means geese—for while it takes four pounds of grain to put one pound of meat on a turkey and three pounds of grain to put one pound of meat on a chicken, it takes only two thirds of a pound of grain to raise a pound of goose. In warm climates, the whole nature of many national cuisines has been shaped by the fact that the olive tree grows on poor soils.

Nature determines not only what the menu shall consist of in any given region, but often as well what selection will be made from the various possibilities and how they will be prepared.

Eating habits are likely to be a result of climate. When I was a boy in New England, I thought nothing of starting the day with a breakfast of steak, fried potatoes, and mince pie, in the winter at least. I would not do it now, and I doubt if anyone does, even those who, at today's prices, can afford a breakfast steak. Those were also the days of winter underwear ending at the ankles and the wrists. The climate of New England, in spite of certain periods when it has been difficult to believe that this is true, has been growing milder for the past fifty years, and central heating has become more general and more efficient. It is no longer necessary to be padded against the cold inside the skin as well as outside. In the constantly damp climate of the British Isles, though the temperature may be higher, the humid chill penetrates, and there the heavy breakfast still holds its own. The weather of Scotland demands oatmeal. The Dutch, also exposed to damp and chill, eat diets heavy in fat (and still wear long underwear), and so do the Germans back from the coasts in the area of typical continental climate. But nearer the Atlantic coast, and of course all around the Mediterranean, where the more equable seaside temperatures prevail, you have the Continental breakfast of *croissants* and coffee and a cuisine that makes more sparing use of fats, or at least of animal fats, and of sugar.

The mention of fats brings us to another of the great dividing lines of cookery. We have noted that one boundary is drawn between the realms of two types of cereal—that of flour and that of rice. Rice is dominant, in general, in Asia and North Africa; flour is dominant in Europe. Within this cereal boundary, Europe (disregarding an Oriental infiltration in the southeastern corner) boasts three main schools of cooking, and this time the boundaries are marked in terms of fats. The Continent is divided among the domains of butter, of lard, and of olive oil. One reason, though not the most important one, for the supremacy of French cooking may be that within her national boundaries France has large areas devoted to each of the three types of cooking founded on these three types of fat. Though each area tends to adhere most faithfully to its own school, none is unaware of the others. Thus at the outset French cooking is gifted with the great asset of variety.

Strictly speaking, what is usually thought of as French cooking belongs to the first of these divisions—the school of butter—and its domain covers the greater part of the country. It includes what has always seemed to me the most essentially French area of France, the region that from the mouth of the Loire sweeps through the Touraine and up through the Ile-de-France toward the northern border; the two great wine regions, Bordeaux and Burgundy, where wine of course enters into and largely transforms the nature of the cookery; the peripheral regions of the Breton peninsula and the Norman coast on the Atlantic; Flanders and its topographically continuous northern neighbors; and the

9

mountain regions of the Jura and the Alps. There are two main subdivisions within the butter school—the *haute cuisine*, which is what has become international hotel and restaurant cooking and appears all over the world on menus whose French is frequently as bad an imitation of the real thing as the cooking is likely to be; and the *cuisine bourgeoise*, which you might translate as home cooking, though it flourishes in many a restaurant. It is hearty, honest, lusty food, the derivative, in spite of its name, of peasant cooking, and it provides such satisfactory dishes, often scorned by the snobbish, as *pot-au-feu*, *blanquette de veau*, and *bœuf bourguignon*.

The second most important of the three schools of French cooking is that based on olive oil. Its country is Provence, the Riviera, and Corsica. In the last two regions, it shades off into Italian cooking.

For the third school, I used above the word "lard," generally understood as referring to the fat of the pig, not wanting to say "animal fats" lest some purist should pop up to maintain that butter is an animal fat. I suppose it is; but I wanted to class together the fat of the pig and the fat of the goose, both of which enter into the same kind of cooking, not only because, as poor-country animals, they are usually found in the same areas, but also because they have a natural affinity for the same sort of treatment and the same sort of accompaniment. We can demonstrate this by reference to the bean.

There is something about shell beans that requires them, when they become main dishes and not mere side dishes, to be attended by the heavy animal fats. Boston baked beans, of course, are accompanied with fat pork. The dish is almost unthinkable without it, especially as a chief dish. The French equivalents of a complete main dish of beans granted the favor of elaborate preparation occur only in pork-fat or goose-fat country. In Alsace-Lorraine, you find such a dish as *potée alsacienne*, red kidney beans cooked with a rich assortment of pork products and sausages. In the goose-fat country, you get wonderful *cassoulets*, in which a smaller yellow bean is used, and while in some varieties the fat is all pork, in the Toulouse type it includes goose or duck. Incidentally, fond as I am of Boston baked beans, made, of course, in a large earthenware pot and cooked slowly overnight with its accompanying fat pork and molasses (especially if it is served with real piccalilli and not what passes for it in restaurants), I feel that I should offer some apology for seeming to put it on the same level with *cassoulet de Carcassonne*, which is likely to flavor its beans with fresh pork, ham, pork shank, cracklings, sausage, mutton, and partridge.

The fact that goose fat and pork fat both harmonize with shell beans justifies, I think, their bracketing as belonging basically to the same type of cooking. I cannot think of any similar bean dishes in the butter school. There you are most likely to be served string beans, with a little butter and chopped parsley—a side dish, not a main dish. The same treatment is given to the more rarely offered shell beans—*fèves* (fava beans, something like the lima, itself unknown in France) and *soissons*, white beans served usually with mutton. In the olive oil country, you do not meet shell beans much either, and not in main dishes; there the chickpea is more apt to enter into elaborate combinations with other ingredients to make a complicated dish.

The animal-fat centers of France are Alsace-Lorraine, where the cuisine approaches that of Germany across the Rhine, but is somewhat spiritualized by the French touch, and the Central Plateau region, of which the Périgord is gastronomically the most famous area. In Alsace the pig dominates, but the goose runs it a close second. In the Périgord the order is reversed, with goose an important item on the menu. Both Strasbourg (Alsace) and Périgueux (Péri-

gord) are renowned for their *pâté de foie gras* with truffles, a product of co-operation, the goose supplying the
liver and the pig rooting up the truffles to garnish it.

The French have no monopoly on the basic fats whose
employment determines to a great extent the nature of the
food cooked in it. The Danes, the Dutch, and the Belgians
have plenty of butter (the last named give you so much
of it that you risk disliking it in the end); the Germans
use pig and goose fat extensively; the Greeks, the Italians,
and the Spaniards wallow in olive oil. How does it happen
that none of them gets the results that the French seem to
be able to produce at will with all three?

Here is where nature gives way and the human being
takes over. French food is what it is in large part because
nature set things up that way, but it is also what it is because of the kind of man the Frenchman is and the sort of
culture he has exposed himself to. Here the term "the
Frenchman" must be understood as representing a compos-
ite, hypothetical, and, in any single individual example,
probably nonexistent being. "The Frenchman" is a many-
sided individual, by which I mean that there are many very
different kinds of individual Frenchmen, so that when you
try to add them together into a single generalization, you
come up with a complicated and highly inconsistent creation. Consider how many different racial stocks have been
brought together within these borders, and what is more
important, within this single culture pattern: the Celtic
Bretons, speaking a language almost identical with Welsh;
the Normans, who came originally from Scandinavia; the
Alsatians, whose patois is more German than French; the
Auvergnats, whose typically swarthy appearance is sometimes attributed (probably in error) to Saracen blood; the
Italianate French of the Riviera and Corsica; the Catalans,
with a language related to Spanish; the Basques, with a language related to nothing; and even a few who for want of

a more precise description can be identified only as French. Yet all of these disparate elements, even those of strong local cultures, like the Basques and the Bretons, have been thoroughly knit together by the major dominant pattern of the French language and French culture.

Perhaps the very diversity of this mixture accounts for one of the most fundamental traits of French civilization as we have it today, the classic French quality of "measure" —the following of a golden mean, the avoidance of excess and extravagance, the guarding of a just sense of proportion. For every tendency brought into the French stream of culture from one source an opposite counteracting tendency has been brought in from another source; each acts as a brake upon the other. In whatever direction you look, whatever realm you inspect, French life seems to be compounded of opposites. You might expect them to annul each other, but they do not; they enrich each other.

Thus the Parisian represents, and with reason, the most urban of men. But he is an urbanite with a taproot thrust deep into the soil. It is hard to find a city-dweller in France who has not somewhere in the provinces a parcel of land to which he is strongly attached and to which, very often, it is his dream at last to retire. There is a peasant beneath the surface of every urban Frenchman; and the peasant, who lives at the source of food, though he may be careless of all other living comforts, usually manages to eat well. No city restaurant can match the *pot-au-feu* of the French farmhouse, where the kettle has been simmering on the back of the stove for years, never being allowed to cool off, constantly being replenished with new ingredients, changing with the seasons. Progress is threatening this dish. Whenever the wood stove, kept constantly burning at no expense with fuel provided by the debris of the farm, gives way to gas or oil or electricity, the immortal *pot-au-feu* disappears.

The urban Frenchman retains his rural roots in part because of the nature of the French family, closely knit but widely spread. It includes cousins of the farthest degree, and the migrants to the cities do not lose contact with blood relatives who remain on the soil. Sometimes the family is so self-sufficient a society that the Frenchman hardly ventures outside it. It is large enough to satisfy all his social needs. It is notorious that he rarely invites non-members of the family to his home: them he meets in a café or a restaurant. But the family gathers in strength at frequent intervals; and in all countries, family reunions are occasions for feasting. So to the solid tradition of country cooking and the habit of making food a festive matter, the urbanized Frenchman adds the refinements of city style, and there you have one basis for great cooking.

There are others, born also out of contradictions in the French character. From abroad, France appears as the leader of Western culture and civilization. So indeed she is, but the distant view reveals only the top of the iceberg, whose massive submerged base remains unsuspected. If France is universally the country of unfailing taste, how do you account for French hotel wallpaper? The fact is that France is not only one of the greatest artistic and intellectual countries in the world; it is also one of the most bourgeois countries in the world. These two tendencies, so hostile in some settings, marry perfectly in the kitchen. What art ministers more directly to the bourgeois ideal of comfortable living than that of gastronomy?

The Frenchman is an individualist. On its reverse side (every virtue is accompanied by its inseparable vices) this may make him selfish and an egotist. He is thus enabled to be unforgiving if he is badly served. His favorite restaurant may have produced for him a thousand superb meals one after the other, but let the thousand and first be unsatisfactory and he rises in wrath to denounce incompetence. I would rather he did not so when I am present, but I am glad that France is full of his kind to keep French cooks up to snuff. We all know what happens to the perfect little restaurant that is discovered by tourists not educated by a lifetime of exposure to French food to the detection of minor imperfections. When it discovers that it can fill its tables quite as readily without taking nearly as many pains in the kitchen—and to the accompaniment of enthusiastic, if ill-informed, praise at that—it proceeds, naturally enough, to take less pains in the kitchen. We need the angry gourmet to keep standards up. They are falling fast enough as it is under the impact of economic changes that have been killing off the great restaurants of France one after the other. Foyot is gone, Voisin is gone, the Café de Paris is a casualty of yesterday, and Larue has suffered the crowning indignity of being replaced by a café-like establishment that refers to itself as Queenie. But who today can afford, even if he has a fine enough palate to tell the difference, to insist that the Cognac poured over the burning fennel twigs above which a *loup* is being grilled should be *grande fine champagne* instead of ordinary cooking brandy? We are doomed in any case to abandon some of the ultrarefinements of gastronomy for the overpowering reason that no one any longer can afford to pay for them. This is one more example of the dependence of a cuisine on the society within which it is exercised.

It is dependent also on the gastronomic traditions of the society and the education of its members. Every country possesses, it seems, the sort of cuisine it deserves, which is to say the sort of cuisine it is appreciative enough to want. I used to think that the notoriously bad cooking of England was an example to the contrary, and that the English cook the way they do because, through sheer technical deficiency, they had not been able to master the art of cooking. I have discovered to my stupefaction that the English cook that way because that is the way they like it. This leaves nothing to be said, as I suppose the rule that there can be no argument about matters of taste applies to absence of taste—in the literal sense—as well.

Social habit would thus explain also the monotony of diet in large areas of the United States. I have been in regions where there was hardly any divergence from the standard meal of steak, potatoes, and apple pie—all excellent things in their way, but which, as the menu twice a day, seven days a week, I should think would finally become as tasteless as water. Perhaps this is the ideal. I once worked in New York with a young man whose noon lunch was invariable—a sandwich composed of the rather startling combination of peanut butter and jelly. I tried once to persuade him to a change of diet, and he gave me the first good explanation of such eating habits I have ever heard. "What difference does it make what I order?" he asked. "I don't like to eat."

This may account for a lack of adventurousness in exploring any but the most obvious foods, a lack I have often noticed in my compatriots. In other cases, it is not a question of timidity in essaying the unknown because it might prove to be unpleasant, but simple fear of being poisoned —by foods which millions of persons have been eating for thousands of years. I remember one American woman who came to dinner with me in Rockport, Massachusetts, and was served a French dish that she praised highly. It was clear that she really liked it, which is far from true of many Americans confronted with the unfamiliar on the dining table; but she didn't know what it was. When she asked me, I imagine I would have done better to have said "Rattlesnake," but I told the truth and answered "Rabbit." She became ill.

Then there was the American naval wife I met in Villefranche-sur-Mer the day after Thanksgiving. We had maintained tradition and dined on turkey with cranberry sauce,

the last an item not easily come by in France (the cranberry exists, but I have yet to meet a French citizen who
knows the name for it—*canneberge*, which grows on marshy
land, or *airelle*, a dry-land variation of it), and so I asked
her if she had eaten turkey. She said no, that her family had
settled for duck. Duck, I remarked, was a noble dish, but
I had been brought up to associate Thanksgiving with turkey and felt cheated if I did not get it. She agreed, but explained she had been so late in ordering that only duck
remained among the canned goods of the ship's stores. I
think I was shocked at this.

"*Canned* duck?" I echoed. "You mean that you ate
canned duck for Thanksgiving? Why, the market at Nice
is full of fresh duck—and chicken, goose, guinea hen, turkey—anything you want!"

"Oh, none of us buy anything *here!*" she told me. "None
of the Navy wives do. We wouldn't dare! Why even as it
is, we all have dysentery!"

"What do you attribute it to?" I asked.

"You know," she confided, "it's the strangest thing! We
just can't figure it out. We can't think of *any*thing we've
eaten that didn't come off the ship."

I suppose we used up all our spirit of adventure on the
frontier.

Eating habits are part of our social habits, part of our culture, part of the environment, mental and physical, in which
we live. In this book I propose to look upon the food of
France as an integral and inseparable element in the whole
pattern of the society in which it has developed.

THE
DOMAIN

OF
BUTTER

The Touraine

The Touraine is the heartland of France. It was here, as much as in any other single locality, that the subtle, clear, precise language of modern France developed, and here also, fittingly, that the subtle, fine, expert cooking of modern France developed. These are only two of France's glories, and they are glories of the Touraine as well. Of France's other claims to fame, the Touraine shares many.

The Touraine is a tiny land. It is encompassed entirely within the borders of the present department of the Indre-et-Loire, itself a mere 2,375 square miles, no more than one ninetieth of France, which has room besides to contain out-croppings of Anjou, Poitou, and the Orléanais.

Much of France's genius has been concentrated in this

small area. Indeed, when one considers the extent of the debt that France owes to the Touraine, it seems almost accidental that the land of France is not called Touraine, that the capital of France is not Tours.

The decisive accident, perhaps, was the existence in the Seine, at the spot now known as Paris, of an island large enough to hold a settlement and small enough to serve as a citadel, with the Seine as its natural moat. Tours was guarded by the Loire on one side only, and the Loire is a capricious river, reduced often to a mere trickle of water threading its bed of sand. Yet the Loire is the longest river of France. Indeed the Seine might be called the Loire today if the river of Tours had not seceded from it in prehistoric times. Once the Loire flowed through what is now the valley of the Loing, a tributary of the Seine; in those days the Seine was a tributary of the Loire.

It was Clovis who named Paris his capital. He looms large in the history of the Touraine as well. It was at Amboise, 17 miles from Tours, that Clovis, in the year 500, joined in celebrating a spectacular feast with Alaric II, King of the Visigoths, whom he was to kill seven years later in Poitou, just south of the Touraine.

Many other kings of France erected palaces in the Touraine. In the year that Columbus discovered America, the Château of Amboise was built by Charles VIII, and it was there that he died. Amboise was a favorite also of Francis I. The magnificent spectacles he produced in its courtyard included fights among wild animals; when a boar escaped from the arena and plunged into the château, it was the King himself who transfixed it with a spear. Louis XIV used Amboise as a prison. It is the property today of the royal family, for its owner is the Comte de Paris, pretender to the French throne, who has no palace in Paris.

Chinon was the residence of the court in the first half of the fifteenth century. Louis XI built the Château of

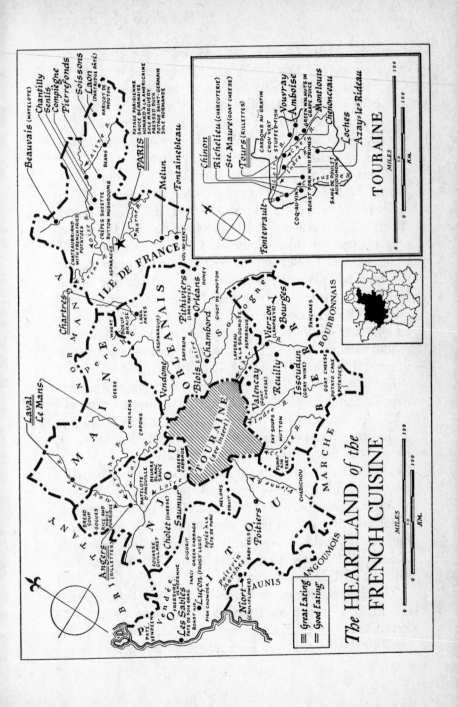

The HEARTLAND of the
FRENCH CUISINE

≡ Great Eating
= Good Eating

TOURAINE

Chinon
Richelieu (CHARCUTERIE)
St. Maure (GOAT CHEESE)
Tours (RILLETTES)
Vouvray
Amboise
Montlouis
Chenonceau
Loches
Azay-le-Rideau
Fontevrault

CARDONS AU GRATIN
CHOU VERT
STUFFED FISH
GREEN WALNUTS IN
GRAPE JUICE
COQ-AU-VIN
ROAST PORK WITH PRUNES
SANG DE POULET
AU DEMI-DEUIL

MILES
KM.

ILE DE FRANCE

Beauvais (MATELOTE)
Chantilly
Senlis
Compiègne
Pierrefonds
Soissons
Laon (PARTRIDGE PÂTÉ)

POTAGE PARISIENNE
SAUCE BÉARNAISE
HOMARD À LA AMERICAINE
SOLE MARGUERY
SOLE NORMANDE
POTAGE SAINT-GERMAIN

HARICOT DE
MOUTON

BEANS

PARIS

CRÊPES SUZETTE
BUTTON MUSHROOMS

CHATEAUBRIAND
WITH FRENCH FRIED
POTATOES

ASPARAGUS

Melun
Fontainebleau

Chartres

NORMANDY

WHEAT

BŒUF
BRAISÉ

GEESE

CHICKENS

CAPONS

MAINE

Laval
Le Mans

BREAD SOUP
BOGUES
RICE AND
MAIZE
PORRIDGE

Angers (RILLETTES)

BRITTANY

Vendée
Oiresiève
GUILLARET
POUASSE À
LA GUILLARET

Les Sablés

Luçon (FROG'S LEGS)

Niort (CAULIFLOWER)

ROAST KID
FISH CHOWDER

PÂTÉ
VENDÉENNE

PÂTÉ DE FOIE GRAS

Poitevin
Marshes

AUNIS

BABY EELS

ANJOU

MATELOTE
D'ANGUILLE
BEURRE
BLANC
SAUCE

Saumur

Cholet (CHEESE)

GIGORIT
POTÉE À LA
TÊTE DE PORC

GREEN CABBAGE
FANCI

MELONS
FRUIT

ORLEANAIS

Vendôme
Blois
Chambord
Orléans

SAFFRON

LARKS
PÂTÉS

Pithiviers (LARK PÂTÉ)
HONEY
GIGOT DE MOUTON

VOL-AU-VENT

TOURAINE
(see insert)

LAPEREAU
À LA SOLOGNOTE

Valençay
(GOAT
CHEESE)
Vierzon

FAT SOUPS
MUTTON

Reuilly

Issoudun
(GRAY WINE)

GOAT CHEESE
POTATO CAKE
POTATOES

Bourges

PANCAKES

BOURBONNAIS

BERRY

MARCHE

PUMPKIN
TART

CHABICHOU

Poitiers

ANGOUMOIS

MILES
KM.

Langeais (where Charles VIII married Anne of Brittany and thus secured that duchy for France) and died at the Château of Plessis-les-Tours. It was the House of Valois particularly which identified itself at least as much with the Touraine as with Paris during the two hundred years of its rule, from Charles V, the Wise, who mounted the throne in 1364, to Henry III, who ceded it to death in 1589.

When the Touraine became part of the royal domain of France for the first time in 1204, during the reign of Philip Augustus (it was not finally so attached until 1584), it was Tours which was added to Paris, and not Paris to Tours, not only because the Ile-de-France had in the meantime added to itself the Orléanais and the Berry, giving it a continuous territory bounding the Touraine, but also because of an accident of history. For the preceding fifty years the Touraine had been English. It was regained by Frenchmen from Englishmen only when a quarrel among the Plantagenets enabled Philip Augustus to recover Touraine (and Normandy) from John Lackland, King of England.

But if it be argued that Paris naturally took supremacy over Tours because Paris had remained continuously French while the Touraine had become English for a half century of its long history, it might be answered that in 1429 Henry VI of England held the title of King of Paris, while Charles VII was only King of Bourges. In that year Charles was set on the way to becoming King of France by Joan of Arc, who singled out the disguised king from the crowd of his courtiers and inspired him to take arms against the English. It would be possible to say that at that time and in that place modern France was born. The place was the Château of Chinon—in the Touraine.

The first meeting of the States-General was held in Paris in 1302, the second in Tours in 1308. Twice Tours has served as capital of France—once in 1870, when the government was driven from Paris by the Prussians; and again in 1940, when the government was driven from Paris by the Germans. On both occasions the reign of Tours was brief. But the Touraine may proudly claim that in the hour of disaster the government of the nation seeks refuge in its heartland.

The title of the Touraine to precedence in the history of France is thus an ancient and an honorable one. Many of the elements which have formed the culture of France, among which her cooking is not the least important, have had their origin here. For that reason our story starts in the Touraine.

The aspects of France are many. There are the sharp bare rocks of the Alps, even in summer flecked with snow; the savage perpendicular fastnesses of the Pyrenees; the wooded hills of the Vosges; the deep-cleft black-green valleys of the Jura. The mountains meet the sea in a clash of hot colors along the Riviera; under a cold gray sky the ocean beats in violent eddies and whirlpools against the rocky headlands of Brittany. There are slagheaps and squalor in the industrial north, and subtle symphonies of parched gray-greens in the semiarid sweep behind the coastal mountains of Provence. Tall scraggly pines cover the Landes. On the heights of the Puy-de-Dôme the plateau stands bare, exposed and waterless. The reeds ripple in the wind above the salt marshes of the Camargue. But these are not the images evoked by the words "the countryside of France." The vision that arises is that of green fields, of poplars lining long roads, of agricultural country, smiling and tender. The Touraine, so often called the garden of France, is the epitome of this landscape.

Its little land is watered by four rivers whose names are as dear to those who love France as any that may be uttered. Possibly only the Seine can be mentioned in the same breath as the Loire, the Cher, the Indre, and the

Vienne. The Rhone is majestic, not intimate, and it is, besides, a foreigner; its source is in Switzerland. The echoes raised by the Marne are martial. The Rhine is German. There are others of which one thinks with fondness: the Eure, as it wanders softly beneath the hill of Chartres, so that you look up from the laundresses beating their linen on its banks to the towers of the great Cathedral above, both fixed in one great and simple and unforgettable image; the Gard where it slips under the leaping arches of the Roman aqueduct that spans it; the Dordogne flowing darkly by the dark caves of prehistoric man—but none mirrors so completely the charm of the French countryside as do the rivers of the Touraine, calm, limpid, lovely, and tranquil.

The great Loire is not always tranquil. Choked in its own silt, it has greatly aged since the days when ocean traffic mounted it as far as Orléans—not so long ago, after all, only half a century. What is fifty years in the history of a traffic that goes back to Gallo-Roman times? Shipping now mounts the river no farther than Nantes, except for bottoms of less than 200 tons, which can dock at Angers. In summer it seems incredible now that ships ever got up to Orléans at all. Even at Tours the river is a stream of sand. A few thin threads of water drain through its center. At Orléans, the rate of flow may be no more than 25 cubic yards per second.

And then the rain falls, in autumn perhaps, or the winter's snow melts, and the sandy bed of the river disappears. Now 8,000 cubic yards of water rush by Orléans every second, at 320 times the rate of the dry season flow. The water slides swiftly by, level with the top of the river bank, level with the road that from time to time approaches it. It is a dirty green-brown, soiled by the earth it is washing away from the garden of France. Trees that have advanced too boldly into the once dry bed raise forlorn marooned heads from the rushing water. But unlike the Rhone, the Loire seldom breaches its banks nowadays as it used to do. The last bad flood occurred in 1910.

Each of the tributaries of the Loire has its own character. The Cher, first to enter it in the Touraine, flows ordinarily through grassy meadows, slow, peaceful, and reassuring. It seems to have been designed expressly to serve as mirror to the Château of Chenonceau, bestriding it on graceful arches. But there are times when the river tears at those arches, dashes itself against them, rears in frustrated whirlpools against their piles, and in a fury of foam roars by too madly to hold the image of the château in its broken flood. There is no room to spare in the river's bed, and so it is over its banks at the first rising of its waters. But as the tourist usually sees it, it is the tranquil glass in which the inverted double of arched Chenonceau quivers and gleams.

The Indre never forgets the function of a mirror. It so serves the château of Azay-le-Rideau, built on its banks. It flows brimful all the year round, brimful but gently, so gently that water lilies grow on its surface without having their roots torn away. Weeping willows dip their drooping branches in its quiet waters. Here and there still stand old mills; their wheels were persuaded to turn by sinking them in a pit so that the idling water had to drop upon their vanes with a force it exerts nowhere else along this dreamy stream.

Last comes the Vienne, sometimes called the little Loire, a broad and peaceful stream, not quite as leisurely as the Cher. A shimmering translucid green, it glides gracefully beneath the weathered walls of old Chinon and traces the western boundaries of the Touraine.

In the waters of these rivers has been reflected an important part of the history of France.

Prehistory, too, is reflected in the rivers of the Touraine. When one thinks of prehistoric man in France, Périgord, more than 500 miles to the south, comes first to mind, where the caves of Les Eyzies and Lascaux are painted with the forms of aurochs and of deer. But Stone Age man lived also in the valley of the Loire. More than 2,000 of his tools may be seen in the museum of Le Grand-Pressigny. Later the Gallo-Roman period, which left so few traces in Paris (the Arènes de Lutèce, the ancient baths upon which the Cluny Museum stands), bestowed its legacy upon the Touraine. Among other remains there is a curious heaped-up pile of stone, which is called just that in the name it has given to the place—Cinq-Mars-la-Pile—and whose purpose remains mysterious. It may have been a boundary mark. Luynes boasts the ruins of a Gallo-Roman camp and an aqueduct. A round tower of the same period, part of the old wall of Tours (whose name, of course, means "towers"), is incorporated into the courtyard of the art museum.

The early history of the Touraine is not lacking in a factor that played a leading part in the shaping of the French spirit—the influence of religion. The greatest bishop of the Gauls was Saint Martin, who first came among them as a Roman legionary. The best-known story about him tells how he cut his cloak in two and shared it with a beggar. His gift of warmth is commemorated in the circumstance that what is called in America Indian summer—the temporary return of warmer weather after the first frost of autumn—is known in France as Saint Martin's summer. The name of Saint Martin is linked with that of Tours. Though the first monastery he founded was established in Poitou, south of the Touraine, the Tourangeaux soon besought him to become their bishop, and he accepted. Many of the churches and chapels he built in the Touraine are still standing. Near Tours itself you may visit today the cells hewn from the rock in which the monks of his monastery of Marmoutier lived. Here Saint Martin entered gastronomic history, for local legend says that the asses of

Marmoutier broke out of their stable and ate all the leaves from the grapevines before the monks discovered what they were doing. The monks bewailed the ruin of their vineyards; but to their great surprise, they discovered the following year that the most severely ravaged vines bore the finest grapes. The art of pruning had come to the vineyards of the Loire.

Frenchmen will tell you that the purest French in the world is spoken, not in Paris, but in Tours. What greater service can any region perform for a nation's culture than to breed its writers? This service the Touraine has offered to France from the beginning, for the Touraine was the birthplace and the lifelong home of the first great French writer.

If you visit Chinon, you can make a trip to its outskirts to see the house where Rabelais was born in the hamlet of La Devinière. Its most notable feature, appropriately, is the extensive wine cellars beneath the building. In Chinon itself, a house once occupied by Rabelais is today a restaurant called the Gargantua. A third building in which he once lived, a Renaissance structure, survives at Langeais.

The fact that French literature may be said to have begun in the Touraine with Rabelais (the only important names later than the time of the troubadours but preceding his were those of Villon of Paris and Froissart of Valenciennes) was no accident. Only a lively intellectual milieu could have nourished so many authors through so many years. Some, like Rabelais, were born citizens of the Touraine. Others, drawn to it by its cultural pre-eminence, remained and became Tourangeaux. There were also those who came and departed again, seduced by its charm, to use it as a background for tales written elsewhere. The Touraine was at once a subject for literature and a home for littérateurs.

In Rabelais's own time there was the lively sister of

Francis I, known to English readers as Margaret of Navarre, but to the French as Marguerite de Valois, or d'Orléans, or d'Angoulême—most frequently the last, for it was in Angoulême, 150 miles south of Tours, that she was born. She was a frequent resident of the Château d'Amboise. Twenty-five years before her death, in 1524, Ronsard was born. He was a native of the Vendômois, just north of the Touraine proper, but still in the cultural hinterland of Tours. Drawn to the greatest city of the region, he made Tours his home, wrote there, and died there, the Prior of Saint-Cosme, in 1585.

The greatest of the old French writers, Rabelais, was a native of the Touraine; the greatest of the modern school, Balzac, was a native of Tours itself. At the Château of Saché, near the more famous Azay-le-Rideau, where he lived from 1829 to 1837, you can see his workroom, maintained as far as possible in the state in which he left it. The name of his native city is enshrined in the title of one of his shorter novels, *Un Curé de Tours*. The valley of *Le Lys dans la Vallée* is that of the Indre. And in Vouvray there stands a statue in memory of a man who never existed: Gaudissart, the traveling salesman created by Balzac, who used Vouvray, a place of which he was fond, as the setting for his story.

The Touraine can boast of artists as well as of writers; at least two of them gave great names to the history of French painting. One was that founder of French art, Jean Fouquet. He was born in Tours early in the fifteenth century. It was about a century later that François Clouet, a court artist of Francis I, like his father Jean before him, appeared on the scene. Jean was Flemish, but the son was a native of Tours. The city also was the birthplace of many lesser lights—the sixteenth–seventeenth–century painter Claude Vignon, whose canvases, betraying the influence of Caravaggio, may be seen in the Tours museum; the seventeenth-century engraver Abraham Bosse, whose genre works are on display in the same institution; and the sculptors Michel Colombe, whose tomb of Charles VIII is in the Cathedral of Saint-Gatien, and François Sicard, whose works may be seen, once again, in the museum of Tours. Lost in antiquity are the names of the painters whose Romanesque murals decorate the church of Tavant and the Charterhouse of Le Liget, which Henry II of England built in the twelfth century to expiate the murder of Thomas à Becket.

But the greatest name in the realm of art, one of the greatest of all time, which is connected with the Touraine, is not that of a Tourangeau, nor, for that matter, even of a Frenchman. Its appearance here is testimony to the intensity of the cultural life of this region, which was able to draw to it from his own surroundings, brilliant though they were, one of the supreme artists of history, Leonardo da Vinci. Francis I brought Leonardo to Amboise, and he seems to have been content there. At least, he stayed until he died in a room of the manor house of Clos-Luce, visible from the terrace of the château, which is still shown to visitors. The grave of Leonardo is not in Italy, but in the Touraine, in the chapel of the Château d'Amboise, the Chapel of Saint-Hubert.

The greatest works of art that the Touraine possesses are its châteaux. To these no names of particular builders can be attached. They are not the work of architects, as we think of architects today; they were the result of the simultaneous operation of many minds, those of their owners, of the contractors, of the artisans, and of many artists, among them Leonardo, whose anonymous contributions are certainly enshrined in some parts of these famous buildings.

Of the châteaux of the Loire, four are considered to surpass all the others, and of these four, two belong to the Touraine: Azay-le-Rideau and Chenonceau. They are of the later period, when the château was no longer a castle, a fortified military stronghold standing, usually, on a height from which the enemy could be seen approaching, and which he would find it difficult to scale, but a palace whose towers and walls were only an ornamental vestige of the military works of the past, and whose windows had broadened from the slits useful only to archers to afford a view of the rivers and the pleasant valleys to which the châteaux descended in more peaceful times. But you will also meet in the Touraine the beetling walls and turrets of earlier and more parlous days—in Luynes, in Langeais, in Chinon, in Loches.

The châteaux were not so much built as rebuilt. Each new king or lord or proprietor added new wings and razed old ones, repaired, redecorated, revised, and altered. Of the older buildings, ordinarily only parts date from the military epoch and recall by their architecture the grim period of constant warfare. Langeais, going back to the middle of the fifteenth century, which is to say to the end of the Middle Ages, was one of the last of the purely military castles to be built, and therefore remains today one of the best preserved. In its park are the ruins of what is believed to be the oldest stone dungeon-keep in France, reared in the tenth century. Luynes is older (it was built in the thirteenth century) and from a distance is an impressive sight, dominating the region with its heavy mass, but it is in precarious repair and cannot be visited. In Chinon and Loches it is not the châteaux alone that are remarkable, but the towns as wholes, for both have retained entire blocks of their medieval buildings and bear the marks of the eventful history of the Touraine—which is the history of France—whose waves have for centuries rolled over their old walls.

Chinon has already been identified as the place where

Joan of Arc recognized Charles VII. It is the scene of other historic events also, some of them tragic. Here, in 1321, all the Jews of the town were burned alive. The same fate was that of half a hundred of the Knights Templar, who were imprisoned in Chinon when their order, become too rich, too powerful, and consequently too arrogant, was dissolved. Richard the Lion-Hearted died in Chinon. To Chinon Cesare Borgia came, bearing the papal bull that divorced Louix XII from Jeanne of France so that he could marry Anne of Brittany. The Château of Chinon (which is really three, combined into a single complex of buildings) was at one time the property of Cardinal Richelieu.

Loches is also a milestone in the intricate journeyings of Richard the Lion-Hearted; he took this all but impregnable point by surprise, in an assault which lasted only three hours. History shows its grim side here, too. Loches was where Louis XI established what he called euphemistically *ses fillettes*—his little girls. The little girls were iron cages in which he confined prisoners he particularly disliked. The most comfortable were six-foot cubes; the least comfortable were so small that their occupants could not stand or stretch themselves or assume any comfortable position; and to make it worse, some of them were slung from the ceilings, suspended in mid-air. These charming inventions had been devised by a prince of the Church, Cardinal de la Balue. A just Providence rewarded him fittingly: he spent the last eleven years of his life in one of them.

Loches is rich also in memories of Agnès Sorel, that remarkable woman who virtually ruled France through Charles VII, to whom she bore four daughters. She was not merely a dweller in the châteaux of the Touraine; she was also a native of the region. Known as *La Dame de Beauté* not, as is the common misapprehension, because of her good looks, but because the King had made her a present of the estate of Beauté-sur-Marne, she lived at

Chinon when the court was there. But when the crown prince, later Louis XI, slapped her in public, she left Chinon and took up residence at Loches. Louis made amends for the humiliation after her death. It had been her desire to be buried in the chapel of the Château of Loches; to that end she had been prodigally generous to the local clergy, but when she died the Church boggled at admitting so notorious a sinner to the sacred precincts. Louis XI was asked to bury her instead in the château. He answered that he would be pleased to do so on condition that the gifts she had made to the chapel should be turned over to the château with her remains. In the light of this royal point of view, the ecclesiastical authorities decided that, after all, the pious wish of Agnès Sorel might well be gratified. She was buried in the château's chapel of St. Ours; but the anticlerical Revolution, paradoxically enough, fulfilled the first impulse of the Church, which the Church itself had failed to carry out. Ignorant soldiers, mistaking the statue over her tomb for that of a saint, broke it down and dispersed her bones. When they were collected again and reburied under the restored monument, a fine fifteenth-century work whose sculptor is unknown, they were placed outside the church, in a tower of the château, where they remain today. Also still visible at Loches is the oratory of Anne of Brittany, another celebrated inhabitant of this château.

Hardly another single spot in France is so redolent with the fragrance of the memory of the masterful mistresses of the nation as the Château of Chenonceau, which is for this reason sometimes known as the château of the six women. The six are Katherine Briçonnet, who built it early in the sixteenth century for her husband, Thomas Bohier, tax-collector under Charles VIII, Louis XII, and Francis I; Diane de Poitiers, the hardy mistress of Henry II (if you have thought of her as a languishing artificial court beauty, you have been doing an injustice to a woman who was accustomed to rise in the biting winter mornings of an era without central heat, bathe in cold water, and then spend two or three hours in the saddle, a woman who never used cosmetics, and who died at 67 with the complexion and figure of a woman of thirty); Catherine de Médicis, who dispossessed Diane as soon as Henry II died (of a lance thrust received in a tournament); Louise de Lorraine, who spent the last eleven years of her life there mourning her husband, Henry III; Mme Dupin, *protectrice* of Jean-Jacques Rousseau and grandmother of George Sand; and, finally, Mme Pelouze, who bought Chenonceau in 1864 and made the world her debtor by devoting her life to its restoration.

There is no space to list all the other châteaux of the Touraine; its soil is sown with them: Amboise, whose most recent historic use was as the forced residence of Abd-el-Kader, exiled from Algeria in the last century, and whose bloodiest chapter is that of the Conspiracy of Amboise in 1560, when hundreds of Protestants, having conspired against the crown, were tortured, hung from the château walls, thrown into the Loire in sacks, beheaded, or ripped apart by horses; Azay-le-Rideau, which has beauty but no history; Ussé, whose shining white stone and fantastic towers and turrets are supposed to have inspired Perrault when he wrote, with this building in mind, the story of the Sleeping Beauty. Vauban, the architect of Louis XIV's fortresses, often stayed here, for it was owned in his time by his son-in-law. Villandry has the only sixteenth-century gardens in France, carefully restored to appear just as they did four centuries ago, laid out on three terraces—the water garden above, the flower garden below, the vegetable garden at the bottom—a vegetable garden without potatoes, for, in the sixteenth century, the potato was not yet a French vegetable. It might, perhaps, have been placed in the flower garden, for it had arrived from the New World about 1540, and was cultivated as an ornamental plant. But it had to wait for Parmentier, who was not born until 1737, to grow it as a food, a service for which he has been rendered immortal by the appearance of his name on menus whenever diced potatoes cooked in butter and sprinkled with chopped parsley are served in France, for this is what is meant by *pommes Parmentier*.

The châteaux are the highlights of the architecture of the Touraine, but they are not its only claim to greatness in this domain. It is true that the Touraine must bow to the Ile-de-France and other territories to the north when we come to consider that mighty creation, the Gothic cathedral. Saint-Gatien, the Cathedral of Tours, is indeed Gothic, and it is of particular interest to students, for it was long building and so constitutes a sort of history of the style in its different parts, even ending with Renaissance towers; but it remains nevertheless a heavy, uninspired structure, and you have only to move eighty-five miles to the north to admire the most beautiful of all Gothic cathedrals, Chartres, which also spans the whole history of Gothic. One might say, unkindly, that Tours offers samples of the worst Gothic of all periods, Chartres of the best. Tours is also overshadowed by Chartres in another field. It might have been famous for its stained glass, for it possesses fine windows of the thirteenth, fourteenth, and fifteenth centuries; but Chartres has thirteenth-century glass, too, and it is not merely fine, but superb. Saint-Gatien is dwarfed in every respect by Notre-Dame de Chartres.

But this does not mean that the Touraine, so French in its every essence, is poor in Gothic buildings. Of their smaller forms it possesses supreme examples. The twelfth- to thirteenth-century church of Candes is a magnificent specimen of the merging of ecclesiastical with military architecture which in the days when the church had some-

times to be a fortress, produced so many striking and powerful structures—like the very different Cathedral of Albi.
The Romanesque style is also superbly represented in the
Touraine, as in Saint-Ours, in the Château of Loches. So
is the Renaissance: see the portal of the sixteenth-century
church of Montrésor. But unquestionably the greatest
work of architecture in this region, the châteaux aside, is
the Abbey of Fontevrault.

Fontevrault was founded in the eleventh century. It has
had a charged history ever since. Today it has come down
in the world; it is a prison. Tourists visiting that part of its
buildings which are under the aegis of the Ministry of
Beaux-Arts are sometimes surprised by the passage of a
group of convicts making their way from one to another
of the structures which in medieval times served as convents, monasteries, and hospitals. Among the edifices open
for the inspection of those who are only temporary, not
permanent, guests of the state, is the fine twelfth-century
abbey church. Its style is Romanesque. Its presence here
may suggest to us another argument to buttress the theory
that the Touraine is genuinely the core of France. It is an
argument that does not admit a weakness in the fact that
the Touraine lacks great large-scale works in the Gothic
style, one of the major achievements of the French genius,
but finds in that lack an affirmation of a more all-embracing,
a more fundamentally French character in the Touraine
than in some other regions where this particular manifesta-
tion of the French spirit has come more completely to
flower.

What is the connection between the Romanesque abbey
church of Fontevrault and the diminishing strength of the
Gothic impulse in the region that surrounds it?

It is this: the Fontevrault church establishes the northern boundary of the style to which it belongs. The four
cupolas carried on its nave are echoed in churches to the

south, but in none to the north. In the same way, the weakening of Gothic in the Touraine is the sign that here we are on the southern boundary of Gothic. With the single exception of Bourges, almost in a line with Tours, the great Gothic cathedrals of France all lie to the north of the Touraine—and Bourges, with its lack of transepts and its five naves, is hardly typical Gothic.

We may thus assert, on the evidence of Fontevrault and Saint-Gatien, that the Touraine is the land where the ecclesiastical styles of the north and the south overlap. Neither is alien here. Neither reaches its apogee here either, but that is because great Gothic is of northern France and great Romanesque is of southern France. The Touraine is neither, but is France *tout court*, France without a limiting adjective. Here neither the Gothic nor the Romanesque is superb, but neither is absent. Both can be embraced by the genius of the Touraine, more catholic, more eclectic, than either the north or the south, than either the Ile-de-France or Languedoc, more inclusively, more completely, more unparochially French than any other province.

Walking around the Abbey of Fontevrault, the visitor cannot fail to notice a curious structure attached like a squat conical exotic growth to the building, at bottom a cluster of rounded towers which dwindles above them to a point, as though it had been crowned with a witch's hat bristling with little round turrets. Its function may puzzle you unless you divine that all these little towers are chimneys. This is the kitchen of the abbey. Beneath the twenty chimneys that rise from its roof are five separate hearths, each destined, it may be supposed, to serve one of the five sections into which the original abbey was divided: the monastery of the men; the convent of the women; the refuge for other women, some of the highest rank, retired here to repent of sins apparently so spectacular that they had to be accorded separate quarters from the nuns; the lepers; and the sick of the hospital. The role of Touraine as one of the principal founts, if not the principal fount, of French cooking is symbolized by the presence here of the only Romanesque kitchen still existing in France.

It is not the fact, of course, that the Touraine alone founded the cuisine of France, and that Paris and the Ile-de-France adopted it only later. Development of the art of cooking could hardly have proceeded otherwise than simultaneously throughout the whole territory already politically linked by the time cooking began to be an art. The court was continually in motion, moving from the banks of the Seine to the banks of the Loire and back again, taking its cooks with it. The Touraine, Berry, Orléanais, and the Ile-de-France, joined not much later by Anjou and Poitou, formed, so to speak, a culinary unit, and even today the local variations in their cuisine are slight. They grew up together, gastronomically, and provided the foundation for French cooking, which is why tourists seeking regional specialities are likely to be disappointed if they enter these territories looking for something different or exotic. In this area they will, indeed, find some of the best cooking of France, but they may fail to be impressed by it precisely because this is the known, the familiar, the accepted standard by which all other cooking is measured. Gourmets have said of the Ile-de-France, and might say also of the Touraine, that it has no regional cooking; but that is only because the cuisine of this region has been so successful that it became first the cuisine of France as a whole, and thereafter the cuisine of great hotels and international restaurants the world over.

We must grant the Touraine at least as large a share in the development of this cuisine as we grant to the Ile-de-France, from which, through the influence of Paris, it spread throughout the world. There is good evidence for the belief that the land of Gargantua was foremost in worship of the kitchen. The Château of Amboise alone offers two scraps of gastronomic gossip which attest to the consciousness manifest there of the importance of food. One concerns the effect the atmosphere of the Touraine had on Louis XIII, who, so far as anyone knows, seemed content elsewhere to eat what his cooks prepared for him. When he came to Amboise to hunt, he gave way to the impulse to invade the kitchen and cook for himself. His tastes were simple; or perhaps his ability as a cook was limited. In any case, what he usually made for himself was an onion omelet moistened with a little local red wine. The other gastronomic note that has come down to us about Amboise is perhaps more significant. It was in this château, the scene of so many historic events of apparently much greater import, that the first incubator for the artificial rearing of chickens was put into service in the year 1496.

The Touraine had certain advantages over the Ile-de-France in that its resources were greater. To begin with, it was wine country. There are few exceptions to the rule that the best cooking is found in the areas that grow wine grapes. It is true that in the days when French cooking was being created, vines grew in the Ile-de-France also. They have left a few degenerate descendants, like the famous vine on the Butte Montmartre in Paris and the trellis of Fontainebleau, whose grapes are still auctioned off yearly. For that matter, there were and are vines still farther north, in the Champagne, which had been politically attached to the Ile-de-France since 1285. But the somewhat sour grapes half ripened in the pale northern sun of Paris could not rival those of the Loire valley, while the grapes of Champagne are of a special character, whose appropriateness for the production of sparkling vintages was not discovered until the seventeenth century, producing even then a beverage of a type that provides us immediately with an exception to the rule just set down above, that good cooking and the production of wine go hand in hand, for Champagne has not inspired an accompanying cuisine.

The Touraine enjoyed other gastronomic advantages over the North. The Loire and its tributaries provided a richer source of fish than the smaller streams of the Ile-de-France. Game was plentiful everywhere in France in those days, but the Touraine, then as now, offered richer rewards to the hunter than the Parisian region. Poultry and cattle were superior. Today one could cite also the fruit and vegetables of "the garden of France," but this factor had no influence on the early development of cooking. In medieval and Renaissance times, man was a carnivorous animal, not an omnivorous one. Except for eggs, he lived mostly on flesh—fish, poultry, game, and, more rarely, butcher's meat. Vegetables rarely appeared on the table, and when they did, only boiled (as in England today). Men got few vitamins in those days. They got gout instead. Early cooking was necessarily simple, if only because of the limitations of contemporary kitchens. Ovens were rare, so there could be little baking. It was usually not practical, in a kitchen that was in essence only the enlarged base of the chimney, to prepare dishes requiring, during their preparation, manipulations more complicated than simple basting. Boiling, and roasting meat and poultry on a spit, ordinarily exhausted the available possibilities.

The favorite dishes of those olden times have disappeared to a large extent from the menus of the Ile-de-France; they have been more resistant in the Touraine. Is this an indication, perhaps, of an earlier origin in this region, which permitted the ancient traditions of the kitchen to become more firmly established in the Touraine than elsewhere, and therefore less susceptible to replacement by the elaborate cuisine later developed about the court in Paris? Another peculiarity of these venerable dishes—both those which have remained in the general repertoire of French cooking and those seldom found today far from the Touraine—points to the valley of the Loire as their place of origin: many of them make lavish use of wine as one of their ingredients. Few wines combine more successfully with meats in cooking than the red vintages of Chinon or Bourgueil. *Coq au vin,* still in honor on menus everywhere in the country, is never better than when made with Touraine wine. Hare cooked in Chinon has even more finesse than hare cooked in Burgundy. These dishes you will find everywhere; but it is not often that you will meet far from Tours *rôtie au vin rouge,* a dish of respectable antiquity, and as for another holdover from medieval times, *sang de poulet aux oignons,* it is today almost confined to the valley of the Loire.

The virtual disappearance of this dish in the Parisian region, while it remains on the menus of Touraine, is perhaps owing in part to the fact that it is easier in the less urban centers of the Loire valley than it is in Paris to provide the essential ingredient that gives its name to this dish, the chicken's blood. This name—it means literally, of course, chicken's blood with onions—is something of a misnomer. It does not describe the dish as a whole, but only the sauce in which the basic chicken, cut into pieces as for a fricassee, is cooked. To prepare the sauce, it is almost necessary to buy your chicken alive in order to be able to catch its blood when it is killed and add to it quickly, to prevent its coagulating, a few spoonfuls of wine. (Vinegar or lemon juice produces the same effect.) The blood is essential to provide a rich binding for the sauce, which begins when you cook the morsels of chicken in butter with small pieces of the chicken's liver, which are removed when cooked. The butter is then enriched by the addition of onions, bits of bacon, and mushrooms, followed in order by a little flour, plenty of red wine, and some soup stock. Seasoning and herbs are then added, and the chicken simmers lengthily in the mixture before the blood, with the wine that has been added to keep it liquid, is poured in at the last minute. For a particularly fine touch, brandy may be added and lighted just before the dish is brought to the table, so that it is served flaming.

The difficulty of obtaining chicken blood at the corner grocery does not quite account for the disappearance of this masterpiece from bills of fare outside of the Touraine, for despite its name it can be made without blood. Purists may insist on this ingredient, but its function seems to be more physical than gustatory. It adds little in the way of taste to the total, but is important as a binding agent. It can therefore be replaced, without great loss, by any other neutral binder or thickener. That other regions have not bothered to do this to preserve a fine dish still popular in the Touraine indicates that its tradition has been stronger in the Touraine than elsewhere. It appears to be the fact that *sang de poulet aux oignons* originated in this region and goes back to medieval times.

The traditional pastry of the Touraine also harks back to the Middle Ages: *cordes, russeroles, cassemuses, fouaces.* Two of these are mentioned in Rabelais. He called the *cassemuses* "*casse museaux,*" or muzzle-breakers, which will give you an idea of the hardness of these cakes. As for the *fouaces*, he gives the recipe, which makes it appear that the medieval version of this cake was rather richer than its modern descendant, for in Rabelais's day it included such rich ingredients as egg yolks, saffron, and spices. Today it is a rather coarse, tasteless bun used chiefly as an aid in absorbing large quantities of the regional wines. Perhaps this is a return to its first character, for originally it was an ash cake, cooked under the ashes of the hearth (*focus*), a word whose corruption provided its name. (It is known in some parts of France as *fougasse*, a word a little closer to the original form from which it is derived.)

If we run through the various departments of a meal, we will find that the Touraine marks its gastronomic importance at the very beginning, with the hors d'œuvre. This country is a rich source of *charcuterie*, a term that strictly speaking should be confined to pork products, but which by extension covers all sorts of meat preparations like sausages, *pâtés*, galantines, and cured meat. *Rillettes* is perhaps the most famous of these products so far as the Touraine is concerned, together with its variants, *rillons* and *rillauds*. When you find *rillettes* on a menu anywhere in France, it will often be described specifically as *rillettes de Tours*, for this constitutes a guarantee of its quality. It is made of finely shredded pork cooked in lard and eaten cold; it has a tendency to be greasy, but the Tours variety, made only of meat from the neck of the hog, with a careful mixture of fat and lean pieces, is finer than most others. Spread a little of it on a piece of French bread, accompany it with a swallow of Vouvray from its own neighborhood, and you have an excellent start for a meal. Amboise is also noted for the quality of its *rillettes*.

Tripe sausages (*andouillette*, the soft variety, generally displayed in long coils, like a length of garden hose, from which the amount you want is cut off, or *andouille*, the hard kind) are also specialties of this region, especially of Vouvray and Chinon, though they are natives of Normandy. *Andouille* is cooked and ready to eat when you buy it, like salami or any other similar sausage; *andouillette*, however, has to be cooked after purchase.

The little town of Richelieu has acquired a considerable reputation for its *charcuterie*. Among its products are *pâtés* of various kinds and in particular a delectable delicacy known as *jambons de volaille*. The word *jambon* (ham) is in this case misleading, for the name is given by analogy to cold boned stuffed chicken legs cooked in wine and later eaten cold. The name is more normal when it is applied to *jambon de gibier*, also a specialty of Richelieu; in this case it simply means that the leg of some game animal —wild boar, for instance—has been treated in the same manner as the leg of a hog which has been converted into ham.

Boudin blanc comes under the head of *charcuterie*, and you may find it listed with the hors d'œuvre on a bill of fare, though it is more likely to be offered as one of the principal dishes. You will find this name on menus throughout the country, especially at the Christmas and New Year holiday season, when *boudin blanc* and *boudin noir* (blood pudding) are traditionally paired on *Réveillon* menus (they are unfortunately disappearing under the influence of the commercialization of these two midnight feasts, whose exaggerated prices restaurateurs have a habit of justifying by forsaking the hearty old dishes for what they consider more elegant and more expensive new ones). Like *boudin noir*, *boudin blanc* is a soft sausage, and its stuffing in most parts of the country is composed largely of bread; but in the Touraine, the bread is replaced by breast of chicken. The Touraine *boudin blanc* is thus the finest variety of this sausage to be found, and there is a further refinement called *boudin de volaille à la Richelieu*, referring again, of course, to the small village already cited above (in spite of its gastronomic fame, its population is less than 2,000), in which truffles and mushrooms are combined with the white chicken meat, and all of them are creamed together in an elaborate sauce. By the time this has been done, one hardly dares refer to the product any longer as a sausage; it is more of a chicken croquette.

Touraine is also the home of a quite unusual appetizer that you will find nowhere else. It is called *cerneaux*, and it is made from green walnuts steeped in the juice of equally green grapes, embellished with chopped chervil. The effect is rather vinegary. It provides a tart beginning for the meal, stirring up the taste buds and inducing a ravenous mood.

It is curious that while most of the regions of France where local cooking shows marked variation from the standard cuisine demonstrate their individuality in their soups, the Touraine has no soups that can be called specifically its own. Perhaps this is because soup was of little importance in the early days of French cooking, when the cuisine of the Touraine was being born. The medieval dishes sometimes classified as soups today were actually much more like what we would now call porridge. Perhaps it would not even have occurred to us to refer to them as soups if it were not for a modern misunderstanding of an ancient use of that word.

When we read today in an old French work (Rabelais, say) the word *soupe* in reference to one of these medieval precursors of oatmeal, we are making the error of transferring to the whole of this concoction a word that when it was written referred only to part of it. For Rabelais, *soupe* did not mean the porridge; it meant a piece of bread boiled in the porridge, then a common practice. The old word, only slightly altered in spelling, still survives in English not at all altered in meaning: sop. In French it evolved. First it was extended to refer by analogy to a piece of boiled meat —not to the bouillon it produced in boiling, but only to the meat itself. The bouillon was not esteemed in medieval times. It appeared only as an accidental by-product of the process of boiling meat, and was usually thrown away. It took some time for cooks to discover that bouillon was good. When they did, the name that had formerly described only the meat cooked in the bouillon was transferred to the bouillon, and *soupe*, having acquired the meaning it bears today, was transferred for the second time to the

English language, in another spelling and with another significance.

By the time cooks began giving conscious attention to soup for its own sake, the period of folk origination was over in the heartland of cookery. Soups were created by professional cooks and became the common property of the whole region, unidentifiable as being of the Touraine or of the Orléanais or of Paris from any intrinsic character of their own, but only in so far as one happened to remember the addresses of the famous chefs who concocted them as individual works of their special art. The Touraine thus has no soups that may be ascribed definitely to it and to no other region.

The situation is different when we reach the fish course. The Loire and its tributaries swarm with fish: *écrevisses* (crawfish), *brochet* (pike), *mulet* (mulet), *alose* (shad), *brème* (bream), *saumon* (salmon), *carpe* (carp), *anguille* (eel). Local gourmets maintain that the Loire produces the best shad, the Cher the best pike, the Indre the best carp; but as the two latter flow into the first, one may be excused for wondering if the distinction is valid. Fish an inch or two long are fried whole, often breaded, and served up by the dozen in a delicious dish called *friture de la Loire*. The bream, a carp-like fish larger and flatter than the true carp, is usually stuffed (*brème farcie*). Two favorite ways of preparing the river fish in the Touraine are not really native to the region: the *beurre-blanc* sauce usually applied to pike, mullet, and shad probably originated in the neighboring province of Anjou, while *matelote d'anguille* is a fashion of preparing this or other fish in wine (old wine is used in the Touraine) which is usually attributed to the Ile-de-France—but they are so popular there as to have become local specialties.

It is when we reach the main dishes of the meal that we recognize most unmistakably the distinctive characteristics of Touraine cooking: simplicity, honesty, unpretentiousness. The Touraine and the Ile-de-France both based their cuisines on the same foundation, the *cuisine bourgeoise*, the hearty fare of the good trencherman. The Touraine chose to rest satisfied with that. Professionalism, in the Ile-de-France, built on this foundation the *haute cuisine*, which, having conquered smart hotels and chic restaurants all over the world, is now what foreigners think of as French cooking. Fundamentally, however, the purest French cooking is the less urbanized, less sophisticated, earthier cheer of the Touraine. Not that the Touraine is not quite as capable as the Ile-de-France of giving you *haute cuisine* if you want it; not that it does not possess its full share of the professional artificers of the kitchen (indeed, it is a notorious fact that a large proportion of the great chefs of France, in the capital and elsewhere, are natives of the Touraine), but because the Touraine prefers art to artifice.

It is interesting to note that the four starred restaurants of Tours, in listing their chief specialties, do not in even a single case name one of those involved dishes smothered in subtle sauces which are assumed abroad to be typically French. The dishes that the best restaurants of Tours emphasize are *tournedos flambé Médicis* (steak), *rognons de veau sautés valleé de Cousse* (kidneys), *dodine de canard en geleé* (cold boned pressed duck in its own jelly), and *noisette de porc aux pruneaux* (roast pork with prunes). Basically, you might call this peasant food; but it is peasant food that has lost its rustic quality. You might also call it bourgeois food, adopting, indeed, the French term, provided that you divorce it from its connotation of stolid lack of imaginativeness. This cooking is bourgeois in the sense that it belongs to a society with a high regard for comfort and for well-being. You must understand comfort here in its highest sense, which makes it more nearly synonymous with luxury than with lethargy.

In all the restaurants of the Touraine you will find featured the same sort of dishes as those cited above, simple homely fare, it might be called, if it were not treated with so much skill and artistry. It is probably significant that this is a great country for roasts. There is nothing so basic and nothing so difficult to do really well, simple though the process of roasting a piece of meat may seem to be. The very simplicity of the roast is what makes it so difficult to produce a fine one. There is nothing to hide behind, no thick sauces with which to cover up mistakes. You are limited to the most transparent of seasonings, the thinnest of gravies. If everything is not exactly right, the defects are glaring. The skill of the Touraine in producing roasts is one more bit of evidence that this is the source from which French cooking sprang. Cross the Pyrenees and you meet the same phenomenon. The basis of Spanish cooking is, almost by definition, the Castilian cuisine; and the great specialty of Castile is roasting meat.

Among the regional dishes named above, you will remember that one was roast pork with prunes. This is typical of the Touraine, but, for once, rather untypical of France. You will meet several combinations of meat with cooked fruit in the Touraine, a result, perhaps, of the presence in this region of many fine orchards. But as a rule, French cooking avoids the simultaneous presentation of sweet and nonsweet tastes. Except for the classic applesauce with pork, you will not often encounter such dishes outside of this region.

Game is another favorite on Touraine menus. Some of it is local, for this is good game country, but the kitchens of Touraine also draw on the Sologne, the best game country in France, which lies conveniently just west of the Touraine. Hare is a particular favorite, but wild boar and venison also combine admirably in various dishes with the red wines of the country. Poultry is often processed in some particularly tempting fashion—in galantines, for instance—especially duck, and fricasseeing chicken is a specialty of the area.

If you follow the French custom of eating a separate vegetable course after the meat, you will find that the garden of France produces some greenery rarely seen elsewhere. It is a fair bet, for instance, that if you do not know the Touraine, you have never heard of *cardons*. The *cardon* belongs to the artichoke family, though it looks more like giant celery. *Cardon de Tours* is what it is likely to be called on a menu, for it is generally admitted that the best *cardons* come from the immediate neighborhood of Tours. A favorite way of preparing it is *au gratin*.

By no means exclusively a product of the Touraine, but particularly good here, is *chou vert*, green cabbage. This is a variety whose leaves spread out like an inverted bell instead of rolling tightly together in the familiar form of head cabbage. It is served locally in the simplest possible fashion, with no accompaniment except the melted butter in which it is doused.

Two other specialties not peculiar to the Touraine, but lovingly produced here, are *champignons* and *fèves*. The *champignons* (mushrooms, of course) of the Touraine are the big ones that reach the table riding inverted on little rafts of toast and brimming with *beurre d'escargot* (snail butter). They are delicious, but avoid them if you do not like garlic; snail butter is mostly garlic, combined with melted butter and chopped shallots and parsley. *Fèves* resemble in looks and taste the American lima bean, but have for the gardener the advantage that whereas the lima is a delicate hot-weather vegetable demanding warm earth and a long growing-season, the habits of the *fève* are those of the pea: it is a hardy plant, up first thing in the spring, and it produces madly. Its seeds are obtainable in the United States under the name fava beans (the Italian word for *fève*, for the plant is grown in Italy also), but the amateur gardener is warned that this bean is not popular in the kitchen. It has to be shelled twice. Inside the general pod, each separate bean is enclosed in its own little case, which has to be removed also. No gadget has yet been devised to perform this chore, and the American housewife is therefore resistant to the naturalization of the *fève*. French cooks being willing to perform any amount of labor to achieve a pleasing result, you will find the *fève* in honor in France, nowhere more so than in the Touraine.

There are many other vegetables that are surpassingly good in this province, though pre-eminence in their production is hotly disputed by other centers. For instance, the little village of Candes, near Fontevrault, specializes in asparagus, and if you see *asperges de Candes* on a menu, do not miss them. Indeed, it is good advice to order any vegetable identified by the name of a local place of production. There is always a reason why the listing is so specific; and the reason, of course, is that the locality named is famous for the product named.

For wine country, the Touraine is unusual in that it produces little cheese. Cheese brings out so miraculously the full flavor of a good red wine, and red wine reciprocates so winningly by emphasizing the savor of the cheese, that it is almost inevitable that both should be produced on the same territory. This, however, is a rule with many more exceptions than that which states that good wine country is good eating country. Normandy is probably the greatest single cheese-producing region in France, but it has no wine.

In the case of the Touraine, the reason is a simple one: the land is too fertile for pasturage, even for dairy cattle, and much more so for goats. It is so valuable for the production of wines, vegetables, and fruit that the Touraine prefers to import most of its milk. It has not far to go for good cheeses, so on the menus of the Touraine you will find those of the Orléanais to the north, Berry to the east, Anjou to the west. The Touraine considers them local cheeses.

There is, however, one exception worth mentioning. This is Sainte-Maure, produced in the Touraine village of the same name. It is a goat cheese, made in the form of a baton. Avoid it from December through April, when it is not at its best.

The Touraine is fine fruit country, where most communities that grow fruit specialize in one variety. The immediate suburbs of Tours itself are renowned for plums and, consequently, prunes; the *gros damas de Tours* is considered one of the finest prunes in the country. The Touraine shares with Agen the distinction of producing the best prunes of France. You will find them on local bills of fare as *pruneaux fourrés*. Preuilly is also noted for its prunes. Revarennes is famous for its *poires tapées* (pears), Azay-le-Rideau for *pommes reinettes* (apples), Rochecorbon for a plum named for this community. Throughout the region you will be offered fine *chasselas* (white dessert grapes); the variety of plum known as *Sainte-Catharine*, which is eaten fresh, never dried for prunes; *poires William*, a variety of pear much prized in France for its pronounced flavor, large, lemon-yellow and highly perishable, so you must eat it during its season, from the middle of August to the middle of September; and the fine peaches of the Touraine, which, while they do not rank with the best in France for eating fresh, are excellent in the local *pêche de Touraine à la royale*, in which it is served in a luscious creamy sauce.

But perhaps you prefer pastry for desert. In this case also you will be well served in the Touraine.

We have already noted the persistence in this part of the

country of some of the oldest forms of pastry known to France. There are many others, described as belonging to the enchanting category of *pourlécheries*. Literally this would mean something that is licked, not once but thoroughly, as a child might go over the sugared fruit-juice dripping from a tart or deprive a cupcake of its icing. It connotes something sweet and succulent, capable of procuring for an adult the same joy he felt as a child when he attacked a lollipop. Here again we find different towns specializing in various forms of pastry, at least two of them producing cakes to which they have given their own names, the *tourangeau* and the *lochois* being, respectively, the cakes of Tours and of Loches. Tours is also famous for its cookies and its barley sugar and Loches for its *cordes*. Ligueil is also known for *cordes*, but even more for macaroons, a specialty that it shares with Cormery.

It is not necessary to go beyond the narrow limits of the Touraine to find all the wines necessary to accompany every course in the rich menu of the region. White, *rosé*, and red, dry and sweet, the Touraine can supply them all. The Tourangeau of today is fond of printing on his menus a quotation from that Tourangeau of older times, Rabelais, which, if memory serves, goes like this: "Empty your full glass. Fill your empty glass. I cannot bear to look at you with your glass either empty or full."

Instead of an artificially prepared *apéritif*, you can very well prelude your meals with a glass of white Vouvray, one of the few French wines that can be drunk pleasurably without the accompaniment of food. For that matter you may, if you wish (there is really no particular necessity for it) use it at the end of the meal to replace Champagne, if you have that habit, for some Vouvrays are natural sparklers (*pétillant*)—that is, they bubble mildly without having to be forced to do so as in Champagne. Some Vouvray is converted into ersatz Champagne, known as *mousseux*, by being put through the champagnization process, but the less said about that the better. Finally, you can even end your meal with *eau-de-vie* without going beyond the borders of the Touraine; Sainte-Maure, which produces the goat cheese, also makes *marc*. This is a distillation of the residue that remains after the pressing of grapes for wine—the crushed skins, pips, stems, and liquid not drained off—and if it sounds like a poor relation of brandy, which is distilled from the wine itself, nevertheless do not disdain *marc* until you have tried it. A good *marc* is golden in color and leaves a rich aftertaste of Thanksgiving in the throat, a murmur of walnuts and raisins. Your chances of getting a good *marc* are better than of getting a good brandy. The latter is sometimes distilled from rather inferior wine; but the producer does not bother to make *marc* at all unless he has pretty good grapes to start with. There is thus a great deal of bad brandy on the market, but very little bad *marc*.

All the Touraine is wine-producing country. For that matter, so is virtually all the Loire valley; but the best wines of the region come from four very small areas—one might almost say two, for in each case you have a pair of regions divided from each other only by the Loire; however, there is a marked difference in both cases between the wines grown on the north and the south banks.

The first two regions are just east of Tours, Vouvray on the north bank, Montlouis on the south. They produce the white wines of the province. Vouvray is the best known wine name of the Touraine. Wine marketed under this name may come from Vouvray itself or from the neighboring communities of Noizay, Vernou, and Rochecorbon, of which the last sometimes manages to get its own name on the label, as the best source of Vouvray wine after Vouvray itself.

Vouvray is a versatile wine. As has been indicated above,

it may turn out to be still or to sparkle naturally, in which latter case the formation of bubbles is not nearly as violent as in the case of Champagne. For some types of Vouvray, the merchant will not guarantee that the wine you buy will prove to be either one or the other. Individual bottles may vary, and the sparkle is not perceptible until the bottle is opened. When Vouvray is turned into *mousseux* by being made to bubble artificially, it is probably as good *mousseux* as is produced anywhere in France, but this is not saying much. The Champagne-lover should not try to find a cheaper substitute for the real thing. There is none. If you like Champagne-type wines, the only thing to do is to buy Champagne, and the best you can get. There is a great deal of bad Champagne on the market, too.

If one epithet can be applied to all Vouvrays, it is perhaps "refreshing." The wines of Vouvray are light, charming, and of low alcoholic content. They are not great wines, but who wants to drink great wines every day?

Some Vouvrays are quite dry, and can be served with dishes that cry loudly for a dry white wine, like oysters. The medium dry Vouvrays are ideal in summer with the fish of the river on whose banks the vines grow—with a *friture* of Loire fish, for instance. Finally, some vintages are almost as sweet as Sauternes, and can be used as dessert wines.

A visit to Vouvray itself is exceedingly pleasant. The wine is stored in natural caves, hollowed out in the chalk cliffs that rise from the river and are carpeted with vineyards. Some of the caves have become improvised restaurants, or at least wine-tasting stations, where you can try a bottle against the background of a bit of bread and cheese or sausage. The pilgrimage to Vouvray used to be an idle and gracious visit, but since the war, unfortunately, the tourist buses have discovered it, and if you want to enjoy its charm, you had better try to avoid the times of their visits. As a result of this development, one or two of the cave-restaurants have turned into something perilously like variety shows, with the winegrower doubling as an entertainer to put his guests into a mood deemed to be favorable to the sale of Vouvray. These are not the places where you buy the best wine.

Montlouis, on the south side of the river, under whose name both the wine of Saint-Martin-le-Beau and its own are bottled, may be described as a producer of secondary Vouvray.

Outside of these two important areas are one or two isolated communities whose white wine is considered sufficiently superior to that of the region in general to be marketed sometimes under their own place names rather than simply as Touraine wine. These are Saint-Avertin, just southeast of Tours, not far from the Montlouis region; Saché, which is in the general neighborhood of Azay-le-Rideau; and Candes, on the Touraine-Anjou boundary.

The other two wine regions are also over toward Anjou, about as far west of Tours as you can go without leaving the Touraine altogether. On the north bank of the Loire is Bourgueil; on the south, Chinon. Both are known for their red wines.

They are earthy wines. The experts seem to have agreed to distinguish between them by detecting a faint flavor of raspberry in Chinon and of strawberry in Bourgueil. You will not have much difficulty in identifying the raspberry component in the taste of Chinon, but you may find that to taste the strawberry in Bourgueil requires either a more delicate palate or a readier imagination. An easier differentiation is supplied by the fact that Chinon is the thinner wine, Bourgueil heavier—more *corsé,* to use a winebibber's term that one might be tempted to translate as "lustier." These differing characteristics of the wines from the opposite sides of the river make it advisable, if you have a hare and a bottle of each, to cook the animal in the Chinon and drink the Bourgueil with it.

Under the name Bourgueil are bottled also the produce of its neighbors, Restigné and Chouzé-sur-Loire, but the best Bourgueil comes from a village called Saint-Nicolas; so look for a label reading Saint-Nicolas-de-Bourgueil if you want to taste this wine at its best. As for Chinon, it is the only label you are likely to find, and it applies to the wine of the whole area, which includes not only Chinon itself, but also Ligré, Beaumont-en-Véron, Huismes, and Cravant-les-Coteaux.

The *rosés* of the Touraine are pleasant natural wines of no particular distinction. They are marketed under the generic name of Touraine, or even Loire, wine, without more specific identification.

Like most wines of comparatively low alcoholic content, those of Touraine are not long-lived. You do not order them to store in your cellar to mature; they are table wines for immediate consumption and everyday use. You would hardly want to go back more than a few years in these vintages. The wines of 1952, a fair year, are already going off. Still holding up are those of 1953, a good year, and of 1955, even better. Also good, and of course not yet too old, are the Touraine wines of 1959 and 1961.

Do not be misled by the use of the word "great," applied in vintage year tables to these wines. The Touraine may have its great *years*, but Touraine wines are never great *wines*. Excellent for daily serving rather than for special occasions, they are well adapted to the cuisine of their own region, which their character no doubt helped to shape—honest, sturdy, appetizing provender with no nonsense about it, a style of cooking in admirable harmony with the character of the heartland of France.

III

The Golden Crescent

[Poitou, Anjou, Berry, Orléanais, Ile-de-France]

Seine is a magic name. The river glimmers in memories all over the world, usually as it has been seen gliding under the bridges of Paris or splitting around the islands of Saint-Louis and the Cité, or perhaps in its more rustic stretches between Paris and Rouen, where it coils placidly through a green countryside, descending slowly to the sea. It is a gentle river, slow and regular in its flow, and by no means a large one. For size it ranks last among the major rivers of France.

Where does the Seine begin? On the eastern slope of the plateau of Langres, the reference books say, and the city of

Paris has erected the statue of a nymph on the spot, perhaps to mark it, perhaps to stop the argument about it. Different geographers have expressed different opinions about just which streamlet is farthest from the mouth of the Seine, and thus entitled to be called its source. It is difficult to be positive, because in different years different experts may appear to be right, depending upon what local precipitation has done for the various watercourses. The Seine is so insignificant a river at its start that in summer it may be dry as far as Châtillon, thirty-one miles from its source—or at least from the nymph.

The oddest thing about the Seine is a perversity quite at variance with the usual nature of rivers. Every river is assumed to cut itself deeper and deeper into its valley as the years go by; but the Seine today is actually some eighty feet higher than it was at the end of the Tertiary Era. The reason is obscure, but the most plausible theory seems to be that the melting of the glaciers that covered the earth at the beginning of the Quaternary Era raised the level of the sea, which flooded what is now the basin of the Seine, filled up the river bed, and then, for good measure, spread a thick coating of silt over the whole region. The Seine is now engaged in digging its trench all over again.

If at the end of the Tertiary Era there had been any men to follow river valleys, and if they had chosen to follow a natural route from north to south, starting at the source of the Oise, they might have progressed down the valley of the Oise, through a short section of the valley of the Seine, through the valley of the Loing (at that time the Loire), and probably, when the rising land began to make the going harder, would have turned westward through the valley that is the route of the Loire today. This course covers an area roughly crescent-shaped. It is not really a natural geographic unit now, for it cuts straight across the Seine at right angles. If you looked at a relief map of France as it exists today, you would expect any cultural area taking in the Paris basin to extend into Normandy and Flanders, and perhaps farther. But the curious fact is that this crescent constitutes a cultural unit that follows roughly the lines of what was once a topographic entity, though it has not been one since an epoch previous to the appearance of man, and hence of culture.

The crescent that starts just short of the northern border and the flat plains of Flanders in the upper reaches of the valley of the Oise cuts across the Seine, continues south along the lines of the valleys first of the Loing and the Loir, then of the Loire itself, and finally swings around the curve to reach the Atlantic at the Loire's mouth. It takes in the ancient provinces of the Ile-de-France, Orléanais, and Berry, and then, passing across the Touraine, embedded in their center, Anjou and Poitou. They are all very much of a piece. They look the same; this is lush, fertile country, with green fields and rolling hills, watered by many streams. Their histories have been similar or have intermeshed ever since the days of the Romans. Most importantly, for the purposes of this book, they have shared very much the same ideas about cooking. There are regional differences within the whole area—the Poitevins are perhaps the most original —but no one from any section of this golden crescent of French gastronomy would find the dishes of any other section particularly exotic. The cooking throughout this region is congruent and it is great.

The Ile-de-France was the kernel about which, over a period of nearly a thousand years, the other parts of France gradually gathered. It covers the area included today in the departments of the Aisne, Oise, Seine, Seine-et-Oise, Seine-et-Marne, and part of the Somme. It was not, however, the first France; and Paris, far from being the capital of that France, was not even included in it. Paris was still Lutetia then, the name the Romans gave it, pleasant enough in sound if you don't happen to know that it describes the place as the City of Mud.

The original Pays de France, the core of the earliest kingdom, still bears that name. It lies north and east of the capital, a somewhat neglected plateau beginning at Saint-Denis, seven miles north of Paris, and extending to Luzarches, twelve and a half miles farther north, with its eastern edge at Dammartin-en-Goële, twenty-two miles northeast of Paris. Paris was in the adjoining "country" (*pays*), the Pays de Parisis, named for the tribe which later bestowed its title on the city. As the domain of the kings of the Capetian line extended, the territory became known as the Duchy of France, and took in roughly the territory from the valley of the Seine to the valley of the Loire. Not until the middle of the thirteenth century did the term Ile-de-France come into being (and it was only constituted a definite province in the fifteenth). In the early days of the Kingdom of the Franks, Paris was less often its capital than were Soissons and Compiègne. Indeed as late as the time of Joan of Arc it was at Rheims—not even in the Ile-de-France, but in Champagne—that she insisted that Charles VII be crowned before she would address him as otherwise than the Dauphin —the crown prince.

The Ile-de-France was given its name—the Island of France—because it is all but carved out from the mainland by the frame of rivers that so nearly encircle it—the Epte, on the northwest, which is the boundary of Normandy; the Eure, on the southwest, in whose waters the towers of Chartres are reflected; the Yonne, in the southeast, which passes by the Gothic spires of Auxerre and Sens; the Marne, to the east, on whose banks the fate of France has twice trembled in the balance; and the Aisne, to the northeast, another river of battles.

This is the lovely, gentle country of soft and subtle contours which inspired the artists who, in the latter half of the

last century and the beginning of this one, made France the
world capital of painters. Unless you have seen the lighting
of the Ile-de-France—especially at twilight, and in the
autumn—you cannot be expected to appreciate fully the
atmospheric effects of Corot. Corot was associated with
half a dozen localities of the Ile-de-France, virtual suburbs
of Paris—Ville d'Avray, whose pools he made famous in
his paintings; Bougival, also inhabited at one time or another
by Meissonier, painter of battles (who was not of the line
of atmospheric painters nor of the Ile-de-France either, having been born in Lyons), as well as by those other ex-
ploiters of the region's atmosphere, Monet, Renoir, and
Berthe Morisot (Berlioz lived here too); and Barbizon,
whose School of Barbizon was founded by Théodore Rousseau (not the Douanier), and whose artist inhabitants included Daumier, Millet, Courbet (and the sculptor Car-
peaux, whose nymphs dance before the Paris Opéra).
There is a school of Argenteuil, too, whose members tried
to capture the peculiar effects of the light of the Ile-de-
France on the surface of the Seine—Monet, Manet, Degas,
Sisley, and Renoir were among them, but it would be difficult to discover reflections from the Seine in the canvases
of one artist who was born here—Georges Braque. Pontoise
furnished a background for Pissaro and Cézanne (before he
left for Aix), Marly for Pissaro and Sisley. Sisley is also remembered at Moret and Monet at Giverny, where he painted
the great canvas called "*Nymphéas*," which hangs in the
Orangerie in Paris, and where he died. Daubigny painted
at Auvers-sur-Oise, and so did Van Gogh, before and after
his adherence to the more brilliant coloring of Provence.
He is buried there, beside his brother Théo, who was so
sturdy a supporter during the Dutch artist's tormented life.
As for Paris itself, Monet is its painter par excellence; Seurat,
the *pointilliste*, also born there, is among those whose treatment of color derives directly from the luminous air of the

Ile-de-France; but Gauguin, a native of Paris, preferred to paint Brittany before he left for the South Seas, and credit can hardly be given to the land for the many painters attracted to Paris by the presence in its neighborhood of the artists who were in touch with its essence, from Toulouse-Lautrec to Picasso—who, in his many metamorphoses, seems to have painted everything except nature; or would it be more exact to say that he never painted anything except painting?

The modern artists of the Ile-de-France are the inheritors of a tradition of artistic activity long exercised in this region. Francis I, who brought Leonardo da Vinci to the Touraine's Château d'Amboise, also summoned Benvenuto Cellini to the Ile-de-France's Château de Fontainebleau. (He also acquired the "Mona Lisa" to hang in Fontainebleau, which is why it is in the Louvre today and not in Italy.) The Ile-de-France was the country of royalty and of the great lords who surrounded royalty, patrons of the arts of painting, sculpture, music, architecture, and cooking. The Ile-de-France and the territories that surround it are strewn thickly with their tombs and their châteaux, and their patronage was a leading influence in making this the greatest center for the French Gothic cathedral. Here are Notre Dame de Paris; possibly the most beautiful of all Gothic cathedrals, Notre Dame de Chartres (in the Orléanais); Beauvais, where the Gothic arch reaches its greatest height (141 feet), but in an effort which exhausted its builders, who were never able to add a nave to the choir that soared so high; Senlis, twenty years older than its sister in Paris; Amiens (in Picardy), with its famous bas-reliefs; Soissons, where hangs Rubens's "Adoration of the Shepherds"; the massive four-towered structure at Laon; the thirteenth-century cathedral of Meaux (in Champagne); and the less well-known twelfth- and thirteenth-century building of Noyon. Saint-Denis, within the limits of Greater

Paris, contains the tombs of all the kings France had during twelve centuries, with only six exceptions—the sovereigns of the family of Orléans are buried at Dreux, not far from Chartres. Napoleon, of course, lies beneath the dome of the Invalides, in Paris itself, "on the banks of the Seine, among the French people I have so dearly loved," in his own words—the words of an Emperor who sent one million of them to death in his wars. As for the châteaux, they include at least two which once sheltered Mme de Pompadour, at Champs and at La Celle-Saint-Cloud; one, Anet, which was built by Diane de Poitiers, and decorated by, among others, Benvenuto Cellini and the sensitive French sculptor Jean Goujon; that of Mme du Barry, near Bougival; and Malmaison, the home of Napoleon's Joséphine. At Pierrefonds stands an immense reconstructed feudal castle. The Château of Rambouillet is today the summer residence of the president of France. The Château of Saint-Germain-en-Laye, a suburb of Paris, has been the backdrop for some eight centuries of history, but is particularly associated with Henry IV. The Château of Chantilly belonged to the great Condé family—not kings, but nevertheless of royal blood. Fontainebleau is one of the most extensive, most elaborately decorated, and most breathtaking palaces of France. Anywhere else, Fontainebleau would be the undisputed masterpiece of its kind. In the Ile-de-France it has to bow to two others—the queen of all châteaux, Versailles, and the largest palace in the world, the Louvre.

When you visit the great châteaux of the Ile-de-France you may be shown state apartments, statuesque staircases, ballrooms, art galleries, chapels, finely furnished rooms—but ordinarily no kitchens. Yet the kitchens could hardly fail to be of interest. Cooking arrangements had to be made on an impressive scale in these great buildings or groups of buildings, each of which harbored as many persons as a small town. There were some 20,000 persons attached to the Court of Versailles at the time of Louis XIV. About 9,000 of them were soldiers, who did their eating in their barracks. Five thousand were servants and other employees, lodged in various outbuildings and dependencies of the château, in most cases with their own eating arrangements. But there were 1,000 aristocrats and 4,000 servants living in the château itself, and a thousand gentlemen of lesser degree quartered about it who no doubt sat often at the tables supplied by the kitchens of the palace. It would be most interesting to be able to see today the kitchens of Versailles with their original furniture, for they marked an epoch in the history of cooking. It was under Louis XIV that the limited number of simple utensils used in medieval cooking was finally replaced with a more varied and more complicated kitchen battery. This being the Grand Century, everything, even kitchenware, had to be executed in the grand manner; so it was not very long after their introduction that in the great palaces the kitchen pots and pans were being made of silver, as they were in at least two great houses not of royal rank, those of the Prince de Condé at Chantilly and of Fouquet at Vaux-le-Vicomte. These two houses are also linked gastronomically by another circumstance—both employed the services of Vatel, a master of banquets whose touch seems to have been unfortunate: in both places his efforts to entertain the king were disastrous.

Everyone remembers Vatel as the cook who committed suicide when the fish failed to appear for Louis XIV's dinner, and therefore remembers incorrectly. Vatel was never a cook, but a sort of major-domo. It has been remarked, indeed, that the famous story that led to the universal misapprehension is in itself proof that Vatel was no cook, for one of the distinguishing talents of the great cook is his ability to make do with what is at hand. A great cook would not have killed himself because the fish was lacking; he would have produced a meal in which the lack would not have been noticed.

At the time of the first of Vatel's two historic and ill-fated banquets, on August 17, 1661, he was in the service of Fouquet, France's chief tax collector, who was not violating the contemporary tradition of tax collecting by making little distinction between the state's money and his own. This enabled him to live in the greatest luxury, which he might have been better advised not to flaunt too obviously in the face of the King when he invited him to a feast on the occasion of his stay at nearby Fontainebleau. The more distinguished of the 1,500 guests took their places at eighty long tables. The others jostled about thirty buffets. The dishes at most of the tables were of silver, but at that of the King the service was solid gold. Louis did not appreciate this attention. He had just been obliged to melt down his own gold and silver ware to help pay for the Thirty Years' War. He glowered through the ballets, concerts, water games, and plays given against the setting of the 1,200 fountains and waterfalls of the estate, stayed for the fireworks, but refused to sleep in the room that had been prepared for him, and returned to Fontainebleau. It was difficult not to divine where the money had come from that made Fouquet able to outshine the court, and Louis would have arrested the tax collector on the spot if the Queen had not dissuaded him. Less than three weeks later Fouquet was in prison, the men who had built his château were in the service of the King, with the mission of constructing Versailles, and Vatel was thus free to enter the service of Le Grand Condé, in which, an almost exact ten years later, he was to serve Louis XIV again and commit the opposite fault. The first time he had provided too much, the second too little.

It is true that Louis set him an almost impossible task.

He came for a three-day visit and brought the whole court along—five thousand persons, all accustomed to eating heartily three times a day. At dinner the first evening the roasts ran out before the last two of the sixty tables had been served and the Controller General of the Mouth of His Highness the Prince lay awake all night grieving about it. In the morning, Vatel was told that the fish had not arrived. He went up to his room, braced the hilt of his sword against the wall and ran himself upon it. A few minutes later the fish were delivered.

If the present custodians of the great houses where such magnificent feasts were a possibility do not see fit to show us the kitchens that provided them, one result of their presence can hardly be hidden—the shape they gave to these structures by the considerable chimneys they demanded. Versailles was too late and too restrained to expose ostentatiously these utilitarian air passages whose proliferation gave a baroque effect to so many structures—but the silhouette of Fontainebleau is dominated by its chimneys, as is that of Henry VIII's Hampton Court across the Channel. The comparison of the two indicates that French cooking had already become somewhat more complicated than English. Hampton Court still had the arrangement that was only rarely still to be found in France—the hearth was in the center of the Great Hall, with a hole in the roof above to let the smoke out. In 1609, not so long after Henry's time, Fontainebleau already had a separate building for its kitchen, in which four of the old kitchens, with their tremendous hearths, were incorporated. (Hampton Court also had other kitchens, and it is one of the few places where visiting tourists can see them equipped more or less as they used to be.) Thus most of the chimneys bristling from the roofs of Fontainebleau are accounted for, not by the kitchen, but by the numerous fireplaces necessary in palaces that antedated central heating.

This royal country of the Ile-de-France, where cooking was an art of the court and of the great houses of the nobles, was consequently a land of sophisticated cooking. The Ile-de-France became conscious of cooking as an art far back in its history. The first French cookbook, the *Viandier* (*viande* at that time meant food in general, not simply meat, as today), was written somewhere between 1373 and 1380 by a court cook, Taillevent, at first chef for Philip VI of Valois, then "first squire of the kitchen and master of the kitchen garrisons of France" under Charles VI. If this date marks the birth of sophistication in French cooking, it does not mean that it had yet reached refinement, even in the great houses of the Ile-de-France and at the court. Delicacy in eating was indeed hardly to be expected when even as late as the time of Louis XIV the King was accustomed to have his closestool brought to him at the dining table, while his guests, less well provided in the way of furniture, were in the habit of relieving themselves on the magnificent steps of the palace of Versailles.

A modern criticism of the cooking of Taillevent's time may be indicated by the change in meaning of the name of one of the dishes then popular. It was made of hashed mutton or chicken, stewed with chopped onions in a meat gravy sauce, and was known as *galimafrée*. The word still exists, but it has changed meaning; today it might be translated as "slumgullion."

Whatever fourteenth-century feasts lacked in refinement was compensated for by quantity. One of the banquets Taillevent served for Charles VI began with an opening course composed of capons with a cinnamon-flavored sauce, chicken cooked with herbs and spices, cabbage (an early appearance of vegetables in formal cooking), and venison. After this appetizer, the servants brought in various roasts, peacocks, hare, capon *pâtés*, and a few other dainties. When this had been cleared away, the guests tapered off on partridge, pigeons, and venison patties, served with jelly. Dessert was composed of cream puddings, pear patties, fruit tarts, and almonds.

It is notable that in so elaborate a meal no fish was included, though fish was already appearing on fourteenth-century tables, especially in the form of *chaudemer*, in which fresh-water fish were first grilled and then stewed in a wine sauce. This was the ancestor of the *matelote*, a dish whose origin is usually ascribed to the Ile-de-France.

Fish appeared more frequently in the time of Francis I. Vegetables were still rare, and so was butcher's meat, game providing the greater part of the fare. Meanwhile Italian influence was making itself felt in the kitchen as well as in art. The inspiration of the Renaissance had not spent itself with the major arts, but extended to the minor ones as well. Catherine and Marie de Médicis intensified this influence by bringing Italian cooks and pastrymakers—the latter then certainly the finest in the world—along with them. Henry IV profited by these immigrations and attached himself to culinary as well as political history by announcing his ideal as a chicken in every pot, while one of the chefs of his time, La Varenne, who directed the kitchens of the Marquis of Uxelles, also linked the two arts by being promoted, if that is the correct word, from cook to politician. Finesse, in spite of the Italian influence, was perhaps still not the word for French cooking, but the guests of Henry IV at the Château of Saint-Germain-en-Laye presumably expected no more refinement from their host at the table than in the grottoes he had had constructed there. They were inhabited by automatons (also the work of Italians) operated by water pressure, and it was Henry's amusement to end a showing of their antics by operating a valve that drenched all those present in an artificial rainstorm.

People went to a good deal of trouble for a joke in those

days. At the Château of Rambouillet, the Count of Guiche was served a large dish of mushrooms at supper, followed by tales of the weird effects of mushroom poisoning. When he woke up in the morning and found himself so swollen that he couldn't get into his clothes, he allowed himself to be convinced at first that it was the work of the mushrooms. Only later did his hosts confess that during the night they had taken all his clothes apart at the seams and sewn them together again on a smaller scale.

Although Louis XIV was too big an eater to be a gourmet, he seems to have been personally responsible for one reform in the direction of more orderly eating. It was he who ordered that the various dishes at the court table should be served separately, one after the other, in contrast to the old habit, exemplified in the meal of Charles VI described above, of bringing on a great variety of different foods indiscriminately in one course. He was also responsible for the appearance of the *entremets*—and if you have wondered why desserts bear this name ("between meats") it is because in the lusty days of mammoth meals that is exactly when this sweet course was served. After a series of courses which would put a modern trencherman *hors de combat*, sweet dishes were served to provide a sort of period for this part of the repast—a period which turned out to be no more than a semicolon, for after the sweets more meat dishes were brought in and the meal began, more or less, all over again, to be ended finally by other sweets and fruit. The addition of a second sweet course to the meal and the daily serving of the *entremets*—a more elaborate dessert than the final one—instead of their appearance only on exceptional occasions was a pampering of Louis's well-developed sweet tooth. He ended his life without a tooth, in his mouth, sweet or otherwise.

Perhaps the beginning of the evolution from stuffing oneself to eating less of more subtly prepared foods occurred when eaters started to transfer their interest from the dining table to the kitchen and to busy themselves with the process of preparing food. This seems to have become a matter with which a gentleman might deign to interest himself by the time of the Regency. Benjamin Franklin reported hearing that when the Regent gave small intimate supper parties, the guests often invaded the kitchen and helped the cooks, or at least enjoyed the illusion that they were helping. The result was not yet quite austerity. A menu for one of these small suppers which has been preserved starts with corned beef, carrots, and potatoes; moves on through two kinds of soup accompanied by a duck; continues with two fish dishes; adds ten entrées, including mutton, chicken, partridge, veal, wild boar, eels, shrimps, perch, pike, sauerkraut—and oysters cooked in cream, a forerunner of the American oyster stew; two *entremets;* a course violating even more than its predecessors Louis XIV's principle of segregation—fried river fish, fowl, sole, and wild duck; four salads; and four cooked desserts. This dainty supper was designed to serve twelve persons.

The interest of the Regent's guests in the kitchen—where they used pots and pans made of silver—probably got no nearer to the reality of the art of cooking than Marie Antoinette's Petit Hameau at Versailles to the problems of peasant living (she also amused herself with a milk house at the Château of Rambouillet, where Louis XVI, for whom agriculture was a hobby, established the national sheep-breeding farm, which still exists—with the object of producing wool, not meat). A more practical cook was Louis XVI's cousin, the Duc de Penthièvre, then living at the Château de Rambouillet, whom Louis, arriving unexpectedly one day, found in the kitchen enveloped in a huge apron and stirring a steaming mass in an enormous cauldron. It was his custom to feed the poor of the neighborhood, and he liked to make personally the stew which was served to them.

This interest in the kitchen, genuine or not (it was at this period that the snobbishness which often afflicts gastronomy began to develop), had at least one effect—it attached great names to a number of the inventions of the leading chefs. This has given rise to legends that one dish or another was originated by some personage of renown. This was hardly ever actually the case, the name being a compliment from the chef, like an author's dedication of his book to a powerful patron. If the dedication did not happen to be by name, the honor was likely to prove ephemeral. *Bouchée à la reine* still appears on French menus regularly, but very few persons who order it know that the name of this delectably filled patty shell refers to Queen Marie Leczinska, wife of Louis XV.

Not everybody, of course, ate as did the great for whom new dishes were likely to be named. If the early history of gastronomy seems to be more a chronicle of the banquets of kings and nobles than of more everyday fare—at least in this aristocratic land of the Ile-de-France—that is largely owing to the theory that only these feasts were worth recording. But another reason is that there were considerable periods when there was almost nothing to be recorded below this level. The great mass of the people were lucky to be eating at all. The best-served commoners were those who, as hangers-on at some court or great house, had a chance at the leavings from the master's table. There are no old restaurant menus to consult, for there were no restaurants. However, Brillat-Savarin does give a menu for a dinner of ten middle-class persons in 1740. It started with a sort of veal pot roast—first the bouillon in which it had been cooked, then the veal itself, together with an undescribed hors d'œuvre. The second course was turkey, vegetables, salad, and custard; and the third and last was cheese, fruit, and preserves. Brillat-Savarin, incidentally, was not highly rated by one of the greatest chefs of the time, Antonin Carême, who wrote a number of books on cooking, was employed, among others, by Baron de Rothschild, the Prince Regent of England (later George IV), and the Emperor Alexander of Russia, and is considered to have been the founder of *la haute cuisine*. Brillat-Savarin, Carême remarked disdainfully, "never knew how to eat." He liked "strong and vulgar things" and "did no more than fill his stomach. M. de Savarin was a big eater and talked very little. At the end of the meal he was absorbed by his digestion and I have seen him fall asleep."

The restaurant was born under Louis XV. (Inns, of course, had been accustomed to feed their guests before that, but they offered no choice; you took what they had at the time when they chose to serve it, and as you had no option, there was no need to present bills of fare which might have come down to us.) One reason why there were none earlier was the existence of a monopoly related to the privileges of the medieval guilds, which, if they were maintained today, would probably lead to prosecution for combinations in restraint of trade. Persons who wanted something to eat outside of their own homes had only two alternatives—to go to an inn or to go to a *traiteur*, a monopolist in the selling of food, who was not permitted, by the rules which bound his profession, to sell less than a whole cut of raw meat, whatever it might be. He was, in a way, a wholesaler of food.

If it was forbidden to sell cooked meat in small quantities for individual consumption on the seller's premises, it was not forbidden to sell the bouillon made by boiling meat. An enterprising bouillon-seller named Boulanger (which means baker), in one of the first high-pressure advertising campaigns on record, gave his soups the name *restaurants*, intended very much in the sense that today we

73

might use the word "pickup." "Boulanger puts out some heavenly pickups," he proclaimed on his sign (*"Boulanger débite des restaurants divins"*) and added, in more classical vein: *"Venite ad me; vos qui stomacho laboratis et ego restaurabo vos"* ("Come unto me, you who are heavy-laden in the stomach and I will restore you"). The word "restaurant" had thus entered the international vocabulary before the thing itself; for Boulanger had not yet quite finished inventing the restaurant. Wishing to add something more substantial to his collection of thin soup, but hampered by the laws which protected the monopoly of the *traiteurs*, Boulanger conceived the idea of producing a dish made of sheep's feet in a white sauce. The *traiteurs* sued him for the illegal sale of a stew. Boulanger maintained that sheep's feet in white sauce were not a stew and the argument was carried all the way up to Parliament, which passed a law establishing, at least *de jure*, that whatever it was *de facto*, sheep's feet in white sauce did not, within the meaning of the act, constitute a stew. The curious hastened to try the new dish—including Louis XV, who ordered it served on his table, once, but never again. A gourmet, Louis apparently agreed with Boulanger that sheep's feet in white sauce were not, *de facto*, a stew or, for that matter, even food. But it proved none the less to be the breach in the monopoly. The restaurant was born. Boulanger had founded a profession.

The new institution flourished. Brillat-Savarin noted that many restaurants prospered chiefly because of certain specialties: "Le Veau Qui Tette for its sheep's feet; les Frères Provençaux for its codfish with garlic; the Véry, for its truffle dishes; Henneveux, for its mysterious boudoirs on the fourth floor." For an infant industry, the restaurants did themselves proud. On Véry's bill of fare, for instance, there were listed daily twelve different soups; twenty-four hors d'œuvres; from fifteen to twenty beef dishes; twenty kinds of mutton; thirty varieties of poultry or game; from sixteen to twenty veal dishes; twelve kinds of pastry; fifteen roasts; fifty *entremets;* and as many desserts of other categories.

The restaurant business might have been expected to suffer a severe blow as a result of the Revolution. The effect was just the opposite. It is true that at first it was considered good form to lean toward the ascetic side in eating in contrast to the arrogant luxury of the displaced aristocracy. But the cooks of the aristocracy had been displaced, too, hundreds of them, trained in the most complicated arts of the kitchen. They began to open restaurants. Even Carême, who had cooked for kings and emperors, presided for six years over a modest popular eating-place, putting his skill at the disposition of the proletariat, which had never tasted such marvels before. A larger public had been found for the skill of the great cooks. It was the basis for the spreading of the *haute cuisine*, whose origin was the elaborate cooking done for the great, and which now developed side by side with the *cuisine bourgeoise*, whose origin had been the never-extinguished fires of the peasants.

From this time on, the cooking of France in general is not particularly distinguishable from that of the Ile-de-France, whose chief characteristics it had borrowed. There is only one item of gastronomic history peculiar to this region and that has been given more importance than it really possessed—the supposed starvation of Paris during the siege of the capital by the Prussians at the time of the Franco-Prussian War. The plight of Paris actually was not nearly so bad as writers have made it appear. There was only one month of real deprivation, when crows, for instance, were on sale at the La Villette slaughterhouses for two and a half gold francs apiece (and for those who had enough gold francs, beef was available even at this period). France knew much harder times under the German occupation of the

Second World War. Thomas Carlyle once wrote that the French were such good cooks that they could make a palatable dish out of a thistle and that it was a shame they had no good butcher's meat. He undoubtedly never suspected that the thistle could actually be made edible, but during the German occupation, when a whole cookbook dealt with ways to use the crumbs that fell unavoidably from the meager amounts of bread available, dishes actually were made from thistles in the South of France.

(The French, incidentally, have plenty of good butcher's meat, but Carlyle was perhaps not aware of the fact that if you cut up a steer, as the French do, in order to obtain from it the best pieces of meat for boiling and stewing, you cannot get from the same animal the steaks and roasts which are the object of the English system of butchering. The difference in the results obtained is so marked that in London's Soho there is a French butcher shop where animals are cut up according to the French system rather than the English one, for the benefit of customers hungry for a genuine *pot-au-feu*.)

It is even truer of the Ile-de-France than it was of the Touraine that its cooking appears to have no regional characteristics, for the reason that the cuisine of this particular area has spread all over the country—and for that matter, all over the world. It has even been said that this area has originated no dishes of its own. This is not so, but the inventions of the Ile-de-France were taken up elsewhere so long ago that their place of birth has been forgotten. It has already been noted above that the *matelote* developed in this region. This is a dish of fresh-water fish or eel cut into pieces and cooked in wine with mushrooms and onions. Local variations of the basic dish bear the names of other provinces, but the Ile-de-France seems to have been the first to have produced a *matelote*. The *vol-au-vent* is probably a native of the Ile-de-France also—a pastry shell filled with any one of a variety of delectable trifles in a creamy sauce. The description "*à la parisienne*" usually indicates a dish accompanied by some vegetable combination including Parisian potatoes, which means the tiniest possible tubers, the size of hazelnuts, sautéed in butter, glazed with veal extract, and dusted with chopped parsley. Deep-fat frying is also a specialty of this area.

Another reason why Paris and the Ile-de-France get less credit for culinary inventions than they deserve is that the attraction which the capital has exerted on persons from other regions has sometimes caused the transfer to Paris of non-Parisian names, which have then been applied to dishes developed in Paris. If you asked most gastronomes to name a food specialty of the tiny Pays du Béarn, in the Pyrenees, they would probably come up quickly and triumphantly with *sauce béarnaise*, one of the most delicious of meat sauces and also one of the most difficult to make successfully. *Sauce béarnaise*, however, was first made in the restaurant known as the Pavillon Henry IV in Saint-Germain-en-Laye, just outside of Paris, and was so named in honor of Henry IV, who came from Béarn. What Saint-Germain lost in fame on this count it gained elsewhere, for one of the best known French soups, *potage Saint-Germain*, a thick pea soup, was actually developed in nearby Saint-Cloud. Then there is the famous case of *homard à l'armoricaine*, a spelling which purists give to the dish otherwise known as *homard à l'américaine*, arguing that the latter was obviously a corruption, since the Armoricain (Breton) coast is great lobster country. The purists do not seem to have been gastronomes, however, or they might have looked at the dish itself, which is obviously not Breton, but Provençal, the lobster being cooked in oil and accompanied lavishly with tomatoes—and indeed until the middle of the nineteenth century virtually the same dish was known as *homard à la provençale*. The most reasonable explanation for this name seems to be the one which ascribes it to a now vanished Parisian restaurant called the Américain, which is supposed to have made a specialty of it. The dish itself belongs in character no more to the cuisine of the Ile-de-France than to that of Brittany, but its present name and its adapted form would seem to be Parisian. As for *sole normande*, this is decidedly an Ile-de-France dish, for it is a *matelote*. Described on menus today as *sole à la normande* (sole in the Norman style), it is incorrectly presented. It is literally *sole normande*, Norman sole, sole that was caught off the coast of Normandy; the preparation of the dish is Parisian.

Although it seems too basic a dish to have been the discovery of any one region, the cut of steak known as *Chateaubriand*, served with French fried potatoes, is generally considered typical of the Ile-de-France. Also from the Ile-de-France comes one of the country's most famous desserts—*crêpes Suzette*. These are the very thin pancakes served flaming in a mixture of liqueurs—usually orange-flavored. There is a story that *crêpes Suzette* were discovered accidentally when a careless cook spilled a bottle of Champagne over his *crêpes* and thought they were spoiled until (again accidentally?) he lighted the Champagne and found he had created a new dish. I do not believe a word of this, not only because Champagne does not enter into any variety of *crêpes Suzette* that I know about, but chiefly because it is not easy to make Champagne burn even when you are trying.

Crêpes Suzette gives every indication of being the sort of dish typical of Ile-de-France cookery—an individual invention, deliberately created. Since the Ile-de-France is, as has been noted above, a land of sophisticated cooking, attracting famous chefs from other regions in addition to those it produces at home, it is the place where many well-known dishes were first introduced by one chef or another;

but these dishes do not, strictly speaking, belong to the regional cuisine. They did not develop naturally from the common contributions of hundreds of cooks, professional or amateur, working in a single tradition (usually evolved as a result of the sort of ingredients obtainable in the area). Each one was *sui generis*, the creation of an artist who produced it in the Ile-de-France, but might just as well have produced it somewhere else. Thus there are a great many names on menus today whose origin can be traced to the Ile-de-France without their being representative of Ile-de-France cooking. It is interesting to note that the list of such dishes includes a particularly large number of soups, which, as we have seen, did not figure largely on the menus of the Touraine. Soup provides a particular test of individual artistry. Anyone can make a passable soup by doing not much more than saving the juice in which meat has been boiled, but a master can ring more various and more subtle changes on soup than on almost any other single division of the bill of fare. A good way to find out how far to go in trusting an unknown French restaurant is to order soup before committing yourself on the main dish. If it produces a good soup, you are safe. It is a trustworthy touchstone.

Among the many soups of the Ile-de-France whose names denote their origin, besides the *potage Saint-Germain* already mentioned, there is first of all, of course, *potage parisien*, a vegetable soup containing potatoes, leeks, carrots, etc. (there is also a chicken *consommé à la parisienne*), and others named for Crécy, Compiègne, Soissons, and Argenteuil (the last asparagus soup, of course, for Argenteuil is famous for its asparagus). Soups using potatoes are popular in the region—*potage Parmentier* is a thick potato soup, *potage bonne femme* combines potatoes and leeks, *potage Santé* is a refinement of *potage Parmentier*. Among those attributable to a single chef is *potage*

Germiny, a subtle, slightly tart egg-yolk-cream-sorrel soup created by Dugléré at the now vanished Café Anglais.

In other departments of the meal, there are many dishes whose names indicate an origin in Paris or the Ile-de-France, to say nothing of those which did come from there, though anonymously. In the hors d'œuvre department there are several items of *charcuterie* so identified—*friands parisiens, hure de porc à la parisienne, pâté de porc de Paris, jambon glacé de Paris*. Any dish described as "Bercy" betrays a Parisian origin; it is along the quay of that name that the great Paris warehouses are located. The pressed duck which is a specialty of the Tour d'Argent is of Parisian inspiration. *Sole Marguéry*, in which tender pink shrimps are included in the sauce that envelops the fish, is, of course, named for the Restaurant Marguéry, which still remained on what had become a down-at-the-heels section of the Grands Boulevards recently enough so that I have myself had the pleasure of eating this dish at the place that created it. Outside the capital, many cities have given their names to local specialties, like the *matelote de Beauvais* and the *gâteaux de Compiègne* and *d'Etampes*. Poultry *pâtés* are identified in many cases by the names of the towns that produce them—they contain partridge at Laon, chicken at Houdan, lark at Etampes and Chartres.

An example of the way in which unfamiliar words are shouldered out of a phrase by more familiar ones, even though the usurpers are meaningless, is provided by one Ile-de-France dish identified on menus as *haricot de mouton*, although it hasn't a bean (*haricot*) in it. *Haricot* here replaces the obsolete word *halicot*, which meant stew—in this case, of mutton, turnips, potatoes, and onions, but no beans.

It is natural for this to be good eating country, for it is a fertile and productive land. On its southwestern rim, with Chartres for its capital, is one of the most renowned agricultural regions of France, the flat plain of the Beauce, which Zola used as the setting for his novel of fertility, *La Terre*. Its produce sinks anonymously into the menu, for its great crop is wheat; but all about Paris is fine market gardening country whose fruits and vegetables load the trucks which rumble nightly through the streets of Paris, upon which they converge from every direction of the compass, to end in the brilliant spectacle of the central markets, the Halles, a tourist must. To this goal come the little button mushrooms known all over France as *champignons de Paris;* the white beans, described universally as *soissons*, though more of them come from nearby Noyon than from Soissons itself; the superb asparagus of Argenteuil, Laon, and Lauris; the tender new peas of Clamart; the string beans of Bagnolet; the cauliflowers of Arpajon; the carrots of Crécy; the artichokes of Laon. Arpajon, particularly noted for its vegetables, holds a yearly "bean fair" at which prize samples of many other kinds of vegetables than beans are on display. The bean presumably gets top billing because Arpajon is the birthplace of a special variety of shell bean called *chevrier*, which, unless your eyes or ears are sharp enough to detect the lack of an accent, might suggest that these beans are fit fodder only for goats. Actually they take their name from the farmer who first produced them in 1878.

This is also good fruit country, where it is standard practice to grow many fruits *en espalier*—that is, against a sort of trellis background to which twigs are tightly attached, with such severe pruning that trees look like bushes or vines (I have seen pears grown this way that you would swear were the fruit of a vine, not a tree). The process seems to increase the thickness of growth of the fruit and the size of the individual pieces so that at the ripening season the trellis seems covered only with tightly packed fruit, which hides the leaves and makes them nearly invisible. This used to be good grape country, and some wine was made here, but since it was never great wine, the more valuable vegetables and fruit the region grows have crowded out wine grapes, though some dessert grapes remain. At Argenteuil, for instance, which used to be a grape-growing center, asparagus has replaced grapes except with a few growers who sell grafts of vines to winegrowers in other parts of the country.

On the grounds of the Château of Fontainebleau you still have the Treille du Roi, the Trellis of the King, which grows grapes from a vine that Francis I discovered in Cahors, Guienne, and had planted in Fontainebleau because, having eaten a few of its grapes by chance, he discovered that grapes were good to eat. Before that time, grapes were not eaten; they were used only for making wine. The grapes from this vine are still auctioned off every year to lively bidding. It is the ancestor of one of the finest dessert grapes of France, the *chasselas* of Fontainebleau, raised in the little town of Thomery, to which cuttings from the Treille du Roi were brought in 1730. Today Thomery has been occupied by the grape. Vines run over the walls and houses and seem to hide all constructions when the great bunches of fruit reach their full size. To walk through the streets is like exploring a jungle of grapes. Most of them are grown on trellises on south-facing walls; if all the walls of this type in Thomery were built in a straight line, they would extend for 150 miles beyond the town limits. It was at Thomery that the discovery was made that grapes could be kept fresh by plunging the stems into water in a room in which the correct degree of temperature and humidity was maintained, and grapes are so preserved in grape chambers until the month of May after each harvest.

Palaiseau, so near to Paris as to be on an extension of the subway, is famous for strawberries, as is Briis-sous-Forges, which also produces beans and seeds. Groslay is the center of a rich fruit-growing region where orchards extend over the plains as far as the eye can see. At Rosny-sur-Seine is the château built by Henry IV's minister, the Duc de Sully, who brought there the sixteenth-century agricultural expert, the appropriately named Olivier de Serres (the name means "Olive-tree of Greenhouses") to oversee the planting of 8,000 mulberry trees. It was to him that Sully pronounced a phrase destined to become a cliché of French political oratory: "Tilling and pasturage are the two nipples of France," a remark which today delights all those who enjoy burlesquing pompous speakers.

In the southeastern part of the Ile-de-France is a region whose food specialty need not be explained, for the name of the area will do it automatically. Here is the country of Brie, which extends into the neighboring province of Champagne, so that there are a Brie Française (in the Ile-de-France) and a Brie Champenoise. From this district comes the name of one of the world's best-known cheeses (and also of the breed of dog known as the Briard). Brie, one of the greatest of French cheeses, or, rather, families of cheeses, is a particular glory of the Ile-de-France, though not its only cheese by any means—Fontainebleau, for instance, produces one of the best known cream cheeses, often eaten with sugar for dessert. A cheese of respectable antiquity, Brie was already a favorite of Charles d'Orléans, father of Louis XII, in the fifteenth century. It has a rather reddish crust, produced by the microorganism that regulates its fermentation, and a pale-yellow creamy center which, though soft, should not run when the cheese is in the peak of its condition. The Bries of Coulommiers and Provins are considered rather finer than the Brie of Melun, but you can find the last in good condition all year round, while the other two are at their best only between October to May. Brie de Melun is saltier and stronger in taste than the other two, and the salt probably acts as a preservative. The big markets for Brie are Meaux, which also deals extensively in grain and cattle, and Melun, which offers grain and poultry in addition.

South of the Ile-de-France is the Orléanais, roughly equivalent to the three modern departments of the Loiret, Loir-et-Cher, and Eure-et-Loir—the first named for a curious river which is not really a separate river at all but a branch of the Loire. This was not perceived when it was named, for though the water of the Loiret flows out of the Loire and then back into it again, its exit is made underground. After tunneling its way for some distance from the main channel, the Loiret pops up to the surface and continues for a mere seven and a half miles before rejoining the parent stream.

Although the Orléanais is historic ground (Joan of Arc, as everyone knows, lifted the siege of Orléans, and she also enters into the history of Sully-sur-Loire), it need not detain us particularly, for it served chiefly as the land bridge between Paris and Tours, and as it joined France in 1198, its destiny was linked early to that of country we have already considered. Part of that fertile crescent which has already been described, and the hinterland of such great cities as Paris and Tours, it has always been a great supplier of food to the cities, though the nature of the food supplied has changed through the centuries—the proportion of game, though still important, has grown smaller, that of butcher's meat and vegetables greater.

The importance of the Orléanais as a game center in the days of venery is underlined by the existence here of the largest château of the Loire valley, Chambord, the precursor of Versailles, whose buildings now outstrip Chambord in size, but whose grounds do not. The wall surrounding the estate of Chambord is the longest in France—twenty miles.

If Francis I, who built Chambord, did not mean it primarily as a base from which to hunt, it is difficult to account for his choice of a site in an isolated and rather marshy region offering no other distractions. It was not rare in those days for great châteaux to start as hunting lodges; that was the origin of Fontainebleau. In any case, whatever the original idea, Chambord was used largely for hunting. Its great terrace provided a place for the women to watch the departure and the return of the hunters. There were three hundred hunting falcons in the aviaries. As for the end result of the hunt, Chambord is one of those châteaux whose outline owes a great deal to its chimneys. It has one for each day of the year, three hundred and sixty-five of them.

Chambord maintains its hunting tradition to this day. The grounds of the château have become a national game-breeding park and wild-life preserve.

The Château of Cheverny, a much later building (1634) also pays tribute to the importance of the region as game country with its Museum of Hunting, which contains two thousand sets of stags' antlers.

The Orléanais is still game country (the Sologne, part of which constitutes the southeastern corner of the Orléanais, is considered the finest hunting region of France, at least for birds), and its food specialties show it. The most famous is the lark *pâté* of Pithiviers, which for two hundred years has been made in the same pastry shop, Gringoire, in the shape of a doll. Pithiviers is also famous for its almond-flavored pastry.

Other towns of the Orléanais make *pâtés* containing such game as partridge, thrush, rabbit, and hare. *Lapereau à la solognote* is a local treatment of young rabbit and *lièvre en terrine* a rich preparation made of hare. But game is by no means the only resource of the Orléanais. Much fine butcher's meat is raised here, particularly in the region called the Perche, which strictly speaking is outside of Orléanais to the northwest, in the province of the Maine.

You know of its reputation for breeding animals, even if you think you have never heard of the place before—you do, that is, if you know Percheron horses. Even the hunting country of the Sologne produces fine domestic animals also—*gigot de mouton de Sologne à l'eau* is a favorite way of preparing leg of lamb, while in the Beauce, which extends into the Orléanais from the Ile-de-France, beef takes the lead—try *bœuf braisé à la beauceronne*. The Beauce is also good poultry country.

Excellent vegetables and fruit are grown throughout this whole region. You will find asparagus from Vendôme noted on many menus, but so far as I know the Sologne has not yet found its way onto bills of fare for this specialty, though in the last twenty-five years or so some of the finest asparagus in France has been grown there. I was taken once to see an asparagus farm of which this region was particularly proud, and while its asparagus could hardly have been bettered, it was not much to look at. All there was to see was bare earth, rippled with the alternation of trench and dike. No greenery is allowed to show above the surface, at least at the time of year when the asparagus is ripening. It grows entirely underground, hilled up in the dikes of earth, and is harvested with a special tool that looks like a carpenter's gouge. The pickers run this implement into the earth with astonishing dexterity, probing for the asparagus stalk, sliding the tool down it with the asparagus cradled in its concave side, and cutting it off cleanly at the bottom with a little twist of the wrist. The object of growing the plant completely underground is to keep the entire stalk white and tender.

An unusual specialty of the Orléanais is saffron, which is grown at Boynes, near Pithiviers. This enters largely into Provençal cooking, but seems out of place here. Its presence accounts for one fine local dish, pike cooked with saffron. Perhaps it accounts also for the special flavor of the famous honey of the region, the *miel du Gâtinais* which you will find on sale everywhere in France.

The chances are that if you asked even a fairly well-informed French gourmet if the Orléanais is wine country, you would be told that it is not—though he should remember that some of the best wine vinegar of France comes from Orléans, and it should be a fair assumption that not all of the regional wine goes into vinegar. The fact is that some light pleasant wines are grown here, but you are never likely to taste them unless you visit the places where they originate. On either side of Orléans, on the hillsides of the Loire valley, Meung, Beaugency, and Sully have some drinkable vintages, and in the department of Loir-et-Cher, as you approach the Touraine wine country, you come upon the small natural red wines of the Blaisois, the Cher, and the Vendômois, and the whites of Trôo, Lavardin, and Moutoire.

The Sologne serves as a bridge from the Orléanais into the Berry, for it lies across both provinces. The Berry, corresponding to the modern departments of the Cher and the Indre, is agricultural country, and though it served as a sort of crossroads for the Romans, has managed nevertheless to stay off the main currents of modern travel. Tourists may make a point of going to Bourges to see its great five-portaled cathedral, but not many foreigners really penetrate into this rural district, where the local patois often largely supplants French, so that the husky pancake known as *matefaim* (hunger tamer) is referred to here as *matafan*, while potatoes are *truches* or *tartouffes*. The potato is much in honor here, as is natural for a region of hearty rustic peasant fare, appearing often in the thick soups of peasant cooking which are encountered frequently in this region. Some families eat soup three times a day. *Soupes grasses*—fat soups—they call them, and they certainly are, especially those which include salt pork. There is also a sort of potato cake called *truffiat*. Pumpkin pie I had always considered definitely an American specialty, with no kin in France; but in the Berry I discovered a pumpkin tart, the *citrouillat*. Later I was to find other examples of this dish elsewhere.

Besides being good game and fresh-water fish country (the lampreys of Vierzon are especially famed), the Berry is noted for the quality of its mutton. The Berrichon combination of lamb and beans is a dish that sticks to the ribs. Goats, which are not generally raised in the flatter parts of France, are fairly numerous in the Berry, and as a result it has some good goat cheeses, like the *crottins* of Chavignol —a name which gourmets remember for another reason. For Chavignol produces some excellent wine (it was much appreciated by Balzac), and so does its Loire neighbor, Sancerre. These wines travel, and you find them even in Paris (Fouquet, on the Champs-Elysées, was serving an excellent Sancerre in carafe as its white table wine at the time of writing). Over on the Cher, Quincy and Reuilly have some fine vintages. Issoudun is a winegrowing town not quite so well known. The best wines of the Berry are the whites, with a distinct flinty taste, and inclined to be heady. There are also the *petits gris*, gray wine, which is likely to be a trifle coarse in taste, but it is a not unpleasant roughness. There is an earthy flavor about it which in French is called a taste of *terroir* but which the Berrichon dialect has twisted into *terre noire*, black earth. The best recent years for these wines have been 1947, 1948, 1949, 1952, and 1953.

Moving westward from the Berry, we slip to the south of the already explored Touraine into the ancient province of Poitou, where Charles Martel saved Europe from the Saracens in 732 and the Black Prince defeated Jean le Bon in 1356. Covering roughly the territory represented today by the departments of the Deux-Sèvres, Vendée, and Vienne, Poitou, like the Touraine and like Anjou, has had its English period, having been part of the dowry which Eleanor of Aquitaine brought to Henry II of England. Philip Augustus won it back in 1203, but failed to hold it. Charles V acquired it a second time in 1369. But not until 1416 was it won definitely on the third try, under Charles VI.

Poitou is another region not too well known to tourists, though it deserves to be. Its capital, Poitiers, where Richard the Lion-Hearted was proclaimed Count of Poitou in 1170 and where Joan of Arc was questioned by the doctors of the university, is a museum of architecture from the fourth century on, while just south of it, at Ligugé, is the place where Saint Martin founded monasticism in Gaul (Huysmans wrote about Ligugé in *Sainte Lydwyne de Schiedam*). Chauvigny, a little east of Poitiers, is a mecca for students of pre-Romanesque and Romanesque architecture, and leads either southward to Civeaux and its Merovingian cemetery, or east to Saint-Savin, whose eleventh-century Romanesque murals are unique. In the other direction from Poitiers, west and a little south, you come to the region known as the "Green Venice," or less picturesquely as the Poitevin marshes, which begin at Maillezais. The land here is threaded with a network of swiftly moving streams, often tunneling through thick foliage that meets overhead, and most of the travel through it is by flat-bottomed boat. Continuing northwest, you move through the Vendée to the coast, coming out, perhaps, at Sables d'Olonne, a fishing village famous for the short-skirted costumes of its women.

Poitou, like the neighboring Berry, boasts many peasant dishes, some of which have remained unchanged for centuries and contain ingredients that offhand do not sound particularly reassuring to timid eaters. Take, for instance, *fressure vendéenne*, which is made of the lungs, liver, heart, and spleen of the pig, chopped up, mixed with coagulated pig's blood, and cooked slowly and lengthily in lard. It is eaten cold, and no doubt in cold blood. After this, *potée à la tête de porc* seems quite aristocratic; the pig's head, cut into small pieces, is cooked in a soup, which is eaten first, after which the morsels of pig's head, slightly flavored with vinegar, are served with rock salt. Pig's head is also stewed in wine and blood, and served under the name of *gigorit*. The *farci* of Poitou is an ancient combination—breast of pork chopped up with eggs, sorrel, green garlic, lettuce, and a selection of hot spices, wrapped in lettuce leaves, and slowly boiled. It is eaten either hot or cold. *Pâté vendéen* is a *terrine* in which wild rabbit with a stuffing made from the same animal is combined with hashed pork.

The Poitevin marshes have a private dish confined to this small region only—*bouilliture d'anguilles*, baby eels simmered for hours in white wine, onion, garlic, and egg yolks. As you reach the coast, you come to the local version of *bouillabaisse* (all seaside regions seem to have one), the *chaudrée*. It is a fish soup combining sole, eel, and plaice in a sauce of white wine, onion, butter, garlic, and spices. This is particularly favored in the Aunis, south of the Vendée, in the region of La Rochelle, by some criteria outside of the Poitou, but not by the gastronomic one. A characteristic of Poitevin cooking is that it is partial to dishes that require long, slow cooking, like this one (as the Ile-de-France is partial to dishes involving deep-fat frying); so the *chaudrée* belongs in the Poitiers region gastronomically whether or not La Rochelle fits into it politically.

If you have been waiting for a favorable occasion to try frog's legs, this is as good a place as any—*grenouilles à la luçonnaise* is the local variety. It is also not a bad region to try kid, which you may have considered an inedible animal. Actually it's an excellent dish, and you have very probably eaten it in your own country under the name of lamb;

most persons can't tell one from the other, so where there's a prejudice against kid, it is simply rebaptized. Here it is *chevreau*, and it is likely to be served sautéed with green garlic and sorrel. Poultry is tasty in this region, which is a good place to try guinea hen—or, for game, snipe, quail, or water hen—and the *pâté de foie gras* of Civray is particularly delectable. Duck patties are also popular.

Among the most renowned vegetable products of the country are its very fine onions, the cauliflower of Niort, the green cabbage of the Vendée, the white beans of Marac, and the local chestnuts and walnuts. Some of these products have given rise to special local dishes—*chouée*, simply the regional way of cooking green cabbage, or *mogettes*, beans with butter or cream. There is a type of *farci*, often referred to as *far*, perhaps to distinguish it from the meat dish described above, which is a sort of vegetable hash—beet leaves, cabbage, spinach, and leeks, first cooked in salted water; then pressed to get rid of the moisture; chopped and allowed to simmer slowly and lengthily in a frying pan with fat pork, diced bacon, and onion; and finally combined with beaten eggs and cream.

This is also goat cheese country, with Chabichou perhaps the best known, and there is a sort of cheesecake made of goat cheese called *tourteau fromagé*. Another dessert is *pâtés de prunes*—plum cakes. There are minor local wines which are pleasant enough for drinking on the spot—the reds of Le Foye Monjault or Pompois, the whites of Loudun or Thouars. You are not likely to encounter Poitevin wines outside their own region, with the possible exception of Brézé, which is often classed with the Touraine vintages.

West of Poitou and the Touraine lies Anjou, a continuation of the Touraine, to which may be applied almost everything that has already been said about the Touraine.

This is still lovely green country, rich in orchards, market gardens, and vineyards. The Loire is broadening as it reaches the end of its course and at Angers, which is actually not on the Loire at all, but on the Maine just before it empties into the Loire, you begin to sense the sea. Above its confluence with the Maine, the name given to the combined waters of the Mayenne, the Sarthe, and the Loir (there is no stream called the Maine higher up, so this wide stream is only six miles long), the Loire carries no traffic; but downstream from Angers, you meet river traffic constantly.

The history of Anjou is linked closely with that of the Touraine, including their simultaneous periods of attachment to the British crown—indeed, Touraine knew that destiny because it had become subject to the counts of Anjou who had wrested the territory from the counts of Blois. It was a member of the ruling family of Anjou who gave its name to an English dynasty, a scion of the house of Fulk (Foulques in French), which included some remarkable individuals running the gamut from saint to devil. The first was represented by Fulk the Good, a tenth-century Count of Anjou who sang in the church choir and interested himself in education at a time when most monarchs were content to leave such hard work as reading and writing to the clergy. The second was Fulk the Black (Foulque Nerra in the local dialect), whose epithet fitted his character, but was actually given to him because of his swarthy complexion. He started early, becoming count at seventeen, and until he was seventy made himself as much of a terror to his subjects in Anjou as to enemies he defeated in Nantes, Tours, Blois, and Le Mans. He was subject to periods of remorse. He made the pilgrimage to Jerusalem three times, and each time had himself scourged in the Holy Land in expiation of his spectacular sins—the last time so thoroughly that he died from the aftermath of the whipping on his way home, to the immense relief of his loyal subjects. It was a Geoffrey of Fulk who married Matilda, granddaughter of William the Conqueror, when he was sixteen and she was twenty-nine. He was something of a dandy and always wore a sprig of heather (*genêt*) in his hat. His son married the divorced wife of Louis VII, Eleanor of Aquitaine, and became Henry II of England two years later, so that the English crown held in France the domains of Anjou, Maine, Touraine, Normandy, Poitou, Périgord, Limousin, Angoumois, Saintonge, Guienne, Gascony, and a certain interest in the Auvergne and the County of Toulouse. The family took its name from the plant which Henry II's father had been accustomed to wearing in his hat—*plante à genêt*, Plantagenet.

It might not seem likely that Anjou, so closely related to the Touraine in geography, products, history, and culture, would differ much from it gastronomically, and indeed the relationship is close—*rillettes*, a specialty of Tours, is also a specialty of Anjou; *matelote d'anguille*, already noted as a favorite dish of the Touraine, is also honored in Anjou; and the Touraine fondness for serving the fish of the Loire in *beurre-blanc* sauce I have already noted was a borrowing from Anjou, where this preparation first developed. As for the green cabbage to which the Touraine gives particular attention, it is even more ubiquitous in Anjou, where it is known affectionately in the regional patois as *piochous* (little cabbage) and constitutes such dishes as *chouée*, which is simply boiled green cabbage doused with butter, and *fricassée de choux verts*, cabbage browned in butter in the frying pan. This is a holdover of the ancient meaning of the word *fricasser*, usually applied nowadays only to this way of cooking chicken, though there is a similar use of the term in the Périgord. A *fricassée à la périgourdine* is achieved when the vegetables are removed half cooked from a *pot-au-feu*, browned in fat in a frying pan, and then returned to the *pot-au-feu* to finish cooking.

But though the cuisine of Anjou and that of the Touraine are very much alike, there is a discernible difference. Somehow the cooking of the Anjou seems to exhibit a more distinctively regional character, though it is hard to say what it is that makes a dish which in the Touraine seems neutral because it is so completely in the main stream of French cooking take on a quality a few miles down the valley in Anjou which reminds you that even the international menu was once a regional one. You might describe the cooking of Anjou as softer, blander, milder than that of the Touraine. It is not quite as professional as the latter (which in turn is much less professional than the cuisine of the Ile-de-France), and so has remained closer to the home cooks who originally produced it. It is a cuisine that has perhaps less aristocracy and more amiability than is encountered farther upstream.

Certainly there is a decided peasant touch to many of the Anjou dishes. *Bijane* is a soup of bread crumbled into sweetened red wine. *Millière* is a rice and maize porridge. *Gogues* is meat pudding with herbs. These are all rustic foods, and so are the coarse pastries, which have no taste to speak of, but are used chiefly to maintain a thirst for the taking on of the fine local wines—the *fouace*, mentioned in Rabelais, and the *guillaret*.

Angers is sometimes said to be a better place to try the Loire salmon than Tours, because it is nearer to the sea and the fish come bigger. While Anjou cooks its pike and shad in *beurre-blanc*, like the Touraine to which it bequeathed the recipe, it has a different treatment for perch and bream, which it serves with a sorrel-flavored stuffing. The poultry of Anjou is admirable and so is its beef, particularly that raised about the town of Cholet, which therefore comes naturally by its chief specialty, jellied tongue. There are some first-rate cheeses—*chouzé*, *caillebottes*, and the cream cheeses (*cremêts*) of Saumur and Angers, which are usually eaten as dessert, with sugar.

The Anjou is wine country, and a good deal of its wine manages to get some distance from home—the light white wine of Saumur, some of which is treated like Champagne, though not with my approval; the *rosés* (*rosé d'Anjou* is one of the varieties of this particular type of wine most frequently encountered on Paris menus); and the Muscadets, fruity white wines that go particularly well with the pike with *beurre-blanc* sauce of the region. Be careful about indulging in Anjou wines, though. They may seem so light as to be almost natural grape juice, but they possess hidden power. A gourmet who was himself from Anjou, Henry Coutant, once wrote of them: "Anjou's wines are like the temperament of Anjou's inhabitants—light and sparkling with an incomparable savor, but also sometimes malicious and treacherous to those who do not know how to confront their caprices with sufficient preparation." Sufficient preparation might consist in laying in a supply of those Anjou pastries, whose solidity in the stomach counteracts the unsettling effects that a too liberal sampling of the wine might tend to produce.

If you start from the Touraine, the first wine region you reach is that of Saumur, on the left (south) bank of the Loire. Proceeding westward on the same bank, the Coteaux de l'Aubance are encountered first, lying along the Loire about opposite Angers, which is on the other side of the Loire and a little way up the Maine valley. Beyond this region, there touching the river but then swinging south of it, behind the Coteaux de l'Aubance and back towards the Saumur wine region, are the Coteaux de Layon. The wines of the first are dry or semidry, but in the second the grapes are picked late, after they have been attacked by the parasite that produces in them the same condition of *pourriture noble* (noble rot) which accounts for the smooth rich sweetness of Sauternes. It has much the same effect here, producing a rather heavy velvety honey-sweet wine. These vintages you are not likely to encounter away from their place of origin. If you reach the spot, some of the best labels hereabouts are those of Quart de Chaume, Bonnezeaux, La-Roche-aux-Moines, and especially Coulée de Serrant.

The westernmost Anjou wines are those of the Coteaux de la Loire, which grow on both banks of the river and along the Maine as far as Angers. Northeast from there are the Coteaux du Loir, on both sides of that river. These are dry and half-dry light white wines. The Muscadets around Nantes are not Anjou wines, politically speaking, since they grow across the provincial border in Brittany, but geographically and gastronomically the whole region is a unit down to the mouth of the Loire. Here you sometimes encounter *rougets*, which are wines in colors about midway between a *rosé* and a *gris*.

The best recent year for Anjou wines has been 1947; 1949 and 1945 were both extremely good, 1952 and 1948 were quite good, and 1950 was not bad. 1953, 1955, 1959 and 1961 are also recommendable.

The Flatlands

[*Picardy, Artois, Flanders, Champagne*]

Across the northern rim of France, lying against the
Belgian frontier, a band of the flattest land in the
country stretches from the sea to the hills of Alsace-
Lorraine. Something about unrelieved flatness seems to discourage cooks and perhaps artists in more elevated realms
as well. Consider, for instance, the gastronomic and cultural
desert of the American Middle West. In Holland, a flat
country, the people eat heavily and often, but I do not
believe that they have ever been accused of finesse in
cooking. In Denmark the food is more imaginative, but

there is, after all, a certain limitation about a cuisine which turns everything into open-faced sandwiches, however tempting.

The northern band of France is unrelieved by much water, and where there is water, it is the sort characteristic of flat land. Streams flow sluggishly and so, apparently, do spirits. The land lying along the western half of France's northern border is the least inspiring in the country. Its cities do not help much either. They are mostly clumsy industrial towns—Lille, the big metallurgical and textile center, its two smaller neighbors, Roubaix and Tourcoing, also cloth-makers, and Cambrai, Béthune, and Saint-Quentin (which does have a fine church). They are important to the economy of France, but they cut no great figure in her cultural life. Arras has preserved some charming Flemish architecture despite the hammerings of two wars which seemed determined to reduce it to the dullness of most of the surrounding region. Dullness is, sadly, characteristic of this area. The blight extends even to food, probably less interesting here than in any other part of France.

The flatlands suffer also from the handicap of lying north of the wine belt. The prevailing drink is beer, which does not provide a suitable basis for fine cooking—until the eastern limit of this region is reached, and you are in the country of Champagne, the wine that enters least well into combination with food. The presence of wine of any kind helps, however, so the comparative sterility of the northern band of France is relieved at its eastern extremity by the lift provided by Champagne, and at its western extremity by the ocean, which helps cooking directly by providing the pungent products of the sea and indirectly by giving the human spirit something more entertaining than flat fields to dwell upon.

Of the four provinces that make up this region, the three western territories are pretty much intertwined, geographi-

The FLATLANDS

MILES
0   50   100

0   100
KM.

Dunkerque
(KOKEBOTEROM)

BELGIUM

Calais
HERRING
CRAQUELOTS

Boulogne
SEAFOOD
HOCHEPOT

FLANDERS

Lille
BEER SOUP!

ARTOIS

PUMPKIN SOUP
EELS■
FISH CHOWDER

PICARDY

Arras
(TRIPE SAUSAGE)

Valenciennes
(WILD RABBIT
WITH PRUNES)

Cambrai

Escaut R.

SALT
MEADOW
MUTTON
Abbeville

FLAMICHES

Oise R.

Somme R.

SMOKED HAMS

DUCK PÂTÉS

ANDOUILLES
ANDOUILLETTES
TRIPE SOUP
Amiens *St. Quentin*

MAROILLES CHEESE

WILD BOAR
GAME BIRDS
JUGGED HARE

Sedan

CAGHUSE

NORMANDY   ILE=DE=FRANCE

CHAMPAGNE

LORRAINE

Aisne R.

Reims
(HAMS IN CRUST)

PIG'S FEET
BLOOD PUDDING
POTÉE CHAMPENOISE

Château=Thierry

Marne R.

Épernay

Ay

(FRUIT BRANDIES)

Ste=Menehould

Châtons=sur=Marne
(CHICKEN IN
CHAMPAGNE)

BRIE CHEESE

= Good Eating

Sézanne
(HOT HORS D'OEUVRES,
TROUT, COQ AU VIN)

DANDELION SALAD

Provins

Seine R.

Troyes
(ANDOUILLETTES)

Aube R.

Sens
(GOUGÈRE)

Chaumont
(CHARCUTERIE)

CHAMPAGNE

B U R G U N D Y

cally and historically. The northernmost, Flanders, lies along the Belgian frontier, reaching the sea at Dunkerque; the modern department of the Nord is identical with what remained to France of Flanders after the creation of Belgium. The southernmost, Picardy, with its ports of Calais and Boulogne, touches Flanders on the west and then sweeps southward at the start of a half circle that brings it back to join Flanders again at the east. Artois thus nestles in their envelopment like the pit of a fruit, with no access to the sea.

The definitive entry of these territories into France was progressive as the French boundary pushed gradually northward, and required about two centuries. Picardy, capital Amiens, englobing what is today the Somme and parts of the Pas-de-Calais, the Aisne, and the Oise, has been uninterruptedly French since 1477. Artois, within the modern Pas-de-Calais, capital Arras, dates from 1559. Flanders goes back only to 1668.

Lying west of all of these provinces and of the Ile-de-France and part of the Orléans as well is the very considerable territory of Champagne, with an important history of its own—though it was absorbed into France as long ago as 1285. Its capital was not Reims, as one would be inclined to guess nowadays, but Troyes. It comprises the modern departments of the Aube, Haute-Marne, Marne, and Ardennes. Champagne, of course, meant simply an expanse of level ground when the region was named, being derived from the word *champ*, field. There are thus dozens of places in France bearing the name of *champagne*, one of which sometimes causes confusion in the minds of foreigners. A region so called near Cognac accounts for the label *grande fine champagne* on some bottles of brandy, to the bewilderment of those who connect the word *champagne* only with the wine thus named. There is, of course, no connection between the wine and the brandy. The

Champagne with which we are concerned is subdivided into two parts, the *Champagne pouilleuse* (miserable poverty-stricken Champagne) and the *Champagne humide* (damp Champagne). The first is flat and monotonous, with poor chalk soil, given over chiefly to sheep. The second has clay soil and is dotted with pools and woods. This part of Champagne looks very much like the fertile Ile-de-France, and it is on the hillsides (wine grapes are not fond of flat land) bordering on the Ile-de-France that the grapes which make Champagne are grown.

If we start our gastronomic exploration of the flatlands at the sea, we are obliged to note to begin with that Picardy takes very little advantage of its portion of coast. There are two notable exceptions to this general rule. One is the summer resort of Berck-Plage, which includes among its specialties a *matelote* of conger eel; jellied eel; and *caudière*, another form of *chaudrée*, which in the last chapter was applied to the fish soup of Aunis, a close relative of this fish soup of Picardy. The other exception is Boulogne, for a commercial rather than a gastronomic reason—it has been an important fishing port at least since 809, which is the date on the oldest surviving document relating to this industry. The catch is predominantly of mackerel and herring.

Other coastal towns do make fish patties, and they consume also a shellfish known elsewhere as *coques*, but here as *henons*. Its shell looks something like a scallop and it is known as the poor man's oyster. But the greatest culinary asset of the sea is here produced on land—the sheep pastured on meadows whose grasses are saturated with salt from the ocean winds which provide the salty mutton known as *prés-salés*. This is a specialty by no means exclusive to Picardy—the Breton *prés-salés* are more highly esteemed —and it is indeed characteristic of the food of Picardy that few dishes seem to have originated here. Picardy has only copied what other regions invented. Among the tastiest specialties are the duck *pâtés* of Amiens and Abbeville, and there is, of course, nothing original about that. Its tripe sausages and tripe soup are borrowings from Normandy, though in Picardy the latter is embellished more with the leftovers of the pig—the muzzle, the ears, the liver, the heart, the spleen, and about everything else for which no other use can be found. Picardy follows Normandy also in the drinking of good cider, as well as of beer. Possibly a more or less indigenous dish is *cachuse*, fresh pork braised with onions. One apparently local creation (though its name seems to point to Flemish origin) is the *flamique* or *flamiche*, a vegetable tart (unsweetened) which may be made of onions, squash, or, especially, leeks. Enthusiasm for the leek embedded in crust may not be unbounded, for it is easy to think of more alluring uses for both the crust and the leek—the latter is happier in soup, and Picardy sometimes so uses it, and also provides a pumpkin soup less admired elsewhere. Otherwise, vegetable specialties are not outstanding here, with the possible exception of red cabbage salad, for a great deal of the land is given over to crops that enter only unostentatiously into the menu— wheat and sugar beets. A well-known Picardy cheese is Marolles (or Maroilles), made from whole milk, salted, dried quickly, and ripened in cellars where it is washed with beer.

Landlocked Artois is too small and has been tossed about historically among too many rulers—it has depended at various times on England, Burgundy, and even Austria, among others—to have developed any distinctive cuisine of its own, though it has some good materials—excellent locally grown vegetables, good beef and mutton, and trout and salmon in the streams. Arras has a specialty in *andouil-*

lettes, tripe sausage, but this of course is not a local invention. Artois eats the food of Picardy and Flanders, which brings us to a school of cooking which, although here represented within the political borders of France, is certainly not French cooking. This is the first time, though it will not be the last, that we have encountered a foreign cuisine naturalized in France.

French Flanders, though its coastline is only about a quarter as long as that of Picardy, derives much profit from the presence of the sea. Although Picardy's Boulogne is a big herring-port, it is only in Flanders that the belt of herring-eaters really starts, extending from here northward along the coast of the North Sea and bringing the Belgians, the Dutch, the Germans, and the Scandinavians into the fellowship of herring-fanciers. (The Dutch paraphrase the "apple a day keeps the doctor away" saying, replacing the apple with the herring.)

Only mildly favored elsewhere in France, the herring in Flanders plays a considerable role, though it is neither so ubiquitous nor so protean in its forms as in the other countries just mentioned. It appears as *craquelots* or *bouffis*, which are treated by salting or smoking to the minimum extent compatible with preserving the fish, which are thus closest to being fresh; *harengs salés*, the familiar salt herring; *harengs fumés*, smoked herring, also known as *gendarmes*, which seems to be a comment on the tough skin these outdoor country policemen acquire; *harengs kippers*, first split wide open and then smoked; herring marinated in white wine; smoked herring marinated in oil; and several other variations.

The importance of the sea in improving the diet of Flanders is suggested by the circumstance that the best restaurant in Lille—which is also the best restaurant in France north of the Paris region—specializes in fish dishes and is named the Oyster Bed (A l'Huitrière). It is unfortunately closed in the biggest tourist month, August, as restaurants which emphasize shellfish often are. However, Flanders, even inland, is richer in food specialties than Picardy, though this is not saying a great deal. Valenciennes, famous for its lace, a town where it is possible to eat quite well, has an engaging dish of wild rabbit cooked with prunes or grapes (*lapin de garenne aux pruneaux* or *aux raisins*).

While such dishes might quite as well be French as Flemish, one whose non-French origin is disclosed by its very name is *kokeboterom*, a specialty particularly of Dunkerque. It is a sort of sweet bun made with eggs and butter and spotted with raisins.

Very Flemish also—and very German, too, for that matter—is beer soup. Some palates seem to delight in the combination of beer and cream in the same dish; I am afraid mine does not. However, I can participate in the enjoyment of another typically Flemish dish, *hochepot*, a thick soup that gives the impression of having been compounded of everything in the kitchen. Its ingredients are pig's ears and tails, breast of beef, breast and shoulder of mutton, salt pork, cabbage, carrots, onions, leeks, and potatoes. The name is an ancient one, but the *hochepot* of the fourteenth century was a different dish, a sort of stew of veal, chicken, or rabbit with a binding of bread crumbs. The modern dish progresses northward, changing as it goes, until it turns up in Holland as *hutspot*, a stew of potatoes, carrots, and meat which is eaten traditionally on October 3 because this mixture is supposed to have been found cooking over a hastily abandoned Spanish campfire when the siege of Leyden was raised on October 3, 1574. A theory to account for the different uses of the name holds that it does not refer to the ingredients of the dish, but to the fact that it requires stirring or agitating of the pot during cooking (*hocher* means shake, *hocher la tête* is nod the head).

When you cross the eastern border of Flanders into Champagne, you encounter at once a complete change in the cooking. The return is to the more or less standard cuisine of France.

Champagne should be French in its cooking, for it is French in its history, even though Reims, its chief city today, was the capital of Gallic Belgium at the time of the Romans (who left a third-century arch of triumph in the city as a memento of their stay). Successively a duchy in Merovingian times and a county under Charlemagne and his descendants, it became a province of France when Philip the Fair succeeded to the throne in 1285. At least two of its cities were for a long time ascendant over Paris in at least one respect—after Saint Remi baptized Clovis there in 496, Reims was the place where kings of France had to be crowned, and Joan of Arc refused to consider Charles VII as King until he had been crowned there; and Sens, not Paris, was the site of the archbishopric for the diocese in which both cities stood until 1622. As though to symbolize this fact, the only medieval residence still standing in Paris is the Hôtel de Sens, which Tristan de Salazar, archbishop of Sens, built about 1500 so that he would have a place to live when he left his capital for a provincial stay in Paris.

Champagne shares with Burgundy the circumstance of having provided the stage for one of the greatest battles in the history of the medieval church, between the intransigent mystic preacher of the Second Crusade, Saint Bernard, whose great monastery at Clairvaux has now almost entirely disappeared (what is left of it, reconstructed, is now a prison) and the rationalist Abelard, whose abbey, Le Paraclet, of which Héloïse was abbess, has now likewise fallen into ruins. However important the doctrinal struggle waged between these two fortresses may have been in the history of the church, it is another abbey of Champagne which has had the greatest effects on the destiny of the modern region, that of Hautvilliers, for it was there that Dom Pérignon discovered, in the seventeenth century, the method for rendering still wine sparkling which transferred the name of Champagne from a province to a beverage. It should not be assumed that the wine went unappreciated before it became *mousseux*, however; Pope Leo X, Francis I, Henry IV, the Emperor Charles V, and England's Henry VIII all had their private reserves at Ay, where some of the best Champagne is grown, before Dom Pérignon was born. Indeed, even much farther back the wine was sufficiently celebrated so that the Emperor Domitian in A.D. 92 ordered the destruction in particular of the vines of Champagne, at the same time as other vines in France, in a rather radical attempt to end the competition of the wines of Gaul with those of Italy. Prohibition worked no better then than on other occasions since, and two centuries later, the Emperor Probus rescinded the order. Later, in a notable reversal of policy, the Romans were to plant grapes in France instead of pulling them up.

Though Champagne plays an important role in the history of France it does not play an important role in the history of French cooking. It presents indeed, the anomaly of being the only important wine region in the country which has not produced on its own soil an appropriate cuisine to accompany its wine. This may be because Champagne does not lend itself readily to combination with food in cooking. Indeed, since the process of champagnization was discovered, the distinctive feature of this wine, its sparkling quality, added to it with such pains, would be lost in cooking with it; and as the process is an expensive one, an additional reason is provided for not using Champagne in the kitchen. Yet it is not entirely unknown. Châlons-sur-Marne has a dish that involves cooking chicken in Champagne, and it does go well in a sauce for the fine trout of the region. Kidneys and pike have also been fried in Champagne, but there is no school of cooking founded on the use of the local wine. In fact, there is no school of cooking peculiar to Champagne at all. The only indisputably local dish that can be ascribed to this region is salad made of dandelion leaves and small bits of bacon, served warm. Most of the other dishes on which towns and cities of Champagne specialize seem to be seepages over the regional borders from the surrounding territory. Thus one of the places with the most interesting list of local specialties, Sainte-Menehould, is close to the border of Lorraine, and its offerings are reminiscent of the definitely regional cooking of that province—pig's feet; blood pudding made from rabbit; *potée champenoise*, which seems clearly inspired by the more famous *potée lorraine*. The region also produces the fruit brandies—*kirsch, prunelle*—so regularly associated with Alsace-Lorraine.

Along the border with Burgundy one finds the *gougère de l'Aube*, which resembles like a brother the *gougère* of Burgundy, a cheese-egg piece of pastry eaten either warm or cold. (It is only fair to report that one theory ascribes the place of origin of the *gougère* to Sens, but if this brings in question the Burgundian nature of the article, it might raise an argument as to whether Sens, credited to Champagne above, actually belongs there or to Burgundy. It is in any case on the border line of a frontier that shifted back and forth for centuries before both territories were merged in France. The French Tourist Office, with commendable impartiality, lists Sens in both Champagne and Burgundy in its series of regional booklets.) Finally, along the frontier of the Ile-de-France, the food specialties are much the same as on the other side of the border—

and as we have seen already, the important cheese-producing region of Brie straddles the border, and this cheese, a link between the two, is made on both sides of it. Sézanne, not far from the Ile-de-France, has a number of specialties reminiscent of Ile-de-France cooking—little hot pastries eaten as hors d'œuvre (*friands champenois chauds en croûte*); trout with crayfish sauce (*truites du Petit-Morin au coulis d'écrevisses*); rooster in wine sauce (*coq au vin de Bouzy*)—perhaps more a Touraine than an Ile-de-France dish—and Brie de la Marne. Bouzy, by the way, is a *red* Champagne wine, which perhaps you did not know existed—I am not thinking, of course, of pink Champagne, made exclusively, I suppose, for Americans and Englishmen; at least I have never seen a bottle of it in France. Sillery and Verzenay are also reds, as were all Champagnes until about the middle of the seventeenth century.

If Champagne offers no particularly original dishes or original variations on standard dishes, it can at least claim to do a particularly good job on foods also to be found elsewhere, because of the good quality of the local ingredients which go into them: A case in point is provided by the famous *andouillette*s (tripe sausage) of Troyes. This is a food produced in many other regions, but the Troyes variety is undoubtedly the only sausage that can lay claim to having saved a city. When Royalist troops moved into Troyes at the end of the sixteenth century, they took first the Saint-Denis quarter, which happened to be the one in which the *andouillettes* were made. Famished by battle, they proceeded to stuff themselves. While they were doing so, the garrison had time to organize a counterattack; and as the Royalists were either too full to have any stomach for fighting, or sleeping as a natural result of overeating, they were quickly slaughtered by the city's defenders.

Almost anything involving mutton is likely to be good in

Champagne because, as we have already seen, the poor soil of the *Champagne pouilleuse*, badly adapted for growing fine vegetables, does produce the kind of pasturage on which sheep thrive. The Ardennes, a thickly wooded plateau which Champagne shares with Lorraine and with Belgium, is rich hunting country, and the *grives* (thrush) of the region are particularly prized. Mezières and Charleville are noted for their thrush and wild boar *pâtés* and their jugged hare. The Ardennes ham so prized in the Belgian Ardennes has crossed the border at Rethel. Reims surrounds its hams with a pastry crust; it also has a specialty of pigeon patties. The picturesque old town of Provins, a favorite excursion spot from Paris, is famous for its fine *poires tapées* (pears).

The wine of Champagne is possibly the most famous single wine in the world—curiously enough, for it strikes me as not being wine at all, in the sense, possibly quite personal, that the word holds for me: that is, of course, of a beverage drunk in accompaniment with food, an integral part of a meal itself incomplete without wine, while the wine can hardly be drunk without food. In this sense of the word, an *apéritif* or dessert wine, which may be taken quite independently of food, like sherry or port, also stands in a separate category. For me, so does Champagne, which can be drunk by itself without food, and is not, to my taste at least, improved by being combined with food. Champagne has its own peculiar values, such as what might be called the literary association that equates it with festive occasions and therefore produces an atmosphere of celebration wherever it appears, but they are not the same kind of values as those possessed by a Bordeaux or a Burgundy. I suspect that the fact that Champagne can be drunk, and is indeed perhaps better drunk, without reference to food, is one of the reasons why Champagne is the only French wine region with no distinctive school of cooking. Another might be the fact that Champagne has no affinity for any particular type of food and can therefore be drunk with any because of the negative virtue of neutrality. It seems, indeed, to be considered in some quarters smart to present a menu for a formal meal with nothing but Champagnes to accompany the food, and I have attended such a dinner in London, with roast beef on the menu washed down with Champagne. Champagne is not exactly pro roast beef, but it is not exactly anti roast beef either—it is not pro or anti anything—so perhaps my regret at this performance was simply for a missed opportunity, for the failure to offer a red wine which would have been enhanced by the accompaniment of fine roast beef. The effect in general seemed to me to be a little like that of drinking water with a meal. The beverage is there to provide moisture, not savor.

I cannot recall ever ordering Champagne to go with food, except *champagne nature,* the dry non-sparkling variety, with a slight bite to it which is a reminder that this grape comes from as far north as any wine grapes grow, an excellent drink with oysters. The sparkling variety I take only when no food is involved. For solo ingestion it is an excellent drink, and in warm weather I am not above ordering Champagne-Vichy, a refreshing beverage half wine, half mineral water. There is no other wine I would deliberately dilute with water.

For whatever the opinion of one not particularly addicted to Champagne (except *nature*) is worth, I might report that my own favorite region is Ay, and I want my Champagne as dry as I can get it—*brut,* without any addition of sugar. I have not drunk enough Champagne to be able to describe the qualities of the different vintages, so I will pass on without comment the estimate of an expert who found Ambonnay characterized by fragrance, Ay by bouquet, Bouzy by softness, Cramant by finesse, and Verzenay by freshness. The Champagne dealers class Ambonnay, Ay, Bouzy, Mailly, Verzenay and Verzy as the top vintages among those made from black grapes (there is also a Verzy made from white grapes, which gets only second rating in that category) and Cramant, Avize, and Oger at the head of the white-grape Champagnes. I suspect that vintage years are less important in Champagnes than their sellers would like us to believe. Champagne goes through a great deal of manipulation before the final bottling, and blending new wine with reserve stores of the past years' production to produce a uniform product is a common practice. Probably the finer the Champagne to begin with, the less likely it is to have any important admixture of wine from years other than that indicated by the label. However this may be, the best Champagne of recent years is likely to be found in bottles dated 1952, 1953, 1955, or 1959. Finally you can, if you like, obtain Champagne not only in the common bottle or magnum (two bottle) sizes, but also in jeroboams, rehoboams, methusalems, salmanasars, balthazars, or neb-ucadnezzars—which hold, respectively, four, six, eight, twelve, sixteen, or twenty bottles. Anything above the four-bottle size is hard to find, and except for festive reasons, it isn't worth the trouble. There is no evidence that putting wine in a larger container than a magnum improves its quality.

Champagne can also provide the drinks you need to precede or follow your dinner. There is a local *apéritif* known as Ratafia, and a *marc de Champagne* is made from distillation of the residue remaining after the grapes have undergone their initial pressing for the making of Champagne.

Normandy

In the last quarter of the ninth century Viking marauders starting chiefly from Norway and Denmark, having been fought off by Alfred the Great, turned their attention from the British Isles to the handiest territory of France, by whose kings they were bought off—over and over again. Charles the Bald paid for immunity from the raids of the Northmen at intervals, only to find that one expeditionary force was not inclined to recognize the bargain struck with its predecessors. Their deckless eighty-foot boats, propelled by sails and oars, ravaged the coasts and penetrated far up the streams—in 886 they even laid siege to Paris—where they pillaged, burned, and slaughtered with hardy Nordic virility. When they found themselves in danger of defeat, they saved themselves by accepting baptism—as often as necessary. Charles the Fat combined the payment of heavy tribute with his gracious permission to plunder neighboring Burgundy, but the Normans found the northwestern segment of France more convenient. Finally Charles the Simple, whose epithet in his time had no derogatory connotations, hit upon the expedient of protecting the land they had been laying waste by making them responsible for it. He met the Viking leader Rollo at Saint-Clair-sur-Epte, the river which to this day is the boundary between Normandy and the Ile-de-France, and prudently keeping the river between his own forces and those of Rollo, made this vassal a present of the land he had been devastating. Thus Rollo, in the year 911, became the first Duke of Normandy, and Normandy itself, a Scandinavian outpost on the soil of France, was born.

The bargain made by Charles the Simple did not so much secure peace as change the setting for war. "On this Norman frontier as much blood has been spilled as on the frontier of the East," wrote the nineteenth-century historian Achille Luchaire. Nor was the suzerainty of the king of France uniformly honored by the swashbuckling dukes of Normandy who succeeded Rollo—William Longsword; Richard the Fearless; Richard the Good; Richard who was only the Third; Robert who was the Magnificent or the Devil, depending on one's point of view; William the Conqueror, who had to defeat Harold the Saxon at Hastings in 1066 to win that title instead of his former name of William the Bastard (he was the illegitimate son of a tanner's daughter); Robert Short Hose; Henry the Scholar, who made Normandy an English rather than a French province and whose daughter, Matilda the Empress, married Geoffrey Plantagenet, thus making the counts of Anjou, who were also to become the kings of England, dukes likewise of Normandy: Henry Short Mantle, Richard the Lion-

Hearted and John Lackland. When the last was defeated by Philip Augustus in 1204, Normandy again became undisputably French. It has remained so ever since.

But the Norman character did not lose itself in the French—nor has it to this day, as reflected in the solidity of Norman building, in its lack of grace, in failure to add ornamentation. Large-scale construction began to flourish after the creation of Normandy ended the period of Viking invasions and provided an era of comparative stability during which it was possible to erect a great abbey before marauders turned up to knock it down. This was the period of the Romanesque, a style that accorded perfectly with the Norman character. The round arch of the Romanesque style, which meant a heavy roof and demanded strong walls, was in tune with the Norman feeling for the massive. But whereas in more southern Romanesque—consider, for instance, the façade of the cathedral of Saint-Pierre at Angoulême—sculpture and ornamentation married itself to the Roman arch, in Normandy walls remained unadorned, bare, simple, austere. In the Norman cathedrals a typical feature is often a heavy central tower surmounting the intersection of the transepts, where later Gothic cathedrals place a delicate lacy *flèch*e (spire, but literally arrow). Such a heavy central tower rises from the cathedral of Coutances, though it is already Gothic, not Romanesque. In Normandy, a heavier feeling persisted into the Gothic than in other parts of France, possibly only because it was earlier—though the old tower of Chartres, just outside the boundaries of Normandy and on the river Eure, which helps to determine the rather indefinite frontiers of the province, antedates many of the great Norman churches, and though it recalls Norman architecture by its austerity, possesses also a soaring quality that is hardly Norman. The two towers of Chartres represent an object lesson in the contribution of Normandy to Gothic ecclesiastical archi-

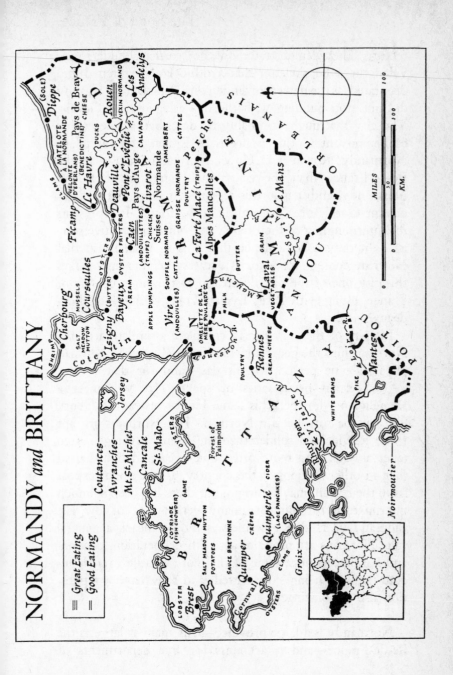

NORMANDY and BRITTANY

≡ Great Eating
= Good Eating

(SOLE)
Dieppe
CLAMS
VELOUTÉ A MATELOTE
A LA NORMANDE
D'EPERLANS) Pays de Bray
Fécamp (BENEDICTINE) CHEESE
Le Havre
DUCKS
Deauville Rouen Les
VEXIN NORMAND Andelys
Pont L'Evêque CALVADOS
Pays d'Auge
OYSTER FRITTERS (ANDOUILLETTES) Livarot
Caen CHICKEN CAMEMBERT
Bayeux
(BUTTER) Suisse Normande
Courseulles CREAM GRAISSE NORMANDE
OYSTERS SOUFFLÉ NORMAND POULTRY CATTLE
MUSSELS APPLE DUMPLINGS La Ferté Macé (TRIPE)
Cherbourg Vire Perche
SALT (ANDOUILLES) CATTLE Alpes Mancelles
SHRIMP MEADOW OMELETTE DE LA Le Mans
MUTTON Cotentin MÈRE POULARDE GRAIN
MILK BUTTER M Sarthe
Coutances Mayenne
Avranches Jersey BUTTER
Mt. St. Michel Laval
Cancale VEGETABLES
St. Malo Couesnon R. ANJOU
OYSTERS Rennes
Forest of CREAM CHEESE
Paimpoint POULTRY
B R I T T A N Y Vilaine R. PIKE Nantes
GAME
(COTRIADE WHITE BEANS
(FISH CHOWDER)
SALT MEADOW MUTTON
POTATOES
SAUCE BRETONNE CRÊPES
LOBSTER Quimper
Brest Quimperlé CIDER
Cornwall (LACE PANCAKES)
OYSTERS CLAMS
Groix Noirmoutier

ORLEANAIS
MAINE
ANJOU
POITOU
Loire R.

MILES
KM.
0 50 100
0 100

tecture. They demonstrate how the Norman builders provided the solid skeleton that Gothic later lightened and decorated, as the newer tower demonstrates. But Normandy did not stop building with the flowering of late Gothic. The city that might justifiably be described as the capital of flamboyant Gothic is precisely Rouen, the capital of Normandy. Rouen is in Upper Normandy, closer to the Ile-de-France than the centrifugal peninsula of Lower Normandy, and it is in this region that most of the flamboyant Gothic of Normandy is to be found. It represents the intermingling of the French and Norman creative spirits. Is it only a coincidence that it is in Rouen also that Norman cooking rises to its greatest heights and makes this city one of the half dozen top gastronomic centers of France, along with Paris, Lyons, Tours, Dijon, and Bordeaux?

In spite of the very nearly complete assimilation of the Normans into the general civilization of France, a Norman physical type persists to this day—and for that matter, so do certain peculiarities of spelling. If you meet a Frenchman who spells his name Henry instead of Henri, you can be sure he is a Norman. The Normans are apt to be heavier and solider than the French average, often taller as well, and more often blue-eyed and light-haired than in other sections of the country, as one might expect from their Scandinavian origin; but there has been so much intermixture through the many generations of the last thousand years that blondness is by no means a general rule. Normans are prone to act with deliberation, caution, and hardheadedness; some of the more volatile French accuse them of being slow-witted; and they have a reputation also for obstinacy.

Normandy is a large province—half again as large as the Ile-de-France—and it accounts for five departments of

France today, the Seine-Inférieure, Eure, Calvados, Manche, and Orne, all but the last touching the sea. It is a varied country. Its coastline starts at the north, just under that of Picardy, about at the seaside resort of Le Tréport, where chalk cliffs drop vertically down to the sea, very much as they do on the other side of the English Channel. This continues as far as Le Havre, at the mouth of the Seine. There the cliffs disappear and low-lying beaches of fine sand beckon summer vacationists to a string of popular resorts, of which the most famous is Deauville. Then the great peninsula of Cotentin juts out into the sea, and the coast becomes rugged and rocky, in anticipation of Brittany to the south and west.

Where the Cotentin peninsula rejoins the main body of France lies the Bay of Mont-Saint-Michel. The almost imperceptible slope of the fine sand that carpets the bay gives it the greatest tidal variations in France. At the time of the high equinoctial tides, the famous Mont may be washed by the sea on all sides, an island (as it used to be) except for the artificial causeway linking it with the mainland. At periods of low tide, you may not see water at all from Mont-Saint-Michel. The tide, which may have risen 45 feet or more between its low and high marks, the national record, and which comes in so fast that it has been known to overtake heedless strollers, may pull back nearly ten miles, uncovering a glistening and insecure surface—there is much quicksand here. Flowing into the bay at this point is the river Couesnon, which marks the boundary between Normandy and Brittany. Reaching the sea through almost flat country, it used to change its course frequently, and on one of its shifts its mouth moved from a position north of Mont-Saint-Michel to a position south of it, thus making to Normandy a present of one of the greatest architectural treasures of France, or for that matter, of the world; and as the lower reaches of the river are now diked, Normandy is sure to retain the Mont. The Bretons have a sour jingle about this: "*Le Couesnon, par sa folie, a mis le Mont en Normandie*," or, freely: "The crazy Couesnon has gone and moved the Mont into Normandy." However, the Breton claim to the Mont was never too good a one, for it was built by the Bishop of Avranches, indisputably in Normandy, to whom the Archangel Michael appeared with a command to erect the structure. The Bishop, a typical Norman, it would seem, was slow to act. The difficulty of crowning the sharp peak of the Mont may have intimidated him. Michael repeated his request once, and when the Bishop still delayed he appeared for a third time and emphasized the demand by thrusting his finger deep into the Bishop's skull. The skull, with the dent made in it by the Archangel's finger, is still on view in Avranches's basilica of Saint-Gervais.

The real Normandy, which is to say that part of Normandy which has least succumbed to the general French atmosphere and has maintained the most individuality, is the Cotentin peninsula and its hinterland—Lower Normandy. The peninsula is known to thousands of Americans whose memories of it cannot be too pleasant: The landing beaches of June 1944 lie along the northern shore of the peninsula, and beyond them is the *bocage* country—the *bocages* being the thickly growing hedges, often combined with ditches, which break the fields of this part of Normandy into small separate compartments. In time of peace the effect is charming. From any point that affords a view at all extensive, the small patches of grassland enclosed by the hedges seem to be swallowed up and the effect is of a completely and pleasantly wooded region. But for the soldiers who had to fight their way across these small patches of land, each one of them contested by an enemy conveniently sheltered behind the natural ramparts of hedge and ditch, this country was a nightmare. East of the *bocage*

country, lying behind the region of low sandy beaches,
straddling Lower and Upper Normandy, is the Pays
d'Auge, one of the most fertile regions of Normandy,
south of which lies Normandy's share of the Perche, the
aforementioned home of the Percheron horse—Normandy
is famous horse-breeding and cattle-breeding country.

Lower Normandy looks toward the sea. Upper Normandy is oriented toward Rouen and Rouen toward Paris
—if only because it is the point at which ocean-going vessels
shift their cargoes for the capital to river barges, so that
Rouen, though well inland and on the Seine, not on the
sea, is in terms of tonnage the fourth port of France,
outranked only by Marseilles, Le Havre, and Dunkerque
—more important even than Normandy's own great harbor
of Cherbourg. This is all fine agricultural country, especially
the section of the Seine valley known as the Vexin Normand, which lies on the north bank of the Seine east of
Rouen, between the Andelle and the Epte, surrounding
Les Andelys, where Richard the Lion-Hearted built the
imposing fortress called the Château Gaillard, whose ruins
still stand. In the center of its eastern border is the region
known, with some exaggeration, as Norman Switzerland;
south of that is the section called, with similar exaggeration,
the Mancelles Alps.

Nowhere better than in Normandy is the principle exemplified that the cuisine of a region is shaped by the food
it produces most easily. The cooking of Normandy is a
function of the importance there of milk, of apples, and of
the products of the sea.

Normans are notoriously big eaters. Perhaps they require
more food because they are larger and heavier than the
average Frenchman; or perhaps they are larger and heavier
because they take on more food. In any case, one of their
eating habits has given a stock phrase to the French vo-

cabulary, *le trou normand*, the Norman hole. These words are usually pronounced jocularly at a bar when Calvados, the Norman applejack, is ordered, as though it were another name for the drink. Actually the origin of the phrase is in the Norman habit, when serious eating is on the program, of eating a good heavy meal and then taking a rest, during which a glass or two of Calvados may be absorbed to kill time. After this pause, or hole, in the meal, one starts all over again, so that the Calvados serves rather the purpose of the *entremets* in the Gargantuan repasts of other days, that of breaking up one very long meal into two only moderately long ones. Another shadow of meaning lurks about the expression also. To the food-logged, Calvados seems to dig a hole in the contents of the stomach, making room for more; presumably the alcohol, of which there is plenty in Calvados, helps digest the food.

If Normans are such lusty trenchermen, that may be partly the effect of the sea—sea air is a wonderful whetter of appetites—but it must also be the result of early training on a rich diet. Norman food certainly is rich, but it has more finesse and imagination than, for instance, Flemish food, which is also heavy, but is more inclined to be gross. The richness of Norman food is attributable in the first place to the importance of Normandy as dairy country and to the habit of absorbing its milk in its richest forms, not only in butter, but even oftener in cream—heavy cream. The habit of eating foods rich in fats has carried over into the use of animal fats also, so that the Normans cook a number of their dishes in a special very elaborate and very rich fat known as *graisse normande*, which is made by combining melted pork fat and fat from beef kidneys, and then giving it flavor by combining with it essences of fresh vegetables, herbs, and salt and pepper.

Cream more than any other single factor determines the nature of Norman cooking, and this in turn has been determined by the nature of Norman cattle. The Norman breed is certainly the most successful in France. Some thirty varieties of cows are raised commercially in France, but the Norman race accounts for about a quarter of the whole. The animal is a mixed-purpose breed, raised for both milk and beef, yet it may be suspected that it is the ancestor of the famous Jersey (of the island that William the Conqueror unintentionally presented to England), in spite of the fact that the Jersey is primarily a milch cow. The chief characteristic of the Jersey is the high fat content of its milk—that is, it is rich in cream—and the Norman breed is also a great producer of cream. The typical fawn color of the Jersey is one of the three colors of the Norman breed, which has a mixed coat showing areas of white, dark brown, and fawn; and the yellowish circles which appear about the eyes of the best Jerseys recall the "spectacles" around the eyes of the Norman cattle, which are so characteristic of the breed that the Norman Herd Book, started in 1883, denies registration to any animal that does not show them. A final reason for believing that the English received the Jersey cow along with the island of Jersey from the Normans is that the very word for the animal in English comes from Normandy—the English "cattle" is the Norman-French "*catel*."

The Norman breed has been successfully reared in other parts of France and for that matter in the world—North Africa, South America, and Madagascar, for instance—but its great success in Normandy must be ascribed at least in part to the fine pasturage. In the region around Caux, the peasants employ a special method of seeing to it that grazing is equal and thorough. They stake their animals out in fields which have been sowed to produce a rich growth of fodder, and then, when it has been cropped down uniformly in a circle about the stake, they move the stake to another position, so that after a while their fields present a curious pattern of tangential circles. On good Norman pasture a steer puts on more than two pounds a day on an intake of perhaps sixty-five pounds of grass; at three years he weighs about one thousand pounds. The quality of the pasture is such that the meat has a slight taste of parsley. (On the Cotentin peninsula, many salt-marsh pastures are used for raising *prés-salés* sheep.) As for milch cows, a good Norman animal should give twenty to thirty quarts a day, and prize animals reach fifty. The butter made from their milk has a slight nutty flavor, and is usually sold throughout France identified by its place of origin. The best is supposed to be that of Isigny, a name you will often find in Paris dairy shops, but Cormeilles and Neufchâtel are almost equally good.

Norman cream is heavy, smooth, the color of ivory. It is used in cooking largely in the form of *sauce normande*, which begins with an ordinary *roux blond*, a sauce made of butter and flour, one fifth more of the latter than of the former. *Roux blond* is cooked rapidly and made just before it is to be used. To this is added a condensed liquid formed by boiling vegetables and herbs until the bouillon has become an essence of their flavors, enriched either by cider, white wine, or egg yolks, depending on the kind of dish for which the sauce is destined. The cream goes in last, along with more butter and spices, plus a dash of lemon. This is particularly good with various egg dishes, but can be used also with fish and chicken.

Either in this form or unprocessed, cream enters into a great many Norman specialties. The Norman fashion of preparing sole uses cream, and is not, as has already been noted above, what goes by the name of *sole normande* in Paris. You are now likely to find this dish described on menus as the *real* Norman sole—*la vraie sole à la normande*—although for purists the difference between *sole normande* and *sole à la normande* would be a sufficient description. Writers of restaurant menus are not always purists, however, or even grammarians, so perhaps the emphasis is necessary. Anyway, the *real* Norman sole is allowed to simmer slowly in cream in a closed dish. (Dieppe has its own special way of serving sole, with shrimps and mussels, cooked in a white wine sauce, and Fécamp has a slight modification of it.) Veal in casserole in a cream sauce is another Norman specialty, and so is chicken in cream, also called *poulet vallée d'Auge*, with an accompaniment of tiny onions. Cooking string beans in cream is also a Norman practice. Finally, Norman soups are likely to be of the *velouté* type, which uses butter and cream, as well as egg yolks, flour, and various other materials. *Potage velouté de crevettes à la normande* is an understatement, for the soup contains not only *crevettes* (shrimp), but also oysters and pike patties. The Dieppe *velouté d'éperlans* adds to the small fish it contains mussels and shrimps— these two are likely to be found in combination in any dish described as *à la dieppoise*. Incidentally, any dish containing cream should be served on very hot plates.

Milk also is the basis for the single type of food for which Normandy is most renowned—cheese.

It would be hard to say which is the best-known cheese of France, but Camembert must rank high. Camembert, a small village in the southern part of the Vallée d'Auge, could not possibly make all the Camembert consumed in France. The cheese to which it has given its name is made throughout the region—and for that matter is imitated in a good many other places as well, in and out of France. A really good Camembert is becoming more and more difficult to find, not only because the proper manufacture of this temperamental cheese is a delicate art, but also because it has its periods of growth and decline and has to be caught at exactly the right moment. A good Camembert should be a light yellow-orange color outside, with no black streaks. If you are allowed to press it in the center, a process on which many cheese sellers frown, it should give slightly but not much. Cut open, it should be a very pale yellow, without holes, and though soft, should not run. If it has a hard white layer in the center it is too old, and has begun to dry up. Don't order Camembert in the summer. It is only good from October to June, and from January to April is its best season. Its slight bitter taste, likely to turn toward the ammoniac as it becomes liquid, is believed to be caused by the oat straw on which it is laid to age.

Here are a few tips on choosing and keeping Camembert. First, if possible, find one made in the Pays d'Auge, the best source. Normandy in general is second best, and after that come the imitations made in Anjou and Gascony. The whiter Camemberts are easier to keep, never run, and last longer. Those whose crust is darker, sometimes approaching a red shade, remain at their prime only for a short period, begin to run when they pass their ripest point, but are often preferred by cheese experts because their taste is stronger and more characteristic. There is a white coating on the crust when a cheese is young which disappears as it matures; don't buy a Camembert on which this coating is too thick—it is not ripe. Also don't buy one that doesn't fill its box (it is running internally) or of which the edges form a raised rim.

This cheese dries easily, so keep it out of drafts and don't put it in the top of the ice chest near the cooling unit. The vegetable drawer is about right for it. If it seems too dry, a few hours in a room of mild temperature and reasonable humidity may improve it.

In Vimoutiers, of which the village of Camembert, three miles away, is a suburb, there is a statue of the reputed inventor of Camembert, Marie Harel. A duplicate of this statue is in Van Wert, Ohio, where an American version of Camembert is made. The statue was presented by Americans to Vimoutiers because an earlier statue to Marie Harel was destroyed by American bombers during the war. The adventure has done Marie Harel no harm—in the new version she appears some twenty years younger than in the original statue, perhaps because the Americans who subscribed to the statue were of the opinion that she had presented a Camembert to Napoleon I, whereas the French who erected the first statue had it that the recipient of the gift was Napoleon III. It could have been either, as Marie Harel lived from 1787 to 1855. There is a story that the first statue, put up in 1926, was also erected by American inspiration, and that Marie Harel had nothing to do with the invention—or reinvention—of Camembert, but was obligingly put forward by the town authorities because of the Napoleonic story when an American visitor expressed readiness to finance a statue to the creator of this cheese. Now that Americans have become thoroughly identified with Marie Harel through her second statue, the question seems to have become a political issue, as so many matters unrelated to politics bewilderingly do in France, and a great deal of heat has been worked up in the French press over the question of whether Marie Harel did or did not invent Camembert. Pro-American papers are sure that she did. Anti-American papers readily prove that she did not.

About the only undisputed fact seems to be that a Marie Harel was born in Vimoutiers. There has long been a legend that the first Camembert was produced during the Revolution, but the anti-Harelists can point to a reference to Camembert as far back as 1680, which describes it as "a very good cheese, excellent for the digestion at the end of a dinner, served with good wines." Some peacemakers have sought to reconcile the two accounts by suggesting that Marie Harel rediscovered a lost method of making Camembert. The explanation is apparently somewhat different, and can give both parties the satisfaction of being partly right. Camembert seems originally to have been a blue cheese, and this would be the one mentioned in the early accounts. At about the time of Marie Harel, a mold, related to penicillin (*penicillium candidum;* penicillin comes from *penicillium notatum*) was added to the Camembert product, and converted it to the present type. The mold was taken from the *bondon* cheese of the Pays de Bray, in northeastern Normandy, which has perhaps since regretted the gift to a competitor, Camembert having become so popular that 90 per cent of all the cheese produced in the department of Calvados is Camembert, and the total production runs to 150,000 cheeses *per day!* As for whether Marie Harel actually produced the new version of Camembert herself (it is not impossible; she was the wife of a farmer) or whether she simply won the credit for it by her presentation of a cheese to one or the other of the Napoleons, no one really knows; and faced by a really good Camembert, no one except possibly a handful of newspaper polemicists really cares.

The Pays d'Auge is the home also of what is probably the second most famous cheese of Normandy, Pont l'Evêque, which is near the northern end of this region while Camembert is at its southern extremity. There is no doubt about the ancient origin of this cheese, which goes back to the thirteenth century. Made of whole milk, it has a crust rather like that of Camembert, but it is likely to be thicker, rougher, and darker, and it is made in square cakes instead of round ones like Camembert. It goes on sale after three or four months ripening in cellars, and is best in summer and autumn.

Of the other Normandy cheeses, the most important are Livarot (made of skimmed milk and aged in cellars where fresh air is not allowed to enter and the walls are covered with mortar mixed with chopped hay), which has

a certain ammoniac taste and is best in autumn and winter;
the *bondon* of Neufchâtel, also made of skimmed milk, but
exposed to exactly the opposite aging treatment—cool fresh
air—cylindrical in shape; and the Gervais cream cheese,
often sugared and eaten for dessert.

The second most important influence on Normandy
cooking is that of the apple. This is the most important
apple-growing area of France, one of the first facts I
learned about that country firsthand, for I had the good
fortune on my original arrival in that country to land at
Cherbourg toward the end of April so that the boat train to
Paris ran for hours through orchards of apple trees in full
bloom as far as the eye could see, one of the loveliest
sights the French countryside affords.

It may seem somewhat surprising that the apple enters
into the preparation of one of the most famous of Norman
dishes, for which it would seem to have no particular affinity, *tripes à la mode de Caen*. Tripe is not a dish for which
I have great affection, but if you are of the same opinion,
I might suggest that if you are going to try this food at
all, there is no better preparation of it. Here is how they
make it in Caen:

The bottom of a casserole is covered with onions and
carrots cut into small pieces. On top of these is laid the
meat from a steer's foot, and the bone that was in it, split
lengthwise. This bottom layer is then covered with the
tripe, cut into squares, and in the middle of the tripe are
thrust several cloves of garlic, a bunch of herbs with thyme
and laurel predominating, and a bunch of leeks. This is
seasoned with salt, freshly ground pepper, and spices, and
covered with thin slices of beef fat. Now the apple comes
in. You pour in cider until it just covers the rest, with a
few spoonfuls of Calvados to give it authority, and then
cover the whole thing with a paste made of flour and
water: this is not destined to be eaten, and is removed be-

fore serving. The idea is to seal the whole thing under this airtight cover so that it will cook beneath it without boiling, which has the effect of keeping the tripe white. The cider sometimes blackens it, and for this reason, some cooks make it with water instead of cider, a substitution on which the honorable should frown. The casserole is now covered, and the dish cooked very slowly in an oven for ten to twelve hours. It should be served on very hot dishes—the best way is in the casserole in which it is cooked, but this is practical only for individual portions, so that the usual practice is to heat separate earthenware bowls and keep the original casserole on the table over an alcohol burner. (There is another town in Normandy which has won itself a reputation for its special fashion of preparing tripe, La Ferté-Macé, which presents it in a rod-shaped form.)

Cider—and Calvados—enter into many sauces which in other regions might be made of white wine, while the whole apple gets into other dishes. There is a *filet mignon* attributed to Saint-Amand, in which the steak is accompanied with duck liver and cooked apples, doused with Calvados, and served flaming. *Bourdelots normands* are whole apples cooked in a crust (*douillons* are pears treated the same way). And a delicious, if rich, dessert, is the *soufflé normand*, in which the soufflé, flavored with Calvados, is stuffed with macaroons and bits of cooked apple. Sugar is also made from Norman apples and used in candy, sometimes under its own name, as apple sugar, and sometimes as barley sugar; this is the sugar used in sweetening Champagne. Finally the apple accounts for the importance of Normandy as a maker of jellies, for apples are rich in pectin, the chemical that makes jellies jell.

We come finally to the influence of the sea. Mussels

are a specialty of this region, coming from natural beds, not artificially maintained ones; at Isigny there is a special giant variety called *caieu*. The oysters of Dives, Luc-sur-Mer, and Courseulles are whiter and firmer than the rather liquid green varieties more common in France, which is perhaps why various fashions of cooking oysters are more common in Normandy than elsewhere; in most parts of France, the idea of cooking an oyster sounds absurd, and indeed it is difficult to imagine cooking *Marennes* or *portugaises*. One tempting cooked oyster dish of this region is *barquettes d'huîtres à la normande*, in which a small boat-shaped pastry base is crowned with two poached oysters, in *sauce normande* enriched with mussels, shrimps, and mushrooms, and crowned with a slice of truffle. *Beignets d'huîtres à la normande* are oyster fritters.

Cherbourg is particularly noted for small sweet shrimp, the variety you get when the menu speaks of a *bouquet de crevettes*, and it shares with Caen and Dieppe a specialty of larger ones, *demoiselles*. The type of clam known as *palourde* is found all along the coast (as far as I know, the American little-neck clam does not exist in Europe). Barfleur is renowned for lobster. Dieppe is the big commercial fishing center, where fine sole, flounder, turbot, and mackerel are brought in daily; a visit to its early morning fish market is well worth making.

In the section on the Ile-de-France, I remarked that *matelote* is made with fresh-water fish. The *matelote à la normande*, made with salt-water fish, is the one exception, and no dish could be more thoroughly Norman, for it embodies in a single confection all three of the great ingredients of Norman cooking—cream, cider, and sea food. It is made of sole, conger eel, and other local fish cut up into hunks, soaked in cider, perfumed with burning Calvados, steeped in a butter sauce, and enriched at the last moment with plentiful gobs of thick cream. It is served surrounded with mushrooms, mussels, crawfish, and poached oysters.

A few other famous Norman dishes should be mentioned. It has already been noted in the first chapter that there are a large number of ways of presenting duck ascribed to Rouen. The original and classic *canard à la rouennaise* seems to be the variety in which a stuffed duck is first lightly roasted. The drumsticks are then grilled separately and strips cut from the body are doused in Cognac and served flaming, and the whole is covered with a rich sauce in which the duck's blood is one of the ingredients.

This preparation is particularly appropriate for the Rouen duck because of the special way in which it is killed. The usual method of killing poultry in France (except for the guinea hen in the southwest, which is often shot down, sometimes the most feasible way to kill guineas, which are virtually wild even in domestication and prefer to perch on the top branches of the highest trees) is to bleed it; but in the Rouen region, ducks are strangled. This leaves the flesh red, and gives it a somewhat gamy tang, distinguishing it from the other famous duck of France, that of Nantes. The Nantes duck, which has a particularly delicate flavor, is also much smaller than that of Rouen—hardly more than four pounds at its heaviest, whereas five or six pounds is normal for a Rouen duck. The Rouen bird is of a special variety raised most intensively in the region of Yvetot, where a subvariety called the Duclair is particularly prized. It is also sometimes crossed with the Barbary, or Indian, duck of south and southeast France (also sometimes called the musk duck because of the pronounced flavor which at times makes it almost uneatable) to produce the mule duck, favored for the production of *foie gras*.

V · Normandy

Omelettes appear in many luscious varieties in Normandy. Everyone has heard of the *omelette de la Mère Poularde*, made by the hotel of that name on Mont-Saint-Michel, which I can remember as being very large, very creamy and classic—not disguised with complicated additions which are so easy to include in an omelette. I will not vouch for this, as the only time I tasted this dish, on a frigid November day when I was the only tenant in the hotel, at the time unheated, was some thirty years back and my attention was distracted from the main business at hand by the unfortunate circumstance that into the first omelette which was served me a bad egg had managed to insinuate itself. I was quickly provided with a second, and on the basis of the revision I can still recommend the omelette, providing that the passage of time and of a good many thousands of tourists has not wrought havoc on it. Rouen serves a rich and elaborate omelette studded with purée of duck's liver, while what is known as *omelette à la normande* is a sweet dish served for dessert, in which the eggs are wrapped around cooked apples doused with heavy cream and flavored with a dash of Calvados.

The omelette, by the way, is a dish whose name has caused some argument among scholars. The most amusing of the various accounts of the derivation of the word maintains that a king of Spain, famished from hunting, entered a woodsman's hut and asked for something to eat in a great hurry. The woodsman hastily whipped together some eggs and produced the first such dish the King had ever eaten. "What a fast worker!" said the King (*"Quel homme leste!"*) and so the word omelette was born. This makes a good story in French but there is one major objection to taking it seriously—the Spanish word for omelette happens to be *tortilla*. Skipping over a few other suggested derivations, it is probably sufficient to point out that the Romans had a dish called *ova mellita* (honeyed eggs). As the honey was beaten into the eggs, and what was made was therefore a honey omelette, there seems no need to search further for the derivation of this name.

It was suggested in the Touraine chapter that the tripe sausages, *andouille* and *andouillette*, were very probably of Norman origin. The fact is not established, but in any case it can be said that the best *andouilles* in France come from Vire, while for *andouillettes*, Caen shares the lead with Cambrai in Flanders and Troyes in the Champagne.

Normandy has a highly individual, well developed, and imaginative cuisine. It is unusual to find such cooking in a region that produces no wine. Possibly one explanation is the cider, which is drunk throughout the meal in Normandy like wine in other parts of France, providing through the juice of the apple the tasty liquid accompaniment to food provided elsewhere by the juice of the grape. Most Norman cider is not as sweet as American cider, but there are limitless varieties of it. The best comes from the Vallée d'Auge, and if you are ordering bottled cider, this is what you should ask for; but in most restaurants in Normandy cider is served lavishly in open carafes, and it is usually good enough. Sometimes it is put on the table whether you ask for it or not, like water, and there is no extra charge for the cider you drink with your meal. This, sadly, is a custom much rarer today than before the Second World War.

Calvados, the distilled juice of the apple, is a powerful drink, and a good deal of the cheaper Calvados sold over bars is a somewhat raw beverage recommendable only to the sturdy. To be really good, Calvados requires aging even more than does Cognac. Fine Calvados is aged in oak casks, into which a few hazelnuts have been dropped. You will not find a vintage year on the bottle because it is never all of the same year. Some of the new distillation is added each year, so that all Calvados is blended, but the first liquid from a new cask should not be drawn off until fifteen years after the first has been put in. If you pick up some Calvados in Normandy to take home, try to get it in the traditional container for fine Calvados, now, unfortunately, becoming rarer—a tall earthenware pitcher-jug with a sprig of apple leaves at the top. After the Calvados has disappeared, the jug remains as a pleasing ornament.

Finally, it should be recorded that it is in Normandy that Benedictine is made. This famous liqueur is a product of the Abbey of Fécamp, where it was first produced in 1510. Credit for it is given to a monk named Vincelli, who first had the idea of distilling a drink from the aromatic herbs that grow on the seaside cliffs of the neighborhood. The distillery is open to the public.

Brittany

In the Middle Ages, there were two principal ways of
acquiring new territories—conquest or marriage. France
acquired Brittany by a combination of marriage and perse-
verance. It took three kingly weddings, two of them with
the same bride, before Brittany became French. Charles
VIII married Anne of Brittany in 1491, but though the
Queen of France was thus also the Duchess of Brittany,
she ruled it separately in her own right. She had not
brought it to France as a dowry. When Charles in 1498
forgot to lower his head as he was passing hurriedly
through a low door in the Château d'Amboise on his way
to see a game of the ancestor of tennis, a widowed Anne

returned to Brittany, whose temporary union with France had thus expired. The foresighted French, however, had included in the original marriage contract a careful clause stipulating that Anne was now obliged to marry the next wearer of the crown. This turned out to be Louis XII, who had courted her when he was still only Louis d'Orléans, but who had unfortunately married in the meantime. He quickly secured an annulment of his first marriage (with the daughter of Louis XI) from the Pope, without, one might guess, much chagrin—his queen had a double hump on the back, deformed hips, and, according to contemporary writers, the face of a monkey. Fifteen years later Anne herself died, at the age of thirty-seven, and her daughter Claude became Duchess of Brittany. Claude, a few months later, married François d'Angoulême, and when, in 1515, he became Francis I, the Queen of France and the Duchess of Brittany were again the same person. Queen Claude was not much interested in matters of state. She preferred gardening; when you order today one of those sweet plums known as Reine Claudes, it is this queen you are commemorating. Therefore she was readily persuaded by the King to cede Brittany to their son, later to become Henry II, before she died at the age of twenty-five from what the not very precise medical science of the time described as a "disease of languor"—perhaps not unassociated with the fact that at this early age she had nevertheless managed to give the King seven children in eight years. In 1532 the perpetual union of the Duchy of Brittany with France was proclaimed, and since then Brittany has been French.

France thus acquired a substantial domain, represented today by the departments of Finistère, Côtes-du-Nord, Morbihan, Ille-et-Vilaine, and Loire-Inferieure. It had already known a thousand years of independent history, counting from the invasions of the Celts; before that period the region had reverted to a savage and historyless state after the barbarian invasions had caused the Roman power to collapse. Long before the Romans, Brittany had been inhabited prehistorically by the men who raised the monuments related to England's Stonehenge, so frequently encountered in Brittany, and then by the Gauls, who called it "the country of the sea"—Armour, a name still encountered on restaurant menus in such combinations as that of the misnamed *homard à l'armoricaine*. (It seems to be Brittany's lot to be credited with dishes that did not originate there, for the many-storied cake known as a Breton did not come from there either, but was created in 1850 in Paris.)

The present name of this section of the country, confusingly reminiscent of that of Britain, was derived quite legitimately from that country. It was Celts from Britain who brought the country back into the annals of history in the latter half of the fifth century, when, having been driven out of the British Isles themselves by the Angles and the Saxons, they moved onto the Armoricain peninsula and gave it its new name. They also gave it their language, fixing it so firmly on the territory that even today, 1,150 years after Charlemagne ended the isolation of Brittany by subduing it, nearly a million and a half people speak Breton. When Breton vegetable- and fruit-growers find themselves with more produce than they can sell at home, they load it aboard the Breton fishing boats, sail around the southwestern tip of England into the Bristol Channel, and there dispose of it to the Welsh, with whom they can bargain easily, Welsh and Breton being practically identical.

Brittany thus represents within the borders of France a distinct and different culture whose ancient roots are intertwined with those of Britain's Celts, not with any stock of France. The Bretons situate the story of King Arthur and the Round Table in Brittany, not Britain, and England's modern scholars agree that British Celts apparently first borrowed the story from the Bretons. Sir Thomas Malory, who wrote *Le Morte d'Arthur*, admitted that he took his details from Breton accounts going back to about the tenth century; on the other hand, it is far from certain that the tenth-century Bretons were not simply repeating traditions their ancestors had brought from the British Isles in the fifth. In any case, they identify the forest of Brocéliande, where Merlin the magician and the fairy Viviane dwelt, with the modern forest of Paimpont, in east-central Brittany. As for the story of Tristan and Isolde, firmly associated in England with Cornwall, England's southwestern tip, the Bretons do not contest the geographical location of King Mark's castle (though if they wanted to they could point out that their peninsula's southwestern tip is called Cornwall, too), but they do have a version of the story which brings Tristan at the end back to his château—in Brittany.

The Bretons, as sharers of Celtic mysticism, are fond of legends and cherishers of superstitions; after emerging from paganism, they diverted their mysticism to a fervent and picturesque devotion to the new faith of Christianity. You will often come across the name Yves in Brittany, for the saint of that name is one of the local favorites—he appears in Celtic Cornwall, too, in the name of the city immortalized in a nursery rhyme, Saint Ives. One of the stories about him is vaguely gastronomic. A judge in the thirteenth century, he is said to have presided over the trial of a beggar haled into court by a wealthy plantiff who was annoyed because of the regularity with which the beggar appeared before the grill of his kitchen windows to inhale the fragrance of the food cooking within.

Saint Yves took out a piece of money and threw it down upon the bench. "The ring of the coin," he said to the complainant, "pays you for the odor of your food."

The contrast of the Celtic enclave with the rest of France makes Brittany one of the most picturesque and exotic parts of the country, especially Lower Brittany, which, like Lower Normandy, being more remote from the mainland, has retained more of its ancient traditions. Lower Brittany, which is the western half of the peninsula, thrust far out into the sea, is called in French *Bretagne bretonnante*, which I suppose might as well be translated Breton Brittany, especially as Upper Brittany is sometimes called Gallic Brittany. It is in the former that most of the speakers of Breton live. Here you will see most often the many elaborate headdresses whose form reveals the place from which its wearer comes. There also are more of the elaborately carved crosses—the calvaries—and more of the ancient stone monuments, cromlechs, dolmens, and menhirs, and this is the country, too, of the religious processions and ceremonies of the pardons. Domestic architecture is humbler and cozier than to the east. Some of the old towns seem in feeling less akin to the solider squarer stone towns over to the west in France than to the villages of England or, skipping across the center of France in the opposite direction, to the towns of Alsace. The dwellers on the sea and the dwellers in the mountains of the Vosges might not be expected to have much in common, but the houses in which they live both seem to exude an anti-urbanism in contrast with the more sophisticated civilization which lies between them. The great cathedrals of the Ile-de-France and Normandy have not been emulated in Brittany. The churches are smaller and simpler. Breton building becomes massive only in fortresses and city walls—especially sea walls, like those of Saint-Malo.

Brittany, especially Lower Brittany, is dominated by

the sea. One is never far from it, even in the central farming country where you cannot see the ocean but can still smell it, for the fields are fertilized with seaweed. Some of the best farming country is within sight of the sea on the northern shore of the peninsula, producing fine potatoes, cabbages, cauliflower, artichokes, peas, string beans, and strawberries. At the extremity of the peninsula the coast is savage and rocky. The tides are high, the currents strong and treacherous, and the fishermen who learn their trade in these stormy, dangerous, rock-strewn waters are master sailors.

They have always been so. Jacques Cartier, who took possession of Canada in the name of Francis I and was probably the first man to report on the practice of smoking (he recorded his astonishment at seeing Indians use tobacco, but left it to Sir Walter Raleigh to import the plant to Europe), sailed from Saint-Malo. This was the most celebrated port of the corsairs, who for something like two centuries were sea scourges for all enemies of France and occasionally of promising victims who were, no doubt by error, mistakenly classified as such; it was not always easy to distinguish between privateers and pirates in those ill-organized days. It is Bretons today who sail their ships across the Atlantic to the Newfoundland Banks to fish for cod and Bretons who make up a large proportion of the sailors of the French Navy. On some of the outlying islands, the rocks on which the Bretons live do not seem to partake of the nature of land at all. They are solidified chunks of the sea, platforms from which its wayfarers can take off. Ushant, the phonetic Anglicization of Ouessant, which means Westerly, and is France's farthest reach in that direction, a desolate outcropping of rock above the surface of the waters, is sometimes thought to be the Ultima Thule of the ancients; but it is more likely that Thule was Iceland. The men of

Ushant spend most of their time at sea. It is so common for them not to come back that a special symbolical funeral ceremony has been developed for those lost to the ocean. Those who do come back celebrate their return to land by setting to on the accumulated housework. Their wives have no time for it during their absence, for they labor the fields and it takes incessant toil to wring a living from these almost bare rocks; yet Ushant does send one superb surplus food product to the mainland—salt-meadow sheep. The Ile de Sein, off the Pointe du Raz, some distance south of Ushant, is even smaller and poorer. All the men are sailors; the women never change from mourning—they would only have to put it right on again for the next victim of the sea—and the place is so poverty-stricken that up to 1958 it was absolved from payment of taxes, a privilege it shared with only one other spot in France, the island of Molène, lying between Ushant and the mainland.

This is hardy country. You would expect it to live on coarse food, hearty but rustic. It does.

Breton food is often spoken of with some disdain. More often it is denied than any really developed regional cuisine exists at all, in spite of the fact that a very considerable proportion of the private cooks of Paris are Bretons. This is less because they have any natural affinity for the kitchen than because it is the nonurban regions peopled largely by those who work with their hands which ordinarily supply the demands of the cities for domestic service. The money-less young girls of the more sophisticated areas provide offices with their stenographers and stores with their sales girls, but Brittany is the big supplier of domestic help. Middle-aged Breton women are preferred as nurses for children in wealthy families, which think it stylish to send the youngsters off to play in the quieter parks with a guardian wearing the Breton headdress—a habit that threatens to convert it into a mark of servitude and kill the picturesque coiffure. Young Breton girls come to Paris as maids of all work for families of more modest incomes, and one of the jobs that is included is doing the cooking. They usually acquit themselves well, so there seems to be no justification for impugning Breton skill in the kitchen, even though the arduous conditions of life on the wind-swept Armoricain peninsula have not been conducive to the development of an elaborate cuisine there.

Certainly the term *à la bretonne* does not apply to a particularly subtle treatment of foods, though it is a filling one. It generally connotes the appearance of white beans. It may mean that the dish itself is accompanied by white beans, as in *gigot de mouton à la bretonne*, in *sauce bretonne;* or it may refer to a *purée bretonne*, in which case the bean dish has been thinned to a soup; or it may mean simply a dish with *sauce bretonne*, as in *sole à la bretonne*, in which last case the beans have disappeared and only the sauce habitually served on them in Brittany remains. *Sauce bretonne* is of two varieties, and if menu writers are meticulous, there will be a distinction in their descriptions. Strictly speaking, *sauce à la bretonne* is a medieval preparation which includes in its ingredients another elaborate classical sauce of those times, *espagnole*, which involved the juice derived from cooking ham, veal, and partridge. This was combined with consommé, butter, chicken jelly, and browned onions, and seasoned with white pepper and sugar. You are not too likely to find this painstaking concoction nowadays, so what you will probably encounter is *sauce bretonne*, made of onions, carrots, celery, leeks, butter, and cream or white wine, depending on the dish with which it is to be served—cream for beans, for instance, wine for sole.

It can be said about Breton food that the country naturally raises products of excellent quality of a nature that does not require elaborate treatment to bring out its flavor—in fact some of the most famous Breton specialties are types of shellfish generally eaten raw. Artifice in the kitchen is therefore not particularly necessary. The technique of a good home cook will do. The fine salt-meadow mutton of Brittany, produced not only on Ushant, as has been noted above, but also in large areas throughout the peninsula, requires little more than expert seasoning and careful roasting to make a fine dish. In Brittany the standard combination is shoulder of mutton with white beans. Partridge and hare from this region have a naturally pungent flavor; all the cook has to do is not to prevent it from making its effect. In the region of Rennes, the capital, fine ducks, turkeys, and chickens are raised. Elaborate dishes can be built up around this poultry, but when it is of the first quality, as the Breton product is, there is no necessity for trying to improve on nature.

The one culinary specialty for which Brittany is really noted is *crêpes*—pancakes. The Breton pancake is less coarse than the American griddlecake, but is still a rather heavy product. It may have been the ancestor of the *crêpe Suzette*, a most delicate derivation, but it compares with it as a gnarled and weatherbeaten farmer with an elegant *parisienne*—although the line of descent does pass through a Breton creation of great finesse, the *crêpes dentelles* (lacelike pancake) of Quimperlé. The ordinary solid Breton *crêpe*, though hardly subtle, is by no means a dish to be despised, and it has the advantage of filling you to repletion at minute cost.

For some reason, a little cluster of Breton pancake places has grown up in Paris around the boulevard Saint-Germain, about midway between Saint-Germain-des-Prés and the boulevard Saint-Michel (offbase, for the classic Breton quarter in Paris is behind the Gare Montparnasse), where I go occasionally for *crêpes*. There is no style. The cook officiates in the dining room in full view of the diners, behind a battery of enormous griddles constantly smoking with batter in various stages of cooking. The only thing on the menu is *crêpes*. I usually order one *crêpe* with butter and eggs or cheese as the main course, and another with jelly or honey for dessert, washed down with a glass or two of cider—the standard liquid accompaniment—and stagger heavily out, hardly lightened at all in the region of the pocketbook. The meal costs about two hundred francs (fifty cents), which is less than half what you would have to pay in even the cheapest restaurant for anything describable as a meal. In this particular place, all the *crêpes* seem to be made of the same flour; the shift from the *pièce de résistance crêpe* to the dessert *crêpe* is made simply by shifting its content from a non-sweet to a sweet. In Brittany there is likely to be a change in the batter as well. Buckwheat flour is used for the first, and it is salted. Wheat flour is used for the batter of the dessert *crêpe*, and it is sweetened.

In the realm of sea food, the two top items in Brittany are lobsters and oysters. The Breton coast is rich both in *homard*, which is practically the same thing as the American lobster, and *langouste*, which corresponds to the spiny lobster which in the United States is found only on the Pacific Coast. In spite of the error that turned *homard à l'américaine* into *homard à l'armoricaine*, a spelling which seems to be encountered less often in Brittany itself than elsewhere, Brittany has developed no particular presentation of lobster other than the standard treatment of boiling the smaller ones and baking the big ones. When you have good lobster to start with, it is in fact rather difficult to improve on this. The small sweet lobsters of Camaret, from the bay between the northern and southern points of the peninsula, are particularly good.

When we come to the oysters of Brittany, we enter upon a subject more complicated than one might expect. The first distinction to be made between the different varieties available here is between the wild oysters brought up from natural beds by the draggers, which have a pungent taste, and the cultivated oysters raised artificially, which are blander. For a time there were practically no natural oysters, for dragging had gone on so enthusiastically that the beds were exhausted. After France forbade dragging and turned to the cultivation of oysters, the beds recovered, and dragging is now permitted under certain restrictions.

In establishing the cultivation of oysters in the middle of the last century, the French went to a source of respectable antiquity—Taranto, Italy, where they studied oyster culture in beds established by the ancient Romans, who were great oyster-fanciers. So were the Greeks, who, you will remember, used to vote, particularly on such questions as banishments, by inscribing their verdicts on oyster shells with styluses. When a Greek was voted out of a community, he was not blackballed, he was oyster-shelled—whence the word ostracism.

Both wild and cultivated oysters are fished in Brittany, and of each kind, both of the two main varieties. The most common French oyster is much more liquid than the American oyster, has a rougher shell, and is green in color; the juice within it is highly redolent of the sea. This is commonly known as the *portugaise*, not quite correctly, but we need not go into that. There is also another oyster of smoother shell, flatter, with firm white flesh and less liquid—a closer approach to the American oyster, though my favorite variety, the Belon, is not nearly so fat as, for instance, a blue point, than which in my opinion it is much more subtle in flavor.

For a while, toward the end of the last century, it seemed that the *portugaises* which, like the Bretons, are extremely prolific, were going to drive out the finer white oysters entirely, but the oyster-cultivators, aided by restrictive legislation, finally succeeded in controlling the turbulent bivalves, and now the *portugaise* variety may be legally cultivated artificially only in the region of Le Croisic, at almost the southern limit of the Breton coast. The biggest oyster-breeding beds are in the Gulf of Morbihan, and they are starters for oyster fisheries in other parts of the country. When you buy oysters described as *morbihannaises* or *armoricaines*, they are direct from the Breton beds. But from Brittany, *portugaises* may also go to Marennes, down the coast, almost as far south as Bordeaux, for fattening, and will then turn up on the market as Marennes. The white oysters may go to Belon, also not in Brittany, or to Cancal, which *is* in Brittany, in the bay of Mont-Saint-Michel, so the oysters make the trip from the southern to the northern coast of the peninsula to be fattened for market, and are then sold as *cancalaises*. Lest this seem like a trick played on the public, which would seem to be getting Breton oysters whatever the name, it may be explained that the locality where an oyster is fattened affects its flavor as much as the place where grapes are grown affects the taste of the wine made from it. The oysters of Marennes, for instance, are much greener in color than those finished anywhere else, due to the minute bits of seaweed and diatoms which exist at this particular spot. The oysters that feed on them acquire both color and savor, just as the sheep pastured on the seaside meadows manufacture tastier mutton from the pasturage they eat.

One thing the various fattening regions have in common —they are always at river mouths, for the mixture of fresh and salt water provokes hypertrophy of the liver in an oyster, which is what makes it fat. The oyster thus has something in common with the goose, which is overfed in order to produce the swollen liver needed to make *pâté de foie gras*.

The Bretons, unlike the Normans, have invented no special dishes in which to use their oysters, once again appearing as somewhat incurious. They have not done much with two other assets they also share with the Normans, either—cider, the universal drink in Brittany as in Normandy, and cream, with which they are well provided also. The Breton cow, a black-and-white animal, though very small—top weight, about 635 pounds—is a fine milk-producer, but the butterfat content of the milk is not quite as high as in Normandy. (A red-blotched variety of the small Breton cow is crossed with the large British Durham bulls to produce a beef animal, much weaker as a milk-producer.) The butter of Brittany is nearly as fine as that of Normandy and it does get into pike with *beurre-blanc* sauce, a dish probably borrowed from the neighboring Loire valley territory, while shad is often cooked with cream. The cream also goes lavishly into the Breton *crêpes*. Little cheese is made in Brittany, aside from the *mingaux* of Rennes, a cream cheese akin to the *crémets* of Saumur.

The Bretons have produced one memorable dish in the sea food category, *cotriade*, which is the local variety of *bouillabaisse*, the mixed fish stew encountered in various forms along all the coasts of France. Bretons say that the more different kinds of fish there are in the *cotriade*, the better it is. There is no fixed list of ingredients, but a dozen different types of local fish may be used, depending on what the day's catch has brought up. Lobster is not included. Onions and potatoes accompany the fish in this stew, and the seasoning is with herbs, especially laurel and thyme. It is served much like the famous *bouillabaisse* of the Mediterranean—the liquid is poured over slices of bread and served in one dish, while the fish and the potatoes are presented on a separate platter as a second course following the soup.

Though Brittany is cider country, it does have some

wine, in the extreme southern point about Nantes, which is at the head of the estuary of the Loire, so that Brittany's wine is really a gift from the Loire region. The vintage here is a dry, fruity white wine that goes well with the local shellfish called Muscadet, because it is supposed to have a slight flavor of nutmeg (*muscade*). The best Muscadets are those of Saint-Herblon and Ancenis on the Loire, and Vallet on its tributary, the Sèvre Nantaise.

Wine grapes are also grown on the Rhuys peninsula, but the less said about that the better. The Bretons themselves have a comment on this wine. To drink it, they explain, takes four men and a wall—one man to pour it, one man to drink it, two to hold onto him, and the wall to keep him from backing away.

The Bordeaux Country

Most guidebooks on France or on Paris inform their
readers that the Place de la Concorde is the largest
in Europe (except the Red Square in Moscow), and therefore most guidebooks are wrong. The largest square is the
Esplanade des Quinconces in Bordeaux, some 140,000 square
yards in area as compared to about 90,000 for the Place de
la Concorde. The pride of Bordeaux is the Grand Théâtre.
It does not outrank the Paris Opéra in size—the Grand
Théâtre seats 1,300, the Opéra 2,200—but when Garnier
built the Opéra he was inspired by the Grand Théâtre—
for instance, the famous curving double staircase of the
Opéra is borrowed from the same detail in Bordeaux. The
city of Bordeaux pays a heavy subsidy to operate its theater,

for it stages its spectacles in so lavish a manner that even if it played to capacity audiences at every performance it would still lose money. The city thinks the result is worth it.

Bordeaux is the second largest city in France in area, the fourth in population, and the fifth port. The exiled Goya picked Bordeaux to live and die in—and provided a minor mystery for the history of art when he was exhumed for reburial in Spain, for the body was found to be headless. "Take Versailles," wrote Victor Hugo, "add Antwerp to it, and you have Bordeaux."

The magnificence of this city results from two factors—first, its geographical position and second, after the first had drawn to the spot the Romans who planted grapevines there, the excellence of its wine.

Bordeaux is on the Garonne River, just above the spot where it joins the Dordogne, the combined streams forming a great estuary called the Gironde. Seagoing shipping can mount the river to the busy wharves of Bordeaux, which provide a natural sheltered inland harbor. There are no topographical obstacles about Bordeaux to cut its hinterland off abruptly, and it is thus the commercial and cultural center for a large region, the coastal territories lying north and south of the Gironde—more particularly south of it—and the interior plumbed by the two great rivers. The Dordogne, which has been called the most beautiful of all French rivers, flows swiftly through that ancient inhabited region of France, the country of Cro-Magnon man, between high banks crowned with old castles and walled towns. The Garonne, rising far to the south in the Pyrenees, plunges in icy foam down from the mountains, slows up after it has passed through another great city, Toulouse, glides through Agen, and as it approaches Bordeaux is flanked on either side by rank after rank of vines as far as the eye can see.

The combination of great wines and great wealth made Bordeaux one of the gastronomic capitals of France, and though its table suffered during the war along with its port (the retreating Germans thought they had blocked the channel for good before they left the region, but the French had it open again by 1946), it remains today one of the great eating cities of France, along with Paris, Lyons, Dijon, Rouen, and Tours. Its Chapon Fin is no longer one of the half-dozen best restaurants of France, as it used to be before the war, but it remains one of the half hundred best, and its atmosphere of nineteenth-century splendor has not changed. It is one of my regrets that I never ate there in the days of its greatness, but my only visit to the old Bordeaux was at the time of the armistice of 1940, when the city was jammed with four times its normal population and no one was able to crowd into the Chapon Fin except influential politicians or their mistresses. But if the Chapon Fin no longer receives three stars in the listings of the French tourist's gastronomic bible, the *Michelin* guide, it still has two, and there are six other restaurants in Bordeaux with one, a remarkable record for a single city.

In this region, the local cooking seems to have originated chiefly in its great capital and to have spread from there to the surrounding territories, petering out as one goes farther and farther from the source. This is rather an exception to the rule that the great cities concentrate and bring to its highest point the cooking of the surrounding region, from which they draw their original inspiration. This is probably the reason also why the borders of the gastronomic region of Bordeaux do not accord with any political borders of the past. In the other areas that we have considered, cuisines developed throughout entire political or geographical units, and though they often reached their culminating points in certain cities within those units, nevertheless there was a more or less homogeneous school of cooking coexten-

The BORDEAUX COUNTRY

MILES
0   50   100

0   100
KM.

≡ Great Eating
= Good Eating

AUNIS (SHELLFISH)

POITOU

ATLANTIC

Île de Ré

La Rochelle

Île d'Oléron

SANTONGE

SARDINE PÂTÉ
SNAIL STEW
WOODCOCK
GALANTINE

Saintes

Marennes
(OYSTERS)

PRESERVED DUCK

Gironde

Cognac

ANGOUMOIS

GIGORIT
STUFFED CABBAGE
PIG'S FEET

LIMOUSIN

GAME

Angoulême

Périgord

Pauillac

Médoc

CHICKENS AND CAPONS

SALT MEADOW LAMB

St. Julien

Margaux

Haut Médoc

Blaye

Bordeaux

GRAVES

SAUTERNES

Libourne

St. Emilion (MACAROONS)

Passac

Dordogne R.

GUIENNE

WILD DOVES

Arcachon

The Landes

GaRonne R.

GRAPEPICKERS' SOUP

OYSTERS

OCEAN

Cérons
(PEAS)

ORTALANS

Marmande
(TOMATOES ASPARAGUS)

Sauternes

Lot R.

Tonneins
(HAMS)

GASCONY

Agen (PRUNES)

Nérac (MEAT LOAVES)

Rouergue

In this area, gastronomic & political boundaries do not coincide. The regions shown in black
on the left are treated in the accompanying chapter. The shaded areas, though part of the same
provinces, are discussed elsewhere – Périgord &
Rouergue, though part of Guienne, with the Central Plateau, & Southern Gascony with the Pyrenees.

sive with the unit. Not so here, where a special cuisine developed in vineyard-surrounded Bordeaux, formed by the influence of the wines on the kitchen, and only partially penetrated the rest of the political territory in which Bordeaux found itself.

This may have been partly because the territory was so vast and so diversified. The elements of which it was composed did not have enough in common to encourage the development of a uniform table. Bordeaux itself was the capital of Guienne (a corruption of Aquitania), a region whose boundaries changed from time to time, including at its peak (the eighth century) Poitou and Berry to the north, which we have already examined; the Marche, the Limousin, the Périgord, and Auvergne, which we shall get to later; and the Saintonge to the northeast, which we shall look at now along with the Angoumois, though politically the latter has never been in the same region as Bordeaux. These last two, north of the rivers that cause Bordeaux to look more readily southward than northward, attach themselves to some extent to Bordeaux because of food products supplementary to Bordeaux's own—for the Angoumois, covering parts of the modern departments of the Charente and the Dordogne, because it is the country of Cognac, producing the natural after-dinner complement to Bordeaux's wines; and for Saintonge, because of its oysters, which accord admirably with the dryer Graves. The latter, rather swampy country, covering part of the Charente-Maritime, had a separate history of its own for a good deal of the period before it was joined to France in 1372. The former is a country of wide valleys and occasional abrupt plateaus overlooking them, in nature and history quite separate from Saintonge or the Bordelais.

South of Bordeaux, in its more closely related hinterland, there is also considerable variety. Beyond Guienne lies Gascony, running all the way into the Pyrenees, itself a much fragmented region. It is difficult to draw a boundary between Guienne and Gascony, partly because it varied from time to time, partly because Gascony was part of Guienne for some four centuries, roughly between 1050 and 1450, and the two thus became confounded. Below Bordeaux along the coast is a strip of long sandy beaches backed by lagoons, some communicating with the sea, some shut off from it. Just back of them is the Landes, covered with growths of rather scrubby pine, with peculiar cultural features all its own. The shepherds go about on stilts, a custom that grew up as a result of the marshy nature of much of the country, but which has persisted in spite of the fact that most of it has now been drained. There is a shepherds' dance performed on the hands and knees, with the face upturned toward the sky. There is a local variety of the bullfight in which cows are provoked to charge and the idea is to avoid the onslaught, but it hardly ranks for danger with the Spanish sport, for the cow's horns are tipped with balls and she is on a long rope that brings her up with a jerk if she runs too far. To the east, the valley of the Garonne runs into ever more hilly country, and as it passes Agen the heights often close in on the stream and its tributaries, of which one, the Tarn, is famous for its deep, savage gorges.

Much of this country was for a long time English—falling under the English crown along with Anjou when Henry Plantagenet, Count of Anjou, became Henry II of England. As Henry's wife was Eleanor of Aquitaine, this vast area became English territory, too, and the English discovery of the wines of the Bordeaux region, which were appreciated with the enthusiasm proper from a country that had no wine itself, had much to do with the development of the Bordeaux vineyards, which share with those of Burgundy the distinction of producing the world's greatest wines.

Bordeaux thus owes to two great colonizing—and importing—nations the evolution of its greatest glory. The Romans planted vines there in the third century. By the fourth, Burdigala, the Roman name for the city, had become a great commercial center and was made the capital of Aquitania Secunda. The fourth-century Latin poet, Ausonius, was a native of Bordeaux and owned a vineyard in Saint-Emilion.

As for the English, whose pronunciation had turned the name Aquitania (in the French of that period, Aguienne) to Guienne, they proceeded, when they took cognizance of the product of the Bordeaux vineyards, to spread the fame of claret—meaning in English a red Bordeaux, though in French the word rather denies the color. *Clairet* is, indeed, applied to red wines, but its specific meaning (our word clear, of course) is that it is only slightly colored—almost a *rosé*. As for *clairette*, whose pronunciation in French is much nearer to that of claret in English, it is a sparkling white wine of the south.

Bordeaux is no exception to the rule that good cooking is found in wine country. The description *à la bordelaise* (Bordeaux style) occurs often on menus throughout the country. It is sometimes confusing. You may meet with some dish so described and then come upon another, also Bordeaux style, without being able to establish any relationship between them. This is because there are several treatments of dishes that have originated in Bordeaux. For instance, *à la bordelaise* may mean that the dish is cooked in *sauce bordelaise*, which is a compound of wine, butter, tomato extract, and marrow seasoned with shallots, thyme, and nutmeg. It may also mean that the sauce is Mirepoix, which is an extract of carrots, onions, celery, and ham reduced to liquid form, and seasoned with thyme and laurel (the ham is omitted when the sauce is to be used for shellfish). A third meaning is that the dish is served with *cèpes*, large fleshy mushrooms. When you meet the *cèpes* alone, *à la bordelaise*, in Paris, the mushrooms will first have been cooked in a closed dish with butter and a little lemon juice, then browned slightly in oil in a frying pan; at the last moment chopped shallots, parsley, and bread crumbs are added. This, however, is not the way they do it in Bordeaux. There the bread crumbs are omitted, garlic is used instead of shallots, the juice of green grapes replaces the lemon juice, and the *cèpes* are not browned in a frying pan. Sometimes they are cooked in oil, but in an earthenware casserole. Finally, *à la bordelaise* may mean a dish accompanied with artichokes and potatoes, with or without other vegetables.

An application of one of these meanings of the description "Bordeaux style" is a specialty of the Chapon Fin known as crayfish, Bordeaux style (*écrevisses à la bordelaise*). This comes under the second heading above—dishes employing Mirepoix sauce. The Chapon Fin makes a very fine Mirepoix, of vegetables only, while the crayfish are sautéed separately in butter, with a seasoning of salt, pepper, and spices. A little Cognac is then poured over them and burned. They are dampened with white wine and cooked in the Mirepoix sauce for about twenty minutes. The crayfish are then removed, and to the remaining liquid yolks of eggs are added, together with butter and seasoning, and the crayfish are served piping hot covered with the resulting sauce.

There is no end to Bordeaux dishes of this sort, with fixed elaborate recipes. This is developed cooking, sophisticated and mannered. Behind it lies a simpler cuisine, closer to the earth—a peasant cuisine. One of its manifestations is *faire chabrot*, a term not understood by many Parisians, but one which your true Bordelais will comprehend immediately. You may hear *chabrot* described as a dish, but it isn't a dish—it is an eating custom. When you are served the bouillon from poultry or meat—no other sort—you wolf it down quickly in order to leave a little in the bottom of your plate while it is still quite hot. Then you empty a glass of red wine into the hot bouillon, give it a few seconds to warm, and finish your soup. This is *faire chabrot* and a tradition says that you should drink the mixture directly from your dish. This custom is falling into disuse, however, and I wouldn't advise you to lift your plate to your mouth unless some native starts first.

An old dish of Médoc—the strip of territory lying along the west shore of the Gironde from Bordeaux to the sea—which you are never likely to be able to taste except in a private home is *lou pastis en pott*, the name being in the old *langue d'oc*. Restaurants do not serve it, possibly because they find the basic ingredients unorthodox—a large earthenware pot, a shelf, and plenty of time. Once these essentials have been brought together, the cook proceeds as follows: The interior of the pot is greased with lard. Two or three fresh fig leaves and a leaf of laurel are laid on the bottom, and aromatic herbs and spices are added to them. Now comes the part that is probably the real discourager of restaurants, or at least of all restaurants that do not buy meat in pieces as large as quarters, for it almost confines the dish to a farm or to some other place where animals are slaughtered. A few alternating layers of pork and beef are laid down, from the scraps left over when the carcasses have been cut up—boned and with the tendons removed in the case of the beef. As many layers go in the bottom of the pot as can be covered by half a bottle of new red wine. When it has been so covered, you let it simmer until it has been reduced to one half its original volume. It is then cooled, sealed (with a layer of fat or other airtight covering), and put on the shelf. Some days later the pot is taken down again. The seal is removed, a few more layers of pork and beef are added, together with as much herbs, salt, and pepper as the new addition of meat demands, covered once more with wine, put to simmer, again until it has been reduced to half its volume, and back it goes on the shelf. This process is continued until the pot is full, when the real fun begins. You help yourself to a serving from the pot—either hot, just after the last cooking, or cold, when it becomes a sort of jellied meat preparation; it's good either way. You then fill up the gap you have created in the usual fashion, simmer once more and return the jug to the shelf. From now on this is the cycle—every time you eat some of the contents of the pot, you replace its ingredients. The process can go on for years, with the contents of the pot growing richer and richer. The wine, specialists in this dish say, should be of the same age as the dish; but it doesn't matter, as the years go on, if you add different wines, provided they are all red Médocs. Wine being the only liquid that goes into this preparation, you can imagine that the resultant dish is redolent of it. It's a little like taking wine in solid form, as the name of the dish suggests—potted *pastis*, *pastis* being the southern name for the anise-flavored *apéritifs* so popular in that part of the country, and so powerful when consumed in large doses.

This is clearly hearty food, very different from the refined, subtle confections of the great restaurants, like the Chapon Fin's *écrevisses à la bordelaise*, but this is a region where both the *haute cuisine* and the *cuisine bourgeoise* (really, here, the *cuisine paysanne*) flourish. Another peasant dish that only the outlander who really penetrates the country is likely to have a chance to sample is the *soupe des vendanges*—grape-pickers' soup, you might call it. As it is served to the crews that harvest the grapes at vintage time, it is customarily made in enormous quantities, the favored utensil being a laundry boiler in the bottom of which are disposed three large clean stones from some nearby beach, carefully arranged in an isosceles triangle—I have no idea why. As large a piece of beef as can be conveniently fitted into the boiler is placed in it, after having had salt, pepper, spices, laurel, garlic, and fresh grape seeds tucked into slits cut in the beef. A large piece of leg of veal is then forced in beside it. In whatever space is left, carrots, turnips, onions, leeks, cabbages, garlic, potatoes, celery, rosemary, and a bunch of mixed herbs are fitted in. A few fresh grapes are added, and cloves are sprinkled plentifully over the whole, which is then covered with water and cooked over a high flame until the water is reduced to one third of its original volume, when it is allowed to simmer to complete its conversion into bouillon. When it is served, the guests customarily sprinkle their portions with a thick layer of pepper before attacking it. As you can see, it is a local variation of *pot-au-feu*, though it commits a heresy that lovers of this dish in other parts of the country consider with horror— elsewhere potatoes are kept strictly out of a *pot-au-feu* because it robs the bouillon of finesse. *Soupe des vendanges*, however, is a concoction that mocks at finesse.

There are some dishes which consummate a marriage between the lusty country cooking and the refined restaurant cuisine. You may find in restaurants, for instance, the typical onion or garlic soup of the region, *tourin bordelais* (if it's spelled *tourain*, you may suspect the place of having lost some contact with the soil, for it has Frenchified the local spelling). In the rustic regional tradition also is *lamproies au vin rouge*, an unusual dish made from the eel-like fish known as the lamprey, one of the few animals whose gastronomic relation with the human race is reciprocal, if there is any truth in the legend that Roman tyrants fed to lampreys—or the related morays—slaves with whom they were displeased. In the competition between eater and eaten, man and the lamprey seem to have achieved something of a tie on one occasion at least—Henry I of England was so fond of lampreys that he died from overeating them. Lampreys swim up the estuary of the Gironde in large numbers in the spring—like the eel proper, they are a migratory race. They are cooked in Bordeaux in a sauce made of their own blood, red wine (contrary to the usual rule that only white wine is used with fish—but this dish is sometimes made with white wine as well), and leeks, with some other seasoning ingredients that vary with the cook. *Anguilles sautées à la bordelaise* is a rather more orthodox way of treating the common eel, but it is not an orthodox way of employing the description "Bordeaux style," as the dish does not fall into any one of the four categories listed above—the fish is fried with herbs, producing a dish reminiscent of a Belgian specialty, except that in the Belgian *anguilles au vert*, elvers (baby eels) are used. Shad is in season at the same time as lampreys and eel and is served in Bordeaux with white wine sauce. And while we are on the subject of sea food, we should mention the oysters of Arcachon, a city south of Bordeaux on one of the lagoons paralleling the coast, in this case communicating with the sea, where some of the finest mollusks in France are cultivated in artificial oyster beds. They are served in Bordeaux with hot truffle-flavored sausages and are such ancient favorites that Rabelais pays tribute to them. The oysters of his day were a flat species, called *gravettes*, found only at Arcachon, which threatened to disappear from the modern menu when disease wiped them out shortly after the Second World War. The beds were restocked with the more commun *portugaises*—but then the choice *gravettes* reappeared, and today Arcachon offers both types.

Another specialty of the region of Bordeaux is the local version of the salt-meadow sheep we have already encountered in other regions, *agneau de Pauillac*, a much appreciated variety of this sort of lamb, raised in the coastal region of Médoc. A suburb of Bordeaux, Caudéran, is famous for its snails. Cérons is noted for peas, Eysines for new potatoes, Macau for artichokes, and Pessac for strawberries. Saint-Emilion, one of the oldest and most interesting towns of the immediate Bordeaux region—the Romans thought highly of it—is noted for its cakes and pastry, especially macaroons.

South of Bordeaux, the Landes provide a number of typical dishes of their own. The sand dunes along the coast, the marshes behind them, and the pine forests behind *them* make it good bird country. The region is known for its *ortolans*, a small bird of the yellowhammer family which is considered the most delicately flavored of all birds in France and has provided a household word for the utmost refinement in eating, *ortolans sauce blanche,* generally used jocularly. Thus a Frenchman reaching the table and finding it set with a particularly economical repast may observe sarcastically: *"Eh bien! Ortolans sauce blanche encore une fois!"* This sort of remark is not recommended to foreigners.

One of the reasons why the *ortolan* is so much prized is that it is not simply shot and served, as are most wild birds. It is caught during the autumn migrations in traps called *matoles,* which possess some screening ability that enables them to catch *ortolans* rather than other birds of the same caliber, and is then caged and fattened on millet until it is judged to be pleasingly plump. In spite of the *ortolans sauce blanche* saying, in the Landes, where they know *ortolans,* the idea of submerging its delicate flavor under a sauce would be considered sacrilege. *Ortolans à la landaise* are cooked by an open fire, either spitted or, preferably, each in a little heavy paper box set close to the flames, in which the birds sizzle in their own fat. No other liquid is tolerated, but the guest may be invited to apply salt and pepper to his own taste as the cooking progresses before his eyes. When the bird is done, pick it up in your fingers and eat it without ceremony, as hot as you dare. They are so small you can put away half a dozen of them with ease.

Salmis de palombe is another dish resulting from the good hunting in the Landes. It is made from wild doves shot during their autumn migration. A *salmis*, strictly speaking, is a poultry dish in which the bird is only about two thirds cooked in the kitchen, in order that the process may be finished at the table before the diner. Perhaps the practice is a reminder of the elaborate feasting of medieval times, when it permitted making a ceremony of the final preparation of the dish before the lord whose hunting party had provided the raw material. In any case, the *salmis* goes back at least to the fourteenth century. The partly cooked bird is cut up, and the pieces are finished more or less elaborately in a sauce, often doused with flaming Cognac, and in combination with such other ingredients as mushrooms. The method of cooking duck in Rouen described in the Normandy chapter is thus a *salmis*.

In this region, grapes enter into a number of combinations that might offhand seem rather improbable, a result of the propinquity of the Bordeaux vineyards. Thus fresh duck liver is served with grapes, and so is hot *foie gras*.

Many dishes found in the Landes—and for that matter in Bordeaux—have made their way northward from Gascony. One is the famous *garbure*, more stew than soup, which we will come to when we consider the cooking of the Pyrenees. Similarly as we move southwestward from Bordeaux through the valley of the Garonne, we find dishes seeping down from the north—the noted gastronomic region of the Périgord—giving this region one of its two distinctive flavors, that of the truffle. The other is garlic from Provence, if it can be attributed to any particular region at all, which is debatable. Garlic gets around.

The cooking of the Guienne region does not vary greatly

from that of Bordeaux, though there is a natural tendency as you penetrate more deeply into the interior for the peasant dishes to take precedence over the *haute cuisine*. As you leave the coast, you get more fresh-water fish—carp and gudgeon—and find new regions of vegetable specialties, like Marmande, a center of tomato- and asparagus-growing. Dessert grapes (*chasselas*) are grown here rather than wine grapes—though there are local wines, such as the reds of Buzet, Perricard, and Marmande and the whites of Côtes Duras, Soumensac, Cocumont, and Saint-Pierre-de-Buzet. Tonneins is noted for its hams and Nérac for its *terrines* (poultry or meat loaves). But the most famous specialty of the region is the prunes of Agen, made from plums grown on plum trees on which choice young grafts have been applied to mature plants.

North of Bordeaux, the seacoast region, the Saintonge, with the minute Aunis north of it, has no distinctive cuisine of its own. It follows the lead of the Bordeaux region, with a heavier emphasis on sea food, in which this coast is rich. Marennes, whose oysters have been mentioned in the chapter on Brittany, is here. The one specialty that might be mentioned comes especially from the Marennes region— *cagouilles*. You will not find this word in a dictionary unless it is more complete than mine, but locally it means snails; they are served either stuffed or in a sort of stew. They are so popular in this region that the people here are sometimes referred to as *cagouillards*.

Further inland is the Angoumois, where the dishes offered are a combination of those of the Bordeaux region to the south and the Périgord to the east. The dishes that seem most distinctively local are likely to be of a rather coarse type—*gigorit*, which is a stew of liver, heart, giblets, spleen, lungs, and so forth; *farée*, which is stuffed cabbage; and the stuffed pigs' feet that I tried recently in Angoulême, not because it is my sort of dish, but because the best hotel there was featuring it as a local specialty. It tasted not much different from highly peppered American country sausage. Angoulême was a somewhat disappointing town from a gastronomic point of view. Its splendid natural situation on a sudden plateau overlooking the valley of the Charente, and the interest of some of its old buildings, first of all the impressive and original Romanesque cathedral whose façade is covered with naïve bas-reliefs, prepares the visitor for cooking affected by them; but though the food was not bad, particularly some mussels from the Saintonge to the west, there was little attempt, aside from the undistinguished pigs' feet, to promote regional dishes.

There are local wines, which accord with the local cooking, as wines customarily do—rather coarse, but agreeable enough. I am told that the best red is Sainte-Radegonde and the best white Saint-Brice, but whether I tasted them or not I don't know. At the Hôtel du Palais the waiter was unable to identify the red carafe wine, which had a slight earthy taste, beyond saying it was local wine, and at the Hôtel de France, the best in Angoulême, though they served a bottled *blanc de blanc* (white wine made from white grapes), the label had no local place name on it. It was fairly dry, with a slight taste of rock which made me think of the Condrieu of Vienne, in the Rhone valley, but with nothing like the finesse of Condrieu, one of my favorites among minor wines.

It is not surprising that there is little local pride about wines, with the great Bordeaux vineyards lying so close. However it is not only because of this geographical fact that you will not hear about Angoumois wines or taste them unless you go to the spot, but also because, interesting though they may be on their native earth, they are not enough so to be worth exporting. The grapes of this region are not particularly good for the making of wine; but they are supreme for the making of brandy. It is on the western border of the Angoumois, and of the modern department of the Charente, that you will find a little town of only 17,500 inhabitants whose name is known all over the world— Cognac.

The word has come to be used generally for brandy, but strictly speaking there is no Cognac except that distilled from the grapes grown in an area of some 150,000 acres surrounding the town of Cognac. Cognac may be made from any one of seven admitted varieties of grape, and the right to market brandy under the Cognac name is forbidden if it is made from any other, but actually the variety of the grape seems to have much less to do with the final result than the place where it is grown—and possibly the cask in which it ages. The combination of Charente grapes and Limousin oak, which is what the distillation is aged in, was discovered accidentally three hundred years ago, and nobody has risked disturbing it since. Surplus wine resulting from several bumper crops in a row was stored in Limousin oak casks that happened to be handy, first being distilled to economize storage space. When its owners returned to it a good many years later, they discovered that it had acquired a velvety quality never before encountered in this sort of liquor. Thus Cognac was born.

The aging process is all-important for Cognac. Distilled liquors, unlike wine, do not develop in the bottle. They age only in the cask, the process being the result of chemical interchanges between wood and liquid with the aid of the air seeping through pores in the barrel—a process during which about one seventh of the contents evaporates. It takes wood that has aged to age Cognac. Put into unseasoned wood, the brandy spoils.

The age of a Cognac is the length of time it has spent in the cask, not the length of time since it was made—hence such terms as "Napoleon brandy" are misleading. A bottle of brandy marked 1815 would be Napoleon brandy, but if it had only stayed in wood to 1816, it would today still be one-year-old brandy. The length of time the brandy has spent in the cask is denoted by the label—more or less. The exact ages represented by the different indications have been explained to me authoritatively by several experts; unfortunately, if the authoritativeness was equal in all cases, the ages were not. The last word probably remains with the Cognac-maker who explained that the proper maturing of brandy is not solely a function of the number of years it has spent in the cask and that therefore age labeling is not rigid. It is safe to assume that any three-star Cognac is five years old or better (the one- and two-star labels seem to have disappeared, probably on the theory that when you offer for sale Cognac younger than five years it is just as well not to call attention to the point). V.O. (very old) has probably had eight to ten years in the cask. V.S.O. (very superior old) is a mark I have again not seen for a long while; it was current before the war, but seems to have given way since to the next grade, V.S.O.P. (very superior old pale), ten to fifteen years old. I have read in an American magazine that there is also a V.V.S.O.P. label (very very superior old pale), but I have never encountered it in France, where Extra Quality is usually the mark on bottles of brandy that has spent more than fifteen years in the wood—and you will not find any of it in ordinary liquor stores. The absolute limit in the wood is from 30 to 40 years; after that there is no detectable improvement no matter how long the brandy is kept. This very old brandy, incidentally, is difficult to drink. It vaporizes in the mouth before you can swallow much of it, so you get it more in the form of gas than of liquid. The taste includes a slight reminiscence of camphor.

One thing brandy's stay in the cask does for it is to give it color. No distilled liqueur has any natural color; distillation removes all elements that could color it. Cognac picks up its color from the wood, and therefore the darker it is, the older it is—very generally speaking. When drinkers discovered this, and dark color therefore became a profitable quality, the habit of adding caramel for color developed, and almost all brandy today is artificially colored beyond the clear amber that would ordinarily be the limit of darkness it would pick up from the cask. This is the meaning of the letter P for pale on the labels of old brandy. It does not necessarily mean that the liquid is pale. Often it is not. It means that no coloring matter has been added, that the tint of the Cognac is a reasonably exact indication of its age. Only reasonably, however. If you visit the home of a Cognac-maker and he gives you some old stock he has tucked away for his private use, it may be almost white— perhaps the pale gold of an old *marc*. No coloring matter has been added to the brandy that was kept for the use of its producer.

There are seven grades of Cognac, though you are not likely to come across more than the top two (*grande fine champagne* and *fine champagne*). The best Cognac comes from the center of the area, and the quality decreases as you move away from the center, though not quite uniformly. The top region is a small area on the south bank of the Charente, which just takes in part of Cognac itself (some of the canton of Cognac lies on the other shore) and really centers about Segonzac. This is the *grande champagne;* so the label *grande fine champagne* has, as we have already seen in the section on the Champagne country, nothing to do with the wine of that name, *champagne* meaning originally simply a country of plains (*fine* means a good quality distillation, and a Frenchman ordering brandy calls for *fine*, not for Cognac; it is assumed that Cognac is what he will get unless he specifies otherwise).

The *grande champagne* is surrounded, except for a minute area on the northern bank of the Charente at Cognac itself, by the *petite champagne*, whose product is usually sold simply as *fine champagne*, as no one sees any need to stress the point that this is the lesser of the two top grades. Just northwest of Cognac is a small area called the *borderies* (borders), in which vineyards grow on the slopes of a group of low, rounded hills; if you find a bottle containing brandy chiefly from this region, the label will read *fines borderies*. Completely surrounding these three districts is the region of *fins bois*, with another little patch so classified lying on the Gironde itself. Completely surrounding these territories, again, is the *bons bois*. This is the end of the system of roughly concentric circles, the Cognac area extending no farther inland, but there are two more regions to the west, in which quality deteriorates progressively as the coast is approached. First comes a strip between the main areas and the coastland vineyards, the Surgères and Aigrefeuilles area, sometimes referred to as the *bois ordinaires* region. Finally, lying along the Atlantic coast, are the *bois à terroir*.

There is also a sweet liqueur wine made in the Cognac area by adding Cognac to certain wine musts: Pineau des Charentes, drinkable as an *apéritif*.

The Cognac vineyards stretch in their western half all the way down to the estuary of the Gironde, across which lie other vineyards that cross the stream at the point where the Cognac area ends, to lie beneath it on both sides of the river. These are the vineyards which produce the wines of Bordeaux, the great glory of the region.

There is a respectable body of opinion in favor of the statement that the wines of Bordeaux are the finest in the world. There seems no particular need to try to establish hierarchies in so delicate a realm, in which certainly differences of kind can be recognized without necessarily classifying them as differences of degree. There are also defenders of the theory that Burgundy outclasses Bordeaux. (There is probably no significant dissent from the proposition that Bordeaux and Burgundy wines are the two greatest categories of France.) I imagine that the average wine-drinker will appreciate no more and no less the suave velvety quality of a fine red Bordeaux or the rich unctuous sweetness of a good Sauternes—or the clean incisiveness of a dry white Burgundy—because he has been informed that it is the greatest (or the second greatest) of the wines of France or of the world.

When you want a fine Bordeaux and order a château wine, you have plenty of choice. There are about 2,500 registered Bordeaux vintages, which in Médoc and Sauternes were once graded into five classes or growths by official judges whose verdicts were not always accepted willingly by the winegrowers. Most winegrowers were happy enough to be allowed to put the rating *deuxième cru* on their labels, there being so very few first growths that to be accorded the rank of second growth was a considerable triumph. Château Mouton-Rothschild, however, though classed at the top of the second growths in Médoc (there are only three first growths there), has always refused to make use of the right to place this distinction on its label. When it was given its classification a little over one hundred years ago, the château adopted the motto: *"Premier ne puis, second ne daigne, Mouton suis,"* ("I can't be first, I disdain to be second, I am Mouton"), and the last two phrases of this device still appear on the Mouton-Rothschild labels.

The Bordeaux wine country begins at the coast south of the Gironde estuary with Médoc, which extends almost to Bordeaux. The first third of this strip of land, lying on the coast, is simply Médoc, with no outstanding wines, but then comes Haut-Médoc, bristling with famous names. Of the four first growths among red wines, three are in the Haut Médoc—Château Lafite, Château Margaux, and Château

Latour. The Médocs are all red, by common consent the greatest of the Bordeaux reds. Subtle, smooth, mellow, and with a fine fragrance that develops over a long period, a good Médoc may take anywhere from ten to twenty years to reach its height, and it will then remain good for perhaps as many more. It will have a rich color, pomegranate when it is young, ruby as it grows older. You will have heard that a fine red Bordeaux should be served warm—*chambré* is the term, chambered, in other words, room temperature, and this is just what it means, assuming a reasonably warm room. Putting a bottle of fine red Bordeaux in warm water to raise its temperature quickly, which I have known some people to do, instead of releasing its perfume will destroy it. Placing it in a warm kitchen some hours before dinner is not so bad, providing you don't think it has to be practically on the stove, but the best way is the way the term suggests —simply bring the wine into the room where it is to be consumed long enough beforehand to raise it from the temperature of the cellar where it has presumably been kept. Pull out the cork an hour or two in advance—it is surprising how much the flavor is brought out by letting the wine breathe a little.

Still on the south (by now more exactly the west) bank of the river, which has now become the Garonne instead of the Gironde, is Graves, the second of the two greatest regions of Bordeaux, if you consider the Sauternes region, which interrupts Graves toward its southern end, as geographically a part of it. Graves can be either red or white, the northern part of the territory producing mostly reds, the southern mostly whites. The reds have a fine delicate flavor, a little thinner than Médocs, and lack a certain arresting quality of the Médocs—it is difficult to drink a fine Médoc rapidly and inattentively: it demands that you notice it. A Graves can slip down easily, and if you are engaged in conversation, it is quite possible not to note particularly what you are drinking; I suppose you could call it an unobtrusive wine. White Graves from the northern part of the territory are likely to be dry; in the south they become sweeter. Although there is no official division of Graves into growths, as for Médocs, a special exception has been made for Château Haut-Brion, rated a first growth along with the three great Médocs, from whose territory it is not far distant.

The Sauternes rank with the Médocs as the top wines of the Bordeaux region, so different that there is no point in trying to compare them as to quality, though you might deduce such a comparison from the fact that Château d'Yquem, the top Sauternes, is also apparently rated the greatest of all French wines, for a special class was created for it alone, above that of first growth, sometimes described as *prémier cru supérieur* and sometimes as *prémier grand cru*. I cannot think of any basis for comparing Sauternes to Médocs, so I will not try to decide whether Château d'Yquem is a greater wine than Château Lafite, but I can report my own reaction when I first met it, at a banquet aboard the now vanished *Majestic* in Southampton harbor nearly thirty years ago. I was served a glass of it at the beginning of the meal, though what could have been served at that juncture to justify this wine I can't imagine today, and having tasted it I insisted obstinately in sticking with it through the rest of the meal. No doubt the wine waiter was disgusted and I realized even then, when my taste for wines was still completely uneducated, that it was a barbarous procedure, but I didn't care. I had had my first sample of Château d'Yquem and I did not propose to let any of it get away from me.

Sauternes are extremely sweet, although they manage to carry off the sweetness without being sickening, because of their very heavy rich body, which somehow takes the curse off so much sugar. There is no such thing as a dry

Sauternes, despite the opinion of the liquor store salesman of Eighth Street, New York, who told me when I observed as much, in a highly superior tone: "*We* have it."

The special distinguishing feature of Sauternes is that it is made from grapes that have been allowed to rot on the vine. This *pourriture noble* (noble rottenness) is the work of a microorganism that converts much more of the fruit into sugar than would normally undergo this change. Hence the honeylike quality of Sauternes.

The rest of the Bordeaux wines take a distinctly second place to the lords of the south (or west, or left) bank of the Garonne. On the other side, in the triangle between this and the Dordogne, is the region called because of this situation Entre-Deux-Mers (between two seas), with a special strip lying along the Garonne known as the Premières Côtes de Bordeaux, and with a small area on the Dordogne, at the extreme eastern limit of the Bordeaux region, known as Sainte-Foy-Bordeaux. This section grows mostly white wines, though there are some reds as well. They are pleasant vintages, lacking the subtlety of the great Bordeaux, but sharing their basic qualities. However, it is only when the Dordogne also is crossed that you come to the region that provides the most interesting vintages after those of the far side of the Garonne. Here is Saint-Emilion, which produces the heaviest wines of the Bordeaux region. They are not officially rated, but of the dozen or so top labels, I might suggest that you try Château Ausone to get an idea of Saint-Emilion at its best. Ausone, by the way, is the modern French version of Ausonius, the Latin poet we met earlier in this chapter; traditionally this property is the vineyard he owned in the fourth century.

Saint-Emilion is an earthy version of Bordeaux, suited better to accompanying some of the peasant dishes we have described above than to being drunk with the more sophisticated restaurant products—or perhaps game, particularly such coarser varieties of it as wild boar. The Saint-Emilion wines are all reds, as are those of its adjoining regions, such as Pomerol, a trifle lighter than the typical Saint-Emilion, and quicker to reach drinkable age, and Fronsac, which produces very respectable table wines. Finally you get both reds and whites from the Bourgeais and Blayais regions, the areas between the Cognac vineyards and the east shore of the Gironde. These are minor Bordeaux that you aren't likely to meet under their own specific names far from the place where they are grown.

One piece of information that may prove useful—when you run into the words "superior" or "inferior" on a wine label, it does not refer to quality; it refers to the altitude of the place that produced the wine.

Wine years are perhaps trickier indications of quality in Bordeaux than anywhere else in France, because of the great number of separate vineyards, any one of which may choose perversely to be different from the others at any given time. However, for what it may be worth, the best recent years for red Bordeaux have been 1934, 1942, 1943, 1945, 1947, 1948, 1949, 1952, 1953, 1955, 1959 and 1961. For whites, the list is 1934, 1947, 1948, 1949, 1952, 1953, 1955, 1959 and 1961.

Burgundy

The traveler who takes train or car from France's third largest city, Lyons, to the capital, quickly finds himself running through a country of green rolling hills, fertile and smiling, with few large towns, but scores of scattered hamlets and many isolated farms. From time to time, through the foliage of screening trees, there is a glimpse of a roof brilliantly checkerboarded in colored tiles, laid often on pert pointed turrets rising from buildings of fairytale picturesqueness. Then the names of the railway stations of the directing signs along the roads become familiar, except that it seems odd to find them attached to towns and villages, for it is a different context in which they have been met before. As the signs succeed one another—Meursault, Volnay, Beaune, Aloxe-Corton, Nuits-Saint-Georges, Vosne-Romanée, Gevrey-Chambertin—you are pursued by the illusion of having, like Alice, been magically reduced in size so that you are able to crawl like a minute insect along a magnified wine card. For the country you are passing through is Burgundy.

Burgundy is as much basic country, elemental country, country of long-rooted traditions as is the Ile-de-France and its attendant territories to the west, and if it is the latter territory which has been described as the most French part of France rather than Burgundy, it is only because its continuous history has been attached longer to the name of France than has that of Burgundy. Burgundy's contribution to what is France today goes back as far and is of comparable cultural importance to that of the Ile-de-France, and its capital, Dijon, is one of the great cities of France, a sort of eastern Rouen, whose buildings attest to its rich past; but three quarters of its history was unrolled under a name other than that of France, and in the days of its greatness it was a dukedom that was the peer of the kingdom of France, and for all any fourteenth-century prophet could have foretold, seemed quite as likely to make France part of Burgundy as the other way around.

At a time when the Ile-de-France had added to its possessions only the Orléanais, the Berry, Champagne, and Normandy, Burgundy had expanded eastward through the Franche-Comté, and possessed also, on the far side of the territories of France, Picardy, Artois, and Flanders, a great part of what today is Belgium, all of Holland (which is to say the southern half of the modern Netherlands) except an island around Utrecht, and the Duchy of Luxembourg. The territories of Burgundy, more extensive than those of France, had the disadvantage of not being continuous; but they had the advantage of pinching France be-

Legend:
- ☰ *Great Eating*
- ＝ *Good Eating*

CHAMPAGNE

LORRAINE

ALSACE

CHEESE

BURGUNDY

GOUGÈRE
(CHEESECAKE)

SALMON TROUT
CHERRY SOUP

Auxerre

CHERRIES
MERINGUES
PIKE
CRAYFISH

PAUCHOUSE
(FISH STEWED
IN WHITE WINE)

PIKE
Montbéliard

PAUCHOUSE
(FISH CHOWDER)
PANADE

FÉCHUNS

●Avallon

MUSTARD
GINGERBREAD
CURRANTS

Dijon

FROG SOUP

FRANCHE

DOUBS

COMTÉ CHEESE

NIVERNAIS

JUGGED HARE
WITH POMMARD

GAME

OGNON

MORILLES

SAUPIQUET
(HAM IN CREAM
SAUCE)

Pouilly sur Loire

Saulieu

Besançon

BRESI

CALVES
HEADS

Nuits St. George

SNAILS

Dôle

COMTÉ

FONDUE
CANCOILLOTTE
POTÉE

●Nevers

Beaune
Meursault

LOUE
FRUIT

Arbois●

Pontarlier

PISTACHIO
PORK

HAM
COUNTRY SAUSAGE
HONEY

SAONE

Forest of
La Joux

CRÈME DE GRUYÈRE

FOUÉE
BACON-WALNUT
BUN

Chalons-sur-Marne

Champagnole

BOURBONNAIS

MEURETTES
(WINE SAUCES)

AIN

Morez
(CHEESE)

SWITZERLAND

BERRY

GAME

Tournus

OYONNADE
(GOOSE STEW)

●Moulins

Cluny

●Gandes

CORN MEAL MUSH

SHEEP TONGUES
WITH TURNIPS

Charolles

BŒUF
BOURGIGNON

SEPTMONCEL
CHEESE

FÉRA
(LAKE FISH)
FISH SOUP

Evian

POTATOES
CHEESECAKE

BEEF

SNAILS

Mâcon

●Gex

(BLUE CHEESE)

AUVERGNE

LYONS FRIED
POTATOES

BRESSE

Bourg

Nantua

VACHERIN

Taninges
(HAMS)

●Vichy

CHICKEN IN
HALF MOURNING

CHICKENS
(BEST IN FRANCE)

CRAYFISH
PIKE FISH-
CAKES

REBLOCHON
CHEESE

Bonneville
(GAME PATTIES)

GOAT
CHEESE

LYONNAIS

Perouges

SAUSAGES

Bugey *Annecy*

SAVOIE

Talloires

Mont
Blanc

LYONS
TRIPE

Lyons

Vienne

Belley
(Birthplace of Brillat-Savarin)

Chambery

Aix-les-Bains

GRATIN
SAVOYARD

LAKE FISH

Celliers
(HAMS)

FOIE GRAS IN PASTRY
TROUT BRAISED IN PORT

DAIRY CATTLE

FARÇON

SASSENAGE CHEESE

CIVET DE LIÈVRE
(JUGGED HARE)

DAUPHINÉ

ISÈRE

ITALY

LANGUEDOC

Grenoble

ST. MARCELLIN CHEESE
CHARTREUSE, WALNUTS
FARÇON
GRATIN DAUPHINOIS

Briançon

Die (CLAIRETTE)

POGNE
(SQUASH PIE)

JUNIPER-FED GRIVES

RHÔNE

Gap

HONEY

Nyons

(GRIVES PATTIES)
GAME

PROVENCE

MILES

0 — 50 — 100

0 — 50 — 100

KM.

BURGUNDY *and the* MOUNTAINS

tween them, which could be decisive in an era with such
well-developed means of communication as our own. Even
then France and Burgundy battled as champions equally
matched. It was the Burgundians, you will remember, not
the English, who captured Joan of Arc; the English only
purchased her from her captors when Charles VII, the king
whom she had crowned, proved too parsimonious to pay
her ransom.

Burgundy as an inhabited land goes back to prehistoric
times. The Stone Age period known as the Solutrean takes
its name from Solutré, near Mâcon, where in 1866 exca-
vators discovered the skeletons of about one hundred thousand horses, covering some two and a half acres to a depth
of three feet, where prehistoric man had disposed of the
skeletons of animals which had been eaten—perhaps the
earliest use for food of the horse, still raised for meat in
France. Earlier remains of man (of the Aurignacian period)
and later implements (of the Neolithic and Bronze Ages)
have been found in the same spot, which is thus known to
have been continuously inhabited since far back into the
Stone Age. It was still before the time of written history
that the Treasure of Vix was placed in a sepulchre near
Châtillon-sur-Seine, to be found twenty-five hundred
years later. These are Gallic remains, going back to before
the Roman invasion (to the sixth century B.C.), including
jewels, a solid gold tiara, a bronze vase nearly six feet high
weighing just under four hundred pounds covered with
bas-reliefs that recall both archaic Greek and Etruscan art,
and other objects consonant with the woman's skeleton
found with them—as well as the remains of a war chariot,
inconsistent unless we assume that this was the grave of a
warlike princess, a sort of Gallic Boadicea.

With the beginning of written records, Burgundy—not
yet called Burgundy, for the Burgundians themselves had
not arrived—began to play an important part in history.

There is little disputing today the theory that Alesia, where Julius Cæsar in 52 B.C. defeated the Gauls under Vercingetorix, who had previously defeated him at Gergovia, is Alise-Sainte-Reine, not far from Dijon. This was the decisive battle of the conquest of Gaul, and modern Frenchmen two thousand years later have still not given up regretting Vercingetorix, who bartered his own freedom for the lives of his men, surrounded by the Roman legions, and was taken to Rome to be displayed in Cæsar's triumphal procession and then imprisoned for six years in the Tullianum before being strangled there.

About the fifth century the Burgundians, a Baltic people, arrived in the valley of the Saône, which might be considered the geographical unit corresponding to the political unit of Burgundy proper, though its borders varied widely from time to time, and established the first territory named for them as a kingdom. They brought with them a culture rather superior to that of their neighbors, and maintained themselves as a separate entity until the Franks managed to absorb them about the middle of the sixth century. But when Charlemagne died, the partition of his empire brought Burgundy back to life. The left bank of the Saône, later to be known as the Franche-Comté, went to the Emperor Lothair and became part of Lotharingia (Lorraine); the right bank was allotted to Charles the Bald and the Duchy of Burgundy was born.

The country spread westward, so that Burgundy was for a time not the valley of the Saône, but the district from the Saône to the Yonne and even to the Loire, where it encroached on the region known as the Nivernais and somewhat on the Bourbonnais and the Lyonnais. France absorbed the territory again early in the eleventh century, but it started another epoch on its own when John the Good made his fourth son, Philip the Bold, Duke of Burgundy. This was the beginning of the heroic age of Burgundy, for Philip, marrying Margaret of Flanders, and his successor, John the Fearless, marrying Margaret of Holland, added the Low Countries to its territories. But Charles the Bold was too ambitious. He tried to extend his domains, and though he succeeded, temporarily, in subjecting Lorraine to his rule, the Swiss defeated him (the basis of the collections of the Fine Arts Museum of Berne is still the booty captured from Burgundy) and he was killed before Nancy. Louis XI brought Burgundy back into France in 1477, and though it maintained a relatively independent status under the French crown for another three hundred years, even adding to its own territories a hundred years after it had become French, its history was thereafter a part of French history and with the Revolution all political autonomy ended.

The soil of Burgundy is strewn with the stones of great buildings. One of France's most famous architects is a Burgundian, Sébastien le Prestre, who was born at Saint-Léger-de-Foucheret, not far from Avallon, in 1633. The name probably means nothing to you, but you will know him by his title, Marquis de Vauban, a name now attached to his birthplace, which today is Saint-Léger-Vauban. Known for the fortresses he built or rebuilt, chiefly for Louis XIV, Vauban was also a specialist at knocking them down, for he was primarily a military engineer, who not only created strong places, but took them—he was a marshal of the armies, a distinction rare among architects.

The greatest constructions of Burgundy came earlier, however—the mighty abbeys which arose on this soil where monastic life during the Middle Ages was as intense as anywhere in Europe, and the churches which give many Burgundy cities, viewed from a distance, a bristling profile because of the number of spires which pierce their skies. There is even a good deal of fine domestic architecture of the Middle Ages in Burgundy, a rarer survival—Dijon, for instance, has whole streets of them, of which the rue des Forges is the most famous.

Burgundy was the battleground for one of the bitterest battles within the medieval Church between two great orders—the Benedictines, whose monastic rules were not overly severe (to this day, the Benedictines constitute a liberal order) and the Cistercians, who stood for austerity —and still do. It is in harmony with the nature of the order that it was the Benedictines who invented, and gave their name to, a rich, sweet, and unctuous liqueur. One would hardly have expected such a development from the Cistercians, whose regulations forbade them to eat meat, fish, eggs, milk dishes, or white bread, and to drink anything other than water. Their menu was restricted to vegetables, which might be seasoned by oil or salt, and dark bread, made of coarse flour. Even today the Cistercians have added only milk dishes and fruit to their menu. They are still forbidden to eat meat.

The origin of the Benedictine order was in Italy, at the famous abbey of Monte Cassino, so heavily bombarded during the Second World War; but its greatest monastery was the one begun in Burgundy some four hundred years after the founding of the order, Cluny. When Cluny became rich and powerful, it was natural that the reaction to its luxury should be expressed in Burgundy also, and it was a native Burgundian, the ascetic and angry Saint Bernard, born of a rich and noble family near Dijon, who embodied it. The mother monastery of his order, situated inappropriately near the famous winegrowing town of Nuits-Saint-Georges, was Citeaux (hence the name Cistercian), which by the middle of the sixteenth century stood at the head of 350 tributary abbeys, while Cluny had nearly 1500 dependencies, many of them, however, outside France.

You can still see at Cluny substantial ruins of its great monastery, although much of it was destroyed during the

French Revolution and the years that followed. Thus was lost the greater part of what was the largest church in Christendom until St. Peter's was built in Rome—and even St. Peter's is only forty-five feet longer than Cluny's Abbey Church of St. Peter and St. Paul. Started in the eleventh century by Saint Hugh and finished in the twelfth by Peter the Venerable, it possessed five naves and five bell-towers as well as two others. A Romanesque structure, its vaults stood more than a hundred feet above the floor. The pointed Gothic arch has risen higher, but the round Roman arch never has.

Of the many great Benedictine abbeys of Burgundy which depended upon Cluny, the second was in the Nivernais, at La Charité-sur-Loire, so named because of the generosity its monks showed to the poor. Known as "the eldest daughter of Cluny," La Charité deserved the title both on the grounds of age (its church was consecrated in 1107) and size (it was the largest in France after Cluny itself, and resembled the latter in having five naves). Much of it still remains.

There are many others—Paray-le-Monial, begun by Saint Hugh, is in some respects a smaller version of Cluny; Charlieu still shows the ruins of monastic buildings parts of which go back to the ninth century; Tournus possessed one of the oldest and largest of the Benedictine monasteries, of which one of the finest remaining rooms is the twelfth-century refectory, which indicates that the Benedictines took their meals in surroundings of considerable splendor. (At the Hôtel Dieu of Tournus you can visit the kitchen and inspect a vast array of the dishes and pewter utensils used in the time of Louis XIII.)

Citeaux, the chief monastery of the Cistercians, has suffered even more from the ravages of time than Cluny, the chief monastery of the Benedictines. Nevertheless, an abbey still exists and still functions in the vestiges of the old buildings, which may still be visited (by men only; women are allowed to enter the church). One of its curiosities is a tulip tree from Virginia planted there in 1865. Saint Bernard did not stay there very long—only three years—but in that time he had imparted a momentum to Cîteaux which it was not to lose. Saint Bernard then moved to Clairvaux, and developed a great monastery there as well, but though Burgundy might lay claim to it, on the basis of the shifting and indefinite nature of ancient boundaries, it belongs more authentically to Champagne. (But Dijon, the capital of Burgundy, maintains a somewhat dubious memorial to the austere teetotaler monks of Clairvaux in its Clairvaux Cellar [*Cellier de Clairvaux*], which is a wine-sampling room; the Clairvaux monks who built it in the thirteenth century never used it for that, of course.)

Burgundy can boast many other important centers of Cistercian activities. There is Vézelay, where Saint Bernard preached the Second Crusade in 1146 (in 1190, King Richard the Lion-Hearted of England and King Philip Augustus of France met here to start out on the Third Crusade). There is Fontenay, "second daughter of Saint Bernard," which has been restored and looks today about as it did in the twelfth century—the refectory and the kitchens are among the rooms on view. There is Sens, which may be mentioned here, as the seat of the Council that granted Saint Bernard one of his greatest victories by condemning Abelard, of the Abelard and Héloïse story, a doctrinal opponent of Saint Bernard, though Sens also belongs more properly to Champagne.

In the struggle between the Cistercians and the Benedictines, which was waged largely on Burgundian soil, it would be impossible to say that any definitive victory was won by either side; in his time, however, Saint Bernard was dominant. But in one realm, victory was foreordained for the Benedictines. When the art of cooking emerged from the monasteries, it had to be Benedictine skills that were passed on to laymen, not Cistercian. The Cistercians had nothing to offer. Even if their ecclesiastical victory had been complete, they could hardly have expected, with their ascetic ideas, to have dominated the gastronomy of a country so fertile and naturally rich in food as Burgundy—rich in other ways, too, as its many fine cities attest: Auxerre, whose skyline, seen from the banks of the Yonne, bristles with the steeples of fine churches; Autun, one of the many cities in Europe whose modern name is a corruption of a Latin one celebrating the Emperor Augustus (it used to be called Augustodunum), which shelters the remains of the largest Roman theatre in Gaul and possesses a celebrated twelfth-century cathedral; Semur, with its old walls and fine church of Notre Dame; Avallon, which has also preserved its fortifications, rising steeply on an abrupt hillside from the Cousin valley; and greatest of all, the capital, Dijon, a magnificent city on which the dukes of Burgundy left the mark of their magnificence. Their former palace is now the city's Fine Arts Museum, but some of its rooms continue to illustrate the life of the rulers who once inhabited it. Among them are the kitchens, one of the best preserved examples of their time—1435. There are six tremendous fireplaces, all of which were operated full blast when a big feast was in preparation. The whole room comes to a point in a big ventilating chimney, the very shape of the ceiling seeming to make visible a sucking upward of the smoke with which the room must in those days have been filled. The scale of the kitchens aids the imagination to seize the lustiness of medieval feasting. Burgundy remains a country of valiant trenchermen to this day, and Dijon is one of the great gastronomic cities of France, with many fine restaurants and a food fair every November guaranteed to send all visitors away several pounds heavier.

· · ·

VIII · *Burgundy*

The gastronomic borders of Burgundy are not coexten-
sive with its political borders. We will split Burgundy here
where the grandsons of Charlemagne split it, along the river
Saône, for the Franche-Comté east of it, part of Burgundy
before the partition and part of Burgundy again some five
and a half centuries later, developed a cuisine of its own during the long divorce, related to the mountain fare of the
Jura. To make up for the loss on the east, we can consider
at the same time some adjacent territories on the west whose
eating has been affected more or less by the strong gastronomic traditions of Burgundy. Northernmost of them
is the Nivernais, capital Nevers, an old and picturesque
city on the banks of the Loire, noted since the sixteenth
century for its fine faïence and glassware. Then comes the
Bourbonnais, capital Moulins, likewise old, picturesque, and
on the shores of a river, the Allier. Finally comes the Lyonnais, the territory surrounding France's third largest city,
Lyons, which almost deserves a chapter to itself, since it has
a cuisine recognizably different from those that surround
it, from all of which it has borrowed and to all of which
it has contributed in a sort of reciprocal culinary osmosis.
But the strongest outside influence is that of Burgundy, so
we will consider Lyons here.

Besides these adjacent regions with culinary specialties of
their own, Burgundy proper includes several recognizable
gastronomic areas within which the cooking shows characteristics peculiar to the locality—three of them attributable to different types of wine, whose influence is felt in the
food served with it. In the north, in Lower Burgundy, of
which Auxerre is the capital, Chablis lies alone, far north of
all the other well-known Burgundy wine centers (there are
a few other wine-producing towns about it, but their vintages do not get outside of the region). The finesse of
Chablis white wine makes for a slightly lighter and more
subtle cuisine (perhaps accounted for partly also by the

propinquity of the Ile-de-France) than is found in central Burgundy, where the full-bodied red wines of the Côte d'Or, the line of hills running southward from Dijon to the neighborhood of Chalon-sur-Saône, accord naturally with the hearty fare which is typical of Burgundy. South of this region there is a gap in the vineyards; then, at Mâcon, there is another stretch of wine-covered hillsides, running from Mâcon almost to Lyons. Here the wine is coarser and the food becomes heavier; the southernmost section, which produces the coarsest wine of all, Beaujolais, has probably affected the cooking of Lyons, too, with its sausages and its potato dishes. Another reason for the earthier fare of this part of Burgundy is the fact that this is beef country, the best beef country in France.

The fourth separate gastronomic region in Burgundy differs not because of a different type of wine (unless you count no wine at all as constituting, for purposes of tabulation, a wine difference, as indeed it does), but because of a different type of terrain. This is the Morvan, a hilly region which extends along the east bank of the Yonne, and has remained somewhat cut off from the influences of the surrounding country, partly because of its steep slopes, partly because it is heavily wooded. Isolated as a whole, it also has a habit of internal isolation. There are few towns, only little hamlets or sometimes isolated farmhouses, an arrangement comparatively rare in France, where the farmers of old tended to cluster together in tight-built towns under the protection of their overlord's castle, trudging long distances to and from their fields because lone farms built among them would be exposed to attack from the marauding bands which in medieval times were likely to appear at any moment. The Morvan, difficult to cross and poor land which offered little booty even if it were penetrated, was bypassed by raiders and the peasants therefore dared to live farther from thick walls. Even if enemies did come, they found the progress across the fields and pastures difficult, for here, as in Normandy, the land is broken up into small squares and rectangles hedged about with thick growths of bushes, each one a possible line of defense.

Poorer soil—though it is not bad pasture country, where the original Morvan cow, an animal with a red pelt, has now been supplanted by the superior Charollais—and the mountainous terrain which always has an effect on food, since mountainers need plenty of energy and an efficient lining against harsh weather, account for the special nature of Morvan cooking. What accounted for another Morvan specialty, which enters possibly into the realm of gastronomy, it is difficult to say, unless it was emulation of the bovine species by the human. In the last century, the specialty of the women of Morvan became the supplying of wet nurses. Many of them went to the large cities—Lyons, Dijon, Paris—to care for children whose well-to-do mothers had fallen in with the contemporary fashion which decreed that it was not well-bred to nurse one's own children. In other cases, babies were sent to the Morvan to be reared there. Baby farming became the most important industry of the Morvan. Unfortunately in this, the most primitive region of Burgundy, sanitation was an unknown concept. Infant mortality was high and a law was finally passed ending the practice.

Burgundy has always been noted for the excellence and abundance of its food. If most of the early tributes are to its wine, like that paid it in the sixth century by Gregory of Tours, the table was not forgotten either; Charles VI praised the cuisine of Dijon (before he became mad); it was his wife, Isabeau of Bavaria, who is credited with the invention of the written menu, then called simply the *escriteau*, or writing, before which time you took what was served you and guessed what it was, so we may assume that a certain philosophic preoccupation with food ran in the family. In the fifteenth century, when Burgundy was at the height of her power and her rulers, known as the Grand Dukes of the West, were more important than the kings of France, the feasts at the Palace in Dijon were legendary. Brillat-Savarin was a Burgundian.

Burgundy is still renowned for good food. Probably no other comparable area in the country, not even the Ile-de-France, can boast of so uniformly high a level of good eating throughout its territory. The *Michelin* guide, which gourmets never fail to carry with them when they sally into the provinces, lists just seven three-star restaurants outside of Paris; four of them are in this region, at Avallon, Saulieu, the Col de la Luère just outside of Lyons, and Vienne.

If the attempt were made to sum up the dominant characteristic of Burgundian cooking in a single word, perhaps that word might be "substantial." Burgundy provides good, solid food. But it is at the same time not simply hearty nourishment. It is much more than that. To the sound basis of its rib-sticking ingredients, Burgundy adds the art always developed in the preparation of food in a country of rich and sophisticated background. The Burgundian does not take a delicate trifle and by the subtle application of refined seasonings transfigure it with an ethereal sauce into a whispering perfection. His dishes demand lusty, full-blooded sauces; but he applies to their confection equal skill in another direction, and achieves instead a trumpeting perfection. The most refined professional Burgundian cooking never gets far from the soil in which it is rooted. This is the *cuisine bourgeoise* at its best, or peasant cooking elevated to its greatest possible heights. It is often said that you need a solid stomach to live on Burgundian cooking; but Burgundian cooking develops solid stomachs. You can dig your grave with your teeth much more quickly on the rich elaborate cooking of the *haute cuisine* than on the sturdy more natural cooking of Burgundy. Burgundians, incidentally, are poor customers of dentists. They attribute their notoriously good teeth to their wine. Perhaps their whole diet has something to do with it. It should be bone-building as well as muscle-building.

The virtues that have been added to Burgundian food in the handling can be attributed to the region's cultural background. The solid basis to which they were applied depends on more elemental features—first the weather, which is vigorous enough to demand heavy food, since Burgundy is sufficiently far from the sea to have a continental climate; then the nature of the soil, which lends itself to the ready production of the sort of food the climate demands. The local ingredients that have done most to shape Burgundy cooking are three, each of a very different sort from the other two—mustard, beef, wine.

Mustard is a very ancient condiment. The Egyptians knew mustard, though apparently they never did anything with the seeds except to pop one or two into their mouths while they were chewing their meat. It was the Romans who brought mustard to Gaul, where the plants grown from their seeds flourished and the seasoning they provided became so popular that by the fifteenth century there was a guild of mustard-makers. The plants were raised with particular success in Burgundy, and Dijon became the greatest mustard-producing center in France—possibly in the world. Half of all the mustard made in France comes from Dijon alone, the city's annual production running to something like eight thousand tons. Few persons would disagree that Dijon makes not only the most, but also the best mustard. The full flavor of the main ingredient is brought out by the tart quality given to it by the juice from unripe grapes in which the flour made from the mustard seed is dissolved in Dijon. (Bordeaux, which makes mustard too, uses must from the wine vats instead.) Dijon also specializes in making a great variety of finely seasoned mustards involving the use of various herbs—tarragon, for instance. Throughout the world, gourmets buy sets of Dijon mustards, small jugs containing perhaps half a dozen different types of this seasoning. Of Dijon's three specialties, mustard is certainly the most widely known. (The other two are currant products and gingerbread.)

Mustard is a strong seasoning. It goes with meat, especially red meat. In sauces, it requires a heavy basis. It would smother the delicacy of more refined confections. It gives high relief to the food it accompanies. It harmonizes, in other words, with just the sort of cooking you find in Burgundy. Perhaps mustard reached its height in Burgundy because it went with the food. Perhaps the food developed along these lines to respond to the mustard. More probably they interacted and Burgundian cooking evolved under their joint influence.

In the category of foodstuffs proper, the most important item is one of the most basic and one of the top energy-providers of all human foods (and one regularly associated with mustard), beef. By common consent, the best beef animal in France is the Charollais steer, developed in the region that surrounds the little town of Charolles not far from Mâcon. Developed fairly recently, it has nevertheless become the second in numbers after the Norman breed, which may put on more meat and develop it faster, but which is second to the Charollais in quality. The Charollais steer, a uniform white in color, has not spread so widely as the Norman race, being raised chiefly in its original breeding-center in southern Burgundy and the two regions just to the north of it, the Nivernais and the Morvan, but there are nevertheless about a million and a half head in France. Charollais steers go to the slaughterhouse at the age of six, not at five, as is the case for many other breeds. The extra year is said to give the beef more flavor, though it also risks becoming tougher; but a properly fattened Charollais steer produces meat so tender to begin with that a six-year-old Charollais carcass may still be tenderer than a five-year-old piece of beef from some other race. The Charollais is primarily a beef animal. Burgundy raises two other types of cows for milk—the brown Swiss, almost entirely a milch cow, and a spotted variety in the Saône valley which is a mixed beef-milk animal.

Burgundy beef is probably the best known of all Burgundian dishes outside of the region, and it appears on menus under exactly that name—*bœuf bourguignon*, which strictly speaking is a misnomer since it refers to the way of preparing the meat, not necessarily to its origin, and is a simplification of *bœuf à la bourguignonne*, beef in the Burgundy style. This means beef cooked in a red wine sauce, accompanied with mushrooms, tiny onions, and small pieces of bacon. A refinement is to start a *pièce de bœuf à la bourguignonne* by inserting the bits of bacon in slits cut in the beef, and then soaking it for six hours before cooking in Cognac—which smacks of treason, utilizing, as it does, a product that comes from the general direction of the rival winegrowing area of Bordeaux. The meat is then braised in Burgundy red wine, and when it is three quarters cooked, the wine is strained to rid it of its accumulated grease and returned to the pot, along with the other ingredients mentioned above, to simmer together for the last stage of the cooking. This red wine sauce with mushrooms, onions, and bits of bacon is what you should expect to find in any dish described as *à la bourguignonne*, except that for a fish dish the bacon is omitted.

The sauce that goes with *bœuf bourguignon* is one variety of what Burgundy calls *meurettes*, a general name for all the wine sauces that are basic to Burgundian cooking. They are usually well spiced, thickened with flour and butter, and appear in varied forms to go with many different dishes of meat, fish, or eggs.

The second most common appearance of the name Burgundy on menus outside of the region is in connection with snails. *Escargots de Bourgogne* are reputed the best in France. In general the most favored snails are those which feed on grape leaves, and wax fat, black, and luscious, but since there are not enough to supply the demand, a smaller gray variety from the south, the *petit gris*, is also to be found on the market. Of the preferred variety, the Burgundy snails are most in demand. To Americans who consider the eating of snails a curious custom, it may be pointed out that it is an ancient one. The Romans liked them, and a certain Fulvius Lupinus is credited with having perfected the method of fattening them. Like oysters, snails are not a summer food. Indeed, their season should be even shorter than for oysters in the opinion of the meticulous, who maintain that snails should only be eaten during the period when they have closed their shells for their winter hibernation. They are allowed to fast for some time to rid themselves of any poisons, for snails eat some plants that are toxic for human beings.

Escargots de Bourgogne does not necessarily mean *escargots à la bourguignonne*, the first referring simply to the place the snails come from, the second to the manner of their preparation. When you pull a snail out of its shell and pop it piping hot into your mouth, which you will wish you had thought to have lined with asbestos first (snails must be eaten very hot), you are likely to consider it a simple dish, and to have no idea how much effort has gone into its preparation. Here is how the Burgundy cook prepares snails:

First the membrane with which the snail tries to protect itself is cut away, the snails are washed several times, using new clean water each time, and then placed for two hours on a mixture of rock salt, vinegar, and a little flour, which has the effect of ridding the animal of any remaining waste matter. They are washed again, and dropped into boiling water for five minutes. They are then dried, cooled, and the meat is taken out of the shells, the darker rear part being cut off. The shell-less snails are then put in a casserole and barely covered with a mixture half of white wine, half of bouillon. Carrots, onions, shallots, and an assortment of herbs are added. The whole is cooked slowly for three or four hours, and the snails are then allowed to cool off without being removed from the juice in which they were cooked. Meanwhile the empty shells have been boiled for half an hour in water containing a little soda, after which they are dried, washed in cold water, and dried again. A small lump of snail butter, otherwise known as Burgundy butter, which is made of the finest butter, finely chopped shallots, chopped parsley, and garlic reduced to a paste, is now placed in the bottom of each shell. The snails are put back into the shell, and the remaining space is filled with a second helping of the snail butter. The refilled shells are now put either on a special snail platter, dented with hollows for each shell, or in any pan with its bottom just covered with a little water, dusted with bread crumbs, pushed into an already hot oven, and cooked rapidly at high heat. They are then served and eaten from the shell—and unless you know how it was done, you would never suspect such ingredients as the carrots and the onions, which never show up on the table at all.

A common ingredient of Burgundy dishes, natural for a country of many cows, is cream. Among the foods cooked in various sorts of cream sauces are pike, chicken, mushrooms, and ham. A special preparation of the last is *saupiquet*, whose very name means "highly seasoned"—more literally "highly salted," as *sau* is from the Latin *sal*, but the word salt was often used generically to mean seasoning of any kind. This is possibly originally a Nivernais dish rather than strictly Burgundian; it consists of ham served with a highly spiced cream sauce. The spicing might lead us to expect that this is an old dish, for medieval eaters liked to be shocked rather than wooed by their food, and the name does indeed go back to the fifteenth century at least, though then it referred only to the sauce and not to the meat plus the sauce as today. An old recipe describes the making of *saupiquet* thus: bread is toasted and then soaked in bouillon. Meanwhile, onions are being fried in bacon. When they are ready, the toast, bouillon, and fried onions are combined with red wine, vinegar, cinnamon, ginger, and mixed spices, the whole boiled together until the sauce is quite thick, and then poured over some such dish as rabbit or a roast. An almost exact reproduction of this ancient sauce is still made in southwest France to accompany hare. However, the sauce of the Burgundian and Nivernaisian *saupiquet* is not the same, since cream, an important ingredient today, did not enter into the old recipe.

Another distinctive regional dish that makes large use of cream is the *fouée*, a pastry, but not a sweet one, in which bits of bacon are imbedded and which is dampened with walnut juice.

Cream country should also be cheese country (and so should wine country). Burgundy does indeed have many excellent cheeses, but in general they are not much known beyond her own borders. Probably the most renowned is Saint-Florentin, also called Soumaintrain, from the Yonne valley, a soft cheese. There is some confusion due to the use of these two names as synonymous, for in Burgundy itself a distinction is made between the true Saint-Florentin, whiter in color, usually eaten quite young, and the true Soumaintrain, yellower, which develops a considerable crust as it gets older (which is the best time to eat it) and is somewhat akin to Munster. It is highly popular throughout Burgundy. The Morvan produces small tasty goat cheeses. Another favorite locally is Chaource, a round white cheese made of whole milk, eaten fresh or sometimes lightly salted. It increases the confusion of the cheese situation by resembling Saint-Florentin but by being made not only at Chaource but also at Ervy-le-Châtel, which is also where Soumaintrain started out.

Most Burgundian dishes are apt to be found almost anywhere in the territory, and in the Nivernais and Bourbonnais as well—but since the different regions all have specialties of their own, it is well when traveling through the country to know what each does best. In the north, about Auxerre, the presence of white Chablis naturally throws the accent toward fish; pike and crayfish from the Cure river are especially good here. The *gougère*, an unsweetened cheese-cake, is eaten cold or as a warm hors d'œuvre. Chablis itself has some dessert specialties—crackers and meringues. The cherries of the Auxerre region are famous.

The Morvan is not only pasture ground for cows and the goats which produce its cheese, but is also a hog-breeding center. The pigs are fed on dairy by-products and potatoes, grown here as animal fodder rather than for the table. Thus ham is an important Morvan product. It appears ceremoniously as an Easter dish, and all the year round creamed. Country sausage is another natural result of pig-raising. The swift-flowing hill streams provide fine trout and the wooded hills are good for game, especially woodcock. Fine mushrooms of many kinds are another Morvan specialty, one variety accounting for a delicious non-sweet pastry, *feuilleté aux morilles*. Morvan honey is excellent.

As the Morvan hills more or less separate Burgundy proper from the Nivernais, the two regions share a number of food specialties. You may run into the unfamiliar words *sansiot* and *jau* on menus in either region. You need not feel ignorant, as most Frenchmen would not recognize them either. The first is calf's head; the second is a variety of *poulet au sang* which must be made from young pullets of that year's hatching. Haunch of fresh pork with pistachio nuts is a delectable dish of this area. The Nivernais raises particularly good specimens of the Charollais steer. Nevers is noted for its nougatine.

Dijon, and the Côte d'Or which runs southward from it, constitute the heartland of Burgundy. In this region many of the principal Burgundian specialties will be found at their best. The area has certain rigid ideas about which wine goes with what—Pommard is always used with jugged hare, the local ground-rule is that with capon one drinks Chambertin, and Volnay is used for the red wine sauce in which chicken is fried. Stuffed roasted suckling pig is a favorite dish. *Pauchouse* is the leading local fish specialty —it is a *matelote* of mixed fresh water fish in white wine— though carp with wine sauce is also found often. Then there is parsley-flavored ham and a variety of creamed mushroom known as *mousserons à la crème.*

Dijon's specialty of gingerbread has already been mentioned. It is made here by a method that involves producing the original dough and then keeping it for six weeks to two months before proceeding to the final stage of its manufacture. There is a special very light variety called *nonette.* As for its currant products, they come under the heads of both food and drink. Some of the currants go into jellies, and others serve to make a strong sweet liqueur, *crème de cassis*, which in France is made almost exclusively in Dijon. The city also has its own private *apéritif*, made by combining the currant liqueur with *aligoté* (white wine), called Kir, after one of the city's mayors.

The Mâcon area in the south of Burgundy is a region of fine beef (the Charollais lies just beside the Mâconnais), of excellent poultry (though the best chickens in France are raised just to the east of this area, in Bresse), and of exceptional vegetables. Hot sausages stuffed with pistachio nuts and truffles—the truffles of this region are no match for those of the Périgord, but still are not as much inferior to them as a critical remark of Brillat-Savarin would lead one to believe—are a particularly piquant specialty of the Mâcon area.

The Bourbonnais, just to the west, contains part of the Sologne, which has already been described as the best game country in France. It is also good country for beef, pork, mutton, and poultry, especially geese. The last two give rise to two special Bourbonnais dishes, sheep's tongue with turnips and a sort of goose stew known as *oyonnade*. Other dishes peculiar to this region are the *gounerre*, which is a *pâté* of potatoes, and the *tarte bourbonnaise*, a sweet cheesecake.

Burgundy has one candy specialty worth special mention. Flavigny-sur-Ozerain, a picturesque old town which grew up around an eighth century abbey, makes Jordan almonds delicately flavored with anise, a seventeenth-century creation of the Ursulines. But it was in Montargis, strictly speaking in the Orléanais, since it is a few miles west of Burgundy proper, that the Jordan almond was first invented. Its creator was the chef of the Duc de Plessis-Praslin, to whom the idea occurred, early in the seventeenth century, of roasting almonds and then coating them with sugar. They were first sampled by the ladies of Louis XIII's court, to whom the duke presented them and by whom they were quickly baptized, after their donor, *praslines*. They are still called *pralines* today (modern French has the tendency to drop *s*'s in difficult places), and the first shop that was set up to make them commercially, opposite the church of the Madeleine in Montargis, is still functioning there today, nearly three and a half centuries after its establishment.

South of Burgundy lies the Lyonnais, which has a distinctive cuisine of its own in spite of the small territory

surrounding the city of Lyons, comprising the two departments of the Loire and the Rhône. Lyons is the third city of
France, with half a million inhabitants to three million in
Paris, and is sometimes described as the greatest gastronomic
city in the country, outranking Paris if its smaller size is
taken into consideration. It is true that *Michelin* grants it
14 one-star restaurants, 6 two-star restaurants, and if the
Mère Brazier at the Col de la Luère, twelve miles outside
of town, be counted, one three-star—but my personal experience has been never to have eaten a really good meal in
Lyons. This may be partly bad luck, and is certainly due
also to a habit of mine, when approaching the city in a
mood for good eating, of trying to push through it to Vienne,
seventeen miles away, to eat at the three-star Pyramide there.
But I suspect that it is due also to the fact that Lyons
is a heavily bourgeois city; therefore, while providing superlative food on the luxurious level to those able to pay for
it, it offers somewhat contemptous treatment to the lower
classes—unlike such a city as Dijon, which may not boast
as many top-notch restaurants, but seems to have no bad
ones. This character of Lyons, a city which has always
vaguely reminded me of Philadelphia, probably accounts
also for my personal preference for continuing to Vienne.
Lyons ought to be a spectacularly beautiful city, with two
big rivers running through it (the Saône and the Rhone
meet here) and steep heights rising from their valleys, but
it manages somehow to be stodgy and self-satisfied. Vienne,
a delightful old city with Roman, medieval, and Renaissance
buildings of great beauty all existing simultaneously within
its limits, has an attractiveness which Lyons lacks, as well
as the advantage of housing what some persons consider
the finest restaurant in France.

The cooking of Lyons fits the character of the city—
it is hearty rather than graceful, and is apt to leave you
with an overstuffed feeling. The cooking of Burgundy is

hearty, too, but there is a livelier imagination connected with it. This is not to say that Lyonnaise cooking is not good of its kind, but its kind is not spirited. The nature of Lyonnaise cooking may be typified by one of the commonest dishes associated with the city's name on menus everywhere—*pommes lyonnaises*, potatoes Lyons style, which means simply German-fried potatoes cooked with onion. Onions are apt to be the sign of a Lyonnaise dish— *omelette à la lyonnaise* is with onions and parsley. One of the most famous Lyons dishes is *gras double à la lyonnaise* —tripe cooked with onions and parsley—again not a subtle dish. Even the most memorable confections of Lyons start with a heavy basis—three which come to mind all fall into the category of succulent but rich and somewhat indigestible sausages. They are the renowned *saussissons de Lyon*, little sausages eaten as hot as you can stand them; *boudin aux pommes de reinette*, blood pudding cooked with apples; and *cervelas aux pistaches et aux truffes poché*, a comparatively bland sausage stuffed with pistachio nuts and truffles. When Lyonnaise cooks set out to be elaborate, they produce rich liver-assaulting dishes even with such a simple start as chicken—for instance, *poularde demi-deuil*, fowl in half mourning, in which the bird is accompanied by sweetbreads of lamb and slices of truffles cooked in Madeira. The Lyonnais has a well-known cheese, Mont d'Or, once made of goat's milk but now of cow's milk, a change which has caused it to lose much of its old savor. It is best from December to April.

Considering the heaviness of the cooking of Lyons, it seems astonishing that the Pyramide at Vienne, politically in the Dauphiné, but gastronomically in the Lyonnais, manages to cook with so much subtlety. Even so the local tradition of richness remains. When the Pyramide attacks trout, possibly the most delicately flavored of all fish, it stuffs it and then braises it in port wine—a triumph, but of the

Lucullan rather than the purist school, which takes its trout *au bleu*—very fresh and boiled with no adornment to detract from the basic flavor of the fish itself. Finally the conclusion of a Pyramide meal, with all the surrounding tables covered with trays of tempting little cakes and pastries of every imaginable variety, is calculated to send the diner away some pounds heavier than when he came. This is Lyonnaise cooking at its best, and you need to be both gourmet and gourmand to contend with it.

Wine is of course the great glory of Burgundy, which shares with Bordeaux the distinction of providing the most famous French wines. The differences between the two reflect with striking accuracy the differences between the cultures of the two regions, reflected also in the characters of their cuisines. Bordeaux, from the ancient city of the Romans—inheritor of the sophisticated Latin tradition—is grown in the region of a great port which has known an urban and cosmopolitan civilization for centuries; it is suave, polished, civilized. Burgundy, from the region of the swash-buckling Grand Dukes of the West, the lusty sons of inland soil, grown where men lived close to the land, remained rustic in richness, and exerted their own influence outward more readily than they welcomed other influences directed inward, is full-bodied, strong, earthy. Bordeaux is city wine, Burgundy is country wine. A fine Bordeaux recalls a man of thorough university training. A great Burgundy is like a country gentleman grown wise in the skillful cultivation of his lands.

In Burgundy as in Bordeaux it was the Romans who introduced the wine grape—the name Romanée, which appears on the labels of several vintages of the Vosnes-Romanée district, is a reminder of that. If the Cistercians, contrary to what one might have expected from the auster-ity of their diet, were responsible for the establishment of many vineyards, it was because they found much of Burgundy wooded, and began the establishment of their abbeys by clearing the forests on land presented to them. Once the ground had been cleared, it was often planted to vines. The rules of the order may have forbidden the monks to drink the wine themselves, but there was no prohibition against making wine for sale to support the monasteries. There was also, evidently, no prohibition against making presents of it; Jean de Bussières, abbot of Cîteaux, which owned the Clos Vougeot vineyard, sent thirty kegs of it to Pope Gregory XI in 1359 and four years later—just about long enough for the wine to have reached drinkable age—he was made a cardinal.

In the northernmost part of Burgundy, around Auxerre, far removed from the other winegrowing areas, is the home of Chablis, one of the best known Burgundy wines, though it is completely divorced from the main Burgundy vineyard region. The soil here is a mixture of chalk, silex, and clay, the grape is the *chardonnay*, which accounts for most of the best Burgundy whites, and the result is a comparatively light wine, dry, fresh, and deliciously perfumed, which should be served very cold. Not far from here, on the other side of Auxerre, a variety of reds and *rosés* are grown, of which Irancy, a *rosé*, is perhaps the best. This also is best drunk thoroughly iced, as is *aligoté*, a name which refers not to the place at which the wine is grown, but to the species of grape. *Aligoté* wines are found in this area, and in some other parts of Burgundy where the soil is not suited either to the *pinot noir*, the favorite for red wines, or the *chardonnay*. The white wine it produces is not as fine as that obtained from the *chardonnay* grape on more propitious soil, but the result is better than could be had from the *chardonnay* in the particular plots sowed to *aligoté* grapes.

It is considerably to the east and south of this area that

the main Burgundy vineyards begin, lying along the slopes of the region known as a whole as La Côte (the Slope). It begins at Dijon and runs south, starting with the Côte Dijonnais, ending at Fixin, a minor wine-producing region of no particular importance. But the next place of any size after Fixin is Gevrey-Chambertin, a name known to all readers of wine cards. Here the famous vineyards begin. From this point on, wine is more than a crop, it is a way of life. The winegrower lives with his product. He occupies the upper floors of his house, the fermenting vats and the hogsheads full of wine fill the lower floors. His chief concern is the quality of his wine. In the south of France, where undistinguished table wines are grown, the wine-grower may get 600 gallons of wine from an acre of ground. From an acre of La Côte—the Côte d'Or, the Golden Slope—the Burgundian winegrower may reap only 200 to 250 gallons; but they are 250 gallons of Burgundy.

The soil of the Côte is chalky, producing wines of strong perfume, with a heavy alcoholic content and a long life. The grapes here are still the *pinot noir* for reds, the *chardonnay* for whites. Some persons serve red Burgundies slightly warmed (*chambré*), like Bordeaux, but Burgundians do not believe in it. They drink their reds at cellar temperature. The stronger Burgundy actually does not need the warmth that releases the full flavor of Bordeaux; like Bordeaux, however, it will benefit by being opened an hour or so before it is to be drunk. The whites of the Côte are served cool, though not as cold as Chablis, but these also may quite readily be drunk at cellar temperature.

The great Burgundy wines grow on the easternmost slopes of the hills; the backhills (*arrière-côtes*) west of them produce wine considerably inferior to that of the favored hillsides, and even to the vintages that continue the Golden Slope southward. These southerly wines are rougher, but there are still some very respectable bottles among them.

VIII · *Burgundy*

Just south of the Côte, in the Chalon region, Mercurey offers excellent red table wines, Givry provided the everyday drink of Henry IV, Montagny is a passable white, and Rully whites are sometimes sparkling. Red sparkling Burgundy can also be purchased in the United States, but so far as I know not in France, and Burgundian winegrowers, though some of them must make it for export, would rather not discuss the subject. Their obvious sense of shame about the existence of such a beverage is quite understandable. Sparkling red wines are an abomination.

After a wineless gap, vineyards resume again about Mâcon, whose best known product is Pouilly-Fuissé, a fine white wine of a greenish golden shade, dry but fruity, which comes close to being in the class of the great white wines farther north. The Mâconnais also produces reds, and Louis XVI favored Mâcon wines, though it is true that he selected them from his table in competition only with wines from the Parisian region, still obtainable in his day. But the more popular reds from southern Burgundy come from the extension of the wine slopes into Beaujolais, a wine region of repute on its own, sometimes spoken of as distinct from Burgundy. There are a number of differences between the Beaujolais area and the chief Burgundy region—the soil, which is underlaid with granite and rich in iron oxide, giving Beaujolais wines a dark color and a strong taste; the manner of cultivation, by individual owners exploiting very small plots, perhaps as little as five acres or so, into which the slopes are minutely subdivided; and the type of grape grown. Here the *gamay* is found, a vine which Philip the Bold, acting the part of "the lords of the best wines of Christendom," an unofficial title which the dukes of Burgundy claimed for themselves, forbade entry into the Côte d'Or, where it was considered inferior to the two favorites. However, it flourishes on the soil of Beaujolais, where it is the major vine grown, though not the only one; for instance if you come across a bottle described as *passe-tout-grain*, that means that its contents come in a proportion of two thirds from the *gamay* grape, one third from the *pinot noir*. Among the best Beaujolais are Moulin-à-Vent, Fleurie, Morgon, Juliénas, and Brouilly. Beaujolais wines should never be warmed before serving.

Because of the considerable spread of Burgundy wine territory, vintage years given for the whole region can be somewhat misleading. Chablis, for instance, is so far removed from the other areas that its good and bad years may be quite different. Indeed recently Chablis has had a succession of years so disastrous that many winegrowers, thoroughly discouraged, threatened to pull up their vines and grow vegetables, although along the Côte d'Or results have been normal. With this much warning, we may now go ahead and suggest that the great years for red Burgundies have been 1929, 1934, 1937, 1942, 1943, 1945, 1947, 1949, 1952, 1953, 1955, 1957, 1959 and 1961. For whites, the top years are 1928, 1929, 1943, 1947, 1950, 1952, 1953, 1955, 1957, 1959, 1961, 1962 and 1963. Chablis was best in 1929, 1937, and 1947, with 1928, 1934, and 1945 as the runners-up. A series of bad years has discouraged growers recently, and made this wine rarer.

The Nivernais has wines also—Tannay, a dry, white fragrant growth from the left bank of the Yonne, which might also be described as a Morvan wine, since it is grown in the region where the two territories melt into each other—and one really superb vintage, Pouilly-sur-Loire. Separated only by the river from the wines of the Berry, which we have already considered (Sancerre, for instance) it should perhaps be listed with these wines, but it is so distinctive, and possesses so much more finesse, that it is worth placing in a separate category. There are two varieties of Pouilly-sur-Loire, one made from the *chasselas* grape, delicate, dry, and a little sharp; the other, from the Sauvignon vine (which produces Sancerre), even more subtle in taste and with a more complicated bouquet, Pouilly-Fumé (not to be confused with the Mâconnais Pouilly-Fuissé).

The Bourbonnais produces some light wines, pleasant enough to drink on the spot, but not sufficiently important to be sent outside of the regional borders. The best known names are Chemilly, Huriel, Vouraud, Chareilles, Billy, Souvigny, and Saint-Pourcin. The most celebrated liquid of this territory, which is exported in quantity, is a mineral water—for Vichy is in the Bourbonnais. Which may lead us to note that Burgundy, great wine country though it is, also produces a considerable amount of hops for beer. Brought in from Alsace, great beer country, hops attained considerable importance in Burgundy when the annexation of Alsace-Lorraine after the Franco-Prussian war removed this source of them from France. Production in Burgundy decreased after Alsace returned to France, but hops are still grown around Dijon, where the quality of the crop ranks with the best produce of the parent region.

Finally it may be noted that the Côte du Rhône wines begin in this area, Côte Rôtie, a rather widely known red, coming from the same neighborhood as the fine sharp white wine of Condrieu, near Vienne, a specialty of the Pyramide restaurant.

The Mountains

[Jura, Franche-Comté, Savoy, Dauphiné]

The eastern frontiers of France are natural borders. Mountains run the length of the country, from north to south. In the north, they do not quite reach the frontier, which is a natural one all the same; it is constituted by the Rhine, back of whose valley rise the Vosges. But toward Switzerland, the mountains take over to draw the boundary. North of Switzerland, the Juras trace the line between the two countries. South of it the Alps begin, and block off Switzerland, and then Italy, all the way to the sea.

This succession of mountain chains includes all three

of the chief divisions of cooking—the school of fat in the north and the school of olive oil in the south, neither of which concerns us now. In the center, the school of butter still holds sway. There are at least two culinary regions here, those of the Jura and the Alps, both of which may be subdivided into two others—the Jura, somewhat dubiously, into Jura and Franche-Comté, meaning really highland and lowland, the Jura being part of the Franche-Comté; and the Alps, perhaps a little more definitely, into Savoy and Dauphiné. Political divisions, which we have found vague and shifting everywhere, are even harder to draw with sharpness and clarity here; the Jura-Franche-Comté distinction is a weak one, as this territory has been pretty much a political unit over most of its history, but Savoy and the Dauphiné have more often been in separate compartments. Culinary and political frontiers do not necessarily coincide, but the latter often exercise some influence on the former.

The situation of the Jura provides one point of view which permits a turning of the tables as between Switzerland and France. One thinks ordinarily of the former as more mountainous than the latter, but if you move northward from Lake Léman, otherwise known as Lake Geneva, through the country that lies behind it and the lake of Neuchâtel, you will find yourself in comparatively level country, but ahead of you a great wall will loom up. The flatter land is Switzerland; the wall is France. The Juras come to an end so abruptly that the effect, as you look toward them, is that of a cliff. There is no gradual approach through foothills, but only this sudden looming of the barrier. This makes the Juras look higher than they are. Actually they are no match for the Alps, and they do not possess the awe-inspiring majesty of the jagged bare pointed rocks of the Alps, stabbing into the sky, and often, even in summer, flecked with snow. The Juras are heavily wooded. The roads that wind up and around them, cutting through thick growths of evergreens on either side, impose serenity upon the spirit. From time to time you find yourself on the edge of a height. The rock of the mountain drops straight downward, and below lies a green valley, comparatively wide in spite of its depth, for another mountain wall rises opposite you with the same abruptness. Through the valley a narrow stream threads. The scene is like a view from an airplane.

Yet the Juras are not inaccessible. Their heights and valleys succeed one another in a regular pattern, roughly parallel, the valleys open at both ends. From the air, they look like a succession of high narrow waves. The highest ranges lie against the Swiss border, and their height decreases as you move into the interior of France, so that the general arrangement is that of a gigantic flight of steps. From time to time the parallel mountain walls are broken by gaps known as *cluses*. Then a stream that has been flowing lengthwise along one step slips through the opening and begins to glide lengthwise along the next one, perhaps in the same direction, perhaps in the opposite one, until another *cluse* lets it drop another step. This makes for long, twisting rivers. The Doubs, which rises fifty-five miles from the Saône, covers two hundred and sixty-seven miles before it empties into it—and at times it seems so unlikely ever to get there that it is named the Doubtful (in Latin, *dubius*, today Doubs). Even after joining the Saône, the waters of the Doubs have to continue with it through Châlon and Mâcon to Lyons to meet the Rhone, which has already been joined above Lyons by the Ain. The Ain, in turn, starting out only nine miles from the starting point of the Doubs, has met the Rhone in a course of a mere sixty-eight miles.

The eccentricities of the Jura streams are vertical as well as horizontal. They have a disconcerting habit of suddenly disappearing into sinkholes in the permeable top-soil, running underground over the water-retaining layers buried below, and at last, when the ground drops away, of gushing forth again from the side of a cliff in what is known as a resurgence. The map of the Jura is studded with names like *Perte de l'Ain, Perte du Lison* (Loss of the Ain, Loss of the Lison), marking the spots at which its streams duck underground. (There was once even a *Perte du Rhône*, where that river, already a wide stream when it enters France from Switzerland, nevertheless plunged completely underground, but a dam has backed the river waters up over the fissure, and though much of the Rhone still flows underground, it does so under water, so that the phenomenon is not perceived.) The official sources of Jura rivers are often not the real ones, but only resurgences. When the names were given to these sources, it was not realized that the floods gushing from cliffsides did not start there, but were only reappearances of streams that had sunk into the earth some distance away. This phenomenon was dramatized in 1901 when dwellers near the "source" of the Loue were delighted to discover that it seemed to have turned to absinthe—weak in flavor, but nevertheless quite palatable. Two days before, the Pernod factory at Pontarlier, where absinthe was made, had burned down, and some 200,000 gallons of it had poured into the Doubs. It was therefore deduced that the Loue was a resurgence of part of the waters of the Doubs. The theory was tested by tinting the Doubs near Pontarlier with a strong green dye. Two and a half days later, the Loue was green also.

The streams of the Jura are among its most picturesque features, for the mountain terrain sends them plunging downward in foaming cascades—of which the most spectacular are those of the Doubs and the Hérisson—or allows them to cut through deep gorges, as do the Doubs and the Ain in particular. Quieter, but no less beautiful, waters are found in the lake region, reached from Champagnole. Magnificent views are afforded wherever the mountains drop abruptly away at the edge of deep valleys, as they so often do here. One such view is that from Mont Rond, on the edge of that wall which the Jura rears along the Swiss frontier; it looks toward Lake Geneva and the Swiss Alps beyond it.

The forest of La Joux includes France's equivalent of the giant sequoia growths of the American Pacific Coast. Although they do not reach the 300-foot height of the sequoias, the pines of La Joux nevertheless attain impressive altitudes. The President Pine is about 160 feet tall and measures thirteen feet around at five feet from the ground; the St. Wenceslas Pine is somewhat higher, but not as thick. Many of these trees, all of which bear plates giving their individual names, put out no branches lower than ninety or one hundred feet from the ground. They are known locally as "the Spaniards" because they are supposed to date from the Spanish occupation of 1556–98.

The forest of La Joux, like all this heavily wooded district, is lumbered systematically, under government supervision, with cutting limited each year to the natural replacement by growth within the same period, which insures perpetual maintenance of the region's principal resource. Because of this controlled lumbering, a communal division of firewood among the local inhabitants had to be instituted, and this has left its mark on the scenery of the Jura. Visitors are often struck by the large wide-eaved roofs picturesquely covering Jura houses, a common enough feature of mountainous country, where one-story buildings covered with low sweeping roofs as protection against wind and snow are frequent, but here the roofs are particularly exaggerated. The explanation is not climatic, but economic. In some communities, firewood is divided in accordance with roof area—and therefore everyone gets just as much roof onto his house as he possibly can. Where roofs are smaller, you may deduce that you are in communities in which division is by the number of persons in each house, or by the number of its fires, whether in stoves or fireplaces.

The climate is rigorous. "We have eight months of snow, two of high winds, but during the rest of the year you wouldn't believe how wonderful the weather is," say the Jurassiens. The rigors of the weather, the hardiness developed in a region in which almost everyone is a lumberjack and where a living has to be wrested from a reluctant soil, no doubt accounts in part for the toughness of the local character. Mountain peoples are usually fierce defenders of their independence, perhaps because their terrain makes defense feasible even against armies greatly superior in numbers, but the people of this region have a particularly proud reputation for resistance—sometimes described by exasperated outsiders as obstinacy. (*Comtois, tête de bois* goes one French saying, which might be translated freely as "those pig-headed people of the Franche-Comté!") They are hotheaded, too—another picturesque French phrase describes the inhabitants of the Arbois region as "wearing their heads close to their hats."

It is a fair question to ask how much the diet of mountain peoples contributes to their sometimes truculent independence. Certain characteristics are shared by most mountain cuisines, which might be summed up as essentially rude. Mountain food is usually heavy to satisfy the demands for considerable energy and for warmth. It is not likely to be subtle or varied; sometimes it is downright monotonous, though the food of the Franche-Comté seems to have escaped that fate, in spite of the appearance here of such not particularly inspiring dishes as the typical *gaudes*, which is simply cornmeal mush; it is eaten either hot or allowed to cool and harden, and then cut into slices for eating cold.

One reason for the shortcomings of mountain food in some regions is the poverty of the soil, which limits the available raw materials as to both quality and quantity. The Franche-Comté has the advantage here that west of the mountains, in the Saône valley, there are fertile plains, one of them gastronomically noted, that of the Bresse, while even in the Juras themselves there are three special assets—the fish of the lakes and the turbulent mountain streams, perfect for trout; excellent high pasturage, which makes this an important source of cheese; and local wines of highly individual qualities, always an inspirer of cooks.

It is still noticeable, however, that the western lowlands of the Franche-Comté provide a more varied and imaginative cuisine than the Juras, even though there is a warm rough heartiness about this mountain food which gives it a rustic charm all its own, and though in mountain regions the first thought seems to be for taking in plenty of food, not for the kind of food to be taken in. "The goat that stops to bleat loses a mouthful," say the mountaineers, and though they profess to prefer wives who are good cooks rather than good lookers, the slant seems to be more toward a full larder than toward a dainty one in the proverb that goes: "It's better to say 'Well, my homely wife, let's have supper,' than 'Beautiful, what have we got to eat?'" Bread is regarded rather as nourishment than as satisfying to the sense of taste by the Jurassien, who prefers it cold —when it is indeed easier to digest—rather than warm, when its flavor is best. "*Jeune femme et pain chaud sont des ruine-outau*"—young wives and hot bread are home-wreckers—is another maxim, *outau* being a word of local dialect replacing the French *maison*. This disdain for woman in her more decorative form would not lead us to look for gourmets in the Jura. In most places and at most times, appreciation of savor in food has usually gone cheek by jowl with appreciation of beauty in women. The pleasures of the table have a natural affinity with the pleasures of the bed.

The plain of Bresse has already been mentioned as a particularly noted gastronomic region. Its fame derives chiefly from the fact that the finest chickens in France are raised here. They are finished on a heavy diet of corn. After they have been killed, they are bathed in milk and then powdered, so that they go to market a glistening white. The flavor is so delicate that in Bresse itself they prefer a simple roasting of the bird to any more elaborate treatment, which might risk detracting from its own subtle savor by giving it competition from other flavors. It is put into a very hot oven, which turns the white carcass a brillant golden brown; and, in order to keep the skin crackly and crisp, is not basted.

When you see *poulet de Bresse* on the menu (or in the most knowing circles, *poularde de Bresse*, for the hen is reputed to be better eating than the cock), you should be getting the finest chicken obtainable in France. But there is a catch to it. Although the Bresse poultry-growers are jealous of the reputation of their birds and send them to market wearing a lead ring attesting to the fact that they come from the Bresse, there are also chickens on the market which are described honestly as *poulets de Bresse* and which bear the lead ring, but which are not of the famous Bresse race. They are chickens brought in from other parts of the country and finished in Bresse, but even if they have lived from the egg up in this region, they are still not the real thing unless they belong to the native species. This is easily recognized if you are buying the whole bird in a market, for the Bresse race is the only one with blue color in legs, wattles, and combs; but as restaurants do not serve their birds complete with these appendages, there is not much you can do in them except trust the management.

By an accident appropriate to the character of Bresse as a food-raising center, the only cloister of the old Benedictine monastery of Brou, just outside the capital of the region, Bourg-en-Bresse, which escaped destruction in the sixteenth century, was the kitchen cloister, which may still be seen by visitors to the monastery and to its magnificent flamboyant Gothic church.

After the chickens of Bresse, the next most important food resource of the Franche-Comté is provided by its cows, white with large brownish-red markings, which graze from May to October on the high Alpine pastures, to which they congregate often from distances of fifteen or twenty miles. The mountain pasturage produces milk that makes particularly good cheese, but the chief reason for disposing of most of the Jura's milk in this form is the prosaic one of difficulty of transport. To bring milk down from these high fields twice a day and then move it to the distant urban regions where it would have to be sent—for the sparsely settled Juras produce much more fresh milk than their own population could consume—would be an onerous process. So the milk is converted into cheese, and in this more readily transportable and less perishable form finally reaches the city markets.

Several types of cheese are made in the Jura. Comté is very much like the Swiss Gruyère made just across the border—the real Gruyère, without holes; the similar cheese with holes is Emmenthal, the next valley from Gruyère in Switzerland. The names of these cheeses have been transferred in popular usage throughout the world, to the extreme annoyance of the cheese-makers of both regions. In the Jura, it is the opinion that the fewer the holes, the better the cheese. Comté is a cheese of good staying powers, which can be kept for long periods without spoiling.

Defective cheeses of this type, which does not mean badly flavored or less edible cheese, but simply those which have become broken or are uneven in appearance, and are thus not considered sufficiently presentable to be put on sale, gave rise to a different sort of cheese known as *crème de gruyère*, or sometimes *fondu*, which means melted, for the original big cheeses were melted down and reworked into smaller and more creamy pieces, often in individual portions. (*Fondu* is not the same thing as *fondue*, to which we shall come in a moment.) This type of cheese became so popular that it is now made from cheeses intended for this process from the beginning, as there would not be enough accidentally spoiled cheeses to meet the demand.

Before leaving the Gruyère type of cheese, we might note the *morbier* of Morez, somewhat coarser than the Comté, made in smaller round cakes. When you cut it open you will find a black streak in its center. Do not assume you have a bad cheese. Each complete cheese is composed of two disks placed face to face; the touching faces have been rubbed with charcoal before being joined.

Two towns in particular make a specialty of blue cheeses of the Roquefort type. Sometimes called *fromages persillés*, they have been described on the strength of that name as containing chopped parsley; actually they do not, the name coming from the supposed resemblance of the green streaks in the cheese to parsley. The color is caused by a mold called *penicillium glaucum*, which is not added artificially, but develops spontaneously in the ripening caves. The variety made at Gex has the peculiarity of always remaining white, instead of acquiring a yellowish-greenish tinge with age, as do most blue cheeses. The little village of Septmoncel makes a similar cheese, but of mixed cow's and goat's milk, whereas Gex is all cow's milk. When the two types of curds are not mixed together, but the one is simply poured in on top of the other before the pressing begins, it is known as bastard Septmoncel. The blue cheeses require two to four months to reach maturity.

Some soft cheeses are also made in the Jura, many of them, in imitation of the similar cheeses of other regions, in small quantities in individual chalets. *Vacherin* is a soft cheese, and so is *cancoillotte*, not only soft, but also strong, as one of its other names, *fromage fort*, makes plain. It is also sometimes called *fromagère*, and is only good between September and June.

Cancoillotte is a word that may confuse you, for it can be applied either to the cheese itself or to a sort of Welsh rarebit made from it, in which this light-yellow liquid cheese is cooked with eggs and garlic. *Fondue* is another cheese dish, made with the Comté cheese, which must have entered the Juras from across the frontier, for it seems pretty certainly to be of Swiss origin—perhaps the only original Swiss gastronomic invention. It is made of cheese melted in white wine, to which a little *kirsch* (cherry *eau-de-vie*) is added just before serving. It is put on the table piping hot, in a wooden bowl that has previously been rubbed inside with garlic, and is eaten in the Swiss fashion —each diner impales a dice of bread on his fork, plunges it into the steaming liquid mass in the common dish, twists it to load the bread thickly with *fondue*, and then plunges his findings into his mouth. Another piece of bread is then stabbed, and the process is repeated. Only dry white wine should be drunk with *fondue*—in Switzerland it is traditionally Fendant, but in France the choice is wider.

Cheese turns up in many Franche-Comté dishes. A fine warm hors d'œuvre with which to start off a meal is a *croustade jurassien*, a fine flaky pastry delicately touched with cheese. The interest of winter squash and potatoes is increased by preparations involving cheese, and another food specialty of the Franche-Comté is combined with this one in crayfish tails cooked in cheese, *gratin de queues d'écrevisses*, a creation of the city of Nantua.

Nantua is the capital of fish dishes for the Franche-Comté. At least two other ways of preparing the fine fresh-water crayfish are named for the city—*queues d'écrevisses à la Nantua* and *mousselines d'écrevisses à la Nantua*. The first is not unrelated to the Bordeaux dish of crayfish already described, starting out with *mirepoix* and involving white wine and Cognac in its preparation, but further enriching elements, like *béchamel* sauce, are added to it long after the Bordeaux dish would have been on its way to the table. The second is a creamy paste in which pike or perch is also included, smothered with *sauce Nantua*, another specialty of the city, itself involving crayfish. It starts off with *béchamel*, a basic cream sauce that goes back to the time of Louis XIV, then adds to it crayfish bouillon and additional cream, and finally puts in crayfish butter, prepared by mixing the butter with *mirepoix* in which crayfish remnants have been cooked, along with a few drops of Cognac and a dash of cayenne pepper.

It is sad to relate that the famous crayfish of the Jura are becoming rarer. If they disappear, the area will still not be destitute of fish dishes. Nantua is famous not only for its crayfish, but also for its *quenelles de brochet*, fat little patties of creamed pike. They are fish cakes by definition, no doubt, but it seems a sacrilege to call them that—though the New England version of this dish is by no means to be disdained.

Among other fish dishes of the Franche-Comté is the *pauchouse*, which we have already met across the Saône in Burgundy proper. Besides the more ordinary varieties of trout, there is a salmon trout in the Breuchin, a tributary of the Saône in the extreme northeastern corner of the Franche-

Comté, which has a particularly rich flavor. The best carp are reputed to come from the Saulon, the best pike from the Ognon.

Wooded mountainous country is ordinarily good for game. Certainly the Jura is. Partridge, woodcock, pheasant, hare, and even wild boar abound. Kid is a favorite dish. Mushrooms of many varieties are plentiful in the high pastures and under the shade of the pines, and the snails of Fourgs are nearly as highly esteemed as their cousins in Burgundy proper.

A food resource that the gourmet is not likely to take into consideration, being accustomed to taking it as a matter of course, is salt. It was not a matter of course in older times when inland regions went to great lengths to insure salt supplies, not so easily obtainable in those days of slow and painful communications and difficult transportation. The salt tax, the *gabelle,* was one of the most important sources of revenue for French kings, and one which the people felt most onerously. The Salzkammergut region of Austria, of which Salzburg (Salt City) is the capital, owed its early wealth to its salt mines. The Franche-Comté has its salt deposits, too. The presence of seasoning may very well have had some influence on the development of its cooking.

The salt deposits of the Franche-Comté have been exploited since the days of the Romans, who found them most advantageously placed in proximity to so much firewood —for the method of extraction was to flood the pits, raise the salt-saturated water, and then boil it until only salt remained. This is in principle the method used to this day, with the addition of powerful modern pumps and great boilers heated by coal, not wood. Visitors can see the process in operation at Salins-les-Bains (which means Salt Deposit Spa; Lons-le-Saunier, near which other salt workings lie, also has the word "salt" hidden in its name). The salt of

Salins constituted the fortune of John the Ancient, an early thirteenth-century noble. The continued importance of salt at a later date can be seen at Arc-et-Senans, where the Royal Works of Chaux were built in the eighteenth century. The plan called for an entire city built in a circle around the salt works, but actually only these utilitarian structures themselves were completed. There are about a dozen of them, and they are sufficiently impressive to remind the visitor of the importance of that very common and therefore little-considered ingredient of almost every modern dish, salt.

If you want to sample some of the hearty, if not exactly refined, food of the Juras, you might try to get in on a hog-killing, when the guests are traditionally served meals composed exclusively of *cochonailles*—pig products. It makes a heavy meal—blood pudding, head cheese, tripe sausage, pork chops, and similar dainties—but it goes with the climate. So does the local version of *potée*, which takes the form of a mixed vegetable stew of which an indispensable adjunct is either a big piece of beef, which has long been hung in the smoke of the fireplace to dry—especially in the valley of Saugeais, where it is called *brési*—or a smoked sausage from Morteau. This is the most famous of the sausages of a region that makes many fine ones. Short and broad in shape, it is made of pure pork, and outside of the *potée* is likely to be accompanied either by hot potato salad or by string beans cooked in butter. Another sausage worth noting is the caraway-seed-flavored product of Montbozon.

Some of the Jura soups may seen a trifle alarming to the uninitiated. *Panade* might be described rather as dull—it is bread soup, very much a peasant dish. There is also frog soup and cherry soup; the latter may have recourse to the cherries grown near Mouthier, in the Loue valley, where fruit trees have replaced the vineyards from which the vines were torn up when phylloxera attacked them. There is a good deal of orchard country in the Franche-Comté, enough so that furniture made from cherry or pear wood is one of the regional exports. There are also many walnut trees, especially in the Pérouges region, where your salad dressing may be made with walnut instead of olive oil.

Féchuns, the stuffed cabbage of Montbéliard, is a typically peasant dish. Two methods of cooking chicken favored in the region by contrast show considerable sophistication. One preparation presents creamed chicken with the black crinkly *morilles* mushrooms in the cream sauce. *Morilles* are among the tastiest of French mushrooms wherever you find them; but these of the Jura, picked in the high pine woods, are particularly rich in flavor. The other chicken dish is cockerel cooked in the wine of Château Chalon, a sweet rich vintage, a mountain Sauternes. Complete urbanism is reached with the *pâtés* surrounded by a flaky crust for which Besançon, the largest city of the Franche-Comté, is renowned.

Except for the *rosé* wine of the Arbois, often served in other parts of France as a carafe wine, the vintages of the Jura are little known today outside their own region. It is necessary to specify "today," for they were more widely known in older times. Probably the comparative ignorance of these wines is owing to their limited production, which prevents them from being commercially important in these days of mass merchandising. It cannot be due to their inability to stand up in competition with other wines, for the Jura beverages are extremely interesting, with highly individual characteristics, and despite the small area from which they come (a strip fifty miles long by six wide), astonishing in their variety.

Knowledge of Jura wines goes back to Roman times, when the area was known as Sequania. In those days growers did not trust to the grape alone to put flavor into their wines. Pliny the Younger and Martial both remark on the taste Romans developed for the flavor of resin and nuts in the wines they imported from Sequania. When they could not obtain the real thing, they sometimes dropped buds from fir trees into Roman wines to imitate the effect. This recalls the modern Greek wines with a similar taste of resin; and for that matter, the Jura has not entirely renounced the resin flavor, though now "pine wine"—*vin de sapin*—has divorced itself from the grape. The Jura shepherds chew the sap that flows from the bark of the pines and then hardens just as New England children chew, or used to chew, spruce gum. They make their pine wine by soaking fresh pine boughs in water along with sugar, barley, and flour. But there is no longer any other element than the grape in Jura wines proper.

The Arbois wines come from the northern part of the Jura wine growing region, with Arbois itself producing the best-liked vintages, and Montigny and Mesnay following close behind. The typical Arbois wine is the *rosé*, or more exactly, especially after it has aged a little, *pelure d'oignon*, onion skin, a name it gets from its color. A good Arbois has a pronounced fruity flavor, nearly submerging the slight rocky taste characteristic of mountain wines and is smooth and velvetlike.

Noted admirers of Arbois have included several Austrian emperors; Rabelais, who mentions it in *Pantagruel* despite his loyalty to the Loire wines of his native region; Francis I; Henry II; Henry IV (there is still extant a letter from him to his mistress, Gabrielle d'Estrées, in which he announces that he is sending her four bottles of Arbois); Henry IV's friend and minister Sully (who may not have endeared himself to the ladies of the court by the manner in which he chose to present them with Arbois wine—he sprinkled them with it); and above all, the man who expressed the opinion that there was more wit in a cask of 1834 Arbois wine than in all the books of philosophy in the world—Pasteur.

If you should visit Arbois, a pleasant thing to do, since it is an attractive historic old town in a fine scenic location, you can see Pasteur's home there (he was born in Dôle, also in the Franche-Comté, but was brought up in Arbois and spent much time there). The exhibits will remind you that the brillant career that inaugurated modern antiseptic methods in medicine, produced a cure for rabies, and delved into the world of microbes, started with the practical problem of discovering a means for preventing wine from spoiling. Pasteurization was applied to wine before it was applied to milk. About two miles from Arbois you can still visit the vineyard owned by Pasteur, on whose produce he performed his experiments on the preservation of wine. Wine is still made from Pasteur's grapes. It is excellent, but is not for sale. If you can persuade its present holders that you are a person of importance, however, you may be given a taste of it free. It is reserved for such visitors.

Just south of the Arbois area, the region of white wines begins. There are two main types—a quite dry white wine, drunk cool but not iced, with a little of the mountain bite to its taste, and one of the most famous regional specialties, the yellow wine, sweet and rich.

The greatest of the *vins jaunes* are those of Château Chalon, another Roman favorite. Nobody knows just how far back the Château Chalon vineyards go. The oldest written document relating to them is dated February 1, 869. The vines were tended and developed by the sisters of the Benedictine convent established there in the seventh century, restricted to the daughters of noble families. The secret of the particular quality of the yellow wines of this region, those of Château Chalon at the top, is that the grapes are allowed to be attacked by an enemy most

winegrowers dread—frost. It is made from the white Savignin grape, which in this area resists all attempts of wind
and rain to knock it off the vine, and does not spoil when
the frosts strike it, perhaps because the pulp of this small
oval grape is particularly thick. The grapes are not picked
until November, which at the altitude of the Juras is
sufficient to guarantee several frosts, if not some snow. The
wine made from it is referred to as "keeping wine" (it has
great staying powers, some bottles having been found to
be excellent after one hundred years) or "frost wine."
The effect of frost on the wine made from these grapes
was known to the ancients, one writer on the wines of
Sequania having remarked that "the wines . . . of Château Chalon cannot be surpassed, at least when they
have been touched . . . by frost on the vine." This
opinion was shared, among others, by Francis I, Henry IV,
and Metternich. The last was dining at the Tuileries with
Napoleon, who praised the Johannisberg wine, grown at
that time by Metternich's family. Metternich thanked the
Emperor for the compliment, but said that France possessed
a finer wine of the same type (from which it must be assumed that the particular Johannisberger in question must
have been of the *Trockenbeeren Auslese* variety, rather than
what you would be likely to get if you ordered Johannisberg
today), Château Chalon. The Emperor sent out at once for
some Château Chalon and agreed with Metternich.

Château Chalon has been compared to Tokay (one
legend adds that the Jura vines came from Hungary,
though actually no one knows the origin of the Savignin
grape; it may have been indigenous to the area, at least
since Celtic times) and to Madeira, though the taste is
very different from either. It is its smooth well-assimilated
sweetness presumably which provokes the comparison.
Another, nearer home, would seem to be with the great
Sauternes. In both the richness is produced by decay, in

the Bordeaux region through the intervention of a micro-organism, in the Jura by frost. As is consonant with its long life, Château Chalon is slow to mature, and requires long and careful treatment before bottling (which unfortunately makes it expensive). It goes into unusually thick small kegs made out of the heartwood of red oak, the older the better, so that the inside will be coated with the tartar deposits of centuries of wine-making. During the first year, it has to be separated from its residue three times. The keg is then sealed, and the wine rests from six to ten years before bottling, after which it remains good indefinitely. I have been told that one cellar in Château Chalon still contains some 1783 wine which is highly drinkable.

A good combination for savoring Château Chalon to the full is to drink it with locally grown walnuts and the also local Comté cheese.

A derivation of the *vin jaune*, an even rarer and more prized specialty of the Jura, is the *vin de paille*, spoken of with awe by connoisseurs, now practically impossible to buy. It is sweet and unctuous, feeling on the palate as thick as a liqueur, with a rich brooding somber undertaste (the straw?) that gives it a most intriguing and elusive quality. The perfume lingers in the mouth, as though the fumes of the wine were heavy and sluggish.

To make *vin de paille*, the grapes are individually sorted and only the best are used. They are spread on straw to dry and it is generally assumed that the grapes pick up some flavor from the straw, but as the grapes are some-times hung in the cellar to dry instead of being spread out on straw (in which case the name is a misnomer), per-haps this is not the case. The grapes are pressed in February, by which time they have really become raisins, giving a thick sticky juice of a dark amber color. The amount of juice is naturally much less than for fresh grapes—a ton of fruit produces about one hundred bottles of wine. Fermentation is slow, so the *vin de paille* has to stay longer in the cask than ordinary yellow wines—ten years or more. It is, of course, a dessert wine. It is also naturally expensive—as much so as fine Champagne.

Continuing southward from Château Chalon, one reaches the territory of another top vintage of the Jura, Etoile. This is the best of the dry white wines, somewhat reminiscent of some of the dry white Burgundies, with considerable alcoholic content though with nothing like the body of the *vin jaunes*, and with a distinct mountain-wine taste to it. Second only to the Etoile in this area is Château d'Arlay, whose vineyards have been owned at one time or another, starting in the thirteenth century, by kings of Spain, England, and France.

Most of the other Jura wines are described as Côtes de Jura. They are quick to mature, and it must be these wines that were in the minds of those who coined the old Arbois maxim: "An hour-old egg, day-old bread, year-old wine, a two-year-old fish, a fifteen-year-old wife, a thirty-year-old friend." Temperature does not seem to make much difference to these wines, so you drink them in accordance with the weather—slightly warmed, whether they are red, *rosé*, or white, in winter; cool, whether they are red, *rosé*, or white, in summer. The exception is the *vin jaune*, always drunk cool.

The best recent years for the Jura wines have been 1947, 1949, 1952, 1953, 1955, 1959. If you get a chance at any of the older Château Chalon wines, try 1893, 1900, 1911, or 1921.

Besides wines, the Jura produces some excellent *marcs*, which are aged in old oak kegs used for this purpose for centuries, and excellent fruit brandies, of which the most famous is the *kirsch* (cherry brandy) of Mouthier. *Prunelle* (plum brandy) is also good, and there are two rather special drinks, one made from pine sap and the other from mountain gentian roots, which produce a very bitter liquid better combined in other drinks (chiefly *apéritifs*) than left undiluted.

The somber wooded Juras lie north of and opposite to the point that Switzerland thrusts into the flank of France. South of that point begin the towering bare rock peaks of the Alps, their summits eternally flecked or blanketed with snow. The mountains opposed a barrier to the march of armies and to the march of trade. It is no accident that the borders of three countries—France, Switzerland, and Italy—meet at the mighty frontier post formed by France's—and Europe's—highest mountain, Mont Blanc. It is one of the most natural frontiers of the Continent.

The mountain ranges impeded some of the more violent currents of history. The Alps participate in all the chronicles of the various rulers of Europe—the Romans, the Burgundians, the French, the Spaniards, the Swiss, the Italians—and their territories passed freely from one hand to another, but often by proxy. Sovereignty could be changed more easily by a signature on a piece of paper than by sending troops into these difficult mountain regions. Meanwhile the peoples of the valleys and the slopes went on with their daily lives, tending their herds of sheep, cattle, and goats, tilling the often poor soil, and cutting the forests, with little regard for the identity of their momentary titular sovereign. This is not to say that the settlements of the Alps, protected though they were, escaped the devastations and destructions that for centuries were the common lot. But they did manage to remain a more sluggish side current of the turbulent flood of European history.

Politically the region we are dealing with now is divided into two sections. Geographically it is also divided into two sections, but the political line is north of the natural one. At about the level of Briançon, at 4,350 feet, the highest city in Europe (there are, however, higher towns and villages), a change occurs in the vegetation and the general character of the country. The influence of the still invisible Mediterranean is beginning to make itself felt. The northern Alps partake of the humid climate of northern France, familiar to all those who know Paris; the southern Alps partake of the dry climate of the Riviera, familiar to all those who know Nice or Cannes.

But the political line dividing the Savoy from the Dauphiné lies much farther north, roughly in the region of Chambéry. Nor does the Savoy run as far west as the Dauphiné, which lies along the east bank of the Rhone after it has finally straightened out and begun its southward course. The two territories parted political company early in the eleventh century, when Humbert of the White Hands assumed the title of Count of Savoy, while Gigues I the Old began to piece together the territories that were to become the Dauphiné. The Savoy, much the smaller territory (it is represented today by the two departments of the Savoie and the Haute-Savoie), was a latecomer to France. It entered the country only in 1860, during the shifting of territories which gave birth to modern Italy, which did not receive this part of the lands of the by then Italian House of Savoy. But the cession was so recent that up to the time of the Second World War there were points along the border where, if you stood on the ground, you were in France, but if you climbed a tree, you were in Italy; the king of Italy had assumed from the House of Savoy the timber rights, which had not been ceded to France along with the soil.

The Dauphiné has been French for five hundred years longer, ever since 1340, when Humbert II, being short of money, sold the territory to Philip VI of France. The Dauphinois did not take too kindly to being disposed of in this fashion, so to mollify them it was decided that the Dauphiné should be granted the honor of having as its special viceroy the eldest son of the king of France. That is why the crown prince of France became known as the Dauphin, in almost precisely the same fashion that the heir to the English crown was regularly created Prince of Wales, for it was to persuade Wales to accept English rule that Edward I promised the Welsh a prince born on Welsh soil, whose first words would not only have been spoken in Welsh, but who would speak no English—and kept the promise by sending his queen to Caernarvon Castle to bear his child, who obligingly turned out to be a son. (In this apposition of the English Prince of Wales and the French Dauphin, history seems to have been intent on making a bad play on words, for *dauphin* means porpoise (dolphin), which shares with the whale the anomaly of being a mammal with the habits of a fish.)

The Dauphiné today is represented by the modern departments of the Drôme, the Hautes-Alpes, and the Isère—the last named from the cold gray-green river that slides swiftly through canalized banks in the Dauphiné's great capital city of Grenoble, so hilly that at one point you cross the river by means of an overhead cable railway which swings you across the stream to a hilltop park high above it on the opposite shore. Though the province reaches the Rhone, we shall deal here only with its mountainous section. Wherever the political boundary may be, the gastronomic boundary is drawn where the mountains end. The cooking of the valley of the Rhone is not the cooking of the Alps. The cuisines of Provence to the southeast and Languedoc to the west have been sucked into the valley of the Rhone by the constant stream of travel which has followed this great north-south artery for as far back as history goes. It has been modified, too, by the greater fertility of the river-washed lowlands, which have given

226

the valley richer resources than the mountains. It is only east of the valley that we are in the region of genuine mountain cooking.

Here we are in an area of higher mountains than the Juras, and at the same time in one to which the luxury of the more urban courts seldom penetrated. As a result, the cuisine is much more typically that of the mountains than is the cuisine of the Jura. It tends to be heavy, hearty, often coarse, and sometimes monotonous. This has not been much modified by the fact that the Alps today are vacation country packed with visitors from the cities, for it is also sports country, and the visitors from the city are active and accordingly more receptive to the type of food preferred by the mountaineers than to the elaborate (and effort-discouraging) banquets of de luxe restaurants. In the winter, this is the great skiing paradise of France. In the summer, mountaineers attack the peaks, lovers of water sports cluster about the lakes. In one or two places favored by the upper crust—Aix-Les-Bains, say, or Annecy—there are luxurious hotels and fine restaurants, but they serve the international menu more often than the fare of the mountains.

The Alps have been consistent in this disdain of sophisticated cooking, in spite of the origin of the French phrase, *faire ripaille,* which means to feast, to banquet, to have a luxurious good time. It might be translated as, "to do as they do in Ripaille," and Ripaille is a château in the Savoy, though not, it is true, in its severer regions, being on Lake Léman, the lake of Geneva. It is in this part of Savoy, if anywhere, that one might expect the stern character of mountain life to have been supplanted by conditions of ease, and it might seem fitting that it is in the monastic buildings attached to the Château of Ripaille that you can visit one of the best preserved old kitchens in France, with all its equipment intact, just as it was used five centuries ago. The fact is, however, that in olden times *faire ripaille* meant just the opposite of what it means today. It referred to the austere life of the Augustine monks who established themselves beside the château. Voltaire used the term sarcastically, in reverse meaning, and somehow or other the new sense supplanted the old one. The expression therefore does not deny the claim of the Alpine areas to be a land of simple living.

As long as the region had to depend upon its own products, it was necessarily a country of unsubtle food—though of healthy nourishment, of excellent quality within its restricted range. Except for its fruits (plums, pears, and cider apples in the Savoy) and nuts (walnuts and chestnuts in both the Savoy and the Dauphiné), the regional crops are not of an exciting character—wheat, rye, potatoes. The mountain potato is of particularly fine quality, however, firm and tasty, and in the Dauphiné this humble vegetable enters so importantly into cooking that any dish described as *à la dauphinoise* is likely to be accompanied by *pommes de terre dauphinoise*, made as follows: thinly sliced potatoes are moistened with boiled milk and beaten egg, seasoned with salt, pepper, and nutmeg, and mixed with grated cheese, of the Gruyère type. The potatoes are then put into an earthenware dish which has been rubbed with garlic and then buttered, spotted with little dabs of butter, and sprinkled with more grated cheese. It is then cooked slowly in not too hot an oven, and served in the dish in which it was cooked. The Savoy is strong on potatoes also, so that *à la savoyarde* likewise has reference to that vegetable. It is encountered most frequently on menus with either one of two meanings. The first is *omelette à la savoyarde*, in which sliced potatoes previously fried in butter and shavings of a Gruyère type of cheese are combined with the omelette, which is made in griddlecake form. The other is the same dish described above for the Dauphiné, but the Savoy uses consommé instead of milk to moisten the potatoes.

The Savoy also has a local dessert made out of sweetened potatoes, *farçon*. This appearance of the potato as an *entremets*, or sweet dish, is in accord with ancient tradition, when the interlude between the two sections of an elaborate banquet, to allow the diners to get their second wind, might be a sweet course following meat dishes, or might be vegetables. The *farçon*, being both, highly merits the name of *entremets;* but if the word is followed even farther back, to the fourteenth century, it did not mean the food with which the spectators toyed "between the meats," but a performance by troubadours, jugglers, dancers, or other entertainers which took place in the middle of the repast, during which these lighter dishes were served. If the term finally came to be attached to the sweets served during this medieval version of the floor show rather than to the vegetables, it may have been because a scenic background of cardboard, representing perhaps a church or a castle, was often set up behind the players, and was later imitated in elaborate structures of pastry which were not only decorative, but also edible.

The cheese that enters into the Dauphinois preparation of potatoes enters also into many other typical dishes of the Alps, being, of course, the produce of the mountain pasturage. The family of *gratins*, to which the potato dish described above belongs, is well represented in both the Savoy and the Dauphiné, where it almost always refers to a cheese dish—though, contrary to the general impression, a *gratin* does not necessarily involve cheese. *Gratin* means a crust formed on various dishes in cooking. It usually results from the use of cheese, which spreads a crust over the surface of the dish to which it is added—sometimes a floating one, as in *gratinée* onion soup—but it may derive from some other ingredient, as in *gratin languedocien*, a dish of tomatoes and eggplant, innocent of cheese, whose crust is formed by bread crumbs.

Almost anything goes into a cheese *gratin* in the Alps— in the Dauphiné, macaroni, hashed boiled meat, the type of mushrooms known as *cèpes*, and the local variety of Swiss chard; in the Savoy, the artichoke-like *cardon*, which we first met in the Touraine; and in both, crayfish tails. The cheeses used are made from what the natives call the "hard milk" of the Alps, provided by the mountain Tarentaise cow, whose fawn color recalls the animals across the Swiss border. Both the Savoy and the Dauphiné produce many fine cheeses, but the Savoy perhaps comes first, if only for Reblochon. This is a rather soft cheese, but without any tendency to run like Camembert or Pont l'Evêque, and much blander in flavor than either. I often switch to it during the summer months when it is difficult to find the more liquid cheeses, like Camembert, in edible condition, although the experts maintain that Reblochon is only an October-to-June cheese, which is not my experience. There is no difference of opinion about when to eat Beaufort, a Savoy version of Emmenthal, good all year round. Vacherin, which approaches Swiss Gruyère, but is softer, is best from November to May. *Tome de Savoie* (*tome* simply means "cheese" in the local dialect), whose most reputed variety is *tome de Sixt*, is a very hard cheese with a rough crust, kept several years before it is released for market. A slight change of spelling gives us also the *tomme de Beauges*, best from September to June, and the *tomme de Boudaye*, whose top season begins and ends a month later. *Tomme de fenouil* is a fennel-flavored cheese eaten between September and June.

The Dauphiné has a *tomme* too, of a quite different type—a white cottage cheese. Saint-Marcellin is the most famous of Dauphiné cheeses, but it is living largely on past reputation. Once made exclusively of goat's milk, it is now mixed, and the proportion of cow's milk has grown so great that the goat component has almost disappeared, reducing considerably the interest of the cheese. Sassenage is a Roquefort type of cheese, with three kinds of milk going into it—goat's, cow's, and sheep's.

After the potato and cheese, the most important natural food resource of the Alps is its fresh-water fish. Mountain streams in France may always be expected to produce fine specimens of trout, but here there are also excellent lake fish, some of them local varieties, such as the *féra* and the *lavaret*, both members of the salmon family. The first is especially succulent when it comes from Lake Léman, the other from the Lake of Le Bourget, both in the Savoy. In the Lake Léman region you will find an excellent *soupe aux poissons*, a fresh-water version of the famous *bouillabaisse*. The Lake of Annecy is associated particularly with a very fine food fish, the *omble chevalier*, which looks like a trout with smooth scales and black spots along the sides, but is actually a salmon (*salmo salvelinus*). The Lake of Bourget also provides choice specimens of this fish, which in the Savoy reaches the westernmost limit of its range, for it is more common in Central Europe.

Game is not as plentiful as it used to be, particularly in the more thickly frequented Savoy, but hare, partridge, quail, and woodcock are still to be found there, and the town of Bonneville is noted for the *pâtés* it makes of them. In the Dauphiné the tiny delicately flavored *grive* is the most sought-after game bird. As *grives* are berry-eaters, their flesh carries a hint of juniper if they have been feeding toward the western limits of this territory (where Nyons makes fine preserves of *grives*), while at the southern border, touching Provence, bayberries account for their flavor. The aromatic mountain herbs give the Alpine region another specialty, too—excellent honey.

The Savoy in particular is noted for its mountain hams,

which are dried and smoked in the open air—the best come from Celliers and Taninges. The Savoyard *civet* may be made either from hare or pork cooked in a highly spiced and seasoned sauce made with the animal's blood, with wine and thick cream. One of the most characteristic productions of the Dauphiné is the *pogne*, which approaches the American pie, differing from it in the summer, when it is filled with fruit, for it has no top crust, but much the same in winter when the customary filling is squash, so that it is almost indistinguishable from an American squash pie. At least, this is what the *pogne* ought to be; but as you get out of the mountains, in the western part of the department of the Drôme, you may find the word applied to nothing more unusual than the familiar French *brioche*.

It may seem surprising to think of the Alps as wine country—in the sense that the land produces its own wine, for local consumption; not much of it gets outside its own region. If you stop to consider the geography, you will realize that the northern part of Savoy, which lies along the shores of Lake Léman, could very well support vineyards, as it does. But it will still seem a startling statement that the moutainous Dauphiné department of the Isère alone produces more wine than the entire Côte d'Or of Burgundy. Burgundy, of course, deliberately sacrifices quantity to quality.

Starting at the north, on the shores of Lake Léman, we have the Savoyard region called La Chablais, which produces a fine white wine with a slight bite to it, Crépy, an excellent accompaniment for fresh fish from the lake. Other Savoy white wines much like it in character are Frangy (grown near Annecy), Chignin, and Aise, of which the last is often champagnized. Follow the Rhone as it leaves the lake and turns south and you come to Seyssel, one of the best-known wine names in the Savoy; Seyssel sometimes manages to get out of its own region, though it is best drunk on the spot. This again is a comparatively dry white wine, often sold as Roussette, which is not a place name, but that of the grape which produces it. (Mondeuse and Altesse, which you may see on Savoy wine labels, are also grape names.) Continue to follow the Rhone and at Yenne you come to Marètel, still a white wine, but this time a sweeter rather syrupy one. Around Chambery you have both whites (Apremont) and reds, the top vintage of the latter being Montmélian, a rather coarse wine, not unlike a Beaujolais. It is followed among the reds by Saint-Jean-de-la-Porte, Conflans, Charpignat, Aigueblanche, Cantefort, and Touvière.

The political Dauphiné can boast of some of the best wines of France outside of the big areas, the Côtes du Rhône wines, but they are not in the gastronomic Dauphiné which we are now considering. This leaves the vineyards of the Isère valley, plus a patch along the Drôme-Isère departmental boundary, which you will find served in carafes in the region simply as local wine—*vin du pays*. At the extreme southern limit of this territory, at Die, is produced one of those *clairettes* mentioned in the Bordeaux chapter. It is a sweetish champagnized white wine made from a mixture of clairette and muscat grapes, and is well enough liked, though not by me, to be sold beyond its own region.

One of the most famous of French liqueurs comes from the Dauphiné, Chartreuse, like Benedictine the creation of a monastery. The monastery of the Grand Chartreuse, near Grenoble, cannot be visited, and though the distillery is open to the public, it no longer permits you to approach the monastery, for a landslide destroyed the original Chartreuse plant, located near the monastery, and the liqueur is now made some distance away, at Voiron. Like Benedictine, its exact ingredients and proportions are a secret, but unlike Benedictine, the secret has been pierced by analysis, and those who know Chartreuse as a very sweet liqueur may be surprised to learn that aside from such purely flavoring ingredients as saffron, cinnamon bark, and the seed coating of nutmeg, most of the herbs that go into it are medicinal. Actually the first use of this drink was as a fortifier for the sick, and even today the more alcoholic of the two varieties of Chartreuse met most often in commerce, Green Chartreuse, is known as "Chartreuse for health" (*Chartreuse de santé*), while Yellow Chartreuse is simply classified, like other distilled after-dinner drinks, as a *digestif*.

The Savoy produces several distilled drinks—good cherry brandy (*kirsch*), *marc*, and a special variety known, humorously one hopes, as *la lie*—the dregs; this is probably because you pour it into your coffee. Chambery makes a well-known vermouth. Cider is a fairly common local product, and beer is brewed in Chambery, Annecy, and Rumilly. Finally mention should be made of one of the best known French table waters, Evian, bottled of course in the spa of that name, on the shores of Lake Léman. It is a non-sparkling water, only slightly mineralized and thus tasteless.

THE
DOMAIN

OF
FAT

X

Alsace-Lorraine

Alsace-Lorraine is a word whose two parts seem destined to remain tied together by their hyphen, but their conjunction is more or less an accident of history. Together they have formed part of the territory of a single sovereignty on several occasions; on others they have belonged to different holdings, and Lorraine in particular has been subdivided now and again, which accounts for its possession of two capitals, Nancy in the south and Metz in the north. Both have been in and out of France throughout the centuries, and oddly enough, it is Alsace, the more foreign of the two, which was earlier attached definitively to France (disregarding the interruptions of the Franco-

Prussian and Second World wars, which gave Alsace and part of Lorraine temporarily to Germany). Alsace, despite a German contrary opinion, has counted itself French uninterruptedly since 1648, when Louis XIV gained it by the Treaty of Westphalia. Lorraine had to wait until 1766, when the death of Stanislas Leczinski, Duke of Lorraine, ex-King of Poland, and father-in-law of Louis XV, caused Lorraine to be added to the kingdom of France.

If historically the two territories we persist in coupling as though they were one have been separated as often as linked, a natural hyphen nevertheless paradoxically binds them together in spite of a geographical separation. This is the Vosges, the mountain chain that runs like a spine along the frontier between the two. It seems as though some common cultural characteristics had flowed down from the crest of the Vosges to the lowlands on either side. More exactly, one might suggest that Alsatian culture, capturing the heights, had flowed down into Lorraine, for Alsace appears to be the dominant member of the partnership, though this may be an illusion caused by the greater foreignness of Alsace, which makes its idiosyncracies stand out more strikingly against the French background.

The Lorraine plateau is more or less continuous with Champagne to the west, and with the flatlands and the Ile-de-France beyond Champagne. Those customs which have seeped in from the west, becoming gradually more and more adulterated as they increase their distance from the fountainhead of French culture in the Tours-Paris axis, do not stand out against the national pattern because they are not particularly different from it. They are quite as typical of Lorraine as the habits that have crossed the Vosges to enter it, but the latter impress us more as regionally characteristic because they are strange and therefore striking. Lorraine is essentially more French than Alsace, par-

ALSACE-LORRAINE

BELGIUM

LUXEMBOURG

GERMANY

CHAMPAGNE

TOURTE À LA LORRAINE

Thionville (BEER)

BACON SOUP

Verdun (JORDAN ALMONDS)

Metz BEER

QUICHE

PARTRIDGE WITH CABBAGE

EAUX-DE-VIE BEER

ROAST SUCKLING PIG
SAUSAGES
FOIE GRAS'
SAUERKRAUT

Commercy (MADELEINES)

Bar-le-Duc (CURRANT JELLY)

Nancy (BLOOD PUDDING) (CHARCUTERIE)

LORRAINE

GEESE

Strasbourg

COLD SUCKLING PIG IN JELLY

POTÉE LORRAINE

HOHWALD (FRUIT)

Vittel

Köenigsbourg

Ribeauvillé

Contrexeville (MINERAL WATER)

VOSGES

ALSACE

Ammerschwihr

Gérardmer (CHEESE)

Colmar

TROUT

Münster (CHEESE)

FRANCHE-COMTE

MUSHROOMS

ZEWELWAI (ONION TART)
CHICKEN
VOL'AUVENT
KUGELHOPF
DUMPLINGS

Mulhouse

Belfort

≡ Great Eating
= Good Eating

MILES
0   50   100

0   100
KM.

ticularly in its northern half, where the lower hills closely resemble the French soil to the west, while the more mountainous southern section tends to follow the example of the Alsatians in their half of the Vosges—for instance, in that pride and attestation of wealth of the southern Lorraine farmer, the great pile of manure in the farmyard, a form of ostentation borrowed from the Alsatians, who in turn imported it from their blood-cousins across the Rhine, the peasants of the Black Forest.

Geographically, the region we are now considering divides itself naturally into three parts—to the west, the Lorraine plateau, subdivided, as we have already seen, into two parts; then the ridges of the Vosges, also subdivisible into two sections—to the north, the clay soil of the lower mountains, to the south, the granite of the higher ones, thickly covered with woods, and likely to assume a characteristic rounded shape that has caused a number of them to be called "balloons"; finally, the plain of Alsace, lying beside the Rhine.

If the Rhine has always been thought of almost exclusively as a German river (though it rises in Switzerland and reaches the sea in Holland) and not at all as a French one, in spite of being a boundary stream between France and Germany for a considerable part of its length, that is probably not only because its most scenic stretches lie north of France, where both banks are German, but also because in the section shared by the two countries, the Germans have advanced to plant their dwellings at the edge of the river, while the Alsatians have retreated from it. This is because the west bank of the Rhine is lower than the east bank, and the river used to flood the Alsatian shore periodically. Thus the line of Alsatian cities which parallels the Rhine does not lie on it. They are built some miles to its west—Mulhouse, Colmar, Sélestat, even Strasbourg itself, which is sometimes described as being on the Rhine, though you have to plunge into its suburbs to reach the bridge that crosses the river to Kehl. The river you have seen in pictures of Strasbourg is not necessarily the Rhine, as most persons assume (though a side stream of that river does enter the city), but usually the Ill. This stream, which runs parallel to the Rhine from the Swiss frontier until it finally spills into the larger river just north of Strasbourg, is the one on which the Alsatian towns are built, the real river of Alsace, although most foreigners have never heard of it, or at least do not realize that they have heard of it. In a sense, they have heard of the Ill if they know the name of the country it runs through, for Alsace, which is Elsass in German and Illsass in the local dialect, means simply "the country of the Ill."

With Alsace, we come to the most genuinely foreign region of France, probably because it is the only one with a culture stemming from a civilization that has retained an integrated independent political identity outside the country, Germany, which has given Alsace its customs, its domestic architecture, its eating habits, and its language. Perhaps the Alsatians would not care to be spoken of as French Germans, but that is unquestionably what they are, and because of the continued existence of a political Germany congruent with a cultural Germany, it is evident that French Germans are foreign in a sense that French Celts and French Basques are not.

Alsatian is a true dialect of German into which a number of French words have crept (a good many have slipped into German proper for that matter). Although it is widely spoken, there are probably almost no Alsatians who do not speak French as well, in spite of the attempts made by the Germans between 1870 and 1914 and again between 1940 and 1944 to stamp the language out entirely. There is a language frontier between Alsace and Lorraine which does not quite coincide with the political frontier but does coincide with the gastronomic frontier. East of it both Alsatian and French are spoken; west of it you will hear only French.

In many ways, Alsace appears even to the casual observer much more German in appearance than French. Specifically, it resembles the Black Forest region just across the Rhine. The women's costumes recall those of Germany (or of some parts of German Switzerland), with the large black bows of their headdresses, laced bodices, and billowing red skirts. So do the men's costumes, though these are worn less frequently nowadays, exception being made for restaurants that go in for local color and therefore impose the regional garb as a sort of livery on their waiters. The houses look German. Instead of the stone rectangles of France, you find wooden cottages, with high-pitched roofs sweeping down for a story or a story and a half; or, if the building is faced with stucco, half-timbered effects or wooden balconies clinging to an upper story.

If domestic architecture betrays the Germanic influence, so does public architecture. City halls apply to their façades the squat triangles carrying a flight of steps on either side which are so frequently encountered not only in Germany, but also in German Switzerland and Holland. The step-gabled façade is everywhere. Exterior decoration is striking, as in the House of the Heads at Colmar, where the heads in question project from a building that is today the setting for an excellent restaurant. Hilltops are crowned with the ruins of old castles and the walls of fortified towns, as in the German Rhineland (in Lorraine, the towns are more likely to nestle lower down on the hillsides). Alsatians, like Germans, apply elaborate sculpture to tombs. Like Germans, they go in heavily for woodcarving and for intricate ironwork, which you may encounter in ship and tavern signs. Like Germans, they have a certain taste for the macabre. When Colmar wanted a Crucifixion for the altar of one of its churches, it imported the German painter Matthias Grünewald to produce one of his frightening realistic pictures. Gustave Doré, whose woodcuts recall the great German masters of that art, was a native of Strasbourg.

If Alsace echoes the culture of Germany, it does so, with a few exceptions, on a smaller scale. Strasbourg, where both Gutenberg and Goethe lived, is the one big metropolis, with 175,000 people. Mulhouse has about 80,000 and Colmar drops down to less than 50,000. Churches and public buildings tend to be modest; there are few monumental buildings. In the field of ecclesiastical architecture, the Gothic cathedral of Strasbourg is the outstanding exception; for military architecture, the castle of Haut Kœnigsbourg. The Renaissance Château of Saverne recalls French architecture rather than German, but it was built in the eighteenth century, when every ruler, including the Germans, was erecting his own private copy of Versailles (as at Potsdam and Schönbrunn).

The same is true of Lorraine, except that here it is French culture which has been duplicated on a reduced scale, with the admixture of some German seepages from Alsace. There are two important cities, Metz, with its Gothic cathedral, and Nancy, whose cathedral is less important, but which has many fine buildings, the beautifully proportioned Place Stanislas, with its delicate iron grillwork, and the imposing governmental palace. Toul has a fine former cathedral and the cathedral of Verdun is quite interesting. Lorraine has had one important painter, as you already know, consciously or unconsciously, for the name under which he is famous is that of his native region— Claude Lorrain (his actual family name was Gellée).

Thus both Alsace and Lorraine, while prosperous and far from isolated, do not possess a culture in the grand style of the Loire-Seine entity or of Burgundy or Guienne. Both, in spite of reasonable urbanization, still remain largely rural.

Their cooking, therefore, is not of high sophistication or great luxuriousness, but is still tasty and hearty. One eats well in this region—especially in Alsace—but quite differently than in the Ile-de-France.

Alsace (today the departments of the Haut-Rhin and the Bas-Rhin) and Lorraine (the Meuse, the Moselle, the Meurthe-et-Moselle, and the Vosges) do not possess on their territories any particularly dominant natural food resources to impose a definite shape on their cuisine, as the cream and the apples of Normandy have formed the cooking of that province. The chief such resource one thinks of in connection with Lorraine is salt, always handy to have on hand in the presence of food, but hardly capable of developing a school of cooking. Alsace, of course, has wine, which in Burgundy and Bordeaux has affected the kitchen profoundly, but it is almost as much as Champagne a type of wine which does not enter with much authority directly into the preparation of dishes, and by the same token it can, like Champagne, be drunk pretty much with almost anything (more gratefully than Champagne, in my opinion).

The cooking of Alsace would seem, indeed, to be to a considerable extent artificial—a borrowing, rather than a school imposed by the nature of the land. The cuisine of Germany has been moved bodily across the Rhine. There it has undergone naturalization, for the better. The Alsatians have added a French subtlety to the often rather unimaginative heaviness of German food. Yet both the individual dishes, like sauerkraut, and the basic principles, such as the use of lard for the chief cooking fat where the territory to the west uses butter, have been imported. Cooking with fat, we have already noted, is likely to be the result of poor land and poor people, who therefore have resorted chiefly to the economical meat-makers, the pig and the goose. Alsace is not poor, for much of its soil is quite fertile, and the pig and the goose might not have installed themselves here quite as firmly if they had not already been fixed in the eating habits of a people who came from poorer soils in Germany, where these were natural foods. The imposition of the goose upon a richer background than this bird is accustomed to at least had the effect of giving us *foie gras*. As the overcharged liver that produces this dish is achieved by stuffing the bird with rich food, it would not have been likely to develop in the customary poverty-stricken haunts of the goose. The Alsatian terrain was more propitious to it.

For somewhat the same reason, Alsace is unbeatable for sausages. The region can afford to treat the products of the pig more elaborately than less favored areas, though here the contrast is less striking, for Germany is of course famous sausage country also.

But if cooking in fat and having lavish recourse to pigs and geese were not likely to have developed naturally on the soil of Alsace, they fitted its climate well enough once they arrived. Alsace is far enough inland to have a typical continental climate; summers may be hot, but winters are often rigorous. While the plain, by the side of the Rhine, enjoys summers warm enough so that tobacco is grown there (the climate is indeed about like that of the Connecticut valley, also tobacco country), the heights of the Vosges are always cool, and in winter snow is deep and temperatures frigid. (Lorraine is also damp and cold.) This is the sort of weather that calls for solid diets with a plentiful fat content. German eating habits are thus not in contradiction with the regional setting, and have therefore taken root and flourished.

If the habit of eating goose was derived from Germany by the Alsatians, the goose itself is French. The Strasbourg goose is a variety of the Toulouse goose, a large race especially suited to the fattening required for making *foie gras.* The common goose of France, known as the ash goose, or farm goose (*oie cendrée, oie de ferme*) is smaller than the Toulouse and Strasbourg varieties. The latter are built close to the ground and have a loose fold of skin on the belly which provides room for fattening, a ready-made reservoir for goose grease. The customary fattening food is noodles. The resulting liver is very light in color, almost a cream, shading to pink, and has a smooth, even, firm grain.

The invention of *pâté de foie gras* is often attributed to Jean Joseph Close (or Clause), an eighteenth-century Norman pastry cook who was brought to Alsace by his employer, the Marshal of Contades, who had been appointed governor of Alsace in 1762. There he was supposed to have created a dish in which he employed the goose liver along with chopped veal and lard, with a truffle in the center, the whole surrounded by a crust. It is obvious, however, that he could hardly have invented *foie gras* itself, which depends upon the manner of feeding the goose, but must have found this ingredient on hand when he arrived in Alsace. The dish became associated with him because he retired in Alsace and put his particular preparation of *pâté de foie gras* on the market there.

Actually the use of artificially fattened goose livers goes much farther back either than Close or the producers of this dish in the Toulouse region. The Romans knew it, though apparently they did not employ the forcible feeding that makes *foie gras* nowadays. They waited until the bird was dead, but lost no time then; immediately the goose had been killed the liver was extracted and placed while still warm in milk. In this state it absorbed a great deal of the milk and became rich, succulent, and heavy—though probably not as heavy as the modern livers, which sometimes weigh as much as two and a quarter pounds, a large proportion for a bird whose top weight after fattening is about twenty-five pounds. The liver, in other words, accounts for one tenth the weight of the goose.

The Alsatian fashion of roasting goose is to stuff it with sausage and serve it with sauerkraut soaked in the juice obtained from the goose as it cooks, further embellished with slices of fat pork and Strasbourg sausages—the sauerkraut sometimes being cooked with the goose. This is *oie à l'alsacienne*, and though *à l'alsacienne* guarantees nothing in particular, meaning only that the dish presented is cooked in the fashion Alsace has developed for that individual item, the chances are pretty good that a dish so designated will be accompanied by sauerkraut. The second best bet is that it will involve *foie gras* in one form or other. Aside from these two applications of the term, it will not be much of a guide to what you are getting unless you happen to know the particular dish to which it is applied.

Alsatian chickens are excellent also. Fowl is likely to be cooked in cream with *morilles* mushrooms. Chicken *vol-au-vent* (in cream sauce in a pastry shell) is also popular.

Sauerkraut (*choucroute* in French) is a specialty peculiar to Alsace in France. *Foie gras* and sausages are produced elsewhere, but not sauerkraut. This is, of course, a German dish par excellence, but the Alsatians do it better. You will hardly need to be told that sauerkraut is chopped pickled cabbage. It is made in Alsace from a local variety of this plant known as the *chou quintal*, and juniper berries are added to it during the pickling process, which takes about three weeks. It is cooked in a pan whose bottom has been lined with fat pork, along with a few onions, each with a clove inserted in it, cut-up carrots, a bunch of herbs, and juniper berries. What goes in then may depend considerably on the fantasy of the cook. If it is *à la strasbourgeoise* it is probably a hunk of pork from the breast of the animal, another piece of smoked pork, and lard, or, better, goose grease. This is covered with consommé, strips of fat pork are placed on top, and it is cooked slowly in a closed dish for about four hours, the pork being taken out after the first hour, to be restored only when the dish is served, along with certain other trifles—thinly sliced ham, cooked Strasbourg sausages, and smoked *cervelat* sausages. It is served with boiled potatoes. A purée of yellow peas is also often produced with *choucroute* in Alsace.

The selection of meats given above is far from standard. All sorts of changes are rung upon the accessories cooked with, or added to, the *choucroute*—smoked ham, smoked goose, partridge, and even crayfish, which seems to be going a little too far.

The various types of sausages with which *choucroute* may be garnished can be chosen from a bewildering variety of Alsace-made prepared pork products, a realm of food production in which this region excels, being the principal home of the pig. Other meats can, of course, produce sausages, *pâtés*, and treated meat products, but pork is most improved by such treatment, and so the French *charcuterie* (which is the equivalent of the American and German delicatessen) is stocked largely with pork derivatives. *Charcuterie* used to cover nothing but pork, and pork butchers were kept strictly segregated from the executioners of other animals, largely because of the sanitary regulations which from the earliest times have always surrounded the preparation of pork—the Romans had meticulous statutes covering it, included in a law known as the *porcella*. The word for sausage, incidentally, comes from the Romans too—it was derived from *salsisium*, itself from *salsus*, salted, but was extended to meats preserved in other ways as well—notably by smoking.

Among the Alsatian sausages there is the Strasbourg sausage, which is the German Knackwurst—mixed pork and beef, seasoned with caraway seeds and garlic, smoked and cooked before serving; *cervelat*, an all-pork lightly smoked bland sausage, served hot, usually with mustard sauce; Mettwurst, mainly beef, with lean pork and fresh lard added to it; *boudin à la langue*, a blood sausage containing tongue; liverwurst, which so far as I know is native to no other region of France, unless you count a somewhat different type of liver sausage made in the southwest; *kalerei*, head cheese; and many others. It was a natural step from these preparations to other varieties of delicatessen—all the *foie gras* preparations, naturally; *pâtés*, meat loaves, and galantines of all kinds; rolled truffled tongue; rolled veal with *foie gras;* and so forth. Ham is, of course, often served in Alsace, but the Alsatian hams do not maintain the superiority over other varieties of this preparation which the Alsatian sausages do; after all, there is no particular reason why Alsace should hold any particular advantage for a form of pork so long and so widely known that it was relished by the ancient Gauls, who used to cure hams by smoking them over aromatic wood fires. *Jambon à l'alsacienne* is served with sauerkraut, Strasbourg sausages, and boiled potatoes.

One of the favorite fresh pork dishes of Alsace is *porcelet farci à la peau de goret*, which is roast stuffed suckling pig not more than two months old. *Schifela* is pork shoulder with bitter turnips. *Carré de porc à l'alsacienne* is roast of pork three quarters cooked in the oven and then finished, as you may have suspected, in *choucroute* and served with the usual Strasbourg sausages and boiled potatoes. Pork chops (*côtes de porc*) may also be presented in the same fashion. *Côtes de porc à la vosgienne* is somewhat different. First the chops are cooked in lard, to which, when they are half cooked, finely chopped onion separately fried in butter is added, one spoonful per chop. This is served with a sauce made of the cooking juices, white wine, vinegar, and concentrated veal bouillon, and with the little *mirabelle* plums cooked without sugar.

In the soup department, *consommé à l'alsacienne* means
only, as usual, that *choucroute* and Strasbourg sausages, this
time sliced, have joined an ordinary consommé, but *consommé à la strasbourgeoise* is more complicated. The original consommé is flavored with juniper berries, tapioca is
added, and then a julienne consommé, meaning one with
finely chopped vegetables in it, the vegetable in this case
being red cabbage. Strasbourg sausage is sliced into it, and
it is served with grated horseradish. The Alsatian list of
soups also includes a flour soup—three spoonfuls of flour
are worked into a paste in cold consommé to avoid the
forming of lumps, and turned into about a quart and a half
of boiling consommé. This is seasoned with salt, pepper,
and grated nutmeg and allowed to boil for five minutes; at
the last moment about a quarter pint of heavy cream and
two spoonfuls of butter are added. Onion soup may not
be of Alsatian origin—it is found widely throughout France,
and apparently no region lays particular claim to it—but
it seems to be made particularly well in Alsatian restaurants.
The onion in any case is popular in Alsace—*zewelewai*, or
flan aux oignons, an onion custard tart, is a local specialty.

There is no lack of good fish in Alsace. The Rhine provides succulent salmon. Trout from the streams of the
Vosges are served *au bleu*—simply boiled, the way connoisseurs prefer them if they are really fresh—in a cream
sauce, or in the local Riesling wine. The best pike are reputed to come from the Ill. *Carpe farcie à l'alsacienne* is
simply the Alsatian version of *gefüllte Fisch* (stuffed
carp) with the fish cooked in white wine, the stuffing made
of other fish in cream, and an accompaniment of *choucroute*
and boiled potatoes. A *matelote* is made of various fresh-
water fish from the Ill, and crayfish may either be cooked
in Alsatian wine or made into a tart.

Dumplings are an important item in German cooking.
They appear in Alsace also—marrow dumplings, liver

dumplings, and unflavored dumplings to be served in soup or with some dish containing a rich sauce, like *civet de lièvre*, also served often with macaroni. *Beckenoffe* is a sort of stew of mutton, pork, and potatoes, cooked in a covered dish, usually prepared at home and sent out to a baker to be cooked in his oven. *Potée alsacienne* is a name that seems to be interpreted individually in almost every restaurant or private home you enter, ranging from a vegetable soup to an Alsatian version of baked beans.

Noodles appear frequently in German cooking; they are also popular in Alsace. The cabbage is a favorite German vegetable; Alsace cooks red cabbage with chestnuts and *chou-rave*, a plant of the cabbage family of which the stem, which swells to turnip shape, not the leaves, is the edible section, in cream. Fine asparagus is raised in many places.

Because Alsatian agriculture leans more heavily upon the pig and the goose than the cow and the goat, there are not many Alsatian cheeses, but one extremely good variety is Munster, soft, a little strong in flavor, but not exaggeratedly so, which is usually served with caraway seeds. It is best from November to April.

Alsatians again resemble Germans in their fondness for pastry. *Tarte alsacienne* is a custard tart with the custard studded with the excellent local fruits—*mirabelles*, cherries, etc. Even more characteristic is the *kugelhopf*, a large light cake baked in a mold, usually with a central hole, though for holidays special molds are used to make cakes for children—in the form of Santa Claus at Christmas, for instance. *Birwecka* is a rich and heavy small cake. *Kaffee krantz* is, of course, coffee cake. Good gingerbread is made in a number of towns.

Compared with the dishes of Alsace, the distinctively regional dishes of Lorraine are less numerous. The region leans heavily on the cuisine of the Ile-de-France area, transmitted through the Champagne, in its western part, and in the east produces its local specialties by ringing changes upon the Alsatian cuisine. Thus perhaps the Number One trademark of Lorraine is the *potée lorraine*, belonging to the Alsatian family of *potées*. The Lorraine version of this dish is made by lining the bottom of a pot with bacon rind, placing on top of it some unsalted chunks of breast of pork and leg of pork, carrots, turnips, leeks, and a whole loose-leaf cabbage. This is covered with cold water and cooked for three hours, a sausage being added half an hour before it is done. The pork used in this dish, incidentally, comes from the Lorraine hog, particularly renowned for the flavor of its meat, considered superior to that of the Alsatian hog —though both are members of the Celtic variety, indigenous to France and the British Isles at least since the time of the Gauls and recognizable by their large floppy ears.

Another famous Lorraine dish is the *quiche lorraine*, which seems to be a native of the region. There are similar concoctions in Alsace, like the onion tart, but it seems likely that in this case Alsace has borrowed from Lorraine instead of the other way around. *Quiche* is a round pastry shell filled with a cream-and-beaten-egg filling thickly studded with bits of bacon, served hot. It is sometimes encountered with cheese added as well, and also with a little onion, but both of these are variants from the classic dish—which you may encounter also under the local name of *féouse*.

Tourte à la lorraine is a particularly tasty prepared meat dish in which slices of veal and strips of pork are marinated in liquid seasoned with aromatic herbs and then, bathed in an egg-and-cream sauce, cooked inside a crust. This brings us into the realm of *charcuterie*, in which Lorraine is not far behind Alsace, Nancy, for instance, being famous for its *boudin* (blood pudding), which, incidentally, is possibly the most ancient food preparation on the French menu, as it was reputedly invented in Tyre by the Assyrians.

Other favorite Lorraine dishes are bacon soup and blood pudding soup; *civet* of fresh pork; partridge with cabbage; and cold suckling pig in jelly. The chief cheese of the region is Gerôme, a corruption of Gerardmer, a town in the Vosges. Made on both sides of the Alsace-Lorraine border, of whole milk, it is sometimes flavored with anis, fennel, or caraway seeds, and is at its best between November and April. Fromgey is a sort of cottage cheese, usually eaten spread on a piece of bread and dusted with finely chopped shallots or onions.

Lorraine has a well-developed sweet tooth. Its best-known cake is the *ramequin*, originally a cheesecake, but nowadays often only a sweet flour-and-milk cake innocent of cheese. Commercy is known for its *madeleines*, a cupcake resembling a dry sponge cake. Nancy specializes in macaroons; Bar-le-Duc is famous for jams and jellies—gooseberry and currant jelly especially. And Verdun, a name that arouses warlike echoes in most minds, specializes in Jordan almonds and opens to the public the factory in which it turns out nearly 50,000 pounds of this confection every month.

On the slopes of the ridge of hills which runs parallel to the Rhine grow the vines which produce wines unlike any others in France, though they do resemble the Moselles and Hocks of Germany. The Alsatian wine region is third in importance in the country, outranked only by Bordeaux and Burgundy, and has been producing wine continuously since the third century. Vines were grown there even before that, but Alsace like Champagne suffered from the Emperor Domitian's unwillingness to allow any competition for the wines of Italy. The vines of Alsace were grubbed up on the orders of the Roman soldiers in A.D. 91, but when Probus saw the light two hundred years later, vines mysteriously reappeared from nowhere and since then have clothed the hillsides that lie back from the Rhine.

The Alsatian wines are almost exclusively white (most persons would tell you they are always white, but a few exceptions do exist), but they are not at all reminiscent either of the dry precise whites of Burgundy nor the syrupy sweet sauternes of Bordeaux. They are instead fruity, approaching more closely unfermented grape juice than other wines, though it would be a mistake to assume from this that their alcoholic content is low. There is a freshness about them which makes them a fine accompaniment to the Alsatian cuisine. Since it is apt to be heavier and sometimes greasier, because of the animal fats used in its preparation, than the cooking of other regions in France, this natural clean-tasting wine serves as an antidote, lightening the general effect. The Alsatian wines are brilliant companions for the Alsatian fish dishes, go very well indeed with the onion tart, the *quiches*, and the *charcuterie* of the region, form an excellent accompaniment to sauerkraut (though not as good as beer), and what is most astonishing, can be drunk readily with dishes including red meat, which is not true of any other white wine. They are, in short, all-purpose wines, drinkable from one end of the meal to the other.

There is a great deal less variation among individual Alsatian wines than among individual Bordeaux or Burgundies, and the exact place where they are grown seems to affect the final result less than in other regions. Thus, almost alone among the wines of France, they bear a varietal, not a place name—that is to say, they are described by the name of the type of grape from which they are made, not by the name of the place in which they were grown. When you buy a Riesling, you are ordering a wine made from the grape of that name; but if it is a particularly good Riesling, the place name may be added also, so that the label describes it as Riesling de Ribeauvillé or Riesling de Riquewihr.

254

Edelzwicker on a wine label in Alsace indicates that the wine is made from a mixture of different grapes—and also that it is a fine wine. An ordinary table wine so blended is labeled simply *Zwicker*. The very rare red wines of Alsace, Ottrott and Marlenheim, you are never likely to see except on their home ground.

The best years for Alsatian wines are 1937, 1942, 1943, 1945, 1947, 1949, 1952, 1953, 1955, 1959, 1961, and 1962.

Lorraine is not known as wine country, but it does produce a considerable variety of locally consumed vintages, pleasant enough drinking in the inns of the country, where they usually appear in carafes. Château Salins, Jussy, Mirecourt, and Coussey are reds; Thionville, Bruley, Sierck, and Contz les Bains are whites; and there are several gray wines —which are really light reds, but without the luminous tint of *rosés*—including Scy, Ancy-sur-Moselle, Dornot, and Toul. These last have a slight flinty taste and should be served very cold.

Lorraine does share with Alsace a specialty for which the latter usually gets all the credit—the *eaux-de-vie* made from the fine fruits of the region. Lorraine produces in particular *mirabelle*, made from a small sweet yellow plum, *quetsch*, from a large violet one, and above all, the *kirsch* derived from the cherries of the Ajol valley. Alsace makes all these and virtually every other fruit brandy one can think of, using especially the fine fruit of one of its most favored agricultural regions, the Hohwald, a picturesque area much favored by tourists—which, incidentally, also grows a sort of cranberry, the dry soil type, not the marshland species of Cape Cod. The queen of all the Alsatian *eaux-de-vie* is *framboise*, made from raspberries, an after-coffee drink of the greatest finesse imaginable. It is also the most expensive, often costing twice as much as a *quetch* or *kirsch* of comparable quality, not only because raspberries are a rather expensive fruit to begin with, but because it takes a great many of them to produce a small amount of the distilled drink.

France is not in general a beer-drinking country, and most French beer, it must be admitted, serves to quench the thirst and not much else. In a region addicted to German-style cooking, however, we might also expect to find good beer and we do. There may be one or two exceptions, but in general the only good beer of France is made in Alsace (where they make pretzels to go with it, too) and Lorraine. The Hohwald grows excellent hops, both hops and barley are produced throughout Lower Alsace, and Lorraine also grows these two crops. Although Alsace is the more Germanic of the two provinces, Lorraine beer is perhaps even better known, Metz and Thionville both being renowned for the quality of their beer. Most of it is light, but dark beers are made also.

Finally it may be noted that two of France's most widely drunk mineral waters come from Lorraine—Vittel, a still water of natural taste, and Contrexéville, which, coming from the next town to Vittel, is very much like it.

XI

The Central Plateau

[Périgord, Auvergne, Marche, Limousin, Guienne]

There is some rather remarkable country in the Auvergne. Much of it may not appeal to lovers of the picture-postcard type of scenery, for savage desolation is characteristic of it. This was once volcanic country—it is still rich in spas, whose mineral water springs, many of them hot, are the inheritors of the volcanic activity of the past. It is also country on which the glaciers of the ice ages made their mark—many of the bleak heights are strewn with the great boulders the glaciers left behind. Much of this higher land seems almost waterless (the motorist will do well to make sure his radiator is full before he starts across the higher points of the southern Auvergne, or the combination of the effort of climbing and the quicker evaporation of high altitudes may leave him with an empty tank in one of these barren stretches where there is no house for miles and no ground water visible). Vegetation is sparse, but it makes good pasture, so the Auvergne is largely pastoral country. In its northern section, the Limagne, fertile land enriched by volcanic ash lies in the valleys of the Allier, the Dore and their smaller sister streams, and here the raising of fruits and vegetables takes precedence over pasturage. But the entire region remains agricultural in one form or another, despite the exception of considerable industry in the one big city of the Auvergne, Clermont-Ferrand. The markets for farm produce, especially for cattle, are the centers of the region's most bustling activity. You will appreciate the richness that the Auvergne draws from its soil if you watch the swarthy, stocky peasants in the black felt hats and long smocks of the region arguing over the merits of the beasts on display in a cattle market. They do not look like men of substance. You visualize them leaving the town for some miserable hovel of heaped-up rocks on one of the arid wind-swept heights above the valleys; and then one of them digs deeply into the folds of his smock, pulls forth an enormous wad of bills, and hands it to another. He has just bought an entire herd of cattle.

The climate of this region is rigorous. It is typically continental—that is to say, very cold winters and very hot days in summer; but the latter are counteracted in many regions by the altitude. Above 3,000 feet the sun may be hot, but the air always remains somewhat cool. The region is not only subject to great changes of temperature from one season to another; it is also noted for the swift changes that may take place within a few hours. In the records of Clermont-Ferrand, one day is remembered for a difference

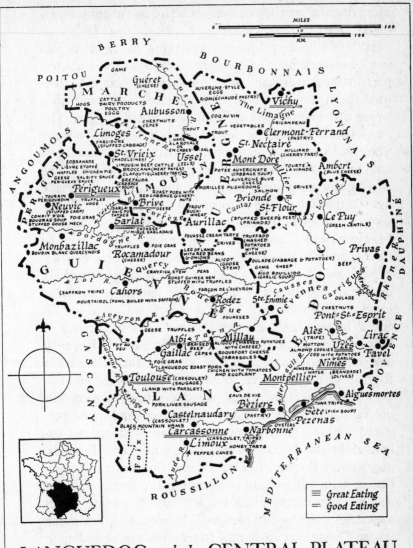

LANGUEDOC *and the* CENTRAL PLATEAU

of 77 degrees between its minimum and maximum temperatures.

It takes a hardy people to stand up to the rigors of this sort of climate, but the dwellers in the Massif Central, especially the Auvergnats, are of tough stock. They take their name from the Arvernes, their ancestors, who built up a strong domain in these hills, with a capital at Gergovia. The name should be familiar, for it was there that the twenty-year-old Vercingetorix, who was an Arverne, defeated Julius Cæsar (who took his revenge later at Alesia). The Auvergnats continued to show themselves indomitable fighters throughout the centuries, so that the counts of Auvergne managed to keep their territory independent of France for a thousand years, though France strove from the sixth century to the seventeenth to add it to her territories. When Louis XIV finally made it French for good and all, he found that the many lords of the Auvergne had been tough toward their own subjects as well as toward outsiders, so he sent royal commissions to Clermont-Ferrand to hear complaints and establish justice. When his judges took one of the first charges so seriously that they executed a seigneur of the Auvergne, the rest of the nobility immediately scattered. The judges passed down other sentences of death with great liberality, but as the condemned persons were not at hand, they made effigies of them and beheaded the effigies. One of the condemned men, Montboissier, lord of Pont du Château, found this idea so amusing that he returned secretly to Clermont-Ferrand in order to watch, from a convenient window, the beheading of his own effigy. "It's highly pleasing," he remarked, "to watch yourself being executed in the street while you're feeling in the pink of health at home."

The Auvergne did not participate in local history alone. Considered relatively inaccessible today, it seems to have been penetrated easily enough in days that we are accustomed to consider as having been less well equipped for travel. Perhaps the explanation of the completeness with which first ancient peoples and then medieval travelers penetrated all sorts of country is that any movement at all was so onerous that the extra difficulties provided by rugged terrain were insignificant by comparison. Nowadays we move about so readily on good roads in fast cars that we tend to bypass any region that does not have the good roads.

Whatever the reason, the Auvergne was by no means divorced from the main European currents, even though its rulers usually did manage, by taking advantage of the defensive possibilities afforded by their mountains, to maintain their independence from outside rule. The Romans, after Cæsar at Alesia had revenged the defeat at Gergovia, poured into the Auvergne, attracted by its warm springs (the Roman civilization, like the American, seems to have laid great stress on the virtue of bathing), and maintained an orderly and prosperous province there for as long as they were able to remain orderly and prosperous at home. On the mesa-like rock of Polignac they established a famous oracle of Apollo. The pilgrims who came to it for guidance made offerings of flowers to the god in a hall at the foot of the rock, accompanied by prayers in which they asked the questions they had come to put to Apollo. They then climbed the rock to the mask of the god in the temple at the top, where they were astonished to hear the mask pronounce the answer to their queries before they had put them. Later ages exposed the secret of the funnel-shaped passage that caught even a whisper in the room at the foot of the rock and carried it, magnified, to the temple, where the priests had time during the pilgrim's laborious upward climb to prepare the answer, which they pronounced by means of a megaphone through the stone mouth of Apollo.

The Auvergne was not so isolated as to be removed from

the artistic and intellectual life of France. Its heights were quite naturally crowned with fortresses, but its ecclesiastical architecture is more interesting—an architecture sometimes closely related to military building, the churches of the Auvergne, mostly in the Romanesque style, being heavy, solid, and massive, surrounded by clusters of chapels recalling the watchtowers of defense works. In their massiveness and their tendency to run to heavy central towers, the churches of the Auvergne have a certain resemblance to those of Normandy, but they tend to cover more ground in proportion to their height, thus appearing more squat than Norman churches. Like those of Normandy, the religious buildings of the Auvergne use sculpture only sparsely; when it is used, it is appealingly archaic.

In a somewhat less elevated field of applied art, the Limousin has given the world the porcelain of Limoges, the Marche the tapestries of Aubusson (where the modern artist, Jean Lurçat, now works).

In spite of conspicuous exceptions, the dwellers of the Central Plateau (especially the most distinct and most prominent group among them, the Auvergnats) are not credited in France with being important contributors to the intellectual life of the country. The Auvergnats are thought of particularly as good businessmen, horse- and cattle-traders at home, and, when they go to Paris, which they do in such numbers that the capital is sometimes referred to as the largest city of the Auvergne, as dealers in coal and wood or keepers of cafés. Their success in these businesses is often attributed to penny-pinching. The French tell about the Auvergnats the same sort of jokes the English tell about the Scots. It is a historical fact that the Auvergne department of Puy-de-Dôme was so named instead of being called, as was at first proposed, Mont Dore, then written Mont d'Or, or Golden Mountain, because a deputy from the Auvergne opposed that name for fear it would remind tax collectors of the legendary prosperity of the people of the Auvergne, who have always been averse to letting the authorities into the secret of how much money they possess. To this day the Auvergnat distrusts banks and prefers to keep his money at home, in cash. It is the country par excellence of the famous French *bas de laine*, the woolen stocking into which the French peasant supposedly stuffs his money before tucking it away in some secret corner.

Because the typical Auvergnat has a dark complexion and black hair, there is a popular legend that there is Saracen blood in the region, supposedly brought into it by Moors fleeing to the mountains after their defeat near Poitiers by Charles Martel in 732. Anthropologists do not share this theory, finding instead that the Auvergnats show strong Celtic characteristics—for instance they are players of the bagpipes, an instrument that appears wherever there are Celts; it is known here as the *cabrette*. The old viol of the hurdy-gurdy type (meaning one played by turning a crank instead of wielding a bow) is also still extant in the Auvergne, and the two instruments together are likely to accompany the dancing of the Auvergne *bourrée*, now rapidly disappearing, which recalls the jigs of other Celtic regions. The enthusiasm and the mysticism with which the Auvergne throws itself into religious rites is also typical of Celts, though in the adjoining provinces to the west, where the Celtic strain is more adulterated, devotion is nearly as strong—Limousin, for instance, holding elaborate "ostentations" at which saintly relics are shown every seven years (1960, 1967, etc.). Of the many pilgrimages and religious processions of the Auvergne, one of the most interesting is that of Besse-en-Chandesse in the Puy-de-Dôme, which combines a religious observance with the rhythm of the pastoral life of the region. At the beginning of the summer, the herds are moved up to the high pasturage, and at the end of September they are brought down again. They are accompanied by the Black Virgin, which is carried up to the heights of Vassivières, at an altitude of nearly 6,000 feet, and brought back to Besse in the fall, where her return is greeted with fireworks and celebration.

The somewhat tenuous connection of this rite with our subject of food, through its relationship to the raising of meat and the production of dairy products, makes it a part of the anecdotage in which foods or their by-products appear in other contexts than the gastronomic one. There are a number of examples of this in the Central Plateau region —for instance the Good Thursday procession, which, since the Middle Ages, has been taking place at Saint-Guilhem-le-Désert by the light of lamps provided by oil burning in snailshells. Another is the explanation of the dark coating on the cliffs of La Barre at La Malène, supposed to date from the burning of a warehouse full of walnuts during the French Revolution, the oil-charged smoke being said to have colored the rocks. Approaching gastronomy more closely is the story of how the celebrated Auvergnat Huguenot fighter, Captain Merle, turned a Catholic ambush from defeat into victory. Attacked in a narrow passage while escorting a convoy of food, he abandoned the wine carts and escaped with his men; then, after giving his enemies time to fall upon the wine, as he had thought they would, he returned to the spot, found them in poor fighting spirit, and defeated them. Finally we approach gastronomy proper with the story of the manner in which the Marquis d'Albignac, driven from his château at Peyreleau by the Revolution, managed to make a living. He had been noted for his skill at preparing tasty salad dressings. Emigrated to London, he turned the skill to account by hurrying from one great dinner to another and mixing the salad dressing, thus turning a comfortable profit from this rather limited talent.

What has been said of the cooking of other mountainous regions has to be repeated for the Auvergne: finesse and sophistication are not to be expected in such rugged country, and are not found; but the food is hearty, of the peasant type, and though somewhat on the fatty side, compatible with the rigors of the climate. Garlic is in general use, for here we are south of the Loire, which provides a rough boundary between the country that uses garlic sparingly and that which has frequent recourse to it. The basic materials are good, with the Limagne region in the northern Auvergne providing fertile soil for the growing of grain, beets, lentils, potatoes, cherries, peaches, apricots, apples, pears, strawberries, and almonds, while the higher regions farther south are given over to pasturage and to the growing of chestnuts and walnuts. The sheep that graze on the high mountain pastures produce mutton of excellent quality; those of Vassivières and Chaudesaigues are reputed the best. First-rate pork is also raised, Maurs being particularly renowned for its hams. There are several races of cows. In the north, a white breed is raised for beef. The Cantal Mountains around Salers have a primarily milch variety named for that town (which has erected a statue to Tyssandier d'Escous, who improved the breed), with a bright-colored, curly hide that loses its luminosity, the local herdsmen claim, if the animals are transferred from the pasturage of this volcanic region to different soil. There is also the Ferrandaise cow, light red with white splotches, raised in the territory between Clermont-Ferrand and Le Mont Dore.

If you ask any Frenchman to name the most characteristic or most famous dish of the Auvergne, he may tell you it is cabbage soup (*soupe aux choux*) or *potée auvergnate*.

Either one will probably be right, for in spite of the evidence of two gastronomic maps that I have before me, both of which inscribe *potée auvergnate* near Clermont-Ferrand and *soupe aux choux* farther south, I am prepared to maintain that these are only two different names for the same dish. The ingredients vary widely, which has helped to confuse the nomenclature, but the two chief invariable components, by whatever name the result is called, are pork (usually salt) and cabbage.

Strictly speaking, the word *potée* means any dish cooked in an earthenware pot, and it appears in this usage in some of the bean dishes, like the *potée alsacienne* in which red kidney beans surround the pork and sausages cooked with them. Step across the fragile border between Alsace and Lorraine, and in *potée lorraine* you have the word applied to what has become its commonest meaning, a soup in which pork and vegetables, most often cabbage or potatoes, are combined with other more variable ingredients. Almost every region with a tradition of peasant cooking has its cabbage soup (*soupe aux choux*)—Burgundy, Languedoc, the Catalan country, and many others—and though other details may be different, pork and cabbage are always there. They belong to the family of the *pot-au-feu*, originally represented by the pot in the farmhouse kitchen which was never completely emptied, which was constantly being refilled, not always necessarily with the same ingredients, and which simmered indefinitely on the back of the stove, year after year, without ever being allowed to grow cold.

You will find described as *potée auvergnate* on some menus a soup with a base of salt pork, accompanied by cabbage, turnips, onions, leeks, potatoes, and garlic—obviously equally describable as *soupe aux choux*. On the other hand, under the name of *soupe aux choux* I have come across a dish in which the liquid character of soup had disappeared under the richness of the ingredients it contained —not only cabbage, and not only one kind of pork, but a shoulder of pork, lumps of lard, fat and lean chunks of pork, a fowl, a leg of veal, and a cut of beef, with some turnips added for good measure. This would seem worthy of being promoted at least to the title of *potée*. The varieties of both are legion, and under either name the dish is likely to be one of the best choices you can make in this part of the country. There is also another dish that might be called *soupe aux choux* but is not, the *soupe au farci* made from a cabbage stuffed with sausage meat seasoned with parsley and garlic.

Another typically Auvergne dish is *tripoux*, for which Saint-Flour, closely followed by Aurillac and Chaudesaigues, is particularly celebrated; these are stuffed sheep's feet. Such prepared meat dishes partake of the nature of *charcuterie*, of which the region affords many other notable examples. *Fricandeau*, which elsewhere usually refers to a slice of veal, here is a sort of pork *pâté* cooked in a casing made from the lining of a sheep's stomach. The *friands de Saint-Flour*, little sausage-meat *pâtés* wrapped in leaves, resemble the similar concoction of the Paris region. Clermont-Ferrand is also noted for various types of *pâtés*. Related to these prepared meat dishes, as it may be eaten cold as well as hot, is the regional *tourte à la viande:* chopped pork and veal cooked in a pastry shell.

The Auvergnats do rather elaborate things with eggs. *Œufs à l'auvergnate* are poached and served on a base of cabbage cooked in lard and fried sausage. Then there is an omelette including diced potatoes and bits of lean pork, to which heavy cream and grated cheese are added just before the eggs are turned over.

Coq au vin is much appreciated in the Auvergne—there is an inn on the very top of the Puy-de-Dôme which makes a specialty of it. Leg of lamb with bits of garlic slipped under the skin is braised in white wine with aromatic herbs and served with red beans and tiny onions, or sometimes with braised cabbage. Though the Auvergne is not as good game country as the Sologne, Brioude has its own special fashion of cooking *grives*. As for fish, the trout from the mountain streams in the regions of Massiac, Aurillac, Marsenac, and Murols have so delicate a flavor that they are usually cooked in the simplest possible fashion, boiled or fried in butter, so that no elaborate accompaniment will destroy the subtle taste of the fish. The salmon of the Allier, of which Brioude makes a specialty, compare in quality with those of the Loire. There are also fresh-water eels, which Ussel puts up in jelly.

Like some other mountainous regions, the Auvergne does a great deal with the potato. *Truffado* is the most typical potato dish of the Auvergne, but there are differences of opinion about how to prepare it. In the Aurillac region, the potatoes are mashed and mixed with fresh cheese. In some other regions potatoes fried with lard and perhaps seasoned with garlic have little cubes of fresh cheese added to them at the last moment. There are other variations, both within the Auvergne and in surrounding provinces, where the basic potato-fresh-cheese combination may turn up under the name of *aligot*, *alicot*, or *aligout*, depending on the regional dialect. At Mont Dore, grated cheese is beaten into liquid mashed potatoes, more grated cheese is sprinkled over the top, and the whole is then covered with melted butter and browned in the oven. The Saint-Flour method of cooking potatoes is to cover the bottom of a cooking dish with a layer of green cabbage previously braised in lard, upon which the potatoes, sliced, are laid, interspersed with cubes of lean pork, seasoned with salt and pepper, dampened with consommé in which a little garlic has been crushed, and covered with grated cheese. The dish is baked in a slow oven. The combination of potatoes and cabbages

appears again in the Cantal Mountains, where mashed potatoes are combined with two thirds of their weight of braised
chopped cabbage, put in a pan and sprinkled with grated
cheese, and browned in an oven. Finally, *pommes de terre
au lard* is found throughout the Auvergne. The dish begins
when diced bacon is browned in lard, together with a few
small onions. The bacon and onions are then removed, and
flour and bouillon added to the remaining liquid, followed
by a small bunch of herbs. This is allowed to boil, and then
the bacon and onions are returned to it, along with potatoes
cut into quarters, and the cooking finished slowly in a covered pot. Chopped parsley is sprinkled over the potatoes
just before serving.

Lentils are much eaten in the Auvergne. Besides the familiar brown dried lentils, Le Puy has a specialty of fresh
green ones. The best peas of the region come from La
Planèze. Mushrooms, especially *morilles*, grow wild in the
woods.

There are many types of pastry in this region, some peculiar to it, others more general. The dry *fouasse* that turns
up in the Cantal region we have met before, and the cream
tarts of Vic-sur-Cère are like similar pastries elsewhere. The
cornets of Murat, cones filled with heavy cream, are a little
more distinctive. Quite local are the *bourriolles* of Aurillac,
heavy sweet pancakes made from buckwheat flour—which
is also used in the *picoussel* of Mur de Barrez, whose filling
of plums seems normal enough, but accords rather oddly
with a seasoning of assorted herbs. Clermont-Ferrand, which
also makes fine fruit preserves, has a number of pastry
specialties—the *angelique*, the *flagnarde*, and the *milliard*,
which is a cherry tart—and be careful when you bite into
it, for the pits are left in. Other pastry specialties: of Thiers,
croustilles; of Riom, the *échaudé;* of Saint-Flour, *bêtises*
and *farces* (literally, stupidities and jokes).

Finally, pasturage country should be good cheese country, and the Auvergne is. Cantal is probably the best known. It is a hard cow's milk cheese, made in very large sizes (110 pounds ordinarily), best between November and May. It is sometimes sold as Fourme de Salers (*fourme* is the same word as the English "form" and refers to the mold in which the cheese is shaped—hence the common word for cheese in French, *fromage*, and for that matter in Italian, *formaggio*). The best Cantal is probably that from Laguiole.

There are a number of "blue" cheeses—cousins of Roquefort, though made of cow's milk, not sheep's milk. Bleu d'Auvergne is the general name, which again may be met as Bleu de Salers, another November-to-May cheese. There is also a Bleu d'Auvergne from the Mont Dore region. Fourme d'Ambert is a blue cheese, too, quite sharp in taste. Saint-Nectaire, small, round, and rather soft, is best from October to July. It comes from the Limagne region, which also produces Murols, Gaperon, and Fourme de Montbrison. Riom produces a cream cheese. Cabecou is goat cheese.

The Auvergne has its local wines, though none of any great importance, so that they are not met outside of the region. Oddly enough, if Auvergne wines do not get around, an Auvergne wine grape does. The *auvernat*, a type of grape grown about Orléans, originally came from the Auvergne. It was popular as far back as Louis XIV's time because it produced a strongly colored liquid. Wine merchants used to mix it with paler products in order to pass the wine off as coming from richer grapes.

The best wine in the Auvergne is grown in the Limagne region, and the red Chanturgue is probably its best representative. You may also be offered Chateaugay, reminiscent of Beaujolais, or Corent. There is a vintage called Fel in the south of the Auvergne, in the Entraygues region. But if you want to be a real Auvergnat, perhaps here you should drink *gaspo*, a favored beverage in this dairy country. *Gaspo* is buttermilk.

The dominant fat employed in the cooking of the Auvergne, the higher, and eastern, sector of the Central Plateau, is, as the inventory of Auvergne dishes above makes plain, that of the pig. In the lower, and western, sector the dominant fat is that of the goose, especially in the Périgord, which has a nation-wide reputation as a region of good cooking. The Marche differs so little from the Limousin that the two may be considered as a single region so far as eating habits are concerned. The Périgord is more distinctive, and its influence reaches southward into the eastern part of Guienne (with the exception of its easternmost tip, which pushes into the mountains south of the Auvergne, the Rouergue).

The rural nature of the Marche is easily demonstrated: its chief city, Guéret, ancient capital of the province, has only ten thousand inhabitants; its best-known town, Aubusson of the tapestries, has six thousand. It is therefore a producer of the raw materials—grain, fruit, nuts, eggs, cattle, mushrooms, game—which the somewhat more sophisticated Limousin, though also primarily agricultural country, has used to compose the dishes common to both. Of the two departments of the Limousin, the Corrèze, which plunges deeper into the hills than the Haute-Vienne, seems to be gastronomically superior. A little Corrèze *bistrot* near the Central Markets in Paris is frequented by the market workers, who know good food; one would never suspect from its appearance that it is a shrine of good eating. The customers look like workmen, the setting is of the humblest, and it appears to be inspired by only one idea—cheapness. It is cheap, but that it has other aspirations became evident to me when I started lunch there with a small individual cubical *pâté*. The delicately flavored meats that went into the *pâté* were sufficient reason in themselves for enthusiasm, but embedded in their center was a whole *grive*. There is no point in giving you the address of the place. It is tiny and always jammed with its regular customers, and if I was able to eat a meal there myself, that was only because I went with a native of the Corrèze who was a friend of the proprietor—with whom I had to stand behind the bar waiting for a table, the *bistrot* being so jammed that there was no other place to wait. The same friend brought back for me from the Corrèze a pot of some local confection of pork which so far as I know is anonymous, but was a miracle of subtlety applied to a not very subtle ingredient. These two experiences alone would be enough to cause me to hold the Corrèze, and the Limousin, in deep respect.

Pork is of considerable importance in the Limousin (the goose enters the picture in the southwestern corner of the region, against the border of the Périgord, the real kingdom of the goose). Fine pigs are raised here, as well as in the Marche, each of which has a special variety of the Celtic race named for its province. *Carré de porc à la limousine* is a favorite way of serving a roast of pork in this country. What it means is that the pork is accompanied by red cabbage braised with chestnuts. Any dish described as *à la limousine* is likely to be embellished by red cabbage prepared in this fashion.

The Limousin is even more important as a beef-producer than a pork-producer. The fine steers of the region are the product of a cross between a native animal and the English Durham breed, great beef cattle.

Probably the most famous single dish having its origin in the Limousin is *lièvre à la royale*, which might be translated as "hare fit for a king." Some cookbooks call it *lièvre à la périgourdine*, thus making a present to a more famous gastronomic region of a creation that nevertheless seems certainly to have come first from the Limousin. *Lièvre farci en cabessal* (or *chabessal*) is also often attributed to the Périgord, but is actually a Limousin dish. It seems an unnecessary transfer of credit, as the Périgord is rich enough in its own right—even in its own private treatment of the hare.

Lièvre à la royale, an old dish, was so popular in the eighteenth century that specially shaped earthenware cooking dishes were made for no other purpose than to prepare it. Its chief distinction was its stuffing, into which went the liver, heart, and lungs of the hare, hashed up together; cooked goose *foie gras;* fat pork; bread crumbs soaked in bouillon; chopped onions previously cooked in butter; chopped truffles and parsley; a little garlic; and the hare's blood. This was cooked slowly in an earthenware dish in white wine, to which at the end was added a sauce made of bouillon derived from various sorts of game, a little Armagnac, and slices of truffles.

Lièvre farci en cabessal also depends for its special flavor largely on its stuffing, in this case a strongly spiced combination of round of veal, fresh pork, and ham, with plenty of shallots and garlic, while the sauce poured on it afterward uses the animal's blood and its liver, which is mashed into garlic and a little vinegar. Tradition requires that it be cooked in red wine in a round dish, so it is tied into a circle, which, in the imagination of those who named it, makes it resemble the circular cloth cushion the women of the region put on their heads as a support for the buckets of water they carry from the wells in this fashion—the *cabessal.*

Other dishes associated especially with the Limousin tend to belong to the rather coarse type typical of mountain regions—the soups especially. Among these are a soup of boiled oats, rather like thin oatmeal; a soup made from rye bread; cabbage soup; and a complication of the latter known as *bréjauda,* in which bacon is added to the cabbage. The Limousins, like the Bordelais, *faire chabrot* with their soups, especially the last-named—that is, they pour a little red wine into the last few spoonfuls of the soup and drink the resulting mixture.

Farcidure is particularly characteristic—a little ball of cabbage leaves, enclosing a stuffing of buckwheat flour, sorrel, and beets; sometimes they are put in cabbage soup to enrich it. Meat *pâtés* of mixed sausage-meat and veal are known as *broccana.* The type of succulent mushroom called *cèpes* is particularly good in the Limousin, and there is a special way of preparing them in the Corrèze, *cèpes farcis à la corrézienne.*

There is quite an assortment of cheeses: Guéret, from the Marche, also called Creusois, best from October to June; the Trappist cheese from Echourgnac, something like Port Salut, good all year round; and the blue cheese of Bassilac, best from November to May.

The *clafoutis,* or unpitted cherry tart, which we have already met in the Auvergne as the *milliard,* is probably the most widely spread pastry specialty of the region, and there are in addition a number of local specialties. Marzipan (*massepain*) is at its best in Saint-Léonard; the spongecake-like *madeleines* are found in Saint-Yrieix; Dorat specializes in macaroons; Uzerches makes meringues; and the southeastern corner of the province is best for little cakes made out of chestnuts. Pancake-like *flognards* and *tourtons,* the latter made out of buckwheat flour, may be found almost anywhere. So may a form of cheesecake.

The Limousin offers little in the way of wine. There are some vineyards in the valley of the Vienne, which produce "gray wines"—Chabanais, Etagnat, Saint-Brice, Aise—and one of them, Verneuil, makes a genuine *rosé* that is quite pleasant, but none of these get outside of the region. In the

Corrèze, Beaulieu produces a sweet, white dessert wine, a rather pale imitation of the *vin de paille* of the Jura.

Just west of the Limousin lies the Périgord, a subprovince of Guienne, where gastronomic greatness bursts forth —not suddenly, for there is excellent solid eating in the Limousin to the east and refined sophisticated eating in the Bordeaux region to the southwest. The meeting and combining of these two influences—the sound hearty peasant cooking of the Massif Central and the rich cuisine of the highly urbanized Bordeaux region—probably accounts for the pre-eminence of Périgord, a name synonymous throughout France with fine food. (The lowlands of the Franche-Comté, meeting point for the mountain fare of the Jura and the rich cheer of Burgundy, provides an analogous case.) The Périgord also has the advantage of long practice. Men have been preparing food here for longer than anywhere else in France, for this is the country of prehistoric man. Add to all this the excellence of the products of the soil, and the good food of the Périgord is amply accounted for. Perhaps a further reason can be found in the fact that of the two items of food most inseparably identified with the Périgord—the goose and the truffle—the second is not particularly exciting in itself, but has the gift of enhancing the taste of other edibles with which it is combined. It is therefore a spur to the ingenuity of cooks, and a constant reminder that in cooking the whole may be greater than the sum of its parts. The truffle must be considered the dominant partner in the pair of Périgourdine specialties. When you order a dish identified on the menu as *à la péri-gourdine*, it may or may not contain *pâté de foie gras*, but it will almost certainly contain truffles.

The truffle is an underground mushroom, and by common consent the best truffles are the black ones found in the Périgord and the department of the Lot just south of it, which is a part of the Guienne most of which belongs to another subprovince, the Quercy. The truffle crop of this region does not suffice to supply the French demand, which therefore has to put up with black truffles from other parts of the country or even with the white variety that comes from Piedmont in Italy and is imported into France in considerable quantities. Where truffles are artificially grown, they can be gathered by hand because the man who has started their spores knows where they are. But for discovering the hiding places of the wild variety, no more efficient way of gathering them has been found than to let pigs root them up, after which a short, sharp altercation with the pig is necessary to secure possession of the truffle. It is therefore not surprising to learn that the Périgord has its own local variation of the Celtic porker; but in spite of the merits of Périgord pigs, the dominant cooking fat is provided by the goose. This is first of all goose country.

On those rare occasions when truffles are served relatively alone, their own taste can be detected as a rather faint licorice flavor, which is usually completely submerged in whatever other dainties it may be accompanying. A dish in which it is possible to taste this original truffle flavor is *truffes sous les cendres* (truffles under the ashes), in which large truffles are seasoned and spiced, each one sprinkled with Cognac, wrapped in a thin slice of salt pork and then in heavy fire-resistant paper, and tucked under the ashes and glowing embers of an open hearth. This is the original way of preparing the dish as it is still made in the Périgord; but thousands of Americans have probably seen a more sophisticated version of it in the television short on eating in Paris made by the Vavin television film organization for the French Tourist Office, in which the truffle was placed on a slice of *foie gras* and folded into a square of dough so that it looked like a piece of ravioli before it was put in the ashes. I may go on record as not being unaware of this version of the dish. Indeed the portly white-haired scarlet-faced diner (if your television set receives color) who eats the truffle in this film is myself.

It is a reasonable guess that almost any dish in which truffles play an important part originated either in the Périgord or not very far from there, but one or two specifically carry the name of the region on menus everywhere. *Tourte de truffes à la périgourdine* you are not very likely to find in other regions. This is a pie whose filling is composed of truffles and *foie gras* doused in Cognac. It is served hot, but whatever is left over is just as good cold. *Truffes en pâté à la périgourdine* comes pretty close to being the same thing in mouthful-sized pieces—each individual truffle, enveloped in a slice of *foie gras* (no Cognac), is wrapped in a ball of dough and baked for about twenty minutes. Truffles are used of course in stuffing for poultry, particularly capons and turkeys, and appear in many types of prepared meats, such as galantines or in *foie gras*. When they cannot be inserted into a dish in any other fashion, *sauce Périgueux* may be added to it; this contains both essence of truffles and small bits of truffle as well—for instance, *œufs en cocotte à la périgourdine*, after the eggs have been broken over a layer of *foie gras* and cooked in a casserole, are served with Périgueux sauce. This subterfuge for slipping the truffles into the dish at the last moment is not employed in the truffle omelette, into which they enter boldly in their own right, or even in *œufs brouillés à la périgourdine*, scrambled eggs, Périgord style, in which chopped up truffles and *foie gras*, separately cooked first in sauce, are added to the eggs when they are nearly cooked, and the whole is served together with slices of *foie gras* and truffles, which have also been cooked separately in butter. (You may meet this dish without the sauce, which is a form of *saupiquet*, a term already discussed above, under the name of *œufs brouillés Rossini*, in other parts of the

country, but it is safe to attribute its origin to the Périgord.)

The goose raised in the Périgord is the giant Toulouse
goose, which puts on fat easily and is thus ideal for the
production of the *foie gras*, which, as has already become
apparent above, is prominent in the Périgord diet. The
goose as a whole has here become almost a by-product of
its liver. Roast goose is not a Périgord dish. Goose is in any
case the fattest of all poultry, and the artificial fattening of
these big Toulouse geese for the production of *foie gras*
makes them almost automatically too greasy for roasting
(though the Alsatians roast them). They produce, besides
swollen livers, great layers of rich yellow fat. This goes
into the cooking of the region. The flesh is then used for
various sorts of goose preserves, which are delicious. Nowadays these goose preparations (*confit d'oie*) are often
canned, but the old-fashioned presentation, in an earthenware container, with a layer of the bird's fat serving as a
seal to preserve it (it will keep for about a year in this sort
of packing) is rather more inviting. As this prepared goose
has already been cooked, it may be eaten cold, but any
number of recipes calls for a second cooking, with more or
less complicated accompaniments.

An attempt to make a complete list of Périgord specialties would be impractical; there are too many of them.
Here, however, are some of the more important ones.
Among soups, there is *bougras*, sometimes listed more pro-
saically as *soupe à l'eau de boudin*, or soup made from
blood-pudding water—which is what it starts with—
though there's a great deal more to it than that. If you
want to taste this soup, you will probably have to visit the
Périgord at Carnival time—that is, just before Lent—for
that is hog-slaughtering season in this region, and that is
when the blood puddings that provide the dish are made.
The water in which the blood puddings have been cooked

is kept, and to it are added hearts of green cabbage, carrots, turnips, leeks, celery, and quartered onions. This is simmered slowly for a little under half an hour, and then thick slices of potato are added, and the simmering continues for a little over half an hour more. About fifteen minutes before the soup is done, some of the vegetables are removed from the liquid, cut into thin slices browned in goose fat, and then powdered with flour and moistened with bouillon from the soup, after which they are popped back into it for the last few minutes of its cooking. This is what the Périgord calls a *fricassée*, as we saw in the section on the Anjou. When the soup is served, it is poured over thin slices of the round French bread placed in the bottom of the soup plates.

Tourain périgourdin is an onion soup containing tomatoes and egg yolks as well. It sometimes becomes a *gratinée* by the addition of grated cheese. *Sobronade* is called a soup, but it's really a whole meal—which is in accord with the peasant habit of living largely from a soup so richly charged with meat and vegetables that it provides all the ingredients of a complete repast in a single course. *Sobronade* includes fresh pork, ham, white beans, turnips, carrots, celery, and onions, and is seasoned with salt, pepper, parsley, garlic, cloves, and a bunch of assorted herbs.

The Périgord gives elaborate treatment to the fish of its rivers and ponds, and Neuvic has developed a variety of stuffed carp in which the flavor of the fish itself is pretty much overwhelmed by its stuffing—*foie gras* and preserved goose. Eggs *à la périgourdine* are stuffed with *foie gras*, too. Some *foie gras* goes into *cou farci*, stuffed goose neck, also, but most of the stuffing is chopped pork, with some bits of truffle added. It is usually, but not always, eaten cold, as an hors d'œuvre or a between-meals snack. In the Périgord, potato croquettes turn up with chopped truffles mixed with the potato.

Poultry appears here in a variety of preparations. *Poularde à la périgourdine* is stuffed, as you might expect, with *foie gras* and truffles, doused in Cognac; after it comes out of the oven, its cooking juices, strengthened with Madeira wine, are used to make the gravy. *Poularde truffée à la périgourdine* takes several days to make, for the stuffed chicken is left for that length of time in an earthenware dish covered with truffle peelings to allow their flavor to permeate the meat. The peelings come from truffles used to make the stuffing, after they have been cooked in chicken or goose fat and bacon along with a variety of spices, laurel, thyme, and grated nutmeg. *Poulet sauté à la Périgord* is young chicken cut up and fried with sliced truffles.

Filet de bœuf à la périgourdine is prepared by inserting small bits of truffle in slits cut in a roast of beef, which is braised in Madeira sauce, and when served is surrounded with slices of *foie gras* fried in butter and little tarts filled with truffles in sauce. In *tournedos à la périgourdine*, this choice round morsel from the center of the filet of beef, cooked in a frying pan, is presented on a little raft of toast, crowned with slices of truffles cooked in butter, with Madeira sauce.

Besides the two dishes made from hare which the Périgord has borrowed from the Limousin, already described above, the region has many ways of its own of treating this animal. *Ballottine de lièvre à la périgourdine* (a *ballottine* is a rolled preparation of boned meat) combines the hare with a stuffing itself made from rabbit, along with truffles and *foie gras* soaked in Cognac, the whole cooked in a rich sauce. It is served hot, though *ballottines* are sometimes presented cold. There is what is essentially a *ballottine* served cold in the Périgord repertoire, though it is called *lièvre étoffé à la périgourdine*, an extremely elaborate confection in which minute separate attention has to be given to the preparation of at least four elements in the completed dish—the hare itself, which is boned, formed into a *ballottine* and eventually, after its cooking, pressed; its stuffing, which is made of its own leg meat, veal, fresh pork, its heart, liver, kidneys, and blood, eggs, Cognac, bacon, *foie gras*, and truffles; the sauce in which it is cooked, which is made from a bouillon obtained by boiling the bones along with a calf's foot, some veal, and pig crackling; and the Madeira jelly made from game juices with which the whole is surrounded after the hare has been pressed and has cooled off. This is cooking in the grand style, a sample of how the Périgord has erected a sophisticated cuisine on the basis of its peasant foundation.

Space will not permit describing other Périgord dishes in detail, though there is no lack of them: stuffed cabbage; veal cooked in a casserole with stuffed *cèpes* (mushrooms); squab with asparagus; *tourtière*—chicken pie cooked in salsify sauce; *cèpes à la périgourdine*—mushrooms cooked with diced bacon, parsley, and garlic in grape juice. The pastries include all the varieties found in the Limousin (and in the Sarladais, to which we are just coming) plus a few others, such as waffles.

The Sarladais, a little triangle of land between the Vézère and the Dordogne in the southeast corner of the Périgord, clustered about the town of Sarlat, which shares with Périgueux, capital of the Périgord, the honor of providing the best food in the territory, offers you the option of considering it as a separate subprovince of the Guienne or as a sub-subprovince of the Périgord, but as it is sometimes called also the Black Périgord, it may as well be ascribed to this region, whose cooking it duplicates, but with the addition of certain specialties of its own. There is for instance a particular way of presenting preserved goose known as *confit d'oie à la sarladaise* which combines it with sliced potatoes and truffles fried in goose fat. This combination seems to be a Sarladais favorite, for *pommes de terre à la sarladaise* is a casserole dish in which alternate layers of sliced potatoes and truffles are cooked together. Corn flour is popular in this region. *Mique sarladaise* is a round ball of corn- and wheat-flour dough mixed, with a dash of pork fat, served instead of bread with dishes like *civet*, not only here but also in the rest of the Périgord. *Milles* (in the rest of the Périgord usually called *milliessou*) is a corn-flour pastry developed in the Sarladais, which probably picked it up from Languedoc, while *cajasse* is also Sarladais pastry. *Roussette*s are corn fritters.

The best known wine of the Périgord region is over toward the Bordeaux region, and is often discussed together with the Bordeaux wines—Monbazillac, a sweet, white liqueur type of wine whose history goes back for many centuries. It has spread far beyond the provincial borders, and for that matter beyond the national ones as well, being particularly popular in Holland for a historical rather than a gastronomic reason—at the time of the Edict of Nantes, a large number of Huguenots from the region of Bergerac, near which Monbazillac is grown, emigrated to Holland to escape persecution. They refused to be separated from their native wine, which has been imported into Holland by the descendants of the exiled French Huguenots ever since. Less well known is another sweet, white wine, Montravel, while you are unlikely to find the nevertheless very drinkable Rosette and Pécharmant reds off their native heath.

South of the Périgord we are in the eastern half of Guienne, whose Western section belongs gastronomically to the Bordeaux region—more specifically, in that part of Guienne known as the Quercy, roughly equivalent to the modern department of the Lot. The influence of Périgord cooking remains strong here, helped by the fact that this region shares with the Périgord the distinction of producing the best truffles in France and is also goose country.

Quercy has, however, many specialties of its own. There is, for instance, crayfish stew. *Fricassée de cèpes à la quercynoise* is another local specialty. There may be some question as to whether or not to award to Quercy the credit for *œufs à l'agenaise*, as Agen, already cited in the Bordeaux chapter for its plums, is in the Lot-et-Garonne, perhaps not quite in the Quercy proper; but the goose fat that enters into this way of cooking fried eggs is typical enough of the Quercy cuisine. Not only are the eggs fried in goose fat, along with a little chopped onion and (added at the last moment) garlic and parsley, but they are also served with diced eggplant fried in goose fat. *Boudin blanc quercynois* is a fat soft white sausage. In the region of Cahors, capital of the province, tripe cooked with saffron is a favorite dish. The Quercy does a number of interesting things to poultry —*poule au pot farcie à la quercynoise* is stuffed boiled fowl, while *pintade rôtie, flambée et bardée de truffes de Gourdon* is roast guinea hen stuffed with what are considered the finest truffles of the Quercy and brought to the table in flaming brandy sauce.

Finally, the best-known cheese of Quercy is Rocamadour, best from November to May, made in the pilgrimage city on whose abrupt rock stands a chapel reputed to have been founded by Saint Amadour—another name for the Zachary who at Jericho, according to the New Testament, climbed a tree in order to see Christ pass.

There is some excellent wine in Quercy, and the only reason one can think of for its not being better known is that it has become overshadowed by the greater wines of the nearby Bordeaux area. As a result, the area in which the wines of the Lot valley, in the Cahors region, are grown has decreased, and fruit orchards have taken over from the vineyards. Nevertheless, the reputation of Cahors vintages is an old one. The vines, brought in from Italy, are of the Aminea variety, which both Virgil and Pliny celebrated. The fame of the wine extended so far that Peter the Great of Russia imported it for his cellars. Nowadays you are not likely to find it far from where it is grown. But if you have the luck to fall upon a bottle of Vieux Cahors red wine, you will find it an admirable accompaniment for, say, the *confit d'oie* of the region.

If you look at a map of the old French provinces, you will see that the eastern extremity of Guienne is shaped something like an animal's head seemingly in perpetual danger of breaking off at the neck. Even from the evidence of the map one would suspect that this oddly shaped appendage is not a natural part of the Guienne; the irregular tracing of the frontier betrays the presence of topographical obstacles. This is the Rouergue, today the department of the Aveyron, indeed a distinct entity so conscious of its individuality that it has recently opened headquarters in Paris to promote the interests of the region, a sort of embassy of the Rouergue to the capital.

The irregular outline of the territory results from the rugged nature of the mountains into which it pushes its way, and it is therefore natural that its cooking resembles more that of the mountainous Auvergne to the north than that of the Guienne to which it has always been politically attached, whose cooking, apart from the exceptions just noticed in the Périgord and Quercy regions, has been that of lowland country, drawing its inspiration from Bordeaux. The most characteristic dish of the Rouergue is *aligout*, already met in the Auvergne with a slightly different spelling—mashed potatoes made with plenty of cream and butter, covered with morsels of local cheese, and cooked in a slow oven. But the most famous food product of the Rouergue is renowned all over the world. Its name is familiar where the name of the province that produces it has never been heard. It is Roquefort cheese.

Roquefort-sur-Soulzon is located in a region of wild and eroded rocks, in which numerous caves have formed, whose air is constantly swept by steady drafts. The caves and the winds that inhabit them hold the secret of the quality of Roquefort cheese. Damp and cold, the drafts favor the development of the fungus added to the cheese as it begins to form, the *pencillium Roqueforti*, whose presence is visible in the green streaks characteristic of this cheese.

That it is actually exposure in these caves which makes Roquefort Roquefort is demonstrated by the fact that at the beginning most of this cheese does not come from Roquefort at all; but it all ends up here, emerging as a remarkably uniform product after ripening in the Roquefort caves. You would have to know only one figure to realize that this small town (population under fifteen hundred inhabitants) could not possibly produce enough milk to make all the genuine Roquefort that eventually comes from here—the present production of this cheese amounts to about twenty-five million pounds a year. Actually the milk is gathered from a wide area reaching well into the Auvergne in the north and throughout the eastern Pyrenees to the south, and it is started on its way to becoming Roquefort on its home grounds, where the first processes that turn the milk into cheese are carried out, the fungus is added, and it is allowed to work for a week or so before the cheeses are taken to the Roquefort caves for aging. Here they are laid out on the floors of the caves in tightly packed rows, thousands and thousands of the great round cakes (it is an impressive array of cheeses, which the public is permitted to inspect). They are brushed and little holes

are made in them to permit the action of the air to penetrate the cheese. Salt rubbed into their surfaces is gradually
absorbed.

Roquefort has another peculiarity besides the aging process in the town's caves; almost alone of modern cheeses,
it is made of sheep's milk. There are a number of French
cheeses which formerly used sheep's milk, but most of them
have shifted to cow's milk in these hurried times, for
reasons which will be clear to anyone who has ever tried
to milk a ewe.

The Roquefort season is from March to September, but
as it keeps well, it does not fall off too badly during the
other months. If you want to choose a good one, look for a
gray crust and a center that is becoming yellowish, looks
a trifle greasy, and is regularly veined with green (or blue,
as many eyes seem to see it). It is normal for Roquefort
to become yellowish as it ripens; a chalky-white cheese
has not matured completely. Roquefort cheese is often put
on sale after thirty or forty days in the caves, but its taste
after so short a period is bland. Roquefort connoisseurs
like a bite in their cheese, and it takes about a year of aging
to produce a really authentic sharpness.

Among the dishes of the Rouergue is one whose name
is easy to confuse with *aligout*—*alicot*, which is a stew
made from the leftovers of goose or duck, simmered slowly
and lengthily, and served with *cèpes* and roasted chestnuts.
(Just to make the confusion complete, there is also a local
cheese called *aligot* and the stew is sometimes spelled *alicuit*.)
Another famous Rouergue dish is *mourtairol*, boiled fowl
with saffron.

On the chalk plateaus of the Causses, thyme and juniper
grow wild. The game birds that feed on them develop
a delicious flavor. Hence partridge is a famous dish of the
Rouergue, and so are *grives*, which are caught in special
traps called *tindelles*. Fine crayfish, trout, and eels are

found in the streams. *Farçon de l'Aveyron* is a special piquant preparation of sausage meat. *Cabassoles* is a dish found in the extreme southeast corner of the Rouergue, the Larzac region, where lambs are raised. It utilizes parts of the animals not always sent to market when the lambs are dressed—the heads, feet, and tripe, which are boiled with ham, veal knuckle, and vegetables, producing a result that makes it appear that the finicky urban purchasers of the rest of the beast have missed something. Finally we might note that Entraygues is noted for the quality of its peas, that the sugared *fouasses* of Millau have been the favorite pastry of the region since the fifteenth century, and that the Le Rozier district produces a pleasant easily drinkable red wine, called Gamay after the Burgundy grape from which it is made.

Sweeping in an arc upward from southwest to northeast, the Cévennes Mountains draw a natural line along the bottom of the region we have just been considering. In looking at them here, we are committing the greatest violation of political boundaries so far, for the Cévennes are entirely within the province of Languedoc. But this is still mountainous country, with a cuisine more closely approaching that of the Massif Central to the north than that of the rest of Languedoc south of this region, an area with a quite distinctive school of cooking of its own, some of whose elements have, however, penetrated into the Central Plateau section and have already received some attention. We have already violated Languedoc by discussing the Velay region about Le Puy with the Auvergne, where gastronomically it belongs, so we might as well repeat the offense for the Cévennes.

The Cévennes belong certainly to the world of the Central Plateau by the nature of their food resources— above all, the great flocks of sheep which graze on the high plateaus, the game birds and the fish of the mountain streams—while the lower land to the east, between the mountains and the Rhone, or to the south, between the mountains and the sea, provides different foods from its fertile fields covered with vines and orchards, devoted more to domesticated poultry than to wild birds. The Cévennes is great chestnut country, and this nut turns up in a number of dishes—entering into many of the sausages and other prepared pork products, for instance. Chestnuts are often made into a purée, like mashed potatoes. The tasty *grives* of the area are sometimes served with a salad composed of potatoes, celery, and chestnuts.

The standard dish of the Cévennes peasant is *oulade*, a cabbage-and-potato soup to which is added a chunk of salt pork, and sometimes sausage. Another favorite soup here is *aïgo bouïllido*, garlic soup, probably a borrowing from Provence, where we shall meet it under a slight variation of the name. The Cévennes approaches Provence not only in a liberal use of garlic, which is not unknown to the west and south either, but also in employing a considerable amount of olive oil in its cooking. The dominant cooking fat, however, remains that of the pig, as in the Auvergne.

Alés, a silkworm-raising community on the eastern slopes of the Cévennes on the way into lower Languedoc, has a tripe specialty, *gras double*—heavy beef tripe, cooked with carrots, celery, tomatoes, thyme, and laurel. And special mention should be made of Sainte-Enimie, one of the few places in this area to grow grapes, if only in tribute to its industry: the earth on the terraced hillsides on which not only grapes, but also almonds and cherries, grow had to be carried up there sack by sack.

Languedoc

Languedoc, as everyone knows, took its name from the tongue spoken on its territory, the *langue d'oc*, or the language in which "yes" is *oc*, as opposed to the *langue d'oïl*, the language in which "yes" is *oui*. Few literate persons are ignorant of this fact, but not so many of them know that Dante first made this distinction, and that in classifying the tongues descended from Latin he includes a third category, which might be Frenchified, to get it into tune with the other two descriptions, as the *langue de si*, the language in which "yes" is *si*. It is not considered a particularly valid distinction by modern philologists—for instance, it makes no distinction between Italian and Spanish, in both of which "yes" is *si*, but then Dante was under the impression that Spaniards said *oc*. The *langue d'oc* is, ignoring the tremendous variety of local variations, Provençal, still widely spoken today, which took its name from Provence, on the other side of the Rhone from Languedoc —for no particular reason, since the tongue was spoken, and still is, all the way from the Alps to the Atlantic south of a line drawn roughly across the country from Bordeaux. If you consider France as she is today, you will find it normal enough that it was the *langue d'oïl* that triumphed over the *langue d'oc* and became French, rather than the other way around, for the north seems clearly dominant over the south, especially if you deprive the latter of the Rhone valley, which as a great highway of travel is not really representative of the hinterland to which geographically it seems to belong. Practically all of the heavy industry of France is in the north; the great cities, beginning with Bordeaux, are mostly in that region also (the most conspicuous exception is Marseilles, which, as the chief Mediterranean port, is like the Rhone valley attributable to a wider frame of reference than the local one); the most noted monuments—cathedrals, châteaux—are in the north; and Languedoc in particular seems somewhat of a backwater. Tourists do not get to it much. They may slip barely into its westernmost reaches to visit the fortress of Carcassonne; they may penetrate its southeastern corner to look at the massive walls of Aiguesmortes, from which Saint Louis sailed in 1248 with a fleet of thirty-eight ships full of crusaders; or they may pass the eastern border by visiting Nîmes—perhaps without even knowing they are in Languedoc, for Nîmes is usually approached from the much frequented Rhone valley and if the tourist thinks about it at all, he may consider it part of Provence. What seems more characteristic of Languedoc than these comparatively frequented localities are such isolated and little visited regions as the mountains of the Cévennes and the plateaux of the Causses above them, which we have already visited; the *garrigues*, lying just below the Cévennes, which we shall come to shortly; and the country of salt-water lagoons lying just behind the seacoast of the low-lying Sète-Montpellier region.

But at the time when the northern and southern languages were still equal contenders for supremacy, the dominance of the north over the south was much less marked. It is true that many of the local lords of southern France presented a rather rustic character in comparison with the brilliant sovereigns of the Ile-de-France-Loire valley region, or even with the dukes of Burgundy, yet this was no inviolable rule. The counts of Toulouse, for example, a family which in recent times has presented France with one of its great modern artists in Toulouse-Lautrec, were not exactly bumpkins. The triumph of the *langue d' oïl* over the *langue d'oc* was owing to the fact that the former became a written language, the literary language of its region, and the latter did not. One reason for this was probably the greater uniformity in the spoken language of the north, resulting from greater ease of movement over its more open country. If you looked at a map of the old provinces of France, you might expect the opposite. The southern provinces—Gascony, Languedoc, Provence—are in general larger than the northern provinces—Ile-de-France, Touraine, Anjou—but in the north the cultural units were larger than the political units, while in the south they were smaller. The courts of the north moved freely between Paris and Tours, or even Bordeaux, and spread the language they spoke over the whole area; and the Burgundians, acquiring realms on either side of the French possessions, and dealing constantly with the French, though seldom amicably, came to talk like them as well. Meanwhile in the south each little lorddom maintained its own version of the *langue d'oc*, and as the lords got around less through the difficult and often desolate, largely mountainous (or, in the south, swampy) areas of that part of the country, uniformity of the language was not achieved.

But a more important reason for the failure of the *langue d'oc* to become a language of literature is probably the paradoxical one that the south of France had become imbued with the Mediterranean civilization earlier than the north. The phenomenon was the same as that which modern times noted with the spread of electrification—on the arrival of electricity, the more backward regions tended to embrace the new form of energy more quickly. Where gas had not yet been introduced, electricity found no competition and there were no expensive installations to be replaced. Technical advance is thus a game of leapfrog in which any revolutionary change tends to make its full force felt first where there is a vacuum to be filled. Cultural changes proceed similarly. Southern France had made Latin its literary language early. It was firmly rooted and hard to dislodge when the spoken tongues resulting from the collision between Latin and the tongues of Gaul began to crystallize sufficiently to be ready to become new languages. Latin was less firmly rooted as a written language in the north. It gave way more readily to the popular speech. And as this became a written language, and exchanges between the north and the south carried it southward before the *langue d'oc* had been committed to paper, the latter remained a dialect and the former became French.

That part of southern France which still retains the name of its old tongue is ancient territory indeed. Agde, on the curve where the Mediterranean coast swings around from an east-west to a north-south direction, was a port of the Phocæan Greeks, who founded it 2,500 years ago. At Enserune, near Béziers, you can visit the ruins of a Celtic settlement of importance which dates back at least to the sixth century B.C. Narbonne, founded by a decree of the Roman Senate in 118 B.C., was a more important port of the Roman Empire than Marseilles. Nîmes was of course a great city of the Roman Empire, under the name of Nemausus (that of the local demigod of the springs about which the city was founded), and its arms today still bear a chained crocodile in memory of the fact that Octavius Cæsar gave lands about Nîmes to the soldiers who had given him a victory over Antony and Cleopatra on the Nile. The best-preserved Roman amphitheater in the world is that of Nîmes, though it is far from the largest— nineteen bigger ones still exist, including that of nearby Arles, which is a few feet larger and wider.

The decline of Languedoc as an outpost of Western civilization was no doubt due in considerable part to the silting up of the ports that had rendered this country so accessible to the Romans. To reach Agde today, the Phocæans would have to sail up the Herault for two and one half miles. A Roman galley could hardly get to Narbonne now, for it is connected with the coast only by a narrow canal. And if modern crusaders tried to duplicate Saint Louis's departure from Aiguesmortes, they would have to drag their ships six miles overland. Only one port along this coast still operates —but it is an important one, Sète, second to no other French port in the Mediterranean except Marseilles—but it dates as a port only from the seventeenth century and the secret of its victory over the sands that have blocked the natural harbors of the region is that it is itself built on the sand bar that cuts off the lagoon of Thau from the sea.

From the days of its glory, Languedoc retains a great deal that is worth seeing, and its comparative neglect by tourists would be something of a mystery if it were not an observable fact that the tremendous increase of *tourist*s in recent years is not an increase in *travelers*—by which I understand persons possessed of enough curiosity about the unusual to be willing to take a little trouble to get to it. Languedoc is not the country for the tourist who wants to be called for by a chauffeur in a private car (if he is well off) or to pile into a bus equipped with a loudspeaker and a guide obsessed with the idea that it must not be allowed to go unused (if he, or more often she, is not so well off), in order to be transported, hermetically isolated from the possible contagion of the surrounding country, to the noteworthy object and allowed to photograph it during the period allotted to it by a travel agency schedule; who then desires to be fed in a restaurant that can give him the same sort of meal he has eaten in every other restaurant he has ever patronized; and who finally requires some sort of standardized entertainment to banish boredom between dinner and bed. Because Languedoc has not yet been completely regimented, this is country which should be particularly attractive to the traveler who has not yet become resigned to being packaged, as well as to the diner who is not afraid to broaden the scope of his collection of tastes. The genuine traveler is advised to hurry if he wants to see Languedoc in something like its pristine innocence. The better-known tourist meccas can hold only so many persons, so the constant mounting of the tourist horde is forcing the flood into hitherto unexplored territories, preceded by travel agents whose duty it is to explain to local populations that tourists travel hundreds of miles from their own homes because they want to find in distant places replicas as like what they have left as possible.

The blight has already begun to invade Languedoc. I remember, nearly thirty years ago, spending a delightful idle aimless afternoon wandering about the Pont du Gard, that remarkable remnant of a Roman aqueduct, then traversing the trickle of river beneath it in the midst of a wilderness where nothing distracted from the spectacle of the weathered stones marching through the country of which they had become a part. But five years ago, when I went back, there were a modern hotel and a restaurant with large windows which permitted you to sit comfortably behind a table and look at the Pont du Gard as if it were on a television screen without establishing any personal contact with it. Someone had been tidying up the place, too—cutting grass, removing brush, and planting other brush where it would never have occurred to an independent bush to establish residence. I would have felt conspicuous to have wandered about and around the bridge and the Gard aimlessly, as I had done twenty-five years before, especially in my customary shameless state, naked of cameras.

The modern building was a violation of the setting, whose essence had been the absence of modernity. By breaking up the unity of the setting, it detached the Pont du Gard from it, too, and it had ceased to be an outgrowth of the country. It had become an isolated object, which might be viewed quite as profitably in a motion-picture theater. You cannot maintain interest in an isolated object for very long. It has to be related to a larger entity to have real meaning. The traveler visits the object on the spot to see it as part of the whole; the tourist visits it, under conditions which safely protect him from any spontaneity, to detach it from the whole and add it to his private collection of trinkets. Unfortunately the elaborate machinery by which he achieves this desire detaches the objects from their settings for all other viewers, too. If, therefore, you are a traveler rather than a tourist, you are recommended to visit Languedoc, still largely unspoiled, and to do it soon. It cannot possibly last long.

The comparative neglect of Languedoc has deprived foreigners, generally speaking, of acquaintance with one of the most interesting big cities of France, Toulouse, which lies at the western border of this region. With well over a quarter of a million inhabitants, Toulouse is the fifth city of France (after Paris, Marseilles, Lyons, and Bordeaux) or the fourth if you compare the populations of the metropolitan areas without regard for legal city limits, in which case Bordeaux and Toulouse change places. It is older than Rome. It has its own saint, Saint Cernin, martyred by being dragged to death by a bull, and the basilica named for him, the finest Romanesque church in southern France, is also the richest in relics, as they represent 128 saints, 6 of them apostles. Toulouse also possesses the finest Gothic church—a style not often found in the south—of this half of France, the Church of the Jacobins. The first Dominican monastery was founded in Toulouse by Saint Dominic himself.

As the capital of the counts of Toulouse, the city gained many other architectural testimonials to its importance, both public buildings like those of which parts have been incorporated into the present city hall, known here as the Capitole, and private dwellings of the rich, like the sixteenth-century Renaissance Hôtel d'Assézat, home of a dye merchant. After the Middle Ages the local quarries became exhausted, so the builders of Toulouse had to shift from stone to brick, with the result that the city has been described as pink at dawn, red in broad daylight, and mauve by twilight. Its intellectual importance is attested by the presence of seven fine museums and the fact that it is almost the only provincial city which has been able to produce a newspaper capable of affecting opinion in Paris.

Moving eastward into the depths of Languedoc from Toulouse, the traveler comes to two places of particular interest almost exactly on a line with each other, both offering the same chief spectacle—walls. The northernmost of the pair is Albi, which shares with Toulouse the use of brick. The walls the visitor gapes at are those of the cathedral, which is of brick, but they do not appear to belong to a place of worship. Albi is possibly the finest example in

France of the fortress-church, built to withstand assault. From without you might easily take it for a castle, not a church at all, if it were not for its tower. The archbishop's palace is likewise fortified, but it is given over to peaceful uses today. It contains the largest single collection of the works of Toulouse-Lautrec.

The other attraction in this region is Carcassonne, the greatest existing medieval fortress in France—perhaps one should say premedieval, for some of the Gallo-Roman masonry of the first stronghold built here still remains in walls added by a succession of later architects, who finally decided the place could be made no stronger in the fourteenth century, when its impregnability won for it the title of "the Virgin of Languedoc."

Long before the fortress had been rendered untakable, somewhere around the year 800, according to ballads of the medieval troubadours, the city was near capture, not because its walls had been breached, but because a five-year siege by Charlemagne's armies had left it without food. In this extremity a noble lady of the city, Dame Carcas, conceived a strategem. She had the last grains of wheat in the citadel scraped together, gorged a goose with them, and threw the bird from the top of the walls. The bird hit the ground at the feet of the attackers, its crop broke, and the grain spilled out. This evidence that the garrison was well enough provisioned to withstand the siege for another five years if necessary disheartened the besiegers and put them in a propitious mood for talking peace when, immediately after the sacrifice of the goose, the defenders sounded the call for truce talks on their trumpets, while the heralds shouted: "Dame Carcas is summoning you"—*Carcas sonne!* Hence, according to the troubadours, the name of the city. One objection to believing it is that a variation of the story, recounting the same basic strategem, is told of at least a dozen such strongholds in Europe, and one begins to suspect the accuracy of its attribution to any single place, or even that it happened at all. Another, even more potent, is that there is good evidence that Carcassonne bore that name long before the time of Charlemagne. One suspects the troubadours of inventing a Dame Carcas for the sake of the story.

Eastward from Carcassonne, one reaches the coastal plain of Bas Languedoc—Lower Languedoc. The characteristic of this coast is the line of lagoons lying just behind it, formed when silt carried to the Mediterranean by the rivers met the resistance of offshore currents and formed sand bars off the original coast line, leaving landlocked lagoons behind them, sometimes with openings to the sea, sometimes completely sealed off. A chain of interesting towns extends along this shore, some of which have been named already—Narbonne, which raised the vaulting of the choir of its Cathedral of Saint-Just almost as high as Beauvais's record altitude, and then ran into the same difficulty as Beauvais, an inability to add a nave and transepts on the same scale (but Narbonne's builders had less trouble with ample proportions when they constructed the fine sixteenth-century house whose three caryatids have caused it to be nicknamed locally "the house of the three wet nurses"); Agde, with a fortified church that looks even less like a religious building than the cathedral of Albi; Béziers, which was razed by crusaders in 1209 after its entire population, including aged invalids and babes at the breast, was slaughtered because of the success there of the Albigensian heresy, but has recovered sufficiently to be today the center of the local wine industry and the site of a wine museum; Sète; and then, back from the sea, another great city of Languedoc, Montpellier.

Capital of Languedoc under Louis XIV, Montpellier, now well inland, is one of those cities which was formerly a port. It was still important enough from this point of view so that it did not rejoice when Provence became part of France in 1482. That meant that Marseilles was becoming French and Montpellier's reign as chief French trader with the East was over. It had been an important role for Montpellier, to which it owed even its name. The spice importers who were its first substantial citizens had chosen to group their dwellings on a hill back from the coast, which was accordingly named the Mount of the Spice Merchants—Monspistillarius, a mouthful which eventually became worn down to Montpellier. Meanwhile the medicinal virtues of many spices had been discovered. Their study, at the point where they entered France, gave rise by gradual degrees to a school of medicine which eventually became the university that is still functioning today. It was here that Rabelais took his doctor's degree, and, characteristically, studied also the wines of Languedoc. Montpellier has been an intellectual center ever since, a fact typified today by its five fine museums.

All along the coast here the country has become a maze of lagoons and salt-water marshes, overgrown with reeds and similar plants, and relatively infertile—a sort of watery desert. As you move east from Montpellier, you hear this coastal territory being referred to as the Camargue, but it is not yet the Camargue, though it resembles it. Strictly speaking the Camargue is the delta between the Little Rhone and the Great Rhone. It is therefore not in Languedoc, whose eastern boundary is the Rhone, but in Provence.

Moving back from the coast toward the arc of the Cévennes, which we have already considered, we come first to a parallel arc of fertile low country which is a winegrowing area from the coastal region around Béziers until it swings north behind Montpellier and passes beyond Nîmes to follow the west bank of the Rhone. Between this outer arc of vineyard country and the inner arc of mountains are the *garrigues*, plateaus on the far side of the Cévennes from the Causses, somewhat lower, but otherwise with many of the same characteristics—chalky soil, an arid climate, and sparse, stunted vegetation best suited for the pasturing of sheep—or for giving flavor to the flesh of the game birds that feed on the thyme bushes and the juniper berries. The west bank of the Rhone remains in Languedoc as far north as the Lyonnais.

Politically speaking, Languedoc, French since the thirteenth century, comprises the departments of the Haute-Garonne (Toulouse), the Aude (Carcassonne), the Tarn (Albi), the Hérault (Montpellier), the Gard (Nîmes), the Ardèche (so rural that it has no well-known city; the capital is Privas), and two that we have already included with the Central Plateau, the Lozère and the Haute-Loire. The six that remain constitute a fairly congruent gastronomic whole.

The cooking of Languedoc is peasant cooking (the *haute cuisine* never developed here). It fits intimately the character and the history of the country. It is solid, like the strong Romanesque architecture of the south, never elaborate like the flamboyant Gothic buildings of the north. It is not the cooking of a poor country, for its raw materials are substantial and they are put together with gusto. It is congruent with the sumptuous living of the counts of Toulouse or the rich spice-dealers of Montpellier, under whose auspices it developed. It never moved in the direction of the effete, as did the inventions of the cooks of the glittering and sometimes precious courts of the Loire and Seine valleys. The comparatively rustic land of the non-literary language of *oc*—Occitania, as it was called before it became Languedoc—provided itself with a rustic table—and a well-furnished one.

The cuisine of Languedoc has been described as having

developed from two influences—the cooking of Rome, which would be natural for this old member of the Roman Empire—and the cooking of the Arabs, who for nearly eight hundred years held substantial portions of Spain, just beyond the Pyrenees, and left traces of their presence in all phases of Spanish culture. Whether Languedoc owes much to Moorish example in the kitchen might be a debatable point, but perhaps not on the grounds most likely to be raised, that reference to the Arabs or the Moors evokes an exoticism not apparent in the dishes of Languedoc. Actually there is nothing particularly exotic about the cooking of the Arabs of North Africa, across the straits from Spain, while in the Near and Middle East whatever unusual influences have crept into the menu are not Arabic in origin but come from non-Arabic Moslems—for instance, the Turks, who themselves, though not immune to ideas arriving from Persia or India, owed a great deal to the Greeks, which gets us back again to the European shore of the Mediterranean. In the same way, it may be inquired, when it is suggested that Languedoc cooking stems from the Roman and the Arab schools, whether it would not be more exact to describe it as coming from the European and African branches of Roman cooking; for it is a fair question to ask from what point the Arabs started. The universal *couscous* of North Africa, made from coarse flours cooked in steam, may be as truly as the universal *polenta* of Italy, made from coarse flours cooked in water, a direct descendent of the Roman *pulmentum*.

Couscous, rather than beans, is the usual North African accompaniment for the omnipresent mutton, which is the favorite Arab meat, possibly because it is also the most available, so the argument in favor of an Arabic origin does not quite hold for the great fondness Languedoc shows for mutton stew with white beans, which itself may be considered as the precursor of the most characteristic Languedoc dish, *cassoulet*. This would seem a natural enough development in any country where sheep are numerous, and a foreign origin hardly seems necessary to explain the dish.

Some of the richer pastries might seem to indicate the Arabic influence more directly. As for the rather heavy use of spices, that could come as readily from the spice-importing center of Montpellier as from medieval Arabs. Everyone used spices heavily in those days because lavish spicing of meat was one of the few possible ways of preserving it in the era before refrigeration. This preoccupation, and not a highly developed taste for exotic flavors (or for the perfumes of Araby to sweeten soaps in the not very fastidious days of Lady Macbeth) sent the Portuguese navigators around the Cape of Good Hope to discover the Spice Islands and enriched the importers of Montpellier.

Perhaps there would have been less spice in the cooking of Languedoc if the port of Montpellier had not specialized in this trade, for the sea and in particular the coastal lagoons back of it provided another important early means for the preservation of meat—salt. A somewhat macabre example of the early Languedocian familiarity with this method of preserving flesh was presented at Aiguesmortes in 1418, when so many Burgundians were slaughtered in a surprise attack that the problem of getting them buried before they became a general nuisance was solved by dumping the bodies into a handy tower and salting them liberally. A somewhat similar example of ingenuity occurred in the history of England, when the problem of how to get Nelson's body back to England in reasonably good condition after his death at Trafalgar was solved by shipping him home in a coffin filled with rum.

Whatever the exact origin of the Languedoc school of cooking, there can be no argument about its substantial, tasty character. It is founded first of all on the excellent produce of the region. The Toulouse-Albi country lies just below the Périgord-Quercy goose-and-truffles belt, and these foods are also found there—indeed, as we have already seen, though Périgord may be more famous for the *foie gras* and other goose products she produces than Languedoc, it is by dint of her borrowing of the goose which was a native of Toulouse.

Along the coast there is a rich variety of fish—not shell-fish, except lobster, for they like colder waters than the Mediterranean, but any number of tasty Mediterranean fish not found on the Atlantic coast. Sheep, as we already know, are plentiful in the uplands—where game birds are also found—while at lower altitudes fine cattle and poultry are raised. In the days when Narbonne was a great Roman port, it was already sending cheese, butter, and cattle to Italy, where they were considered to be of particularly high quality. The whole region is wine country, always an aid to good cooking. It is also given to much garlic, which has never been a discourager of the arts of the kitchen.

The outstanding dish of Languedoc is *cassoulet*, white beans cooked in a pot with various types of meat, which takes its name from the dish in which it is cooked, the *cassole*—an old-fashioned word no longer in current use. Originally it belonged to the family of farm-kitchen dishes, like *pot-au-feu*, which remain on the back of the stove indefinitely, serving as a sort of catch-all for anything edible that the cook may toss into the pot. Anatole France claimed in his *Histoire Comique* that the *cassoulet* he used to eat in a favorite establishment in Paris had been cooking for twenty years. It is to be doubted that any restaurant could be found today in which the stoves had not been allowed to cool off in that length of time. Modern fuels may be more convenient to handle than the farmer's wood, but they are too expensive not to be turned off between meals.

This sort of a dish is obviously likely to vary with the

individual cook, or even with what the individual cook happens to have at hand (my own cook makes a first-rate *cassoulet*, but the ingredients are likely to be different every time). The one thing that does not change is the beans. Nevertheless, you can work up a hot argument among *cassoulet*-fanciers at any time about the ingredients of the real *cassoulet*. It is a subject as touchy as the correct composition of a mint julep in certain regions of the American south. With the caution that this is a most variable dish, even when made on the same spot by the same person, what seems to be majority opinion on the standard varieties of the dish, which then serve as points of departure for individual fantasy, is offered here:

There are three main types of *cassoulet*, those of Castelnaudary, Carcassonne, and Toulouse, of which the first seems to have been the original dish. It is therefore, in principle at least, the simplest, combining with the beans only fresh pork, ham, a bit of pork shoulder, sausage, and fresh pork cracklings. Carcassonne starts with this, and adds hunks of leg of mutton to the mixture (in season, there may also be partridge in this *cassoulet*). Toulouse also starts out with the Castelnaudary base, but adds to it not only mutton (in this case from less expensive cuts), but also bacon, Toulouse sausage, and preserved goose. The last ingredient may sometimes be replaced by preserved duck, or there may even be samples of both.

This would seem to make everything plain—Castelnaudary, only pork; Carcassonne, distinguished by mutton; Toulouse, distinguished by goose. However, an authority I have just consulted, which lays down these distinctions very sternly, then goes on to give two recipes for *cassoulet de Castelnaudary;* one of them contains mutton and the other contains goose. The conclusion that must be drawn is that *cassoulet* is what you find it.

The only invariable rule that can be stated about *cas-*

soulet, with whatever name it may be ticketed on the menu, seems to be that it is a dish of white beans, preferably those of Pamiers or Cazères, cooked in a pot with some form of pork and sausage. After that it is a case of fielder's choice. Other points various forms of *cassoulet* are likely to have in common are: the use of goose fat in the cooking; seasoning that includes assorted herbs, an onion with cloves stuck into it, and garlic; and enough liquid to give it plenty of thick juice, sometimes provided by meat bouillon. The approved method is first to cook meat and beans together —they are likely to enter the process at different times, depending on their relative cooking speeds—and to finish the process by putting the whole thing into a pot, coating the surface with bread crumbs, which gives it a crunchy golden crust, and finishing the cooking very slowly, prefer- ably in a baker's oven. There is a tradition that the crust should be broken and stirred into the whole steaming mass again seven times during the cooking.

One might think that *cassoulet* would have replaced *pot- au feu* in Languedoc, but it has not. The region goes in for both, though it sometimes appears that the Languedoc ver- sion of *pot-au-feu* is only a more liquid *cassoulet*. Thus the Carcassonne *pot-au-feu* not only includes beef and mutton along with the vegetables customary in other regions (car- rots, onions, perhaps leeks and turnips), but also adds some lean bacon, stuffed cabbage—and the white beans of *cas- soulet*. Another variety of *pot-au-feu* popular in this re- gion is made with stuffed fowl instead of meat—probably a borrowing from the Pyrenees, specifically Béarn. *Pot- au-feu albigeois* builds the soup around stuffed goose neck, but *pot-au-feu à l'albigeoise* (always assuming the menu writer is meticulous) includes beef, mutton, raw salt ham, dried country sausage, preserved goose, and the usual list of vegetables plus cabbage. *Pot-au-feu à la languedocienne* differs from the classic variety only by the addition of salt pork. The *oulade* of the Cévennes, a cabbage and potato soup, becomes cabbage and white beans here. The proper way to prepare it is to make two soups separately, and turn them into the same dish only when you are ready to serve. Sète, as you might expect, makes a fine fish soup.

In the realm of *charcuterie* and hors d'œuvres, Toulouse sausage, a long fat soft sausage whose filling must be chopped by hand, occupies a leading place. It emerges from the hors d'œuvres category to become a substantial main dish when presented as *saucisses à la languedocienne*, in which it is rolled up in a spiral, transfixed with spits to keep it that way, sautéed in pork or goose fat, cooked in a covered dish with garlic and herbs, and finally served in an elaborate sauce including tomato extract, parsley, and capers. Languedoc also makes the closest approach to the Alsatian liverwurst, which though it is called pork-liver sausage actually includes only one quarter liver to three quarters of pork, mixed with the pig's blood, thus making it a relation of *boudin*, blood pudding. The best hams of the region come from the Montagne Noire just north of Carcassonne. The little pastries of Pézenas, also known as *petits pâtés de Béziers*, the nearest sizable town to Pézenas, are eaten not only as hors d'œuvres, but also, with sugar added, as dessert.

Generally speaking, a dish described as *à la languedocienne* should be accompanied by tomatoes, eggplant, and *cèpes*, and seasoned with garlic, but there seem to be more exceptions than examples for this rule. The Languedoc fashion of frying eggs comes pretty close to it, however—the eggs are arranged in a circle on the plate, each egg poised on a slice of fried eggplant, and in the center is a thick garlic-and-tomato sauce. Only the *cèpes* are missing. *Poularde à la languedocienne*, which appears surrounded by whole tomatoes and eggplant, and with garlic in its sauce, might appear at first sight to have left out the *cèpes*, too, but they are there—chopped in the stuffing that fills the tomatoes. But *carré de porc rôti à la languedocienne* has no relation at all to the presentation supposedly associated with this term. The roast of pork is larded with bits of garlic twelve hours before being put in the oven (or on the spit) and allowed to absorb oil, salt, and spices, poured over it at the same time, preparatory to the cooking. There is of course no rule against serving the Languedoc trinity of tomatoes, eggplant, and *cèpes* along with the pork, but it is not part of the dish. Actually it would appear that in giving this accompaniment to main dishes the title of "Languedoc style," the taxonomists of food have allowed themselves to be led astray by a few dishes, and those probably seepages across the not very tight gastronomic frontier with Provence, which exchanges a good many dishes with Languedoc. The *cèpes* may be considered characteristic of Languedoc, though even they could be wanderers from the Périgord-Quercy area to the north, but the tomato-eggplant combination is typical of Provence.

The eating habits of Languedoc and Provence nevertheless remain distinct enough, in spite of the common cultural background of a common language and in spite of a common reservoir of the same original foods provided by the Mediterranean. The same sea washes both coasts, and it is to be assumed that the same fish can be taken out of it at Sète as at Toulon; but eating habits seem to have imposed a different selection from what is available. The closest relationship appears to be in cod dishes, made of a salt fish not obtained from the Mediterranean at all. *Morue à la languedocienne* is the creamy dish compounded of cod, potatoes, and garlic, all merged together in the cooking until they become a homogeneous mass in which one ingredient cannot be separated from the others; but it used to be served to me on the Riviera under the name of *morue à la provençale* in defiance of the fact that another version of the dish bearing that name contains tomatoes, practically the trademark of Provençal cooking. The Languedoc *brandade de morue* also suggests a Provençal dish, for it employs olive oil, though oil is not at all unknown in Languedoc, particularly toward its eastern limits. In this dish the cooked cod is crushed into a paste along with garlic, milk, and olive oil, and up to this point might be suspected of belonging to Provence; but then it is garnished with slices of truffles, which serve as its naturalization papers.

An exception to the rule that the Mediterranean is weak in shellfish is provided by the Thau lagoon behind Sète, where there are oyster beds, but Atlantic oysters are usually considered better. Palavas, a little farther along the coast in the direction of Montpellier, is noted for lobster; it is also a fishing port from which boats set out to net various Mediterranean fish, especially tuna. This is not quite the same fish as the Atlantic tuna—for one thing it grows to only about one fifth the size of the deep-sea variety—and it is known in the local dialect as *thounina*. Palavas is credited with a dish called tuna tripe by many gastronomic writers, but it must be only for the record, as the general public is not likely ever to get a taste of it. I have never seen it on a menu, and so far as I know there is no way you can sample it unless you go out on a fishing boat yourself and have it aboard, where it is made. When the fish are cleaned, some of the inner adjuncts, including the roe, are cooked in white wine and sea water with various herbs and wolfed down by the hungry crew.

A great deal of mutton and lamb is eaten in Languedoc, as has already been suggested; Toulouse is particularly noted for its manner of cooking a quarter of lamb with parsley; and the thick white sauce that appears in the classic *blanquette de veau*, a stand-by of the *cuisine bourgeoise*, is applied here also to lamb. The good beef has inspired both Albi and Carcassonne to produce their own special versions of braised beef, and the former has its own variety of tripe. Both of these towns share with Toulouse a reputation for good cooking; on the coast Narbonne, also with its own variety of tripe, joins the company (and is famous for honey also); while in the east the two top gastronomic centers are Nîmes and Uzès, which was saluted as a "city of good cheer" by the poet Racine, sent there by his family as a young man to keep him away from the theater of Paris, for which he had a silly desire to write plays. His tribute to Uzès occurred in a jingle not meant to be entirely complimentary: it admitted that twenty caterers could make a good living there, but added that a bookseller would starve to death. Nîmes is noted particularly for the quality of its *brandade de morue*, its preserved green olives, and its almond cookies. Uzès must have a sweet tooth, too, licorice candies being one of its specialties. But a sweet tooth is no rare thing in Languedoc—Castelnaudary, Carcassonne, Narbonne (honey tarts and one cake called romantically "the arm of Venus"), and Limoux (pepper cakes) all make exceptional pastry, while candies come from Albi (*gimblettes* and *janots*), Pézenas (caramels), Mèze (Jordan almonds), and Carcassonne (candied fruits), among other places.

The wines of Languedoc have no great standing in comparison with more famous vintages, but it would be a distinct mistake to underrate them. They go wonderfully with the local food and are distinctly superior as *vins du pays*. One of my own small list of pleasant surprises in the way of discoveries of unknown vintages is attached to this area—a rich crusty red Vieux Limoux, a wine of which I had never heard before it was served to me in a restaurant in Carcassonne.

If Languedoc wine names do not appear often on tables of other regions, that does not mean that the wine does not. A good deal of it is grown here, in a few spots in the higher regions of western Languedoc, and in a more or less continuous band from the lower ground south of this area along the coast to the Rhone. The Albi territory has Gaillac, one of those *clairettes*, white sparkling wines, of which we have spoken before. This is also the nature of the wine of the Domaine de Cheminières, near Carcassonne, and Limoux, as well as the red mentioned above, also produces a sparkling white wine, the Blanquette de Limoux. West of these areas, against the border of the province, are the white, *rosé*, and red *rancio* wines, sweet and liquorous, something like Madeiras, or like similar growths on the other side of the Spanish frontier.

The continuous sweep of vineyards begins in the Narbonne area, runs past Béziers, the wine-marketing center for the region, and on to Montpellier—reds, whites, and *rosés*. Toward Montpellier, at Frontignan and Lunel, the muscat wines, with their nutmeg taste, grown from plants imported by the Romans, are found. Past Nîmes, almost over to the Rhone, are Tavel and Lirac, the former especially, an apparently light but treacherous *rosé*, being likely to turn up as a table wine far from its home grounds. Here we are in the Rhone valley, whose wines, on whichever side they grow, can most usefully be considered together; so we will leave Rhone wines until we cross the river and find ourselves in Provence. We might note first, however, that it was on the Languedoc side of the river, at Pont-Saint-Esprit, that Stendhal helped himself so generously to the local vintage that he clasped a waitress to him and went into a wild dance, moving Alfred de Musset, who was present, to make a sketch of the scene which still exists.

A number of liqueurs are made in Languedoc, Pézenas

being the marketing center for them. One of France's best known table waters, Perrier, which sparkles naturally, comes from the Languedoc. The spring that produces it is about one third of the way to Montpellier from Nîmes, just off the main auto road, N113. The bottling establishment is open to visitors.

THE
DOMAIN

OF
OIL

Provence

The most magical of all the provinces of France is Provence. Here the Latin civilization which is today the basis of the national culture took root earliest. Here nature and man are in closer harmony than anywhere else in France. Buildings are not excrescences on the face of the earth; they have become part of the landscape, baked into it by the synthesizing heat of the Provençal sun. The land is antique, but it is not old. You cannot live there long without becoming conscious of the vigorous pulse of the south. In comparison, Paris seems jaded.

The Romans seeped early across the Alps, spread into the land beyond them, and found themselves so much at home that they called the land their province—Provence. (Later, when they crossed the Rhine, they knew they had met a mentality hostile to the Latin genius—as it still is, which is probably why German scholars have been foremost in studying the ancient Mediterranean civilizations, analyzing them as only outsiders could—so they announced that here they had founded, not a province, but a colony —Cologne.)

Perhaps seeped, an effortless word, is not the right term for the Roman move into Provence. Drove, thrust, or pushed might be better. The passage from Italy into France by way of the Riviera may seem an easy way today, along the low coastal route beside the sea which avoids the stark Alpine passes above; but that highway was not open when the Romans came. In their day the mountains marched straight into the sea. The coast was accessible only where there was a break in the wall, like that hollowed out by the deep bay of Villefranche, into which the Romans sailed and called it Olivula, and into which the Saracens also sailed, leaving behind them a covered street like those of the Middle East when they abandoned it to the Christians of the Middle Ages, who called it the Port of Olives. There was then no travel from point to point along the coast. The mountains barred the way between anchorages. Only in this century were the three cornice roads drilled through them. The Romans followed the crests, leaving behind as the mark of their passage the high-perched ruin known as the Triumph of Augustus crowning the tip of the great rock of La Turbie, from which today's tourist looks down a thousand feet to Monte Carlo and the sea.

The land route into Provence was arduous. There was an easier way by water. Six hundred years before the beginning of our era, the Phocæan Greeks established a colony about a harbor from which it was an easy journey to the only non-mountainous route to the north, the valley of

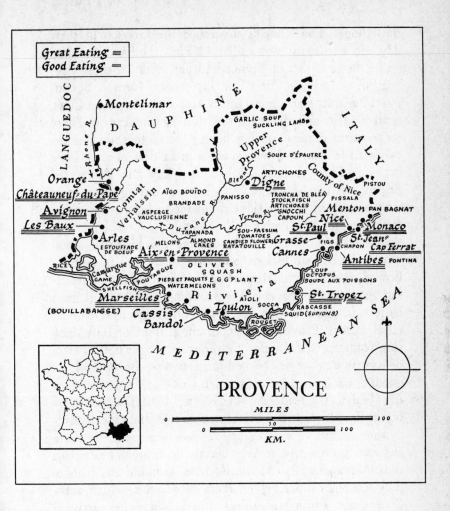

Great Eating ═
Good Eating ─

LANGUEDOC

DAUPHINÉ

• Montélimar

Rhône R.

GARLIC SOUP
SUCKLING LAMB

Upper
Provence

SOUPE D'ÉPAUTRE

ARTICHOKES

• Digne

Bléone R.

County of Nice

ITALY

PISTOU

Orange •
Châteauneuf-du-Pape

Avignon
Les Baux

AÏGO BOUÏDO

BRANDADE

ASPERGE
VAUCLUSIENNE

Comtat
Venaissin

PANISSO

Durance R.

Verdon

TRONCHA DE BLÉA
STOCKFISH
ARTICHOKES
GNOCCHI
CAPOUN

PISSALA

MENTON

St.Paul

PAN BAGNAT

Nice

Monaco
St.Jean
Cap Ferrat

Arles •

ESTOUFFADE
DE BOEUF

TAPANADA

MELONS

ALMOND
CAKES

SOU-FASSUM
TOMATOES
CANDIED FLOWERS
RATATOUILLE

Grasse

CHAPON

FIGS

Aix-en-Provence

Cannes

Antibes

PONTINA

RICE •

Camargue

GAME

POUTARGUE

SHELLFISH

OLIVES
SQUASH

PIEDS ET PAQUETS EGGPLANT
WATERMELONS

LOUP
OCTOPUS
SOUPE AUX POISSONS

Riviera

St.Tropez

Marseilles

AÏOLI

SOCCA

RASCASSE

(BOUILLABAISSE)

Cassis

Toulon

SQUID (SUPIONS)

Bandol

ROUGET

MEDITERRANEAN SEA

PROVENCE

MILES

0 ————————————————— 50 ————————————————— 100

0 ————————— 50 ————————— 100

KM.

the Rhone. The Romans succeeded the Greeks. In their day the settlement was called Massilia. Today it is Marseilles, largest port of France and her second largest city.

From Marseilles the Romans under Consul Sextius moved against Entremont, the capital of the Ligurian Celts, destroyed it, and replaced it with a Roman camp. There were warm mineral springs here, a detail that always impressed the Romans, who spent a great deal of their time bathing. They therefore called the place the Waters of Sextius—Aquæ Sextiæ, today Aix, or, to distinguish it from a multitude of others similarly named, Aix-en-Provence, for the region of which it is the capital.

The valley of the Rhone became the highway along which the Roman legions, and after them Roman culture, flowed to the north. Meanwhile the Romans were spreading out through Provence and stamping it with the Roman pattern it wears to this day. Some of the greatest Roman cities were in Provence, as important as those of Italy, barring Rome herself. Under Nero one of the greatest centers of Roman culture was Nîmes, just across the border in Languedoc, but in essence very much a city of Provence. Under Trajan, the leadership had shifted to Arles, indisputably in Provence, which celebrated its two thousandth anniversary recently, a considerable understatement, as there has been a settlement at Arles certainly for much more than two thousand years. As the Romans mounted the Rhone, they left their cities behind them—Tarascon, which antedates them, for it was already there when they arrived; Orange, whose early inhabitants slaughtered one hundred thousand soldiers of the first Roman legions that tried to conquer them, but which became so thoroughly a Roman city later that its pride to this day is the Roman theater rising impressively in its center, known simply as The Wall; Vaison la Romaine, where modern excavations have uncovered a French Pompeii.

Roman rule withered, but the civilization that had been installed so firmly in Provence remained. It was Provençal, not French, which was the language of the troubadours— though it is true that most of them came originally from the territories on the western side of the Rhone, which spoke the *langue d'oc,* either from the heights of the Massif Central, from Languedoc, or especially from the ebullient territory of Gascony. They were drawn to Provence by the opportunities to exercise their talents provided by the great thoroughly civilized once Roman cities, which became the hosts of the celebrated Courts of Love. One of the most famous was at Les Baux, today a ruined stronghold without inhabitants perched on a high mesa so spectacular in appearance that visitors are now giving it animation again and one of the half dozen best restaurants in France has appeared there. Les Baux was not distinguished solely for its devotion to love. One of its rulers was the fourteenth-century Raymond of Turenne, whose idea of entertainment was to force his prisoners to jump from the château on the edge of the cliff to the plain beneath. It was by a marriage in the ruling family of Les Baux that Orange gave its name to the ruling family of Holland, through William the Silent (and thus also to the Orange Free State in South Africa), and remained a Dutch possession until Louis XIV won it back. Meanwhile Avignon had become the capital of the popes, Rome being insecure. Popes and antipopes succeeded each other there for about a century, and even after they had left the territory belonged to the Papal States until the Revolution.

The great days of Provence have left their monuments scattered far and wide over the countryside. The most imposing is no doubt the Palace of the Popes at Avignon; it certainly looks solider than the medieval walls of the city, which are picturesque but hardly impregnable. More typical of the country is architecture on a less grandiose, but,

it seems, more solidly seated kind—the Romanesque buildings looking as if they had grown out of the ground on
which they stand. They do not tower, but they are self-
assured and in perfect harmony with their environment.
The hill towns, often still behind their ancient ramparts,
cling to the mountainsides like parts of the rock on which
they are built. Along the sea coast, where the colors become spectacular, the houses glow in pastel tints. In the
quieter inland rural areas, the typical buildings are the low
clusters of one-story whitewashed farm buildings, the *mas*,
clinging close to earth. Throughout the countryside one
comes upon the oratories, the unobtrusive shrines, less striking than the calvaries of Brittany, but easier to live with.
An attempt to catalogue them has caused some thirteen
hundred to be listed, but there are certainly more. (Across
the Rhone, the word "oratory" has become transmuted
into "*oradour*," so that a score of settlements that grew up
close to shrines bear this name, a fact the Germans did not
know when, during the Second World War, they mas-
sacred the entire population of Oradour-sur-Glane in re-
taliation for a resistance raid on a military train near Ora-
dour-sur-Vayres.)

The first fact of life in Provence is the sun. Not only
does it beat down hotly during the summer, but it is also
present almost all the rest of the year, too. Local inhabitants may grumble about the spring and fall, especially the
fall, but northerners find Provence particularly blessed all
year around. There is not much grumbling during the winter, even from the natives (whose grumbling is in any case
on the good-humored side, for the people of Provence are
in general as sunny as their climate), for after November,
often a damp month, the clouds disappear. The one draw-
back is the mistral, the wind that roars down the whole
length of the horizontal chimney that is the Rhone valley
and usually, once it starts, keeps it up for three or four days

without faltering. Even Provençal tempers fray after seventy-two or ninety-six hours of this constant buffeting, but the sun is a great healer. The mistral is so striking a feature of the climate of Provence that it does not seem surprising that the writer who took it upon himself to try to make Provençal a literary language should have taken the *nom de plume* of Mistral. What is surprising is that it is not a *nom de plume*. Frédéric Mistral was born with the name. No doubt it shaped his destiny.

The sun has made Provence a country of painters, some native, some attracted to it by the luminosity of its colors. Cézanne was born there, a native of Aix-en-Provence. The Montagne Sainte-Victoire which he painted over and over again is in its neighborhood. When Van Gogh, who had used a dull, muddy palette in Holland, came to Arles, his canvases exploded with light. Renoir, born in Limoges, transferred himself to Cagnes-sur-Mer to get its rosy light into his painting. Matisse, born in the foggy north, found his brilliant colors on the French Riviera. Picasso deserted the sun of his native Malaga for many years in Paris, but at last returned to a southern clime—and brighter colors—in Vallauris.

Where Provence begins exactly, or if it even has a definite boundary, I do not know, but coming from Paris I always feel myself first in the Midi at Montélimar. This is the first place with the broad open spaces that betray a city living much of the year outdoors. The squares and broad streets are lined with squat trees pruned strongly back so that their boughs spread out flatly not far above the ground, while the thin bark of a warm climate peels in patches from their trunks and reveals pale green Hans Arp-shaped bared splotches beneath. If it is warm weather, shop doors are open and bead curtains hang in them, letting in the air and keeping out the flies. Somewhere within sight, or at least within the hearing of metal clinking against metal, a game of bowls, here called *pétanque,* is being played with rapt tensity. This is the South.

Provence is a unit in many ways—through its language, its climate, its history, its architecture, its cooking—but there are certain very distinct subdivisions within it. The first is the one by which we enter it when we come via Montélimar, the way most persons enter it coming from Paris—the valley of the Rhone. This is the most Roman part of Provence, or at least the most Imperial Roman part of Provence, meaning the most anciently cosmopolitan (the Riviera is modern cosmopolitan), as it was two thousand years ago the main artery for Roman armies, Roman culture, and Roman trade. Here are the great cities and the most fertile part of Provence—almost the only really fertile region, for here the waters of the Rhone provide moisture, which elsewhere, except in the Camargue, the sun dries up. On the eastern bank of the Rhone, the area of natural fertility has been extended from Montélimar to the sea by irrigation, begun by the Romans, who not only led water from the great river to adjacent arid land, but also drained the marshes of the Crau, on the other side of the Rhone from where the Camargue still lies among the not-yet-drained marshes of the river's delta.

Some distance south of Montélimar, in this fertile valley region, lies the Comtat Venaissin, named for the now sleepy and nearly forgotten village of Venasque, clustered about one of the oldest churches in France (seventh century). It differs from the surrounding area only in political history. This territory belonged to the popes. It seems pleasant country today, but in the fourteenth century the Italian poet Petrarch could not find words harsh enough to describe Avignon, as he urged the popes to return to Rome, where no doubt he himself desired to return. Perhaps his discontent was less with the region than with the ill luck he had encountered there, first in finding that his Laura, whom he met in a church in Avignon, was not only already a wife, but even a faithful one, and then in losing her to the plague in 1348. Nevertheless he remained there for sixteen years, in Vaucluse, near the famous "fountain," actually the point at which the river Sorgue bursts from its underground course to run in the open.

To the west from the Rhone is the area essentially more Provençal than any other, the bare earth unrelieved by the distraction of the great river or of the Middle Sea. This is the region over which Aix, a great university town and the intellectual capital of Provence, reigns supreme. The coastal mountains cut it off from the humidity of the Mediterranean. The spurs that merge into the Alps farther east shut out rain-bringing breezes from north or east. It is dry country, and it looks it. It seems painted in monochrome, gray-green; but when your eyes become accustomed to the palette of Provence-Behind-the-Sea, you will marvel at the never ending gradations of greens, though they never become lush or tender or shining, but remain in tune with the grays of the rocks. Grass grows sparsely, and it is almost a surprise to come across a field where there has been enough of it to cut for hay. (Yet melons, the most watery of fruits, grow here profusely.) The country around Aix, sealess Provence, grass-roots Provence (and that is almost all there is to the grass here—spreading, thirsty roots with only scanty blades), may not trap the eye at first sight, but it provides lasting satisfaction to those who stay. The subtle nuances of all those thousands of greens and grays offer new education daily to the eye. Across the mountains, on the coast, the colors shout brilliantly, but in half an hour you have sorted them all out, and they give no more work to the spirit. They are without shading. You begin to ache with desire for a cloud to cross the unwinking blue of the sky. The coast can provoke love at first sight, but love at first sight frequently leads to quick divorce. It takes longer for the interior to penetrate your understanding, but when you grow to love it, your affection is unshakable.

One area of the coast, however, produces this same effect by other, similar means.

This is the Camargue, the triangle of land lying against the frontier of Languedoc, between the Little Rhone and the Great Rhone. If interior Provence to the east is a near desert of solidly sun-baked land, the Camargue is a watery desert that sends the reflections of the southern sun shimmering back from the surface of its lagoons and marshes. The water in them is salt, or at best brackish. The vegetation consists of reeds or such other meager plants as can put up with salt. There is a desolate grandeur about the Camargue. Here again variations are subtle, and to perceive them the mind is forced to that effort without which there can be no genuine perception.

Human habitation in the Camargue is represented by isolated clusters of farm buildings, every one the headquarters of a single family, with probably no neighbors in sight. Each of these little human islands is the center of a herd of beef cattle who splash through the innumerable pools to reach their meager pasturage, chivied by cowboys mounted on the small quick horses of the Camargue and armed, not with the lasso of the American cowboy, but with lances that make them resemble the picadors of the Spanish bull rings, who, indeed, come to the Camargue to buy their horses. Hordes of waterbirds, finding this a secure nesting area (they have been given an absolutely inviolable one in the national wild life preserve of the Vaccarès lagoon) fly overhead, among them pink flamingos and snowy-white egrets.

The sheep that used to share the Camargue with the cattle during the winter, going up to the high plateaux of the Causses for the summer, are growing fewer. What the area is losing in one department of food production it is gaining in another. The Camargue raises less mutton, but more rice. The combination of heat from the sun and of soil covered with water naturally suggested rice. The water was unfortunately salt, but that was not an unalterable disadvantage. The marshes are being drained, the salt water pumped into the Etang de Vaccarès, and fresh water is being brought in from the Rhone. Already the rice crop of the Camargue supplies one third of all the needs of France. After rice has been grown here for a few seasons, the soil will be ready for other crops. From marginal land, it will graduate to first-rate agricultural country. Crop rotation will become possible, the vacant spaces will fill with new farm buildings put up on drained dry land, the poor but picturesque Camargue will become prosperous, and one more of the few remaining places of solitude in Europe will disappear. It will be a pity.

The coast on the other side of the Rhone delta is very different. This is the part of France that the rest of the world knows best after Paris, the Riviera. It is by no means uniform. From Marseilles to Toulon, pine woods carpeted with needles and without underbrush run down to the sea. Here and there fingers of the Mediterranean probe deeply into the land—the *calanques*. After the great naval port of Toulon, the character of the coast changes. High hills sweep down to the edge of the sea, the Mountains of the Moors. At Saint-Raphaël begins what many vacationers think of as the Riviera proper, though for a good many the Côte d'Azur conjures up only the last section from Cannes onward. Behind the coast are the wooded heights of the Esterel. Along its edge runs the famous Corniche d'Or road, cut through red rocks and red earth, looking down into gulfs far below where water of limpid green or limpid blue is so clear one sees easily to the bottom. At Cannes there is another change. The colors of nature become a little less startling, the soil not so red, the waters not so luminous, but the works of man now crowd in more thickly. From Cannes eastward, the coast is closely built up. Past Antibes sandy beaches give way to pebbles. Back from the sea are the hill towns—Grasse, the capital of perfume-making, Cagnes-sur-Mer, Vence, Saint-Paul-de-Vence. From Nice onward, the buildings crowd even closer, pinched between the sea and the mountains that rise in cliffs of bare rock sometimes straight out of the sea. The hill towns become more spectacular—Eze, incredibly perched upon its rock; La Turbie, a shelf overlooking Monaco; Roquebrune, which has tunneled into the cliffside. Down below is the incredible toyland of Monte Carlo; then Menton with its lemon trees, and beyond it Italy.

From Nice onward, we have been again in a region with a political history different from that of the rest of Provence, the County of Nice, French only since 1860 (indeed a small slice of it entered France's boundaries only in 1947). Here Italian influence is evident. To Italians, Nice remains Nizza la Bella. Many of them maintain that it is in the wrong country. Yet Nice has never belonged to Italy. When Italy was put together, the County of Nice remained outside; and its rise began with its annexation to France. It had 45,000 inhabitants then. It has more than 200,000 now, and is the sixth city of France.

At night a grove of olive trees looks like the phantom of a forest. In moonlight or even starlight the leaves are of a spectral ashen hue. The boughs, low, widespread and gnarled, twist and turn in grotesque tortured shapes. The grove is eerie and ghostlike, wearing a macabre beauty.

Even in broad daylight the olive tree looks unreal. Each breeze that ruffles it blows a wave of silver through its foliage as the dusty undersides of its leaves are raised and dropped again. It is a silver not metallic, not like shining polished silver, but dull and deadened. The dry trunk and limbs appear the dead skeleton of a tree. The soil from which it grows often increases the impression of death and desolation. The olive will make do with the barest soils; sometimes one sees olives rising from ground covered with small stones, where no soil at all is visible.

When the olive does not seem dead or dying, it at least seems ancient. Many individual trees are. The peoples of olive countries call the tree immortal, and it is true that no one knows its maximum possible age. Italy has trees reputed to go back to the time of republican Rome, but their histories are doubtful. The oldest more-or-less authenticated record is of a tree seven hundred years old. But the olive is not quite immortal. The unprecedented cold weather that swept southern France in February of 1956 killed one third of the olive trees of Provence.

The olive tree looks like death, but to the countries where it grows, it sometimes literally means life. Where it thrives, often nothing else can flourish. If its trunk and even its leaves look dry and sapless, that may be because every droplet of moisture has been squeezed from the rest of its growth and deposited in its fruit, as though purposely to make it available to man. The olive is as much the savior of man in semiarid areas of poor soil as the date of the oases is in the desert. Where the soil is better and moisture more plentiful, the quality of the fruit improves, and as it takes so little from the earth, shade-loving vegetables can be grown beneath its boughs. In the almost desert areas of Spain, where the olive is virtually all that grows, and it in shrunken, dwarflike forms, the fruit is somewhat bitter. In Provence, more fertile and less dry, olives and their soil are richer and more unctuous. They are outdistanced by the Italian olives, which grow on soil that is hardly rich, but is more abundantly watered by the streams pouring down from the mountains.

Man has been tending the olive for a long time (the trees

of Provence are said to have been introduced by the Greeks 2,500 years ago, and nobody knows how long the Greeks had been cultivating them before that), and in the process he has diversified it greatly. There are at least thirty distinct types of olive, with subdivisions producing perhaps twice as many recognizably different sorts of trees. The fruit may be small or large, dry and hard, or soft and juicy, white, green, purple, or black. It is more versatile than one might think, at least in the form of oil.

In Provence, the fruit is crushed into a pulp (if you want to see the sort of mill in which this was done a millennium ago, visit the museum in the old castle of Cagnes-sur-Mer), and from the pulp is pressed the virgin oil, the top grade that you buy in the groceries (*huile vierge*, the label says). To the residue after this first pressing, cold water is added to replace some of the moisture that has been squeezed out, and a second pressing produces second-grade oil, marketed in France as *fine* or even, perhaps somewhat exaggeratedly, as *extra-fine*. Olive growers sometimes add warm water, a greater encourager than cold, and produce a third pressing, but this is not for the market; his own family thus gets the leftovers from his crop. But this is not all. The olive oil used in soap comes from still another pressing. The dry remains of the pulp make fertilizer. The pits provide a lubricating oil. The hard tight-grained wood of the olive, often beautifully marked with whorls as tortured as the live trees' misshapen limbs, is prized by woodworkers. It is also prized by salad-makers, who find the ideal salad bowl one carved out of a single piece of root from an olive tree. As everyone knows, a wooden salad bowl should never be washed, only rubbed clean after each using, so that the oil impregnates the wood and adds its contribution to the dressing, each new salad becoming more fragrant than the last. There is a theory that no wood performs this service better than that of the olive, and it seems after all only natural that olive wood should show an affinity for olive oil. (If you have such a bowl, it goes without saying that you should never make a salad in it with any other oil than that of the olive.)

Many other plants mark this southern part of the country (and in particular the Riviera) as of a different clime from the north, but the olive symbolizes Provence. They know that in Nice, where an olive has been planted in front of the boys' high school in recognition of that fact. I seem to recall that later, as an afterthought, a fig tree was planted on the other side of the high school door, but no matter how great an admirer of that incomparable fruit one may be, it is necessary to admit that there can be no comparison between the influence the fig and the olive have had on the eating habits of Provence. The fig offers only itself. The olive, providing the basic fat in which everything else is cooked (and the chief element in the dressing in which many raw foods are eaten), enters into virtually every other food until the cheese and dessert courses are reached. The grease in which the food of a country is cooked is the ultimate shaper of its whole cuisine. The olive is thus the creator of the cooking of Provence. A local saying points this up. "A fish," it runs, "is an animal that is found alive in water and dead in oil."

There is a second universal influence in the cooking of Provence almost as important as that of the olive: garlic. It is less exclusively associated with Provence than the olive, for as has already been remarked, garlic is an important element in French cooking from the Loire southward. It increases in favor as you go farther south, but more rapidly in the southeast than in the southwest. The greatest saturation point is reached on the French Riviera—if you eat, that is, where the local population eats, rather than in the luxury hotels where the cuisine has been emasculated. Garlic may not belong to Provence alone, but at least it gets special recognition there. It has even been called "the truffle of Provence."

A third element must be noted as particularly typical of Provençal cooking—the tomato, which manages to get into almost everything. Unless you know the contrary, it is fairly safe to assume that any dish appearing on a menu as *à la provençale* will be accompanied by cooked tomatoes strongly seasoned with garlic. The few exceptions will certainly be distinguished by garlic. There may be dishes Provençal style which contain neither of these two ingredients, but none comes to my mind at the moment.

The variety of Provençal food is endless, but it is not uniform throughout the whole territory. There is most variety in Nice, which draws upon both Italian and Provençal cooking and also enjoys the riches of the sea, of which the interior is more or less deprived. The poorest region for food is the Camargue, on the sea also, but on a low-lying sand-choked shore, where sea and land are often confounded, making approach to the former difficult, while the nature of the coast seems less propitious to variety in sea food than the rockier area to the east. Besides, the men of the Camargue are as a rule more versed in the ways of cattle than in those of fish.

They do go to the sea for at least one thing, however—an accompaniment for the rice that is becoming yearly a more important product of the Camargue. Why *riz de Camargue* is sometimes called *riz à l'américaine* is difficult to divine, for it means rice served with sea food of a type that most Americans eschew—mussels are the least debatable, but this form of rice may turn up mingled with octopus (*poulpe*) or squid (*seiche* is the name of the animal, but on Provençal menus it is more likely to turn up as *supions*, a smaller and less horrendous variety). I find this last fish a little too adventurous eating in the form in which it often turns up in Spain (*calamares en su tinto*), when the beast is served *in toto* swimming in the black secretion that gives it its popular name of inkfish; but *supions* with rice is quite inoffensive in appearance, little bits of white meat mixed in with the rice, and though it may be a trifle rubbery, its taste is excellent.

Because the Camargue is beef country, it is natural that one of its characteristic dishes should be *estouffade de bœuf*. If beef is preferred in this fashion rather than in the comparatively unadorned form of roasts and steaks, that is because the sparse pasturage of the Camargue obliges the steers of this region to wander far afield for their food. At the same time that they put on flesh they develop muscle. The Camargue is not grain country, so its animals, or at least such of them as are consumed in the region where they are raised, are not finished off on grain, which would make them tenderer. They are tough when slaughtered, and therefore lend themselves particularly to this sort of dish, which involves long softening cooking. When an *estouffade* is meant to be consumed in the middle of the day, the beef goes into the pot the night before. The meat is cut up, combined with tomatoes and black olives, and set to simmer in red wine, usually from Languedoc, in a covered earthenware vessel. By the time it is ready to be eaten, it would never occur to you that it was once tough.

Another dish that takes overnight to cook is *pieds et paquets* (feet and packages, literally), a dish for which Marseilles is particularly renowned, but because it is a sheep-country dish the Camargue, which still raises some sheep, though not as many as a few years ago, has it, too. As it is made today, its name is somewhat misleading. The dish is sheep's tripe stuffed with salt pork flavored with onions, garlic, and parsley, cooked slowly in white wine and tomato sauce. This constitutes the package, but the feet seem to have disappeared from the combination. Probably the dish used to be cooked together with calves' feet, as it still is in Nice, where, however, it has perversely abandoned the name that doesn't make sense in the Camargue, but would make sense in Nice, and is described simply as *tripes à la niçoise*.

The Camargue is also, naturally, a good place to eat wild waterfowl in season.

When we move over to the Rhone valley and the inland territory west of it (the Riviera is pretty much a separate realm), the menu immediately becomes more diversified. A feature of the cooking is the widespread use of a variety of highly aromatic herbs. They grow well in the sun-parched hilly dry regions of inland Provence, and Provençals like plenty of taste in their food. The herbs go especially into the cooking of game, like the plentiful *grives* and *chachas*, a local term for a local bird, while the rabbits of this area hardly need herbs; having fed all their lives on thyme, they have inbred seasoning. Individual cooks are likely to add assorted herbs to their own particular taste, even when the general recipe doesn't call for them—as in the very characteristic *tomates à la provençale*, cooked in plenty of olive oil, redolent of garlic, and sprinkled with parsley. Eggplant (*aubergines*) and summer squash (*courgettes*) turn up with this treatment, too, and very often herbs other than parsley will be added. If all three of these vegetables are stewed together with the same accompaniments, minus the parsley, though not necessarily without other seasonings, they constitute one of the most popular of Provençal dishes, *ratatouille*.

Consonant with the Provençal delight in pungent flavoring is what this region does to mayonnaise. Mayonnaise is a rich and unctuous sauce to begin with, as everyone knows, but it is rather bland. The Provençal is disposed to approve of mayonnaise because it is made largely from olive oil, but he wants to make it more exciting; besides it contains no garlic. These two defects are cured simultaneously by mixing the mayonnaise with crushed garlic—a great deal of crushed garlic—and sometimes, though not necessarily, with chopped parsley as well. The result is *aïoli* (*ail* meaning garlic), sometimes referred to as the butter of Provence. If you see the word *aïoli* alone on a menu, it will probably appear smeared copiously over a dish of mixed vegetables—the exact contents may vary with the seasons, but carrots, potatoes, and string beans form a combination often encountered. It is delicious when the vegetables are hot, and also when they are cold. *Aïoli* is also particularly good on many egg dishes, even better on fish, and superb with lobster.

There would be no difficulty about making up an all-Provençal meal in this part of the province (we will consider the specifically Riviera dishes later). Beginning with the hors d'œuvres, one of the most natural things to order would be olives—the wrinkled fresh black olives that you will see filling giant hogsheads to the brim in Provençal groceries; or green preserved olives flavored with rosemary; or even better, *tapanda*, which is preserved olives crushed into a sort of paste, mixed with olive oil, and strongly spiced. Perhaps at this point in your meal you might try *panisso*, made either of chick-pea or maize flour, boiled into a sort of mush, then allowed to cool and become more solid, when it is fried. This is sometimes sugared and eaten as a dessert. Then there is *socca*, a chick-pea flour pastry, more common along the coast than in the interior, however. Garlic sausage from Arles is another possibility.

The collection of soups may be headed by *soupe à l'ail* (garlic soup), a testimonial to the Provençal fondness for this item, for here garlic, usually employed to accompany more substantial ingredients, is pretty much the be-all and the end-all. A lot of it goes into the soup—twenty-four cloves of garlic to two quarts of water (when you start; as you boil it twenty minutes, there's much less water when you finish), along with which you drop in a sprig of thyme, another of sage, a clove, and salt and pepper. You strain the result through a sieve and pour it over small slices of round French bread which have been soaked in olive oil, covered with grated cheese, and placed in the oven just long enough for the cheese to melt. Give the bread time to soak up as much of the soup as possible before you start eating.

Other soups that do not vary greatly from this make major use of garlic also—*aïgo bouïdo à la ménagère*, in which there is a little less garlic, a little more herbs, and some olive oil, and the slices of bread over which the soup is poured are adorned with chopped parsley, not cheese and oil. Or eggs may be poached in the bouillon of this same soup, after which they are placed on slices of bread and the soup is poured over them. *Aïgo à la ménagère* is more complicated. In this case, you start by frying a chopped onion and three chopped leeks in olive oil just long enough to give them a little color. Then you add two crushed tomatoes without their seeds, four cloves of garlic, also crushed, a sprig of fennel, a bit of dried orange peel, a bunch of mixed herbs, four cut-up potatoes, and a pinch of saffron. Pour in two quarts of water, add salt and pepper, and boil strongly for a quarter of an hour. You then take out the potatoes, powder them with chopped parsley, poach one egg per person in the soup, and then take the eggs out also and serve them on top of the potatoes. The soup you eat separately, poured over slices of bread. A Provençal version of *pot-au-feu*, made elsewhere usually with beef, or beef and veal, is *soupe d'épautre*, in which a shoulder or leg of mutton is boiled with onions and cloves, carrots, turnips, leeks, celery, and, of course, garlic. In *soupe de mariage*, no doubt served originally for wedding banquets, mutton, beef, and chicken are all put in the same pot; it is thickened with rice.

334

There are any number of varieties of *œufs à la provençale*, most of which employ eggplant. Poached eggs Provençal style are served on half tomatoes previously cooked
in oil, drowned in tomato and garlic sauce, with diced eggplant also fried in oil in the center of the dish; the whole is
covered with chopped parsley. Fried eggs (fried in oil, of
course) are also served on halved tomatoes, likewise
cooked in oil, and on top of that goes a slice of eggplant,
similarly fried in oil—in fact, even the sprigs of parsley
which accompany this dish are so fried. For another treatment, an earthenware casserole is rubbed with garlic, slices
of eggplant already fried in oil are placed in the bottom,
the eggs are broken on top of them, and the whole is then
cooked in the oven. Provençal sauce is added before serving, a complicated addition we shall examine later. Cold
jellied eggs *à la provençale*, a wonderful dish for a hot day,
are made by starting out with a soft-boiled egg, which is
bathed in mayonnaise with tomato extract added to it, and
decorated with a leaf or two of tarragon inside a coating of
jelly—chicken jelly preferably. The egg is then stood on
end in a scooped-out tomato, which has itself been marinated in a mixture of oil, vinegar, salt, and pepper, and is
packed in place with a salad of diced potatoes and eggplant
in *aïoli*, after which the whole thing is surrounded with
chopped jelly. Arles makes a special type of scrambled
eggs which begins when long summer squash (of the zuc-
chini type, for instance) are cut in half and cooked in oil
after most of the pulp has been removed. The pulp is cut
up and mixed with the eggs, along with tomato extract and
garlic, and the scrambled eggs thus prepared are placed in
the scooped-out squash halves. Enough squashes are used
so that one half of each squash suffices for the eggs. The
other halves, covered with grated Parmesan cheese and
soaked in melted butter, are quickly browned in the oven
and served with tomato sauce together with the eggs. As

for a Provençal omelette, that is made with diced tomatoes and garlic, previously cooked together in oil, mixed into the omelette.

The Provençal fashion of roasting pork recalls that of Languedoc, at least in that the preparation begins twelve hours before the cooking, though the flavors the pork is encouraged to acquire during this period are not quite the same. Instead of inserting bits of garlic in slits in the meat, as in Languedoc, the cooks of Provence tuck sage leaves into the slits. If this difference seems inconsistent in that part of France most enthusiastically devoted to garlic, it does not mean that garlic is being banished from the dish— quite the opposite. After the meat is seasoned with a mixture of salt and ground thyme and laurel, it is covered with crushed garlic and olive oil is then poured over it; and after its twelve hours in this bath of fragrances, it goes into the oven along with the garlic. This is *carré de porc rôti à la provençale*.

Daube de bœuf à la provençale starts with boiling beef cut into large cubes, marinated in white wine (unusual, for ordinarily red wine is combined with beef in cooking), Cognac, olive oil, onions, sliced carrots, parsley, thyme, and laurel. After two hours soaking in this mixture, both it and the beef go into the pot, to which are added bits of pigskin, diced bacon, sliced carrots, chopped onions, chopped raw mushrooms, peeled and seeded tomatoes, crushed garlic, pitted ripe black olives, a piece of bitter orange peel, and assorted herbs. Veal bouillon is poured in, the cover of the pot is sealed, and it is cooked slowly for five or six hours in the oven. Less complicated is *bœuf bouilli à la provençale*, in which the beef is again cut into cubes, browned in butter and chopped onions, seasoned with garlic, boiled, and embellished at the very end of its cooking with tomato extract.

Mutton is also particularly good in Provence, where

336

sheep graze in the department of the Basses-Alpes, Provence's farthest north, in fields of lavender. This pasturage gives their flesh a particularly delicate flavor. A favorite dish of Provence is *agneau au lait*, suckling lamb, from animals slaughtered much younger than is ever the case in the United States. In Nice alone at least two shops sell nothing else, opening for perhaps two months in the year at the lamb-killing season and remaining closed the rest of the time.

Poulet sauté à la provençale fries the chicken in oil with chopped onions, tomatoes, garlic, white wine, and veal bouillon and surrounds it when cooked with ripe olives, mushrooms fried in oil, and strips of anchovy. *Cèpes à la provençale* cooks these large fleshy mushrooms in oil with chopped onions and crushed garlic. *Pommes de terre à la provençale* treats potatoes with considerable elaborateness. They are bathed in a sauce in which marinated tuna fish and hard-boiled eggs have been worked into tomato extract, covered with bread crumbs, and cooked in the oven.

Other dishes presented as *à la provençale* may be so saluted because they are served with *sauce provençale*. For a warm dish, whether it is eggs, fish, meat, poultry, or vegetables, this means tomatoes, chopped onions, and crushed garlic, cooked in oil and seasoned with salt and pepper, to which white wine and veal bouillon are added at different stages of the cooking, with chopped parsley sprinkled over it as an afterthought. There is also a *sauce provençale* for cold dishes, such as salads. In this case it means a seasoning of oil, vinegar, salt, pepper, and crushed chopped tomatoes, with an addition of hard-boiled eggs, capers, pickles, chopped parsley—and, of course, garlic.

Provence also has a sauce that is chiefly garlic and has been employed in this part of the country since the Middle Ages—*sauce à l'ail à la provençale*. It is unusual among Provençal specialties in not employing olive oil. The garlic is first simmered instead in consommé along with mixed herbs, and when it has boiled down to a rather thick consistency the garlic and herbs are taken out, basic thick white *velouté* sauce and egg yolks are added, and the final result strained and enriched with a little butter and lemon juice.

There is also a special old sauce for *brandade*, a dish we shall consider in a moment, sometimes used for other fish as well. *Sauce brandade à la provençale* starts out with what is called German sauce (*sauce allemande*), which itself starts with *velouté*, adding to it egg yolks, veal or chicken bouillon, and butter. Having achieved this, the Provençal cook continues with grated nutmeg, pepper, crushed garlic, lemon juice, and salt. After this has been well cooked, with constant stirring, it is taken from the fire and a copious portion of fine olive oil is poured in, and at the last moment a little more lemon juice and chopped chervil or tarragon is added.

The *brandade* on which this sauce customarily goes does not often appear on menus with the description *à la provençale* because it does not require this ticketing, *brandade* being a dish so emphatically of the south (Provence and Languedoc) that no specification is required. It is salt cod crushed into a paste in a mortar, into which olive oil is worked gradually and thoroughly while the cod is hot— which is somewhat hard on the cook, for it is usually done with the dish at least half in the oven. Crushed garlic is also worked in, and the resulting creamy mixture, while definitely not the sort of dish that is likely to be served at the Tour d'Argent, is a feast for any admirer of the *cuisine paysanne*, southern style.

No one who has lived in Provence can turn his thoughts to the vegetables of the local cuisine without thinking at once of artichokes. They are ubiquitous in the region, and show considerable variety, from the very large green ones, big enough so that the base of each leaf contains a quite considerable quantity of the edible pulp, to very small dark-brown ones requiring a good deal of work to get at very little substance; but what you do get is well worth the trouble, it being true of the artichoke as of many other foods that the tiniest specimens are the sweetest. In the Vaucluse area you may be surprised if you order something listed on the bill of fare as *asperge vauclusienne*, for it is a joking name in the tradition of Scotch woodcock or prairie oysters, and what you will get is not asparagus at all, but artichoke. It will be a very festive artichoke, however, stuffed with chopped ham and highly seasoned with a mixture of those herbs that seem to develop particular pungency in the dry hilly terrain of upper Provence.

Another very Provençal dish is *barigoule*—artichoke hearts, mushrooms, chopped sausage meat, bits of bacon, and, of course, much garlic. The artichoke may be the most characteristic Provençal vegetable and the tomato the most used, but close behind comes the onion, eaten raw. Then there are eggplant and summer squash, both of which have also appeared above; *cardons*, here served with a cream sauce; fennel, employed not only to add taste to other dishes but as an independent course, boiled or sautéed; and peppers.

What the artichoke is among Provençal vegetables, the fig is among fruits; and as with the artichoke, its most succulent variety is the smallest. The great purple figs, bursting open with ripeness, are marvelous eating (those who have only tasted dried figs can have no conception of what the fresh fruit is like), but the best is the little green fig that does not even look ripe, usually known as the *figue de Marseille*. In Italy an excellent hors d'œuvre is formed by combining slices of paper-thin cured ham with ripe figs, but so far as I know this delicious combination has not crossed the frontier to the Riviera, as so many other Italian dishes have and as one might have expected this to have done because of the wealth of figs along the Côte d'Azur. Perhaps it is because France (except in Corsica) has no native ham comparable to the Italian *prosciutto*, which goes best with figs.

Another Provençal fruit sure to attract the attention of any traveler through Provence, at least if he passes through the country around Aix or follows the Rhone south from Avignon through Cavaillon, famous for this specialty, is the melon. Fields are thick with them. They are of a type approaching the American honeydew rather than of the canteloupe variety. This is the only part of France where the watermelon is at all common also. Called here *pastèque*, it is better known along the Riviera, and particularly in the area of Marseilles, than in the interior; and though there seems no particular reason why it should not get farther north, it simply does not. Once in a great while one sees a watermelon in a Paris market, but it is a rarity, and as there seem to be few takers, the grocer who has displayed one or two as a curiosity is not likely to repeat the experiment. (The same is true of the sweet potato—*patate*—which can, by exercise of diligence, be found occasionally on Paris markets, though not easily; it is more frequently found in Provence, but even there is not much eaten.)

The flowering of the fruit trees in the early spring is a beautiful sight in Provence, as it is everywhere, but here the great variety of trees and the perfect backgrounds—whether the duller hues of the arid country behind the coastal mountains, or the quite different florid coloring of the Mediterranean coast—seem to intensify the spectacle. All of the common fruit trees are to be found here—peach, apricot, quince, cherry, but few plums—though the apple is conspicuously missing. However, the almond, one of the loveliest of all when its white flowers burst out, makes up for it. There are other fruit trees that are not found elsewhere in France—for instance the pomegranate (*grenade*) and the persimmon (*kaki*), though they do not seem to be much eaten.

Another fruit tree of the south is the *nèfle du Japon*, which may have a name in English, but if so, I do not know what it is. The *nèfle* proper is the English medlar, which resembles a crabapple, but the *nèfle du Japon* seems to be no relative to it. Its Japanese name is *biwa*. The fruit looks like a small apricot and has two stones. Its flesh is firm, refreshing, and a little tart—at least that of the tree which grew in my back yard at Villefranche-sur-Mer was. In this part of Provence, the Riviera, there are also of course all the citrus fruits—lemons, oranges, tangerines (*mandarines*, the French call them), the very sweet blood oranges (*sanguines*), and grapefruit—which, not quite so big and luscious as the California variety, are most properly described on French menus by the English word, while the Riviera type is called *pamplemousse*. (This distinction seems to be disappearing except in the most careful restaurants, and either variety of the fruit may turn up nowadays under either name.) Bananas grow on the Riviera, ripening some years and failing to ripen in others, depending upon the season. An edible banana is more of a freak than a dependable specialty on the Riviera. As for the big bunches of dates you see in the palms growing along the Promenade des Anglais in Nice, they do not ripen. As far as I know, the only date palms in Europe which deliver ripened fruit are those of Alicante in Spain.

Elaborate pastry and desserts are not particularly common in Provence, which is understandable when you consider the climate, though it offers some specialties in this line, such as the *bugnes* of Arles and the almond cakes (*calissons*) of Aix. What Provence does do is to candy its fruits and even its flowers. Apt and Avignon both specialize in candied fruits, the latter using slices of the melons of the region. Grasse is the largest of half a dozen towns that make candied flowers. Tarascon produces chocolate candies named for its most famous (fictitious) citizen, *tartarinades;* Carpentras offers Jordan almonds; and though almond-and-honey nougat may come from anywhere in the Vaucluse, Basses-Alpes, or Allauch regions, Montélimar has established most firmly the right to be called the nougat capital of France.

The most distinguished wines of Provence are those that fall under the heading of Côtes du Rhône—more a handy way of lumping together a number of different vintages that do not fall into other well-defined winegrowing areas than anything else, for if these growths have the shared characteristic of appearing on the banks of the Rhone, they have little else in common. They occupy patches here and there along the river, often separated from each other by considerable distances, and many of them fall outside the Provence area, but may be considered here as conveniently as anywhere.

Farthest north, in the Lyonnais, we have already mentioned the white Condrieu, with which we might also have named the less distinctive moderately dry Château Grillet of the same region, as well as the fine red Côte Rôtie, one of the better-known Rhone vintages. Crossing the river to the eastern bank and descending it nearly to Valence brings us to another well known name in the Dauphiné, Hermitage—a rich, rather heavy red, velvety, but with a hint of bitterness. Just opposite Valence, back on the west bank, is the quite dry, pale-yellow, rather fragrant Saint-Péray. Hopping the river again, for the last time (the west bank south of here has already been covered in Languedoc), we finally find ourselves again in Provence in the Avignon region, which produces some of the best Rhone wine, including one which ranks with the great vintages of other regions, Châteauneuf-du-Pape. This is a rich, generous wine with a high alcoholic content, which should let it travel well; and you will indeed find it almost everywhere. Yet my personal experience with this wine has born out strikingly the wisdom of the advice that the place to drink any wine is where it comes from. I have drunk Châteauneuf-du-Pape in many places, but there are just two occasions when I remember being particularly struck by it. One was at Villeneuve-les-Avignon, just the other side of the Rhone from Avignon, and the other was at Châteauneuf-du-Pape itself, where I not only had a remarkable bottle of red Châteauneuf-du-Pape, but learned for the first time that a white Châteauneuf-du-Pape exists —Château du Raya, I believe it was called. I have never encountered it since and that was some time ago—on May 10, 1940, to be exact, a date not difficult to fix, being the day the German Army poured across the frontiers of France, Belgium, and Holland, catching me, as a newspaper correspondent, far off my base in the wine fields of Châteauneuf-du-Pape. The two bottles that I drank on that day were both 1929, a fine year, but rather far back now, even though the Rhone wines often take many years to age. The best recent years for Côtes du Rhône are 1943, 1945, 1947, 1949, 1950, 1952, 1954, 1955, 1959 and 1961.

When you leave the Rhone and strike across country through the heart of Provence, north of the coastal ranges, beyond Aix you run into vineyards stretching all the way to the valley of the Var. These are the Côtes de Provence wines, none of them distinguished, but very drinkable table beverages usually served anonymously in carafes. Aix can point to a distinguished patron of these wines in the fifteenth-century ruler of Provence who has gone down in history as the Good King René. He first planted muscat grapes in Provence, and enjoyed himself working in his vineyards.

The region produces reds, *rosés*, and whites, but in recent years has had most luck with the last. There has not been a really good year for reds since 1933, nor for *rosés* since 1935, but whites have been good in 1935, 1937, 1939, 1944, 1945, 1947, and 1949. One of my best memories of the whites of this region is of the *blanc de blanc de Provence*, Clos Mireille, of the Château de Selle in the Domaine Ott (many of the Provence wine holdings are known as domains). Most of the properties produce wines of all three varieties, but for whites especially one may recommend Meyreuil and Villars-sur-Var, and for superior Provençal wines of whatever type, the vintages of Château de Saint-Martin, Château de Sainte-Roseline, Domaine des Moulières, Domaine de la Croix, and Clos Cibonne.

The Cote D'Azur and
the County of Nice

France's famous Riviera is part of Provence. All the
dishes of Provence will be found there. But because the
coastal strip, cut off from its hinterland by the mountain
ranges along the coast, has in addition many creations of
its own, it has seemed worth while to consider them separately.

What might seem more surprising than the difference in
food between the coastal strip and the interior, separated
by a natural barrier, is a discernible difference in the favorite dishes of different sections of the coast, not a very long

strip—less than two hundred miles from Marseilles to Menton by the shore road, and of course considerably less measured along a straight line. These differences seem to result from the persistence of eating habits going back to the time before the coastal roads existed, when every indentation in the shoreline was cupped in the mountains that ran into the sea on either side, cutting off land communications between each pocket and its neighbors. There was of course nothing to prevent the fishing boats of one bay from sailing into the next—nothing except the rivalry still evident today wherever fishermen of different regions draw on the same reservoirs of sea food for their sustenance. In less efficiently policed ages it was probably prudent for fishermen to put into the ports they had sailed from. Thus each port developed its own variations on the regional cooking, and these have not altered much over half a dozen centuries. The rigidity of such patterns, once formed, is demonstrated by one of the chief differences between the food of the coastal region and that of the interior—the richness of sea food on the coast, its virtual nonexistence just back of it. That was natural enough in the days when no means existed to keep fresh fish from spoiling in a climate that never produced natural ice and when transport was not fast enough to move perishable goods very far before they spoiled. It makes no sense now, when fish from the coast can not only be packed in artificially made ice or dry ice, but can also be moved from, say, Saint-Raphaël to Aix in two hours. Nevertheless, the interior still does not eat salt-water fish because it has never been used to eating salt-water fish. On the other hand, preserved fish—salt cod, which goes into the Provençal and Languedocian *brandade*, principally—is an important article of the diet of the interior, and having always been a better traveler than fresh fish, has also pushed down to the coast. It seems somewhat odd to find that a number of the

favorite dishes of the Riviera, whose waters are teeming
with fresh fish, are compounded from the salted or preserved variety, but it is the fact none the less.

Nice with the region about it is a law unto itself, but
there is a political reason for that—the separate existence
of a County of Nice, under the sovereignty of the House
of Savoy, for a period of nearly five hundred years. Nice
had been a part of Provence continuously for some four
hundred years before that (the city had been founded by
Greek merchants about 350 B.C., but its history as part of
the Roman civilization and of its inheritors had been interrupted by barbarian and Saracen occupations), so its
basic institutions and cuisine were Provençal. Perhaps language is more ephemeral than cooking; the private patois
of the country, Niçois, which mixes Provençal and Italian,
draws more heavily on Italian elements than on Provençal.
Thus there is a marked difference between the speech of
Nice and that of Cannes, only twenty miles away—when
Nice sets out to call a spade a spade the word is *pella;* in
Cannes it is *ramassa.* The cooking of Nice, however, is
basically more Provençal than Italian, though it includes
some very substantial Italian borrowings.

Possibly the contrast between preponderance of Italian
influence in language and preponderance of Provençal influence in cuisine does not indicate that either one or the
other is more resistant to change, but results simply from
the time when Nice became subservient to the counts of
Savoy—1388. By then Provençal cooking had already attained a stable character and had become firmly rooted in
Nice. Language, however, was still in a state of flux. Latin
remained the literary language of the learned. Provençal,
though it had had a literature at least since the eleventh
century, and was at its height in the twelfth, was still not
so much a language as a group of related dialects. No one
variety had acquired ascendancy over the others, as Floren-

tine had for Italian. Thus Italian was a stronger idiom than Provençal and was able to supplant it to a considerable extent in Nice. The situation was not the same for cooking. Although nearly two hundred years later Catherine de Médicis would still be able to bring to France Italian cooks capable of giving lessons to the French, this was the cooking of Florence contributing to the cooking of Paris, the older sophistication educating the younger; but the more earthy cooking of the French Riviera had no basic lessons to learn from the Italian Riviera. Individual dishes crossed the frontier, but not a style. The style was already fixed, Provençal, the basis of the Nice cuisine. To it had been added, coming from the west, the riches of the subdepartment of Provençal cooking which belonged to the Riviera alone. And as an overlay there filtered in from the east the cooking of Italy's Riviera Ponente.

If we start at Marseilles, with the intention of working our way eastward, we are obliged first of all to consider the dish most definitely considered to be Marseilles's own, *bouillabaisse*. Just how Marseilles acquired this reputation is not quite clear, for *bouillabaisse* occurs all along the coast, each locality having its own variation of the dish, and almost every cook having his own variation of the variation. Indeed the same cook may not make *bouillabaisse* in the same fashion twice running. There is no general agreement on all of the fish which must or must not appear in this fish chowder for it to be saluted as an authentic *bouillabaisse*, and the exact constituents of any particular *bouillabaisse* may depend therefore on what the nets have brought up that day. Marseilles may stake its claim to being the *bouillabaisse* capital of the world on the theory that it is made best there. Many persons would agree that it is. I cannot assert that it is not. However, I have not personally had the good luck to encounter a particularly remarkable *bouillabaisse* in Marseilles, though I have tried it at several restaurants there. The best *bouillabaisse* that I can recall eating on the Riviera I had at the Voile d'Or in Saint-Jean-Cap-Ferrat; but the best in my entire eating career was served me, not on the Riviera, and not even in France, but, however extraordinary it may seem, in New York—at the Restaurant du Midi, before society discovered it, when it was still a rendezvous for French sailors.

Marseilles can hardly claim *bouillabaisse* on the ground that it originated there unless it changes the account of its origin that the Marseillais will tell you quite unblushingly (Marseilles is a city of tall stories). According to this legend, *bouillabaisse* would have to be considerably older even than Marseilles, with its twenty-five hundred years of existence. It is based on the superstition that fish chowder made with saffron is a soporific (it is not, but any food taken in on the gargantuan scale that *bouillabaisse* encourages is likely to make the eater sleepy). The story goes that *bouillabaisse* was invented by Venus to put her husband Vulcan to sleep when she had a rendezvous with Mars. Possibly the Marseillais see in this story a chance to claim the dish by inheritance, as their city, long held by the Greeks, may look upon itself as the heir of Greek divinity. In any case, one may sympathize with the contention that *bouillabaisse* is divine.

More prosaic accounts also give the dish a Greek origin, pointing out that ancient Greek literature contains references to fish soups resembling *bouillabaisse*. Perhaps the Greeks who founded Marseilles did bring with them the ancestor of *bouillabaisse*. We know that they did introduce the olive into Provence, thus providing at least one important ingredient of the soup. However, whether the Greeks imported the first *bouillabaisse* or not, it would have been almost inevitable for Marseilles to have developed some such dish, even without outside inspiration. The really strange thing would be for a fishing port to fail to develop a fish chowder. Every coast of France has its own *bouillabaisse*, whether it be called *cotriade*, as in Brittany, *chaudrée*, as in Poitou, or *ttoron*, as in the Basque country; or even inland, where it is necessarily made of fresh-water fish, like the *pauchouse* of Burgundy. But when these soups are mentioned, they are often described as the *bouillabaisse* of their own regions, in unconscious tribute to the special excellence of the Riviera—or Marseilles— variety of fish chowder. The tribute is justified. *Bouillabaisse* is a great soup. One would be tempted to use a superlative to describe it if there were not so near at hand— on this same coast—two serious rivals for top place among soups, *soupe aux poissons* and *pistou*.

The subject of *bouillabaisse* is a complicated one. It is also one of those about which tempers rise easily. Everyone has his own idea of what constitutes the real *bouillabaisse* (all others are imitations), and if a contrary opinion is suggested, he acts as if his honor had been impugned. The easiest, and least subtle, way to provoke a discussion guaranteed to end a lifelong friendship forever is to bring up the issue of lobster. There are two chief schools of thought about this. One is that a man who would put lobster in *bouillabaisse* would poison wells. The other is that a man who would leave it out would starve his children. I have had excellent *bouillabaisse* with lobster and excellent *bouillabaisse* without lobster. Of course only one of them is the real *bouillabaisse*. Unfortunately, I do not know which.

There are other points about which I must claim ignorance. What are the fish that go into *bouillabaisse*—and this time I am not thinking of the arguments, of which there are plenty, about which fish ought to go into *bouillabaisse* and which, in the name of morality, should be kept strictly out of it, but even when the cooks have agreed on the selection, what fish are they? I know their names in

French, I know what they look like, I know what they taste like—but have they any names in English? Do they exist in any English-speaking country? If they do not, English has no occasion to name them. Bilingual dictionaries are not as useful as you might think. They sometimes give, with an air of perfect assurance, an equivalent term that may translate one word by another word, but does not translate one fish by exactly the same sort of fish in another country. (You do not even have to cross language borders to get into this sort of trouble; just try to get an Englishman and an American to agree on what "partridge" means.) "Perch" is *"perche"* in French—but is any fish the French might call a *perche* (and they scatter the name around about as freely as we do the word "perch") necessarily a fish we would call a perch? Columbus reached the New World two centuries before Linnaeus was born. In the interval Europeans encountered new fish, birds, animals, and plants, and named them for home species that they vaguely resembled. And even after Linnaeus had provided a sort of Bertillon system for the identification of species, a good deal of naming was done by persons unacquainted with it. Add to that the propensity of species for varying when their environment is changed, and the identification of exact equivalents becomes well-nigh impossible. Not so many years ago, French streams and lakes were stocked with American rainbow trout and smallmouthed black bass, species previously unknown in France. Are their descendants now identical in taste with the trout and the bass of North America? Or have they undergone a metamorphosis, like the oysters that are moved from Cancale to Marennes, and proceed to become Marennes, quite different in quality from *cancalaises?*

The Mediterranean is rich in good eating fish. I know them on their home grounds, but they do not exist on my native New England coast. Perhaps some of them may be

found in the Gulf of Mexico—I have been told that the
rouget, regularly translated as red mullet, is found there—
or in California, where the French *langouste* is supposed to
appear, the New England lobster being of course the
equivalent, though not, my palate tells me, the exact equivalent, of the French *homard*. But how about the *chapon*?
Here the difficulty is increased because even French dictionaries ignore the *chapon*. There is no definition for it in
my *Petit Larousse*—except "capon," which does not fit
this case. Even the fat *Larousse Gastronomique*, with its
more than one thousand pages devoted to defining nothing
but food, only adds to the literal meaning its figurative
sense (also from Provence and Languedoc) of a slice of
bread rubbed with garlic and dampened with oil and vinegar, added to a salad.

Yet the *chapon*, one of the fish that go into *bouillabaisse*,
when you can get it, is one of the tastiest fish of the Mediterranean. It is advisable to say "when you can get it" because it is becoming very scarce. When I was living on the
Riviera, I had a standing order with my fishmonger to save
me a *chapon* whenever he received any. I seldom got more
than one a month. It is a solidly built fish with an enormous
boxlike head about one third the size of the whole animal.
The flesh is white, firm, often somewhat flaky when baked,
and admirably adapted to absorbing the aromas of thyme,
laurel, and the like. Has it a name in English?

What is *rascasse?* It is a coarse fish, armed with spines,
which lives in holes in the rocks, and would be allowed to
stay there if it were not for *bouillabaisse*. Alone it is not
particularly good eating, but it is the soul of *bouillabaisse*.
Cooked with other fish, *rascasse* is one of those catalytic
foods, like the truffle, whose own contribution to taste
seems meager, but which has the gift of intensifying other
flavors. My French-English dictionary has no idea what
rascasse is. Sculpin, perhaps? It is also mute on the subject of

saint-pierre (though it knows that *Saint Jacques* is a scallop). *Larousse Gastronomique*, doing better, says it's called John Dory in England, but none of my English friends know what a John Dory is. I can only describe it as a fish of firm, tasty white flesh. Its name comes from two round spots on either side, where, legendarily, its ancestor was held between the thumb and finger of St. Peter the firsherman when he lifted it from the water. As for *fiélas* and *sarran*, both likely to appear in *bouillabaisse*, no dictionary at my disposal names them at all.

These are minor difficulties of definition. The major one is to describe *bouillabaisse* in terms that all its champions will accept. Even the basic statement, that *bouillabaisse* is a sort of fish chowder, we shall have to qualify shortly; but for the moment we can let it stand. One indisputable fact is that *bouillabaisse* should be brought to a violent boil and cooked quickly. It shouldn't take more than fifteen minutes to cook a *bouillabaisse*. For the ingredients, only one fish is agreed upon by everyone—*rascasse*. It is also generally agreed that *rascasse* alone could not make a *bouillabaisse*—there must be other fish in the stew. No two lists are the same, and *rascasse* is the only name common to all of some half dozen recipes I have just compared.

The condiments and the seasoning play just as important a part as the fish in the quality of the finished *bouillabaisse*. Everybody agrees that it is not a *bouillabaisse* if it does not include olive oil, tomatoes, and saffron—which gives it its typical orange color. There is virtually complete agreement—on the Riviera—that none but Mediterranean fish should be included, and specifically that mussels have no role to play in a *bouillabaisse*. (Mussels are not, as some persons think, foreign to the Mediterranean, but are not as good there as in the cold Atlantic waters.) This is the main point that distinguishes *bouillabaisse à la parisienne* from the Riviera variety: Parisians insist on putting mussels in it. This does not mean that whenever you order this dish in Paris it will contain mussels. There are plenty of Mediterranean cooks in the capital who think this sacrilege. You may even find a Riviera restaurant here or there which makes its *bouillabaisse* in the Parisian style, but this will be more rare.

This list of ingredients gives little idea of the riches of *bouillabaisse*, for it contains only what everyone is agreed on. But everyone is also agreed that there should be much more than this, even if the lists are not the same. First for the fish: one school holds that the classic *bouillabaisse*, whatever other fish it includes, must contain *rascasse*, *congre* (conger eel), and *grondin* (a fish that belongs to the same family as the *rouget*). A Marseillais who was very firm with me about what ought to go into *bouillabaisse* left out the *grondin*, but as he put in its cousin, perhaps it amounts to much the same thing. His list was *rascasse*, *chapon*, *saint-pierre*, *congre*, *baudroie* (this last is a fish with a big head, like the *chapon*, which is perhaps related to it), *rouget*, *rouquier*, *merlan* (vaguely whiting), and *loup*, which in the opinion of my dictionary, for which I take no responsibility, is sea perch. Another recipe calls for *rascasse*, *saint-pierre*, *fiélas*, *baudroie*, and *sarran*. A nineteenth-century writer puts down the essentials as *rascasse*, *rouget*, *orade*, *pagel*, *saint-pierre*, *loup*, and *galinette*, this last a fish that glares out at you through eyes set in a thicket of spikes. (My Marseillais objects to the omission of *merlan* here, but does not seem to mind the absence of *congre* and *grondin*.) Finally, Nice has provided me with a quite different aquarium—moray, conger eel, *rascasse*, *chapon*, deep-sea eel, *baudroie*, "and others." Perhaps it may be summed up by saying that *bouillabaisse* is made of *rascasse* and as many other kinds of Mediterranean fish as the cook can lay his hands on.

Once the principle of putting shellfish into *bouillabaisse* is admitted at all, there seems less argument about what has to be in. There is agreement about what has to be out, as has already been noted—mussels, clams, and the like are considered inadmissible. But almost anything in the lobster-crab category seems to be all right. *Langouste* (spiny lobster) is almost *de rigueur*. *Homard* (our Atlantic lobster, or at any rate a close relative) ought to be ruled out on the same grounds as the mussel—though not unknown in the Mediterranean, it is better in colder waters. Nevertheless, it sometimes turns up in *bouillabaisse*. So do crabs, including the variety known as sea spiders.

It would be too complicated to go into all the variations of the other ingredients. Here is the Marseillais assortment: chopped onions (or onions and leeks), pressed seeded tomatoes, plenty of garlic, fennel, shredded parsley, thyme, laurel, dried orange peel, the best olive oil, salt, pepper, and powdered saffron.

All of the ingredients except the softer fish, which take only about half as long to cook as the others, go into the pot together and are covered with water or with fish bouillon. The latter gives a thicker richer soup, and the bouillon of *bouillabaisse* should be a little thick, though Riviera cooks do not like the Paris practice of making it so by adding butter. This, they hold, is committing treason to the olive oil; and besides it makes the bouillon too thick. If the proper materials go into the *bouillabaisse*, they add, the bouillon will be rich enough without butter. They do not quite accuse Paris of skimping on the ingredients and covering up with butter, but if you draw that conclusion they will not contradict you. Under any circumstances, a Riviera cook considers it something of a presumption for a Parisian to attempt *bouillabaisse*.

The *bouillabaisse* is served in a fashion that makes it the whole meal unless you are still able to eat dessert afterwards. Bouillon and fish are served in separate dishes, giving you two courses. The bouillon is poured over slices of bread, which your true *bouillabaisse*-lover insists should not be tampered with, but should be placed in the dish in the state in which it left the oven, not toasted, fried, or sprinkled with grated cheese, as it sometimes is. In Marseilles, they are so fussy on this minor point that a special kind of bread, called *marette*, is made, whose sole destiny is to be submerged in *bouillabaisse*.

The separate serving of the fish may have produced a change in the cooking of *bouillabaisse*. Every recipe I have seen directs that the fish should be cut into several pieces, all of the same size, regardless of the dimensions of the original animal, but I cannot recall ever having been served a *bouillabaisse* in the two-plate fashion when the fish were not whole. Presented separately, they look better that way. Apparently cooks only cut up the fish now when they intend to serve everything in one crammed bowl—or perhaps the size of the pot available determines whether the diner is going to get his *bouillabaisse* in one dish (small pot, cut-up fish) or in two (large pot, whole fish). Nice goes the serving tradition one better by making it three courses—the *langouste* (and crabs, if any) are served on a separate platter from the fish. This may indicate that Nice is the home of the *bouillabaisse* with lobster; but Marseilles also seems to use lobster almost invariably these days. Toulon is sometimes more austere, holding to the fish-alone theory. Some restaurants give you a choice, probably thinking of your purse more than your palate—lobster in the *bouillabaisse* increases its cost considerably.

Some restaurants offer you grated cheese to sprinkle on your *bouillabaisse*. This seems rather unnecessary; enough excitement has been provided for the taste buds already, and the bland addition of grated cheese is a letdown rather than the opposite. If you are going to try to top the flavor of *bouillabaisse*, what you require is a bold stroke—not a soothing additional taste, but something to give you a real jolt. This is provided by *rouille*.

Rouille is a classic product of Riviera cooking, excellent in *bouillabaisse* and even better with *soupe aux poissons*. It does not seem to be easy to find any more; certainly the Riviera restaurants do not suggest it unless you ask for it. This may be partly that *rouille* is a little troublesome to make, but I suspect that the chief reason is that the Côte d'Azur has been overrun for too long a time by Anglo-Saxons whose taste buds are cursed with a limited vocabulary—Americans who study the bill of fare with panic and finally ask for ham and eggs, and Britons who bewail the difficulty of finding a bit of cold boiled mutton. Restaurateurs may have learned their lesson by putting soup containing *rouille* before customers without warning them. Even less limited eaters should perhaps be told what to expect the first time. *Rouille,* properly made, is hot. The effect on the mouth is a little bit like that of those innocent-looking red and brown pastes that accompany Indonesian food, and which, when tasted, make you comprehend instantly why the accepted drink with *rijsttafel* is not wine, but beer: it is useful to put the fire out.

Rouille is made by crushing garlic and a red pepper together—the more of the pepper, the hotter the result and the better the *rouille*—together with bread crumbs, olive oil, and fish bouillon. It has the consistency of heavy cream and the color of reddish mustard. A spoonful of it is ladled into the middle of the soup, and remains floating on its surface like sour cream on borsch. One might think that so hot a condiment would banish all other taste than its own. On the contrary it brings out brilliantly the diverse flavors of the *bouillabaisse,* apparently promoting them to its own high key of intensity.

Bouillabaisse de sardines, made with fresh sardines, of course, deserves the name, for except for the change that its name denotes—the only fish in it is sardines—it follows the definition well enough, containing all the other essentials—oil, tomatoes, saffron—and about the same additional ingredients, plus sliced potatoes. But at least two other dishes bearing the name might be accused of appearing under false pretenses, for neither of them contains fish. These are the exceptions to the statement that *bouillabaisse* is a fish chowder, which we will now find it necessary to qualify somewhat. However, they are the sort of exceptions which prove the rule, for the name was applied with sarcastic intent. This is particularly obvious in the case of *bouillabaisse borgne*, since it means one-eyed *bouillabaisse*, a description not intended as a compliment. Actually it is a quite respectable soup with a less contemptuous name also—*aïgo sau d'iou*. It is made with a bouillon concocted of olive oil, chopped onions and leeks, white wine, crushed tomatoes, crushed garlic, thyme, laurel, salt, pepper, and saffron, all cooked together in water. Potatoes are sliced into this bouillon; when they are cooked, eggs are poached in it. The bouillon, poured over slices of bread, is then served in one dish and the potatoes and poached eggs in another.

Bouillabaisse d'épinards (likely to be offered under its Provençal name of *boui-abaisso d'espinarc*) is particularly popular in Marseilles, but you will not find it in tourist restaurants, only in those frequented by the citizens of the port themselves. This is made of spinach first boiled separately, then pressed to get rid of all moisture, and chopped. It then goes into an earthenware casserole with sliced potatoes, garlic, fennel, salt, pepper, and saffron, is covered with water, and cooked slowly, covered. When the potatoes are done, eggs are broken on top of the dish, and when *they* are done, it is served in the vessel in which it was cooked.

There is also a *bouillabaisse de morue*, in which salt

cod and potatoes replace the fish of the coastal dish; but this is made chiefly in the interior, in an attempt to approach with salt fish the famous Riviera dish made with fresh fish. It must be admitted that the attempt is not very successful.

As though the *bouillabaisse* situation were not complicated enough, it becomes further involved by the existence of *bourride*, usually described as a special variety of *bouillabaisse*. It is sometimes difficult to determine in any given case whether a certain soup is *bourride* or *bouillabaisse*, the former, like the latter, appearing in many variations along the coast. One work generally considered authoritative explains that one of the distinguishing features is that there is no saffron in the *bourride;* unfortunately on another page the same book gives a recipe for *bourride*—one only, no variations permitted—and calls for saffron. Generally speaking, the distinction appears to be this: *bourride* uses only fish of white flesh, never includes shellfish, and is usually made of rather smaller fish than is *bouillabaisse;* it mixes *aïoli* into the bouillon; and often it adds egg yolks also.

Marseilles provides the flavor of fish in soups for all pocketbooks. After *bouillabaisse* with lobster, necessarily expensive, one descends to *bouillabaisse* without lobster, then to *bourride*, and finally to the most economical means of providing the sea food taste, the use of fish leftovers. This appears in *soupe de poisson au vermicelle à la marseillaise*, in which fish heads, tails, fins, backbones, and other unwanted morsels abandoned when the fish was used for other purposes are cooked in the bouillon to give it flavor and, of course, strained out before the soup is served. If this sounds like a poor man's dish, as in a sense it is, it does not taste like one, for the bouillon is rich with the fragrances of olive oil, chopped onions, tomato extract, garlic, parsley, laurel, thyme, and saffron. The vermicelli goes in toward the end, and the fish flavor is just as authentic as if it had been derived from nobler portions.

Marseilles has more or less of a monopoly of one sort of sea food—bivalves. Shellfish in the oyster-clam-mussel-scallop category are usually better in colder waters, as we have already hinted, and though they occur in the Mediterranean, are not much eaten here. The Marseilles region is the exception, probably because the lagoons lying beyond the low coast provide the best possible conditions for the raising of these shellfish, allowance being made for the water temperature. Marseilles gets some rather unusual ones. Besides mussels and *praires,* a clam that resembles in taste the American cherrystone, also found on the Atlantic coast, Marseillais eat *clovisses,* a delicately flavored clam distinguished by the lustrous mother-of-pearl lining of its shell (the somewhat similarly shaped clam sold in Paris under the same name is different from the Mediterranean species and, for once, not as good) and *violets,* which you may not care for if you are not used to them, their iodine taste being quite pronounced. I do not recall ever coming across scallops on the Riviera, though in Paris I have been served *coquilles Saint-Jacques à la provençale,* in which the scallops were cooked, not in the creamy cheese sauce with which their large shell is ordinarily filled in Paris, but out of the shell, in a thin delicate sauce of which I should imagine the ingredients were not much more than garlic and white wine. They were delicious, and I can recommend scallops prepared in this fashion, but I include it here with reservations, as it does not appear to me, in spite of the name, to be a Provençal dish—it includes neither tomatoes nor olive oil, and I suspect the chef who served it to me of having named it himself with more regard for the amount of garlic (not exclusively Provençal) which he used in his sauce than for the ordinary meaning of the label *à la provençale.* He himself came from the Jura.

An unusual sea food dish that is definitely Marseillais

is *poutargue des Martigues*—Martigues is on the Etang de
Berre, that tremendous lagoon which lies behind the coast
back of Marseilles—a Provençal substitute for caviar. This
is the roe of the gray mullet, grated into olive oil. Sea
urchins are much eaten in Marseilles also, but the city has
no monopoly of them—they are popular all along the
coast, and are plentiful everywhere, almost too plentiful
in the view of bathers, who have discovered that you can
develop a very sore foot by stepping on one of them.

Among other dishes for which Marseilles is especially
known are the *pieds et paquets*—the tripe preparation already described—and its own variety of *aïoli*. The Marseilles *aïoli* puts this garlicky cousin of mayonnaise on a
mixture of boiled cod, snails, carrots, string beans, and potatoes.

Eastward from Marseilles is Toulon, the great Mediterranean naval base, which I always associate with good
fish, not because it has any monopoly of the fine varieties
found throughout the Mediterranean, but simply because
it was there that I first happened to taste *rouget*. It was
cooked in the simplest possible fashion, sautéed in oil
almost without seasoning, and the natural taste of its subtle
flaky flesh could hardly have been bettered by even the
most skillful additions. In spite of the fact that it is translated in all dictionaries as red mullet, I remain skeptical
about this definition. It is a sort of *grondin*, which I do
not believe would be considered a mullet, though local
usages for such terms differ so widely that it is difficult to
be sure—*muge* or *mulet* should be the French equivalent
for "mullet," but the fish these names represent looks
nothing like a *grondin*, which is translated as red gurnet.
Rouget translated literally would come out "redfish," but
I can assert that it is nothing like the fish known by that
name on Cape Ann, where I have eaten it often, flying in
the face of the local superstition that holds that the scabs

which often appear on this fish are cancers that will infallibly be passed on to the eater. Redfish are not bad eating, but they are not even in the same world as the *rouget*. For the benefit of ichthyologists more learned about fish in the uncooked state than I am, I can describe the *rouget* as a rather small fish (in the restaurant at least it does not get over one foot in length), with tender flesh, a delicate orange-rose color, two long tentacles striking backward from its lower jaw, and rough scales, which are generally left on when it is cooked. This (and not their taste), plus the fact that the smaller *rougets* are often cooked without being cleaned, is probably what led Brillat-Savarin to call them the woodcock of the sea. But the comparison on the basis of taste would be defensible enough also, for the *rouget* is as subtle and as satisfying in the category of fish as the woodcock in the category of game.

Rouget, chapon, which has already been discussed, and *loup* constitute the trinity of great Mediterranean fish— from the gourmet's point of view, that is; I believe sportsmen have a different classification. *Loup,* or *loup de mer,* literally sea wolf, is described by the dictionaries as sea perch, and again I have my reservations. It is also held by French dictionaries to be nothing but the Mediterranean name for the *bar,* an excellent eating fish from the Atlantic, but the identification is at least clouded by the fact that there are two Atlantic fish described as *bar.* In any case it is a firm-fleshed fish, with white meat and is larger than the *rouget.* While the latter has so distinctive a taste of its own before any art on the part of the chef has intervened that it seems blasphemy to disguise it, *loup,* while excellent before treatment, is also neutral enough to be a splendid carrier of other aromas. As a result, the favored, appetite-provoking method of cooking it on the Riviera is on the table before the eyes of the diner over a little fire of twigs, usually fennel or grapevine shoots. The twigs are often doused with brandy, and the fish may have been stuffed beforehand with some preparation containing an assortment of the aromatic herbs so much used in Provençal cooking. One reason for my skepticism about the identity of the *loup* and the *bar* is that I have never seen the *bar* treated this way in the north, and a rather exhaustive cookbook that I have consulted gives sixteen ways of dealing with *bar*, but not this one, which is almost the only way you get *loup* in the south. Indeed the cookbook gives a recipe for *bar à la provençale* which has no relation to the Riviera manner of cooking *loup*—it is sautéed in oil, then covered with *sauce provençale*, powdered with bread crumbs, moistened with more oil, and finished in the oven.

The use of *sauce provençale* marks this as belonging definitely to the regional cuisine, but I am not quite so sure about *sardines aux épinards à la provençale*. In this case fresh sardines rolled in egg and bread crumbs are fried in butter and served on a bed of spinach also cooked in butter and seasoned with crushed garlic. I have never encountered this dish on the Riviera or anywhere else in Provence, and I strongly suspect that, like *coquilles Saint-Jacques à la provençale*, it was named by an outlander overimpressed by its garlic. Frying the sardines in butter is particularly suspicious. This may be a misnamed northern variation of the way fresh sardines are cooked in Antibes, *sardines à l'antiboise*, which also uses the egg-and-bread crumb coating, but fries the fish in olive oil and serves them with that other trademark of Provençal cooking, tomatoes, in this case in the form of a highly seasoned tomato extract plus, of course, garlic.

If none of the fish described above may be ascribed specifically to Toulon, one dish, and a very special one, was developed here—*esquinado toulonais*. It starts with crabs, which are cooked in water to which a little vinegar has been added. The meat and, if any, the eggs, are then scooped out of the shells and combined with an equal quantity of mussels, which have been cooked separately, in a sauce made from the water in which the mussels were cooked. The combined ingredients are then put back into the shells and placed in the oven to brown.

Continuing eastward, the next place that might attract our attention is Saint-Tropez—a delightful little town that used to be a quiet hideaway off the main routes of travel, at the end of its peninsula, but which has now been "discovered," and has become something of a three-ring circus. I connect Saint-Tropez with *soupe aux poissons*, one of the three great Riviera soups. Saint-Tropez has no monopoly on *soupe aux poissons*—every town along the coast makes it, but every town makes it differently—but it is impressed on my memory of Saint-Tropez for a number of reasons, one of which was the difficulty of getting it. Saint-Tropez claims that its *soupe aux poissons* is unique because it employs fish highly local in their habits. They are taken in the Gulf of Saint-Tropez, but nowhere else in the Mediterranean. I do not vouch for the statement, but simply pass it on—though I was shown the fish that went into it, and one at least looked totally unlike anything I had seen in the Nice fishmarket. It was small, rather flat, and a brilliant chemical-looking green with a metallic shine to it, as abhorrent a color as those that automobile manufacturers apply to their cars, possibly to sicken pedestrians. It did not seem that so artificial-looking a color could appear in nature, but there it was.

I met this fish on my last day in Saint-Tropez. I had been clamoring for the local variety of *soupe aux poissons* for a week or so, but could not get it. Its makers, in Saint-Tropez at least, are less willing to compromise with the ingredients than the creators of *bouillabaisse,* and no one would produce it without the correct dosage of all the half dozen or so different fish supposed to go into it. They were not all available because the mistral had been blowing without a let-up during that whole period. This is supposed to discourage the fish, or at least some of the fish, which do not allow themselves to be caught in weather they feel is unsuitable for the purpose. The effect of the mistral on the fish may be a legend, but the effect on the fishermen was observable. They preferred to stay ashore and play *pétanque*, and no one who observed the violent bouncing of the yachts anchored within the shelter of the break-water of the little port, as they tossed up and down along the seawall to which they were attached, would have been likely to blame them. The mistral was still blowing, rather more softly however, on the day I was to leave, and I had given up the idea of trying the Saint-Tropez version of *soupe aux poissons;* but at noon my host, an amateur cook of great skill, arrived beaming with a collection of fish and announced *soupe aux poissons* for lunch. I think it was the best I have ever tasted. I ate so much of it and sat at the table so late that only a sense of obligation to the family that ran the Restaurant de la Ponche where I had eaten so often took me there for an early dinner before I left. I had to say good-by, but I had not made up my mind when I went into the place whether I would attempt to down something light or postpone the chore of eating until later—much later. But Renée, the handsome daughter of the house who waited on the clients, let out a whoop when she saw me come in, and her mother dashed out of the kitchen wiping her hands on her apron to announce that for my last meal in Saint-Tropez she had managed to round up just enough of the right fish to make a *soupe aux poissons* for one (she had made enough for half a dozen). So I had another tremendous helping of the Saint-Tropez version of this dish. It is the only time in my life, I think, that I have had enough *soupe aux poissons.*

Other parts of the country where this name is applied

to soups like *bouillabaisse* serve you the soup and the fish that have been cooked in it—for that matter, you may even come across this sort of fish soup on the Riviera, though if the menu-writer is alive to the subtleties of his art, he will set it down as *soupe de poissons*, not *soupe aux poissons*. A dish providing soup and fish is not the geniune article, as the Riviera understands it. In *soupe aux poissons*, no fish is visible. It is there all right, but it has disappeared into the liquid. The body of the fish has gone. The soul remains. The fish is ground, crushed, pulverized, and then cooked until it has become liquid itself, and the soup is then strained to eliminate any telltale traces of the ingredients that provided its greatness. For it is really a great soup, more subtle than *bouillabaisse*, which is a great soup, too. The seasoning of both seems to be very much the same. I cannot vouch for it, for I am unable to find a recipe for *soupe aux poissons*. It must have gotten into some cookbooks somewhere, for it is made all up and down the Riviera, but I can find no trace of it, and not even a mention in the guidebooks. The fame of *bouillabaisse* seems to have obliterated knowledge of the other great fish soup of this region, perhaps because it requires a better educated sense of taste on the part of the eater to savor *soupe aux poissons*, whose technique is that of the rapier, than to appreciate *bouillabaisse*, which slugs you over the head with a bludgeon. It would be hard to say which is the better; but it is safe to assert that *rouille* shows up to more advantage in *soupe aux poissons* than in *bouillabaisse*.

It may seem strange that Cannes, the yachtmen's mecca and the playground of royalty, seems to have contributed nothing to gastronomy. But it is easy to see why. These cosmopolitan vacation centers cater to an international population, and provide it with the international standardized hotel cuisine. The majority of the restaurants' customers have no roots there and provide no encouragement for regional cooking—and their presence corrupts the natives. What is odder is that the wealthy society (and now motion-picture) coterie that flocks to Cannes does not even receive particularly good service from its practitioners of the international cuisine. Cannes is a curious spectacle, a luxury city without a single really good restaurant (there are a few within easy reach of it, however). Similarly Monaco has, so far as I know, added nothing to the Riviera repertoire, in spite of the fact that a couple of not particularly exceptional soups bear the name of Monaco, probably the inventions of individual chefs; but they are not products of a school of cooking. Perhaps there are not enough Monegasques to have developed one. At least Monte Carlo has several rather good restaurants, which is more than can be said for a number of other society rendezvous in addition to Cannes. It would seem that high society, if there is such a thing any more, is not particularly interested in eating.

A little way behind Cannes, cradled in hills back from the coast, is Grasse, the perfume center, which has some specialties to its credit. During much of the year the slopes are carpeted with entire hillsides of lavender and other flowers destined to go into the perfumes, and the rather heavy fragrance of the 85,000 acres of flowers might seem likely to discourage appetites. Perhaps Grasse goes in for somewhat coarse dishes as an antidote to the cloying scent of the flowers. One of her specialties is *sou-fassum*, which does not require much imagination to convert from the local form of Provençal into *chou farci*, stuffed cabbage, and which is a little more than that, for the cabbage after being stuffed is then cooked in a *pot-au-feu*, either the conventional beef-veal type, or one in which mutton substitutes for these meats. Also rather to the rustic side is *tourte de courge à la grassoise,* an impressive title for squash pie. Less unexpected from this flower-growing city is its *fleurs pralinées,* candied flower petals.

Back on the coast, about halfway between Cannes and Nice, Antibes boasts a considerable number of local dishes for a small place. It is also, however, a very old place, the Antipolis of the Greeks, who founded it in the fifth century B.C. Like Grasse, it raises flowers, but for their own sake, not for perfume, and it shares with Grasse the stuffed cabbage specialty, though it spells it *lou fassun* (for *le farci*—the cabbage has disappeared from the name). The Antibes method of preparing sardines has already been mentioned. At least two egg-dishes carry the town's name. *Œufs poêlés à l'antiboise* is made first by browning newly hatched fish and roe rolled in flour in a frying pan (the recipe I have before me says to use butter, but I am certain that in Antibes they use oil), after which very small dices of Gruyère cheese and crushed garlic are added. When the cheese melts, the eggs are broken on top and the frying pan goes into the oven for finishing. The eggs are served with chopped parsley sprinkled over them. *Œufs brouillés à l'antiboise* starts off with scrambled eggs made in one pan and slices of summer squash sautéed in oil in another. When both are done, a layer of the eggs is laid in the bottom of a casserole, followed by a layer of the squash drenched in tomato extract, and layers are thus built up alternately until the casserole is full, the last layer being of eggs. This is then covered with grated Parmesan cheese, doused in melted butter, browned in the oven, and served with tomato sauce.

Beyond Antibes we come to Nice, sixth city of France. From here to the Italian border, except for the enclave of Monaco, is the territory of the County of Nice, which also extends back from the coast to take in the mountainous hinterland. It is not a very considerable territory—part of the present department of the Alpes-Maritimes, with only one other town of any size, Menton, but it possesses a particularly rich cuisine. Many dishes bear the label *à la niçoise*, which usually indicates the presence of tomatoes and garlic.

Nice is the country of *pistou*, one of the finest soups I know. It seems undoubtedly to have come across the border from Italy, deriving from a Genoese sauce called *pesto*, which it is the boast of Genoa cannot be made properly anywhere else. If we apply this statement only to *pesto* proper, we can perhaps accept it, for the *pistou* of Nice is not made with exactly the same ingredients as the *pesto* of Genoa. But if the two are to be compared, my vote would go to *pistou*.

Pesto, it has been stated above, is a sauce, not a soup. Strictly speaking, *pistou* also means not so much the whole soup as the special seasoning added to it which has given its name to the soup. The Genoese make *pesto* by using a pestle and mortar to mash together leaves of sweet basil, Sardinian sheep's milk cheese, butter, garlic, and olive oil. They put it into soup, but they also use it on macaroni, meat, and fish. In Nice I have never encountered it except in soup. The Nice formula for the paste that gives the soup its soul omits butter and uses cheese of the Gruyère type. The sweet basil is known locally as *basilic*, which may be the same thing as the plant by whose name it is translated into English, but if so it seems to have developed somewhat different characteristics. It is a tender herb, growing only in the warm south; hence *pistou* is unknown in Paris.

The soup in which the *pistou* is placed, giving it its flavor and its name, is a form of *minestrone*. One Nice recipe gives the vegetables that go into it as white beans, tomatoes, and summer squash. Another names string beans, potatoes, tomatoes, and vermicelli. My cook, who comes from Fréjus, which is outside of the County of Nice, but still in the *basilic* belt, and who makes the best *pistou* I have ever tasted, says it does not matter what vegetables you put in *pistou*, as long as there are plenty of them. What does matter is that into this rich mixture of a thick liquid crowded with vegetables you put the *pistou* (whose composition is sacred and must not vary) at the very last moment—just before the soup is removed from the stove to be served.

Nice food is outdoor food. A great deal of the region's eating is done in the open, for a number of months in very hot weather, which accounts for the development of many specialties having a picnic air about them. One of them is a famous local creation, *pan bagnat* (French, *pain baigné*; English, bathed bread). What the bread is bathed in is olive oil. A round bun is sliced in half, soaked in the oil, and between the halves are placed various items of the Nice repertoire—always tomato, green pepper, and black olives, sometimes slices of onion, slices of hard-boiled egg, radishes, or anchovies—or all of them. The proper place to eat this is on the beach, in the sun, between dips. It is a wonderfully refreshing hot weather snack; it is all you will want to eat in the middle of a hot Mediterranean day, and you will want the ocean handy to wash the oil off your chin when you have finished.

In the same category of hot weather outdoor food is *salade niçoise*. This is a salad innocent of lettuce, but it contains many other ingredients, all variable except two— it contains tomatoes, which must be cut into quarters (if they are sliced, it's not a *salade niçoise*; the local population is adamant on this point), and it is abundantly laced with olive oil mixed with *pissala*, which means anchovies ground into a paste in a mortar. Black olives are almost invariably included, and so are slices of green pepper. Filets of anchovy may be, in addition to the *pissala*, perhaps the lima-like beans known as *fèves* (raw), radishes, and occasionally hard-boiled eggs. In Paris I have been served a so-called *salade niçoise* containing cooked string beans and even potatoes, necessarily cooked, but a purist would regard either of these, particularly the last, with horror. A genuine *salade niçoise* should contain nothing cooked, with the possible exception of hard-boiled egg, a rather dubious addition not often permitted in Nice itself.

Pissala accounts also for the name of *pissaladiera*, an Italian gift to Nice, related to the famous Naples *pizza*. As made in Nice this is a large pie-shaped pastry shell filled with cooked onions, black olives, and anchovy filets. A variant is covered with tomato sauce; sometimes the round shell is filled half with one version, half with the other.

Two vegetables are often eaten raw as hors d'œuvres—*fevettes*, the tiny first early *fèves*, and the early small artichokes, with olive oil dressing. The artichoke is a favorite vegetable of Nice. More different kinds of this vegetable are to be seen than you would imagine existed in the gay animated open-air market of the rue Saint-François-de-Paule, which the municipality is rumored to be about to suppress in a misguided gesture toward modernity. Fortunately no municipal council can abolish the old town of Nice, in which the market stands, so it is to be hoped that eventually it will be decided that there is no point in eliminating the market. It is one of the most brilliant spectacles of Nice, with its hundreds of small merchants, many of whom are also the growers of the produce they sell, putting into the sale of food a gusto capable of inspiring in the buyer an equal enthusiasm for its eating. The food market is continued by the brilliance of the flower market. In narrow, twisting side streets, through which handcarts bear down ominously upon you are fish stores so crammed with every kind of Mediterranean water-animal that you have the impression that you are shouldering your way through the fish as through a crowd; butcher shops with long rows of naked calves' heads turning their placid sightless gaze on the passers-by; horse butchers displaying entire carcasses of fat horses with artificial roses running down their spines and ribbons fluttering from their flanks; shops that sell nothing but macaroni and noodles, in all shapes and even several colors; other shops that sell nothing but olives and olive oil. If you leave the old town and cross the Place Masséna to Caressa, you will find one of the most fascinating luxury food shops in the world. Its counters of cheeses and sausages seem to offer every known variety of both, domestic or imported. It scours the earth for exotic foods. One of its window displays some years ago was made up entirely of packaged foods from China. What was in them nobody knew; the only language on the cartons was Chinese. But in the middle of the labyrinth of ideographs which decorated one package was a picture, not quite authentically Chinese—the familiar drawing of Mickey Mouse.

The richness of the Nice markets is the outward token of the richness of its food. The crowded fishmongers are a reminder of the crowded Mediterranean. It seems something of a miracle that it remains crowded, given the existence of a certain Niçois specialty, *poutina et nounat*. These are barely hatched fish, taken at the time when they emerge from their eggs, so that fish and roe are often mixed together. By a special dispensation the Nice area is absolved from the usual conservation regulations which elsewhere protect fish at this time. They are taken in special nets in April and May, and are boiled and eaten with olive oil and lemon juice, or cooked in omelettes (or in the Antibes egg dish described above) or fritters.

When the fish become a little larger, but not much larger, they appear as *petite friture de la rade*. Smaller than sardines, they can be cooked whole, without cleaning, and eaten entire—head, tail, fins, bones, and all. They are rolled in flour and cooked in olive oil. The next stage of growth presents them as *friture de poissons*, cooked in the same fashion, but now too big to be eaten entire. Finally they reach the age of individuality, and each fish gets the special treatment due its species.

Nice treats the major fish in standard fashion—*loup* grilled over twigs, *chapon* baked with herbs, *rougets* sautéed and served sizzling on a hot plate. It also has its own variations. *Rougets à la niçoise* are cooked in oil on a bed of tomatoes and served with anchovies and lemon juice. *Loup*, whiting, and other fish are often boiled in a rich bouillon fragrant with herbs, and are drenched with olive oil and lemon juice before being served. *Sartadagnano* consists of small fish worked together into a sort of paste with olive oil so that it can be cooked like a griddlecake: boiling vinegar is poured over it when it is served. *Supions*, the small squids or cuttlefish already mentioned, are a specialty of Nice; a good place to try them for the first time, in a *risotto*, is the small pleasant Gambrinus restaurant on the rue de l'Hôtel des Postes or the more expensive Garac, by the old port, which specializes in sea food. *Poulpe à la niçoise* is octopus cut into small pieces and cooked in a spicy tomato sauce. It has to be well pounded before being cut up to make it tender enough to eat.

Nice joins in the curious devotion, for a seaside region, to salt cod; but it has a specialty of its own for the utilization of preserved fish called *estocaficada* in the local dialect, otherwise *stockfisch*. This is cod not only salted, but also dried, imported from Norway—from the Lofoten Islands, on a guess, for this is where you see cod hung up to dry by the thousands on racks made of sticks—hence *stokk-fisk*, in Norwegian (if the fish are simply laid out on the rocks of the cliffs to dry, as is sometimes the case, they become *klipp-fisk*). The *stockfisch* as the Nice housewife buys it does not appear to be edible at all. It looks and feels

exactly like a chunk of wood. It requires three days' soaking in water, which must be changed from time to time to
get the salt out, before it can be used. It is then stewed in
olive oil, along with potatoes, tomatoes, black olives, sweet
peppers, onions, leeks, aromatic herbs, garlic, perhaps a
dash of brandy—and a local variety of tripe which perhaps
you might as well think of by its Niçois name of *bedeù* instead of translating it into French (*boyaux*) or English
(bowels). Despite this rather alarming word, *stockfisch* is
a marvelously savory mess, one of the really great dishes of
the regional cooking of Nice. The difficulty is to get it.
Restaurant-owners feel that it is earthy peasant fare, as of
course it is, not worthy to be put on the menu for their
clients, especially not foreign clients. So they keep it for
themselves. I got my first taste of real Nice *stockfisch* at
the small, unpretentious and pleasant Hôtel de la Darse in
Villefranche when I caught Mme Morelli, its proprietor,
making some for herself. It was not on the bill of fare, and
she tried to argue me out of insisting on so plebeian a dish,
but I finally got a portion. It made regal eating, especially
in that setting—the open veranda of the hotel, with the old
citadel built by Vauban rising out of the water at the left,
the barracks of the *chasseurs Alpins* (the Blue Devils)
providing incidental music in the form of bugle calls at the
right, and in front the yacht basin filled chiefly with dirty
and disreputable craft that everyone knew had arrived with
smuggled goods from Tangier.

The Italian component in Nice cooking has presented it
with a number of dishes belonging to the macaroni-noodle
family. *Canelloni* is a favorite form of these *pâtes* (Italian, *pasta*). These are large cylinders of dough rolled
around a stuffing whose nature may vary, served in sauce,
usually tomato. Nice *ravioli*, the familiar stuffed squares of
macaroni dough, come in a smaller size than the ordinary
Italian or American varieties. The filling varies, usually con-

taining chopped meat, but one excellent type uses chopped spinach; the sauce really makes the dish, also variable, but always tasty. *Gnocchis à la niçoise* is a form of dumpling whose appearance here is something of a mystery, for it is peculiar in using a mixture of flour and potatoes, a distinction it shares with the *gnocchi* of Rome, but not with the variety made just across the Italian frontier on the Italian Riviera, the form in which one would have expected this dish to enter France. There is no particular reason why Nice should have added potatoes to *gnocchi;* it is not potato country. Nor can the skipping over of the intervening territory by the Roman variety of this dish to arrive finally at Nice be explained by attributing it to a sea passage in the days of the ancient Romans. They ate *polenta*, from which *gnocchi* would be an easy derivative, so they may have known this dish, too; but they could not have known it in its present form, for the Old World was not to make the acquaintance of the potato for another fifteen hundred years. The cooks of Nice, undisturbed by worry over the origin of the dish, make *gnocchi* delicious by the tastiness of the sauce poured over it, often the same as is used for beef, a rich wine sauce. (A sauce becomes *à la niçoise*, incidentally, when the anchovy essence, *pissala*, and chopped tarragon is added to the ordinary recipe.)

Nice does not do much with eggs. *Omelette à la niçoise*, which combines extract of tomatoes, parsley, and chopped garlic with the eggs, and adds anchovy filets when it is served, is one of the few exceptions. But it does have some special preparations of chicken. *Poulet sauté niçoise* calls for sautéeing the cut-up chicken in oil along with white wine, tomato sauce, and garlic. It is served with artichoke quarters, lumps of summer squash, new potatoes, and black olives, and is sprinkled with chopped tarragon. *Poularde à la niçoise*, chicken fried whole, is a name covering at least two different ways of presenting the bird. One is much like the *poulet sauté*—it surrounds the chicken with artichoke quarters, pieces of summer squash, new potatoes, and black olives, and serves it with a sauce of veal bouillon, tomatoes, white wine, and garlic, finally sprinkling it with tarragon. The other method finishes it in a casserole after the frying with tomatoes, diced summer squash, new potatoes, and black olives—no artichokes, but the same sauce and tarragon as for the first dish.

An *entrecôte à la niçoise* is a steak cooked in oil, accompanied by tomatoes, new potatoes, and ripe olives, and with gravy made from the cooking juices, white wine, and veal bouillon mixed with tomato extract. *Petits filets de bœuf à la niçoise* is *filet mignon* mounted on a slice of bread fried in oil, accompanied with string beans and new potatoes, with a filet of anchovy poised on each piece of beef, the whole served with a sauce of the cooking juices, veal bouillon, tomato extract, white wine, garlic, and chopped tarragon. Chopped parsley is then sprinkled on top. *Filet de bœuf froid à la niçoise* is a fashion of presenting cold roast beef which is excellent for outdoor eating. The roast beef is put into a mold and surrounded with meat jelly flavored with tarragon, and containing bits of white of egg, truffles, and whole tarragon leaves. The slices of beef, each in its frame of jelly, are served with hollowed-out tomatoes marinated in oil, vinegar, salt, and pepper, filled with truffles cooked in Madeira; artichoke hearts filled with asparagus tips; and olives whose pits have been replaced by anchovy butter. *Piech* is brisket of veal (sometimes mutton), with a stuffing of rice and *blète*, a local variety of Swiss chard. *Menon* is roast kid. The Nice fashion of cooking rabbit is in tomato sauce. It has already been noted in the previous chapter that tripe is cooked in Nice with the calves' feet that have disappeared from the *pieds et paquets* in other regions, accompanied by a piquant tomato sauce.

The top vegetable dish is probably *ratatouille*, described

in the Provençal chapter, often spelled here *ratatouia;* the recipes say that peppers as well as tomatoes, eggplant, and summer squash go into it, but I have never been served it in that form. A special variant of it at Puget-Théniers, one of the hill towns above Nice, back of the coast, adds white beans to the other ingredients. *Tian* is a non-sweet tart with a filling of *fèves,* spring peas, chopped artichokes, and spinach or *blète.* Somewhat like it is the *troucha de bléa,* which includes young peas, chopped artichokes, *blète,* little edible pine-cone seeds, and sometimes raisins—the last two only when it is sweetened and served for dessert. *Socca* is a sort of croquette of chick-pea flour. *Capoun* provides us with another change on the stuffed cabbage dishes—in this case the cabbage is stuffed with rice and sausage meat. The summer squash flower is often picked here before the fruit has developed, stuffed, and cooked in olive oil. *Cantarèu* are little gray snails, served cooked in tomato sauce.

A number of desserts originated in Nice—fritters containing various fillings, such as the squash flowers mentioned above or acacia flowers; *ganses,* a cookie fried in deep oil, eaten with powdered sugar; and *chaudèu* (French, *échaudés,* which means scalded), a hard circular cookie flavored with orange flowers. The same thing is encountered in Grasse and Vence, but made in the shape of a grill, under the name of *fougassette.*

In running thus along the coast of the Mediterranean, noting in each locality the dishes connected with it, we have missed a great many common to the whole area—too many to attempt to list them all. The most important, perhaps, are *aïgo saou,* another fish soup in which a number of different kinds of white-fleshed fish appear, cut into small pieces; the stalks of *blète,* which are somewhat celery-like, cooked in a cream cheese sauce; and *polente,* which is nothing more than the familiar Italian *polenta,* corn meal mush.

377

Vines grow everywhere along the Riviera. Most of the wines appear anonymously in carafes on the local tables. A large proportion are *rosés*, good hot weather and outdoor wines. They do not get around much outside of their own territory, at least not identifiably so (they do go for blending purposes into various mixtures most of which are sold under trademarked, rather than place names). However, though they have no great distinction, they are quite pleasant to drink on their own territory.

A few Riviera vintages have, however, attained a certain reputation under their own names. Farthest west is Cassis, with pleasant light white wines. Bandol, next along the coast, produces a Muscat. At Toulon, before the war, I made the acquaintance of a wine labelled Campo Romano and later met it again under a French version of the same name, Champ Romain. I recall it as a slightly harsh but interesting red, but have not come across it or heard of it since the war. It is not listed in any reference book I can find, which is not particularly surprising, as it would be impossible to register every local wine in a country whose every hamlet, south of the line drawn by the thermometer, has its own vintage. Nor is it even recorded in the official booklet of the association of Côtes de Provence winegrowers, but this may simply mean that the producers of Champ Romain have not joined the association.

The wine of Nice is Bellet. It comes in both white and red, and is very much a summer wine—so much so that the red as well as the white is served iced. Although it is a genuine red, not a *rosé*, which customarily gets this treatment, it turns out to be excellent cold. Of all the Riviera wines I have tasted, I would rate Bellet at the top.

XV

Corsica

About two or three times a year, dwellers sufficiently high up on the cliffs that tower above the coast of the French Riviera from Nice to Menton look out of their windows across the Mediterranean in the morning and see in the distance an island where the day before there had been nothing but empty water. It appears quite distinctly. Its mountains are sharply outlined, the wooded valleys between them clearly defined. They are thus reminded that a piece of France exists over the curve of the sea. The island is Corsica.

Corsica is not normally visible from the mainland. It is rather more than one hundred miles from the coast (it lies only half that distance from Italy), and the rare phenomenon of its appearance is owing to some sort of mirage. It happens only on winter days when the sky is covered with a continuous blanket of cloud with clear air below it, and only in the morning. When the sun rises higher, the image disappears. (Even rarer is the apparition of Elba, which I saw from the heights of Villefranche in 1951, according to the local press a spectacle that can be expected only once or twice a century.)

It is perhaps not a bad thing that the mainland should be reminded of the existence of Corsica now and again, for Corsica is a somewhat neglected region. It is not inaccessible. You can board a boat in Marseilles or Nice in the evening and get off at Ajaccio or Bastia, Calvi or L'Ile Rousse, early the next morning. You can take a plane at Nice and be on Corsica in half an hour. There is no difficulty about getting there. It just does not occur to many persons to visit Corsica, which makes it all the better for those who do.

Corsica is uncrowded, not only so far as visitors are concerned, but by its own population. Its 3,367 square miles (greatest length 114 miles, greatest width 52) are inhabited by not many more than a quarter of a million people, and there is a steady drain to the mainland. Corsicans have large families, but the population has decreased 10 per cent in the last fifty years. The interior is pretty much undeveloped, and consists of mountainous, dry, scrubby land (in spite of being surrounded by water, Corsica has an arid climate) overgrown with brush, the famous *maquis*, whose name gained a new meaning during the German occupation of France from the association between the wild country in which resistance fighters used to hide from the occupiers and the savage backlands of Corsica, which not so long ago had provided comparatively safe shelter for the island's bandits. The last of them, the celebrated Spada,

Good Eating

Cap Corse

SEA URCHINS

PATRIMONIU

L'Ile Rousse   Bastia
Calvi   MISSISSA
           Lagoon of
ZIMINU   Biguglia
(FISH CHOWDER)

CHESTNUTS   EELS
  PRIZZUTU   Cervione
 (CURED HAM) CHESTNUT PUDDING
LONZO   COPA (SPICED PORK)
Mt. Cinto   Corte
STUFFATO   MERLE
        BROCCIU CHEESE
           TROUT
CAPONE (ROCK FISH) ACCUNCCIATU
                   PREMONATA
          ROAST KID
LOBSTER   WILD BOAR
       TAGLIARINI
Ajaccio   CHEESECAKE

          MISSIASOGA
         POLENTA
ANCHOIADE   CEDRATES
(ANCHOVY PASTE) SHEEP TRIPE
Sartène   Porte Vecchio
        FIGATELLI SAUSAGE
          STOCKFISCH

   Bonifacio

MEDITERRANEAN SEA

CORSICA

Miles
0   50   100
0   50   100
Km.

was put out of business by what almost amounted to a French expeditionary force not long before the war.

There is a desolate grandeur about the *maquis*, a grandeur that is anything but desolate about some of Corsica's magnificent mountain scenery, and a spectacular and rugged beauty about its jagged rocky coast. It has not become too civilized, and has not yet found it necessary to get in step with the pace of mid-twentieth-century life. The *maquis* particularly seems remote from the rest of the world, with its dry wilderness of hardy shrubs (*maquis* is from the local word *macchia*, which means "brush")—arbutus, thorn, myrtle, juniper, heather, wild mint, and asphodel, the flower of hell. The fragrance from these plants is so pronounced that it can often be smelled from the sea as boats approach the island. In some regions they grow close to the ground, as these species usually do; but there are areas where the brush rises to a height of fifteen feet.

There are considerable forest areas, too. Corsica is a modernization of Korsai, believed to be a Phoenician word meaning "covered with forests." The *laricio* pine, a species confined to this island, has been known to reach a height of two hundred feet. The Romans cut them to make masts for their galleys and they are still being used for masts of modern ships. Nelson urged Britain to take the island with an eye to using its wood to build vessels of war. The Genoans and the Pisans drew upon Corsican forests for wood for their fleets. Corsica is also rich in cork oaks, which provide one of her principal exports, chestnuts, and, of course, olives.

If Corsica is left relatively alone today, in this age of fast and far-ranging transportation, which hardly encourages stops in regions of unimportant industry and resources, it was not so much neglected when slow sailing ships needed every island to break tedious journeys and provide fresh food and water. The Corsicans would perhaps·have preferred neglect. From the time when the Phocæan Greeks arrived in 560 B.C., Corsica was fought for and over by every sovereignty within reach. Often the outlanders were fighting each other primarily, but the Corsicans were in the way and were slaughtered abundantly as well. Perhaps no other area so small has so much history, almost all of it bloody. The rare exception that comes to mind is the plague of 1576, which killed off two thirds of the population. Corsica was invaded, ravaged, or governed—and in its history, "governed" and "ravaged" turned out to be virtually synonymous—successively by the Etruscans, the Carthaginians, the Romans, the Goths, the Lombards, the Moors, the Franks, the Papal States, the Pisans, the Genoans, the Aragonese, the Milanese, the Barbary pirates—whose raids were so bad that at one period the fertile seacoast was practically abandoned and reverted to marshland—the Turks, the French, the Germans, the Spaniards, the British and the Sardinians. The Corsicans also had trouble from time to time with their own feudal lords.

Corsica's various masters and their common penchant for limiting their interest in the island to what they could carry away from it provided at least two of its local folkways. One is the vendetta, the blood feud. This derived from the fact that the overlords of the mainland did not bother to set up a judicial system, but left the islanders to take care of that themselves. They used the simplest method—direct reprisal. If one family clan felt that a member had been wronged, it took vengeance on the clan held responsible. A nineteenth-century investigator studying a period of twenty years estimated that within that time 28,-000 persons had been murdered on Corsica in vendettas. The practice died out only recently—if it has died out. Feud killings were still being reported before the last war, but they seem to have disappeared since; possibly large-scale killing discouraged small-scale operations.

The other habit that may be traced to the attitude of Corsica's absentee governors is dietary. Corsica used to produce much grain on its fertile eastern land. The Pisans and the Genoans found the grain a convenient commodity in which to collect taxes. They were accustomed to impound and take to the mainland the totality of the crop or as much of it as they could lay their hands on before the peasants secreted it. With the greatest obviousness, this was killing the goose that laid the golden egg. The peasants stopped growing grain, and even today there is not nearly as much cereal production on Corsica as there was in the Middle Ages. Meanwhile the Corsicans, left without flour, turned to their chestnut forests. They ground the chestnuts into meal. Corsicans still give an important place on their menus to chestnuts and chestnut-flour dishes.

In 1768 Genoa sold Corsica to France, and her subsequent destiny has been less tormented. Having no doubt too much history to remember, and perhaps having no great desire to dwell on the sort of history they had, Corsicans seem for the most part to have decided to settle for concentration on one item in their 2,500 years of records, which falls within the French period, and to forget the rest. The tourist sometimes has the impression that the only event of note which occurred in Corsica was the birth of Napoleon Bonaparte. It was Corsica which supplied a dictator for France and perhaps in emulation, on a minor scale, the Corsicans ever since have been credited with providing the police force of Paris, as the Irish are credited with providing the police force of New York.

The corrolary to this predilection for the police force on the part of those who leave the island is the ambition that seems to be universal among the Corsicans who stay on it to find some sort of government job. The result is that other activities suffer, and instead of processing their own produce on the island, Corsicans send it elsewhere for finishing. The finest Corsican chestnuts go to Nice, and are made into *marrons glacés* there. Corsica starts cheeses and then sends them off to Roquefort for ripening, in the fashion already described. This is Roquefort's most distant source of cheese.

Many of the Corsicans are now employed in the tourist industry, which has become quite important, but not so much so as to overcrowd the island and rob it of its greatest charm, precisely its isolation. This characteristic has not operated, however, as it sometimes does (for instance, in the more inaccessible valleys of the Alps) to preserve such customs as the wearing of local costumes. The Corsican costume has almost died out. Except when it is worn self-consciously for the benefit of the tourists, you are not likely to come upon it nowadays, certainly not worn by the young. At some village festivals, old people occasionally maintain the tradition. The men wear wide velvet trousers; striped or checkerboard shirts with red or blue on white, giving an effect not unlike a lumberjack shirt; open vests; red flannel cummerbunds; and black felt hats with extremely wide brims. The women wear long full skirts over layer above layer of petticoats, pinched in tightly, however, at the waist. There is a satin or brocade blouse, and the hair is covered with the *faldetta*, a shawl folded into a triangle and tied under the chin.

The purest survivals of folk traditions are the religious processions and festivals. Corsicans are in general strong believers and equally convinced followers of superstition. Many of them believe in the evil eye. Some of the Easter rites are reminiscent of the processions of penitents in Spain. There are many shrines to which pilgrims walk barefoot, the most important being those of Erbalunga, where there is a miraculous picture of the Virgin wearing a silver crown, to which throngs of Corsicans flock on September 8, and of Bastia, where a fishermen's procession at the beginning of May has for its objective the Black Christ of that city. Ajaccio, capital of the island and birthplace of Napoleon, celebrates Assumption with particular brilliance because it is both a religious holiday and the date of the Emperor's birth.

If these celebrations, the local costume, when it appears, and other folkways of the Corsicans, such as their fondness for singing, especially to guitar or mandolin accompaniment, give the island an air more Italian than French, that is only natural. The two closest points of the French and Corsican coasts are 106 miles apart; to the mainland of Italy, the distance is 54; Sardinia is separated from Corsica only by a narrow strait. In spite of the many waves of invaders which have swept over the island, almost all of its inhabitants are of Italian descent; the others, from time to time, came, saw, and sometimes conquered, but went away again. The chief exception is a Greek colony that has existed at Cargese for some three hundred years. The inhabitants whom the Phocæan Greeks disturbed when they first came to the island probably originated in Liguria. The language remains Italian, very much like its Sardinian dialect, particularly in the south, nearest Sardinia, but retains some Tuscan and Ligurian peculiarities also. Because the language of the schools is French, the Corsican dialect is spoken mostly in families and among intimates, and French is used by the same persons for more formal contacts. Corsica being in so many aspects more Italian than French, its cooking is, not surprisingly, Italian also.

Corsican food is essentially simple food. It is not today as simple as it was when a Corsican would announce that he was going to dine "out of the drawer"—meaning the drawer in which he kept his supply of chestnuts, likely to be his staple diet on those occasions when non-Corsican overlords left him little else. Unless he lived in the interior, however, it is hard to visualize a period when he could not also have lived, to some extent, out of the sea. The sea is one of Corsica's most dependable reservoirs of food. Its most famous offering here is lobster. At a time when the price of this crustacean has become astronomic in most parts of France, one can still eat lobster in Corsica without concern for the cost.

The interior offers fish also—trout in the many fast-flowing mountain streams, the sort of water in which this fish delights. The *maquis*, as one might expect, is game country, and the aromatic herbs and berries of the brush give a piquant flavor to the flesh of the birds. The nature of the land is not conducive to the raising of cattle, so there is not much beef, but sheep and goats are plentiful. Pigs feed in the chestnut forests on the nuts that fall to the ground, and thus develop particularly delicious meat. Most southern vegetables and fruit grow well on some part of the island—a specialty is a sweeter variety of lemon called a *cedrat*, also found occasionally on the Riviera. There is not, however, as much variety in vegetation in Corsica as one might think from the extremes in climate, which are a function of altitude. While the seacoast is quite warm all year around, it forms a rather narrow base from which the hills rise very quickly—Monte Cinto, the highest peak, reaches 9,020 feet above sea-level—and in the mountains the climate can become quite rigorous. But as the higher lands are in general rather barren, plants of the temperate climate do not grow as readily as do those of warmer regions, which flourish on the more fertile strips of soil along the coast.

The Corsicans like strong spicing, carrying a little further the Provençal predilection for much use of herbs. In Provence, cooks make delicate and subtle use of such flavors as those of thyme, laurel, and sage. In Corsica, they are more likely to set out to shock you with hot peppers and strong spices. For instance, Corsica has its own form of *bouillabaisse*, in which red peppers and pimentos provide a hotter seasoning than in the Riviera version. The local word for it is *ziminu*. The lobster, the best of the Mediterranean, is usually served boiled or stewed, but try to find it somewhere *à la calvaise*. The Calvi preparation dishes it up in a highly spiced tomato sauce. Just as Corsica has the best lobster, so it has the biggest *rascasse*, known here as the *capone*. But the Corsican, like the Riviera variety of this fish, is not highly esteemed for eating by itself. It goes into the Corsican *ziminu* as its smaller relative goes into the Riviera *bouillabaisse*. Corsica shares with Nice a fondness for *anchoiade*—crushed anchovies, worked into a paste in olive oil together with chopped shallots and parsley, which is spread on squares of bread soaked in olive oil. It is then powdered with a mixture of bread crumbs, chopped garlic, and parsley, anointed with a second coating of oil, and slipped into the oven to brown. *Stockfisch* is also prepared as in Nice. The small fish of the inlets are fried in oil, stewed or served *au gratin*. Sea urchins are particularly popular; they are eaten as hors d'œuvres with dry white wine. As for the inland fish, trout are usually grilled in Corsica. The lagoon of Biguglia is famous for its large eels, fished in November and December, when boats are sent especially from the Italian ports of Leghorn, Piombino, and Naples to carry part of the catch to those cities, which are particularly fond of the Corsican eels (which they call *capone*, the same word Corsica uses for the *rascasse*). The favored method for cooking them is to cut them into small pieces and grill them on a spit or over a charcoal fire. Finally, the lagoon of Diane produces oysters—natural, not cultivated—of irregular shape and not the equals of the Atlantic shellfish, but as palatable as any in the Mediterranean.

In the department of *charcuterie*, the peppered smoked ham known as *prizzutu*, the closest French approach to the

Italian *prosciutto*, is especially notable because it carries that chestnut flavor which results from the diet of the pigs. Corsicans would be more likely to name first in this category their favorite between-meals snack, *figatelli*. These are sausages made of a mixture of pork liver and pork, dried and spiced. They are served after having been grilled over a wood fire between slices of a special type of bread designed to blot up the grease that oozes from the hot sausage. *Lonzo* is a highly typical Corsican hors d'œuvre—boned filet of pork pickled in brine containing aromatic herbs, then dried and served in paper-thin slices; it is also made into sausages. *Copa* may also appear in two forms—as the hotly spiced shoulder of pork it is originally, or as a sausage.

Among main dishes of pork, pork stew with fava beans is typical. *Missisa*, strips of smoked marinated pork, is grilled before eating. One of the rare beef dishes is *premonata*, braised beef with juniper berries. Kid probably occurs more often on the menu in Corsica than anywhere else in France. *Cabiros* (*cabri* in French), may appear as whole roast kid or be used in a stew, or the legs and shoulders may be roasted separately, with rosemary-garlic stuffing and oil and vinegar dressing. *Missiasoga* is strips of goat meat cured by being dried in the open air. *Stuffato* is stewed mutton, and *accuncciatu* is a stew combining mutton, lamb, and horse meat with potatoes.

Sheep are the usual furnishers of tripe. In *tripa*, the stomach lining of the sheep is stuffed with spinach, Swiss chard, and herbs, mixed with the sheep's blood, sewed up into sausage shape, and cooked in salted water. *Tripes à la serra* powders it with grated cheese. *Tripettes à la mode corse* is sautéed in tomato sauce.

The game of Corsica is famous, the most delicate meat, in the opinion of Corsicans, being provided by the blackbird (*merle*). This puts the Corsicans at odds with France, one of whose most common proverbs, the equivalent of the English "half a loaf is better than none" is "*faute de grives, on mange des merles*"—"when you can't get thrush, you can always eat blackbird." The Corsican prefers the blackbird. It is true that his *merle* is especially succulent because of the diet it finds in the *maquis*. It feeds on the fruit of the olive, the juniper, and the *lentisque*. The last is related to the pistachio nut, and as it grows on the Greek archipelago (where its sap is collected and made into the powerful drink known as *raki*), the Greeks probably brought it to Corsica. *Merle* is roasted with sage, served in a *salmis*, or made into *pâtés*. Woodcock is also common; it is usually roasted over a fire of myrtle twigs. It may also appear *alla cacciatora*.

Corsica has larger game also, but its most spectacular item is now very rare, so that you are unlikely to be able to taste its famous *ragout de moufflon*. This wild mountain-sheep has now almost disappeared, and the few remaining animals are protected; but poaching is not unknown in Corsica. It is not necessary to poach, however, to find wild boar (*sanglier*, or, if it is a young animal, *marcassin*). This will appear either roasted; *en daube* in a conventional red wine sauce with herb flavoring; or in the highly spiced local sauce called *pibronata*.

Since Corsican cooking is an offshoot of Italian cooking, *pasta* is of course popular. One of its favorite varieties is *ravioli*, whose stuffing here is oftenest made with herbs and *brocciu* cheese. It is served with a tomato sauce, usually made from the highly concentrated tomato extract called *coulis*, which appears often in Corsican cooking, and grated cheese. *Tagliarini* is also often served. This comes in the shape of thin flat strips instead of the familiar straw shape of spaghetti, and appears with a great variety of sauces. *Stufatu* is macaroni with mushrooms and onions, often served with stewed mutton.

Italy has also bequeathed *polenta* to Corsica. It may be made, as in Italy, of corn meal, or of chestnut flour instead. It is usually eaten with warm milk and *brocciu*. *Panizze*, a corn meal cake borrowed from Italian cooking, has undergone a similar treatment; it is quite as likely to be made of chestnut flour.

As on the Riviera, eggplant and summer squash are among the most popular vegetables, but they are likely to be treated somewhat differently. The former is usually fried or stuffed and baked in an oven; the latter turns up often in salads. Artichokes grow profusely in the dry sandy soil of Corsica, exactly the sort of earth they like. The small purplish variety is most common, the type preferred for the hors d'œuvres known as *artichauts à la grecque*, which means with an oil-and-vinegar dressing. Hearts of artichokes with spring peas is another common combination, or they may be stuffed with *brocciu* cheese. *Morilles* mushrooms are common and are used most often in omelettes. *Brocciu* also makes a good omelette.

Brocciu, which comes from the word for brush, referring to the pasturage of the goats whose milk makes the cheese, comes in three forms, a sort of cottage cheese, a semidried-out variety, and finally a drier cream cheese of the *petit suisse* type. The fresh liquid cottage cheese is eaten with sugar and a dash of liqueur, *kirsch*, or rum. For its frequent use in cooking, it is sold in attractive little wicker baskets. It is best between March and January. Other well-known Corsican cheeses include two cream cheeses, Venaco and Niolo, best from October to May, Asco, recommended for the same period, Calenzana and *petit Cap Corse*.

The useful *brocciu* turns up again in some Corsican desserts. *Falculella* is a cheesecake made of *brocciu*, milk, sugar, and eggs, and baked on chestnut leaves. The vanilla-flavored *fiadone* and *embrucciate* are cakes with *brocciu* filling. Chestnut flour enters into a number of others—*brilliolo*, a light chestnut-flavored cake served with hot milk; *castagnacci*, a chestnut flour pudding; and *migliassis*, which is roughly *falculella* with chestnut flour replacing the cheese. *Torta* is a round, flat tart powdered with crushed almonds. There is a variation of it which uses edible pine-cone seeds (*pignons*) instead of almonds, often flavored with anis. Anis appears also in *canistrelli*, cookies of irregular shape, sweetened with sugar that has been given an anis flavor, being allowed to stand some time mixed with anis seeds. A bun that appears especially at Easter, the *panette*, is sweetened, contains eggs, and is spotted with raisins. The *cedrats* of the island make jellies, preserves, and candied fruits.

Corsica is abundantly supplied with wine. It is somewhat harsh, but quite drinkable, and some of it finds its way to the mainland. Most of the wine regions produce reds, whites, or *rosés*. Vines grow almost everywhere on the island, but the best-known vintages are these: Olmato, a little south of Ajaccio; Sartène and Porte Vecchio in the south; Cervione, on the east coast, whose dry whites and reds are equally good; in the north, Patrimonio and Malvoisie (both white and dry *rosé*), Centuri and Porticcioli, for their white muscatel, and Cap Corse, which in addition to wine makes a famous *apéritif* under the same name. The wines of the interior are in general less important, but Corte might be mentioned.

In the *apéritif* category, the favorite drink of Corsica is *pastis*, a cousin of absinthe, forbidden by law. Corsica pays little attention to this. A local tradition holds that it prevents fever, and no doubt its medical qualities are considered justification for ignoring the law. It is a yellowish licorice-flavored drink, of which an inch or two is poured into the bottom of a tumbler, which is then filled with water, which promptly becomes a clouded light-green. It has a mild, slightly sickly sweet taste and may seem to be something of a woman's drink, but do not allow it to deceive you. If you take too much of it you will learn why it is forbidden.

Corsica also makes a number of *eaux-de-vie*—from the *arbuste*, cherry, myrtle, and wild mint particularly. But its top contribution to the category of after-dinner drinks is *cédratine*, a rich, sweet, syrupy liqueur made from the lemonlike fruit that is a specialty of the island.

THE
PYRENEES

Butter, Fat, Oil

XVI

Gascony and the Basque Country

The Pyrenees are not so high as the Alps, but their passes and valleys are so oriented that they are harder to penetrate. The symbol of this inaccessibility is the existence of Andorra as an independent state. This minute country would hardly exist today if larger, more predatory powers had been able to get into it easily. In winter there is only one entrance even now, by the road from Seo de Urgel, in Spain: you can stand on French territory and look into Andorra but you cannot enter it. Not until the snow melts may Andorra be breached from France.

The mountains have divided the Pyrenean territory into a mosaic of boxes. Communication among them is difficult.

As a result each has developed and crystallized its own habits with a minimum of interference from the habits of its neighbors. Each little box has, to a certain extent, its own culture. It has as part of that culture its own eating habits. That is why the Pyrenean region, though it is natural to consider it as a whole, does not fit entire into any of the categories we have set up this far on the basis of the fundamental cooking mediums. The west, influenced no doubt by the example of the territories to its north—Gascony, Guienne, the Périgord—has accepted fat, especially goose fat, as the dominant cooking grease. The center, where a mountain cow appears, leans more to butter. The east woos olive oil. Yet in every region devoted to one of these substances, some dishes call for another. There are recipes in which two of the usually separated greases are called for, and even some that combine all three. And here gastronomic divisions are respecters neither of political divisions nor of natural divisions.

If you move along the Pyrenees from Atlantic to Mediterranean, you will count many fewer political divisions than natural ones. Politically the list is: the Basque country; Béarn; then, after an interval occupied by territory politically attached to Gascony, itself bound to Guienne, to the north, the County of Foix; and finally, the Roussillon. But if account be taken of natural divisions and political subdivisions, which tend to follow natural lines, the list of recognizably different societies is much larger. The Basque country divides itself into three provinces, Labourd, Lower Navarre, and the Soule (and the last has a subdivision, the High Soule). The Béarn follows. Then comes the Bigorre, once a separate county. The Comminges, next west, has also been an entity under its own rulers from time to time. The County of Foix lies north of Andorra, west of which three separate territories run from north to south—the country of Sault, a natural rather than a political division;

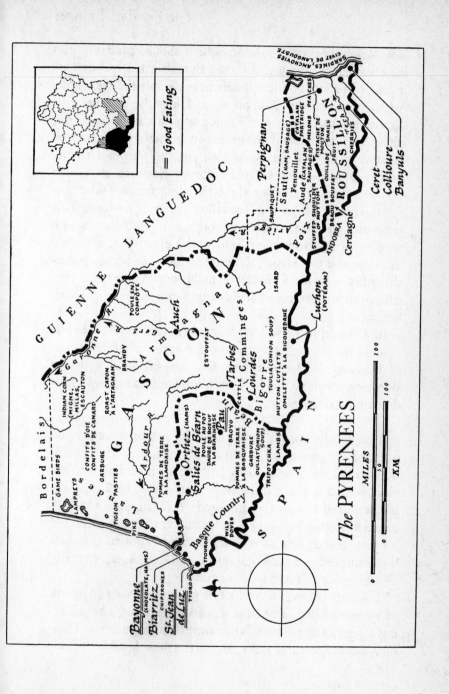

The PYRENEES

the high valley of the Aude, which should probably also be classified as a natural division, though it has had its moments of partial political independence; and the Cerdagne, which was a distinct province straddling the Pyrenees, so that today part of it is in France and part in Spain. This, along with the rest of the territory to the west, was considered as part of the Roussillon for the purposes of the cession of this territory to France by Spain in 1659, but actually there is another three-tiered section of intervening territories before the Roussillon proper is reached. This time they are, from north to south, the Corbières, which used to be the frontier of France; the Fenouillet, a natural division; and the Haute Vallespir, which has been a political entity at various epochs of its history. With the Roussillon proper, we reach the coastal lands along the Mediterranean.

In addition to these Pyrenean territories, it will be convenient for our purposes to consider here the southern part of Gascony, whose northern area was included with the Bordeaux country, and whose most important single subdivision is Armagnac.

The word Gascon, through the efforts of novelists and operetta librettists, has become synonymous with "swashbuckler." Time has probably lent some enchantment to the view, which it could do with particular ease because there is a period of at least two hundred years (ninth to eleventh centuries) when romance is in no danger of being corrected by fact. About that stretch no facts are known. Gascony then suffered the most complete of Dark Ages, virtually dropping out of recorded history.

The part of its story which is known allows for plenty of swashbuckling. The land was broken up into a bewildering congeries of counties, viscounties, and seigniories. Their boundaries were not static, nor were their loyalties. Their inhabitants fought back and forth for centuries, in the small-scale wars that offer so much more scope to individual feats of derring-do than better organized ones. Even when France and England were fighting over this territory, the times were still propitious for the romantic version of warfare—or at least they seem so looked at through the wrong end of the twentieth-century telescope.

The name of Gascony is an error. Gascon is the same word as Basque, but the Gascons are not Basques. When they came up from Spain, they were called Basques (Vascones, at the time, in conformity with the principle of the interchangeability of *b* and *v* in Indo-European languages) because Basques lived in the general region they came from and the age was not one of nice distinctions. The *v* became transmuted into *w*, but as French abhors *w* and prefers to convert it to *g* (William equals Guillaume), the country became Gascony, the land of the Basques, exactly what it is not.

Relating the ancient Duchy of Gascony to modern territories is difficult because the ancient borders changed so much. At its most stable, it included what are now the departments of the Hautes-Pyrénées, the Gers, and the Landes, and parts of the Basses-Pyrénées, the Haute-Garonne, the Lot-et-Garonne, and the Tarn-et-Garonne. This takes it from the estuary of the Gironde down to the Pyrenees, and in a number of areas right into them and to the Spanish border. At times it included the Basque country and parts of the Bordelais. The capital was Auch. It disappeared into Guienne about the end of the eleventh century, and though it is difficult to separate the two territories from then on, all of the combined Aquitainian domain did not become French as a unit. The north of the Guienne-Gascony area was under the French crown as early as 1453, but the southern border of Gascony did not become the southern border of France until 136 years later.

For the purposes of this book, Gascony is being considered as the strip of territory between the Bordelais (thus some of its northernmost territory, which eats as Bordeaux does, is omitted) and the Pyrenees (leaving its occasional incursions into those mountains to be dealt with when we reach the highland areas, whose food differs from that to the north). Gascon cooking is related to the various schools of Pyrenean cooking, and includes many of the same dishes, but the two are not entirely congruent. It does not deny the swashbuckling theory. Gascony has a heroic cuisine. It may well have nourished soldiers. It should appeal to the hardy.

The western part of Gascony, which lies along the Atlantic, is a continuation of the Landes, which we first met when we visited the Bordeaux region. The coast here is one long beach whose sands stretch all the way to the Spanish frontier; but as it is rather bare, uninviting country, it has not attracted many vacationists. One of the few frequented watering places along this coast is Hossegor, and even that is far from famous. (The most renowned beach resort of the vicinity, Biarritz, is in the Basque country, south of the territory we are considering now.) Lagoons lie beyond the coast, blocking access to the beaches. Atlantic gales blow the sand into the interior, piling it up first in dunes, which until a century ago were constantly being shaped and reshaped by the winds until they were finally fixed by the planting of pines and other vegetation to hold the soil in place. Draining of the marshes behind the dunes made this pineland, too, and the chief impression one has of the Landes today is that of an infertile area overgrown with vast forests of rather scrubby pine. Not much can be expected in the way of food, as the direct produce of this poor earth, but to make up for it the woods shelter much small game and the lagoons are rich in fish.

Besides the *ortolans* and wild doves mentioned in the

Bordeaux chapter, this more southern section of the Landes also offers woodcock, quail, *grives*, and *bec-fins*. What the equivalent of this last may be in English, or if there is an equivalent at all, I have no idea. It refers to a small bird not unlike a lark, but a trifle larger, and it seems to be a name sometimes applied indiscriminately to a number of birds of the same type—as sardine is applied to small fish of various species. Farther east the name becomes *bec-figue* (fig beak, presumably a reference to its diet in the fig country). Whatever its identity, its reputation is of respectable antiquity. The Latin poet Martial speaks highly of it (as a native of Spain, Martial lived in the *bec-fin* area). Brillat-Savarin was in such a hurry to get to the eating of the bird that in the "recipe" he gives for it he neglects to mention the detail of cooking it, describing simply how to hold the bird by the beak and pop all the rest into the mouth.

Bec-fins à la landaise are wrapped in a slice of bacon and then in a grape leaf; spitted in threes with a piece of buttered bread between each pair of birds; seasoned with salt and pepper; and cooked in a long dish in a fast oven, basted with fat from *foie gras*. While the birds are cooking, a sauce is made with meat bouillon and Armagnac, warmed with grape seeds in it, and this is poured over the birds just before they are removed from the oven.

In the fish department, the chief products of the lagoons are eels, lampreys, shad, and pike.

One thing that does grow in poor soil is potatoes. The Landes produces them and has its own method for cooking them, *pommes de terre à la landaise*. Onions and Bayonne ham, both diced, are first cooked in goose fat. Diced potatoes are then added, seasoned with salt and pepper, and the pan is covered to finish the cooking. (It should be shaken from time to time to prevent the potatoes from sticking to the bottom.) Just before the end of the cooking, chopped garlic and parsley are added.

Preserved foods enter largely into the repertoire of the Landes. *Foie gras* from goose and duck is esteemed equally. *Confits d'oie* and *confits de canard* are also both made. The special Landaise dish made from preserved goose is sometimes described on menus as *confit d'oie à la landaise,* but more often as *confit d'oie aux petits pois.* This is made by cooking little onions and diced Bayonne ham in goose grease. Fresh spring peas are then cooked in this mixture, dusted with flour, covered with water, seasoned with a little sugar, parsley, chervil, thyme, and laurel, and cooked in a covered casserole slowly for forty minutes. Then a quarter of preserved goose goes into the casserole, and the whole cooks for twenty-five minutes more. Landes ham is cured raw and so eaten.

The sandy soil along the coast produces grapes from which is made what is known as *vin de sable*—sand wine. Its alcoholic content is high and its taste recalls the odor of seaweed—violets steeped in iodine is one description given of it. The best is probably that produced in the region of the Current of Huchet, the outlet which drains the water of the Lagoon of Léon into the sea. Back from the coast, in the Chalosse region along the banks of the Adour River, some pleasant local table wines are found.

As one moves back from the coast out of the Landes, the variety of foods becomes richer. This is all *garbure* country, like some of the Bordelais territory, but because this dish originated in Béarn, we will save it for consideration when we reach that territory.

Omelette à la gasconne has the stick-to-the-ribs qualities associated with the local food, adding a touch of swagger to this sometimes pallid egg dish. Diced ham and finely chopped onions are browned separately in goose fat. They are then beaten into the eggs, along with chopped garlic and parsley, and the omelette is also cooked in goose fat, in pancake shape.

Pigeon pasties (*croustade de pigeonneaux à la gasconne*) are a delicious specialty of this region, but *épaule d'agneau à la gasconne* is more in the hearty tradition of the country. The shoulder of lamb is stuffed with a mixture of hashed raw ham, bread steeped in meat bouillon, onions, garlic, chopped parsley, egg, and high seasoning. It is then braised in the oven in fat *pot-au-feu* bouillon with pieces of green cabbage, carrots, an onion with a clove stuck in it, and assorted herbs, and quartered potatoes are added toward the end. *Côtes de porc à la gasconne* is also filling. The pork chops are first marinated for an hour in oil with a little vinegar in which thyme and garlic have been crushed with salt and pepper. They are then fried in butter or goose fat just enough to dry them of the liquid in which they have been steeped, and are transferred to a covered dish for slow finishing, along with a plentiful helping of garlic. When the chops are nearly finished, stoned olives are added, and finally the whole is dampened with a gravy made from the cooking juices, veal bouillon, and white wine, and chopped parsley is dusted over the finished result.

After these heavy meat dishes, it is appropriate to take a simple salad in the Gascon style. One of the frizzly forms of lettuce is preferred—curly chicory, escarole, or something of the sort. The salad bowl is rubbed with crushed garlic, a round piece of bread dampened in oil and vinegar and impregnated with garlic is left in the bottom of the bowl, and the classic simple oil-vinegar-salt-pepper dressing is used.

This is maize country, where Indian corn has been raised ever since it was first brought to Europe from America in the sixteenth century. Corn is not eaten on the cob, the local varieties being closer to American field-corn than to the highly developed types grown for table use in the United States, but there are many corn meal dishes. Indeed cornmeal was at one time the chief bread flour (corn meal bread was called *méture*), but wheat flour has now replaced it. However, corn meal still appears in the form of *miques* (as in the Sarladais), *millas* (also a Sarladais dish), and the more local *escauton*, corn meal mush cooked in goose fat. Corn meal noodles are also used to fatten geese for the production of *foie gras*.

In the heart of Gascony, around its capital of Auch, is a region of special gastronomic excellence, Armagnac. It is almost exactly the same territory as the department of the Gers, and though it is the core of Gascony, it managed to keep out from under the French crown until 1607, while Gascony as a whole had become French in 1589. This is an indication of the particular toughness of the Armagnacs, who had a reputation for being hard fighters, and were borrowed from time to time by foreign monarchs to win battles for them, though not after 1445, when Emperor Frederick III of Germany used them to fight in Switzerland, where they were resoundingly beaten.

The excellence of food in Armagnac may be owing in considerable part to the encouragement provided to good eaters by the fact that this is the country of the other brandy. Strictly speaking, there are only two genuine brandies, Cognac and Armagnac, and though the latter is less well known, partly perhaps because there is less of it, it can hardly be considered as second in quality to Cognac. Both are excellent.

Like the wines of the Cognac region, those of Armagnac are not very pleasing in themselves. They are mostly whites with a high alcoholic content and a strong harsh flavor. But, again like the Cognac vintages, they lend themselves admirably to distillation. The methods used are different. Cognac is made in batches, from blends of different wines. Armagnac is made by the method of a continuous distillation of unmixed wines. For Armagnac, as for Cognac, the barrel in which the liquor is aged is important; but whereas in Cognac barrels are used again and again, the oldest kegs being the most prized, Armagnac uses new casks made from the tight-grained heartwood of local oaks. The characteristic taste of Armagnac suggests peaches to me, but apparently to no one else. At least I have never seen it so described.

Lower Armagnac is held to produce the best brandy, especially in the neighborhood of Nogaro, Cazambon, and Gabaret. However, Lower and Upper Armagnac, as well as the Ténarèze region that separates them, all produce the top-grade Armagnac made from the wines approved for this purpose and carrying a certificate known as the Acquit d'Or. Armagnacs made from other wines are entitled to display the Acquit Blanc. Liqueurs from the Armagnac region with the Acquit Rose certificate are not true Armagnacs—not grape brandies, in other words—but *eaux-de-vie* made from such other fruits as currants and quinces, and even walnuts.

It is natural in this country that many dishes should be cooked with Armagnac; and as this is still game country, woodcock, partridge, and jugged hare are all prepared with sauces into which Armagnac enters. Roast capon *à l'Artagnan* (who, you will remember, was a Gascon—and a historical character, too, born at Lupiac, in the Armagnac region, not an invention of Dumas) also has Armagnac in its sauce.

Poule en compôte is chicken stew, probably a variant of a dish that originated in the Béarn. Cabbage in cream is another favorite dish of Armagnac. Finally, it is perhaps the birthplace of *estouffat* or *estouffade* a word that can mean almost anything cooked in a closed pot, but refers particularly to the liquid in which such dishes are likely to be stewed. It is a rich concoction, made by boiling down to their essences a large number of ingredients—lean beef, shank of veal, marrow bones of both, pork cracklings, ham, meat fat, carrots, onions, garlic, and assorted herbs.

South of Gascony, lying against the sea to the west and the Spanish border to the south, in France's extreme south-western corner, is the country of that strange people, the Basques. Their origin is a mystery. One theory holds that they came from parts of Spain other than those the Spanish Basques now occupy, the descendants of the people the Romans called the Iberians—which, even if generally accepted, would not throw a great deal of light on the Basques, almost nothing being known about the Iberians. Another school of thought considers them to be lighter-colored Berbers (the non-Arab North African race), whose exact origins are also somewhat mysterious, even though there is at least a contemporary population to be studied. A third idea gives credit to the legend of Atlantis, and suggests that the Basques are the sole survivors of a vanished Atlantic continent or large island, adding for good measure that the Guanches, the original inhabitants of the Canary Islands, were also Atlantidians. This might seem a fairly safe assumption, for the Guanches did not long survive the Spanish discovery of what had previously been called the Fortunate Isles, but modern scholarship claims the Guanches as Berbers, throwing the third theory about the Basques back into the arms of the second, and making the hypothesis of an Atlantis superfluous. Finally, one group of scholars has saved itself the need of worrying about where the Basques came from by suggesting that they did not come from anywhere, but have always lived about where they are now.

The Basque language might seem to bear out the last theory. It does not particularly help any of the others, as no one has succeeding in demonstrating its relationship with any other language. It does not belong to the Indo-European group of languages, which may be one reason why some scholars have tried to establish a kinship with the only European group of languages also outside of this family, the Finno-Ugric (Finnish, Estonian, Magyar). One German classification lists it among Caucasian languages; philologists, of course, are not required to explain how the Basques traveled from the Caucasus to the Pyrenees without leaving traces of their passage on the way. And there have been attempts to prove that Basque is related to Berber, a Hamitic language.

It is in any case quite primitive, which is consonant with the idea that it may have crystallized a very long while ago, among a people whose speech was not exposed to the transforming influences of contact with other tongues during migrations. Like some American Indian languages, it builds up words by tacking on suffixes to a basic root, so that a verb may have an ending that expresses its subject, direct object, and indirect object. The words in the vocabulary which refer to tools indicate tools of stone, which might mean that the speech became fixed in the Stone Age. Other signs that the Basque culture is a very old one unmodified by movement are the persistence until very recently of the two-tined digging fork, the *laya*, instead of the plough, and the fact that the Basques, alone of all western European peoples, still practice practically all the types of dances known among primitive people—for whom dancing is often a magical or religious rite.

Possibly millennia, not centuries, of living together on the same territory, as well as the possession of a language hermetic to all those not born to it, has held the Basques so tightly together and maintained their customs and institutions, though they are divided by a natural frontier that has existed as long as there have been frontiers. Spanish Basques and French Basques share the same habits as well as the same language; and on the French side of the frontier, it is certainly indisputable that of all the different peoples of France, the Basques have resisted most successfully the inroads of the larger culture and have preserved a Basque society intact within the French civilization. *Zaspiakbat*, the Basques say of their land—"seven in one." It is the expression of the unity of the Basques, despite the fact that of the seven provinces, four—Guipúzcoa, Alava, Viscaya, and Navarre—are in Spain and only Labourd, Lower Navarre, and the Soule are in France.

The most striking physical characteristic of the Basques is probably their agility. The earliest known written reference to them, dated 778, speaks of this characteristic, which modern times have reasserted in giving tennis player Jean Borotra the nickname of the Bounding Basque. The universally played game of handball, especially in the more sophisticated form of *jai alai* with the wicker basket-scoop (the *chistera*) strapped to the wrist and replacing the hand as a bat, is a particularly active form of sport—rather hard to reconcile, perhaps, with another recognized Basque sport, eating, in which regular competitions are held to see who can put away the most food.

Socially, the outstanding quality of the Basques is perhaps their strong democratic trend. Throughout their history they have always maintained the equal rights of individuals, have given women a status of legal independence rare until recent times in other groups, have maintained civil rights against all sovereigns, and have customarily filled offices by processes of free election. Only two categories of Basques were barred from membership in their legislative bodies—lawyers and priests—on the ground that these two corporations are automatically on the side of tyranny. (But the Basques are deeply devout, so that it appears they made a distinction between religion and clericalism.)

Basque conservatism accounts for the survival without

adulteration by the French and Spanish cultures of the many habits and customs which are the trademarks of a land noticeably different from the country about it—the architecture of the asymmetrical houses of whitewashed stucco, sometimes with timbers showing as in the Tudor style, with wooden balconies and tile roofs; the ceremonial dances, in which women rarely participate; the music performed by a single musician on a three-holed vertical flute, the *tchirulä*, played with the right hand, and a snare drum, the *ttun-ttun*, played with the left; the berets of the men and the staffs they carry (*makhuilas*), larger at the bottom, which is clasped in a pointed iron ferule, than at the grip, covered with leather; the *espadrilles* worn by everyone, a sort of slipper with a cloth upper and a rope sole; the fleece-wrapped yokes that the slow Basque oxen carry on their horns, not on their shoulders—and, of course, the food.

The Basque country is a small territory. All three of its provinces—Labourd, on the coast, capital Ustaritz; Lower Navarre, in the hills behind it, capital Saint-Jean-Pied-de-Port; and La Soule, deep in the mountains, capital Mauléon —constitute together only a little more than one third of the modern department of the Basses-Pyrénées. Yet it has managed to maintain a strikingly different individual cuisine little affected by French cooking, with a considerable variety of dishes. It suggests Spanish cooking, especially in a free use of pimento, which might seem natural enough, as the major part of Basque territory is in Spain and it is probable that the French Basques represent the overflow pushed across the Pyrenees by a growing race originally entirely confined to the southern side. Yet the French Basques, who share so many other things in common with the Spanish Basques, are differentiated from them to some extent by individual eating habits, while the Spanish Basques them-

selves have a cuisine quite different from that of Spain—
whether by Spanish food you mean the classical cooking
of Castile or that of the Galicians, to the west of the Basques,
possibly the peninsula's best cooks. The most famous single
dish of the Spanish Basque country, *angulas a la bilbaino*
—baby eels fried in oil—is not likely to turn up on the
French side of the frontier; and although salt cod dishes
are, as we have seen, oddly popular along the fresh-fish
coastline of the Mediterranean, the French Basques much
prefer their own fish to the preserved cod, while the Spanish Basques go in for *bacalao a la vizcaina*, their version of
the Languedoc or Provençal salt cod dish. Wines are different, too. The rather vinegary green wine—*chacoli*—of
the Spanish Basques has nothing in common with the reds
produced on the French side of the frontier.

The Basques have borrowed more from the French than
from the Spanish. Although their own dishes are characteristically different from those of France, they have added
to their list, sometimes giving them a naturalizing touch of
their own, borrowings from the cooking of their Pyrenean
neighbor, Béarn. Béarn is a sort of focal point for good
cheer and has exported its creations in a number of direc-
tions, so it is natural enough that the Basque country has
taken its share of them, especially as there is a kinship between the two cuisines in any case. Thus the famous Béarn
garbure has moved into the Basque country as well as into
Guienne and Languedoc. So has the *poule au pot*, which we
shall come to when we reach Béarn.

Basque cooks are naturally highly conscious of the products of the sea. This is a usual, but by no mean invariable,
result of propinquity to the sea. We have seen that Picardy
is inclined to neglect the possibilities of its coast (it is true
it has not much seafront) and that Languedoc does not ex-
ploit the fish of the Mediterranean as much as the Côte
d'Azur does. But the Basques were not likely to make this

mistake, having always been great fishermen. The Basques, indeed, were the earliest whalers.

Biarritz and Saint-Jean-de-Luz were the principal whaling ports. They began hunting these great mammals of the sea in the eleventh century. It was offshore whaling, with the harpooners setting out in their cockleshell open boats from the beach, a technique that has probably disappeared everywhere now except in the Azores, where whales are still taken in this fashion. At Biarritz, which still has a hunted whale on its coat of arms, a lookout was posted toward the end of September, the season at which the whales appeared (one of the high lookout platforms still exists in the port), and when he sighted the animals he raised the alarm by means of a smoke signal. The whale, still classified as a royal animal in England—which means that theoretically at least any whale taken off the British coasts is the property of the crown—apparently was considered in somewhat the same light in medieval France. In any case, part of each catch went to the king. Bayonne, more astute than the king, managed to secure for itself the privilege of receiving the tongues of all whales taken at its dependent port of Biarritz—for the tongue was the tastiest morsel, and Bayonne then, as today, was a city always alert about fine food. Whale is not today considered highly as a food, but that was its chief attraction in those days. For that matter, it is still sometimes eaten in Norway.

In the course of centuries, whales disappeared from the Basque coast. The last one taken in the Gulf of Gascony was harpooned in 1686. Giving up whales, the Basques were among the first to sail across the Atlantic to fish for cod off Newfoundland. When the French lost Newfoundland, the Basques found a use for their ships by becoming privateers like the Bretons. They are not generally remembered today as having vied for fame with the corsairs of Saint-Malo, but they must have been considered redoubtable in their time. Their exploits won them the right to keep their hats on in the presence of Louis XIV.

Today the Basque fishing fleet has returned to more peaceful pursuits. Tuna is the big food fish pursued off these coasts, Saint-Jean-de-Luz being the chief port of the tuna boats—an industry developed since the war. Other fish frequently taken off the Basque coast are bonito, sea perch, gray mullet, and conger eels. As this is on the Atlantic (cold water) side of the Pyrenees, crustaceans and mollusks are better here than in the warm Mediterranean. Inland, the streams of the Pyrenees, like mountain streams everywhere, provide trout (this is one of the places that have been stocked with American rainbow trout), and there are salmon in the Adour, the Bidassoa, the Nive, the Nivelle, and a number of other streams.

Although oxen are used as work animals, the type of pasturage available is not particularly suited to beef or dairy cattle, so the Basques concentrate on raising smaller animals. There is a special Bayonne variation of the Celtic race of hog, and sheep are plentiful in the hills back from the coast. To compensate for the lack of cows, a breed of sheep called the Manech is one of the rare examples of this animal bred for milk rather than for wool or even meat, but a special Basque race of sheep also gives fine wool. The skill of the Basques as sheepherders is so widely known that they are imported into the United States to care for the great herds of sheep on Western ranches.

As for products of the soil, we are again in maize country. It is the chief food crop of the region. In spite of the far southern position of the Basque country, the combination of cold air from the Atlantic and the altitudes of the Pyrenees back from the coast makes it good country for that chief fruit of the temperate zone, the apple. There is even a theory that the apple orchards of Normandy and

Brittany were planted originally with trees brought from
here.

Two other growing things not particularly restricted to
the Basque country and not even exceptionally prominent
there, combined, however, with one food that is very
much a regional specialty, make up the accompaniment to
various dishes, particularly meats, known as *à la basquaise*.
This is constituted of *cèpes* sautéed, potatoes cut into regular cylinders and cooked in butter in the oven, and a pow-
dering of chopped Bayonne ham.

This last introduces us simultaneously to what is probably the best known single specialty of the Basque region,
the renowned *jambon de Bayonne;* a category of food in
which the area is particularly rich, its *charcuterie;* and what
is certainly the gastronomic capital of the Basque country,
Bayonne.

That Bayonne became a gastronomic center is owing to
the fact that it has always been rich, and therefore able to
afford luxuries. Its wealth has come from its port; though
it is some ten miles up the Adour, at the point where the
Nive enters it, the river is broad enough so that ships up to
25 feet draught can mount it to Bayonne. In older days
this meant most shipping, and the prosperity of Bayonne
was only interrupted when the entrance to the Adour was
blocked by silt, a fate with which it is constantly threatened by the churning up of the sand along the coast as a
result of the battle between the swiftly flowing river as it
enters the sea and strong currents which pass there, to say
nothing of incoming tides. The whirlpools stirred up are
so impressive that tourists visit the Bar of the Adour to
watch the swirling water. Modern dredgers now keep a
channel open, but in older days it was often blocked.

The great days of Bayonne were during the Hundred
Years' War, when Aquitaine, then including the Basque

country, was part of the Plantagenet kingdom, and the fleet of Bayonne sailed with the English fleet; the end of the sixteenth century, when access to the port was restored after a period of blockage by silt; and the end of the eighteenth century, when Bayonne became a free port, attracting a great deal of trade, while her privateers brought in spoils that enriched the city even more than the cod fishing that had been their previous occupation. During this period of her greatness Bayonne was celebrated for ironworking, and particularly for the making of weapons. The city produced one that has spread its name through the world, though few persons who use it give a thought to its origin—the bayonet.

The specialties of this rich city with its taste for fine food are many, but one is so widespread today that it is difficult to credit it with having had its origin in a single place, and that quite recently. Bayonne is famous for its chocolate. What few persons aware of this realize is that as recently as the seventeenth century, Bayonne was the only place in France where chocolate was made. The popularity of the chocolate flavor has spread so rapidly and become so habitual that it is taken as a matter of course. But if you set aside mentally the familiarity of this flavor and fix your attention upon its characteristics as one seldom does for what is well known, the exotic nature of chocolate, for a dweller in the temperate zone, will at once make itself felt. Chocolate came up from Africa to Spain, brought by the Moors. There it stayed until the Jews were expelled from Spain. Some of them came to Bayonne and taught that city the art of preparing it. It seems to have been a hotter product in those days. When Mme de Sévigné tried it, she wrote to her daughter: "It pleases you for a little while, but then all of a sudden it kindles a mortal fever in you." This has not prevented a modern company from giving its fine chocolates the brand name of Mme de

Sévigné. She may have been not without justification. Not
only does the chocolate proper seem to have come out from
its processing a good deal harsher in those days, but spices
were added to it to increase its piquancy. The Spaniards
still dose their chocolate heavily with cinnamon. In the
seventeenth century it was apparently loaded with clove
and other strong spices.

Among other specialties of Bayonne is another sweet,
pâté de cedrat, made of the lemon-like fruit we have already encountered in Corsica. Bayonne also produces a
variety of sausages and related products, of which its blood
pudding is particularly famous. The local variation of
garbure is enriched with chunks of preserved goose or preserved pork, which is put up in much the same way, and is
another regional creation. *Côtes de porc à la bayonnaise*
starts out like the Gascon version of the same dish by mar-
inating the pork chop, but after frying the chops lightly in
pork fat, adds to them *cèpes* separately cooked in oil and
new potatoes whose cooking has been started in the pork
fat, and finishes the whole together in the oven.

But the number one specialty of Bayonne is of course its
ham. The reputation of *jambon de Bayonne* is widespread,
but Bayonne does not quite deserve all the credit. Most
"Bayonne" hams come from Orthez, which is not even in
the Basque country, but in Béarn. However, the hams are
cured by having Bayonne salt rubbed into them. The ham
is otherwise raw, and is often so eaten. *Canapés à la bayonnaise* are slices of bread spread with butter mixed with
herbs, with a thin slice of Bayonne ham on top. Bayonne
ham is often used in cooking to add flavor to sauces or
stews, and when cooked for its own sake, goes particularly
well with various egg dishes. But if you want cooked Bayonne ham, you can hardly do better than to order it prepared in the local fashion, *jambon à la bayonnaise*. After it
has been well soaked, with several changes of water to get

rid of excess salt, it is boiled until it is about three quarters cooked. It is then taken from the water, skinned, scraped to get rid of grease on the surface, and then finished by being braised in Madeira wine. The customary way to serve it in Bayonne is with a rice pilaf including tomatoes, button mushrooms, and the little spicy *chipolata* sausages cooked in butter. Madeira sauce made from the juices of the final cooking of the ham is poured over the whole.

Many other specimens of *charcuterie* are to be found in Bayonne, but are not peculiar to this city. They exist throughout the Basque country. Two of the most typical are the *loukinka*, a small garlic sausage, and *tripotchka*, a type of blood pudding made from veal. The soft parts of the intestine and lungs of the calf are chopped up together and boiled. This is added to frying onions and is strongly spiced with pepper, salt, red pimento, nutmeg, and parsley. The calf's blood is used as a binding agent to make the whole into a thick paste, which is worked into a casing of intestine. It is then cooked slowly for five hours in a bouillon to which leeks, carrots, and a bunch of herbs are added.

The Basque fashion of making consommé starts out with an ordinary consommé, that is, one boiled down from meat and vegetables, to which is added some *julienne*, a concentrated essence of vegetable consommé, sweet pimentos, tomatoes, rice, and chervil. Tasty as this is, it cannot be compared to the greatest triumph of Basque cookery among soups, *ttoro*. This is a rich fish chowder utilizing a variety of the small fish of the Atlantic coast—the *bouillabaisse* of the Basque country.

Probably the most typical sea food dish of this coast is *chipirones*, inkfish. These are popular also in the Spanish Basque country, but there are likely to appear rather alarmingly swimming in their own black liquid, a forbidding looking substance. The French Basques either stuff them or serve them in some sort of casserole dish that provides them with a disguise reassuring to timid eaters.

Another characteristic Basque preparation is *piperade*. This is usually described as an omelette containing pimento and tomatoes, but everywhere that I have had it it has been, not an omelette, but scrambled eggs. It is served either as a separate course or with some other main dish, instead of a vegetable. *Œufs frits à la bayonnaise* is an interesting variety of one of those egg dishes with *jambon de Bayonne* referred to above. As many eggs fried in oil as the eater can manage are piled on a piece of bread also fried in oil, with alternate slices of Bayonne ham likewise fried. *Cèpes* go along with it. The same entry on the menu, but described as *sur le plat* instead of *frits* is just ham and eggs—finished in the oven, though—with Bayonne ham. It is likely also to come with an accompaniment of sautéed *cèpes* flavored with garlic and parsley.

It has already been noted that preserved goose is cooked in *garbure* in the Basque country. Another way of serving it is *confit d'oie à la basquaise*—a quarter of a goose cooked in goose fat and served with *cèpes* sautéed in a mixture of goose fat and olive oil, to which chopped garlic and parsley are added at the last moment. Biarritz has its own fashion of serving chicken, *poulet sauté à la biarrotte*. It is fried in oil and anointed with a sauce in which white wine, tomato sauce, and crushed garlic are combined with the cooking juices. Meanwhile *cèpes*, diced potatoes, peeled eggplant, and sliced onions have also been fried in oil and are served, each separated from the others, in little attendant heaps about the chicken.

From domestic birds one can progress to wild ones. Wild doves are a much relished sort of game in the Basque country as in the Landes, but the Basques have their own peculiar way of catching them. During the migration season they net the birds in the air as they fly through the mountain passes, shying white wooden disks at them as they fly by to frighten them into the desired direction. It is explained that the doves take the disks for hawks and fly blindly into the nets in their haste to escape, an ingenious theory, but one which has always caused me to wonder what dove revealed this bit of insight into his mental processes. One might be inclined to think that a dove might try to dodge any object thrown at him, even if he took it for a white wooden disk, but this story is told so regularly and so authoritatively that it would be rude to doubt it.

A vegetable preparation worth noting is *pommes de terre à la basquaise*. For this, long potatoes are selected and partly hollowed out in the direction of their length. They are then boiled for about five minutes and taken out of the water. Then the hollowed-out section is stuffed with a mixture of tomatoes cooked down to a concentrated essence, a sauce of which the principal ingredient is sweet pimentos cooked in oil or butter, and Bayonne ham chopped up with parsley. The stuffed potatoes are then placed in a deep buttered pan, seasoned, butter or oil is poured over them, and they are cooked slowly in the oven. Just before they are done, the pan is removed from the oven and the potatoes are covered with bread crumbs and butter, and put back in the oven to form a crust. They are served with a sauce made from veal bouillon.

The Basque dessert of which one hears the most is *ttouron*, a cake with crushed almonds and hazelnuts mixed with the flour embellished with bits of pistachio and candied fruits. More in the tradition of this country of maize is a dish more likely to be served to natives than to tourists, *milhassou*. This is made by bringing a quart of milk to a boil, moving the pot off the fire, and stirring into it half a pound of fine corn meal. When the mush thus created has about half cooled off, half a pound of butter and eight eggs go into it, along with half a pound of powdered sugar or four serving spoons of barley-sugar syrup. It is then flavored with orange-flower extract, lemon, or vanilla, poured into a mold, and cooked in a very slow oven.

Basque wines are likely to be a little thin, but are quite pleasing. A good accompaniment for fish is the dry white Herrika-Arnoa. Near Bayonne, there is a rather heady white, Anglet, which is a sand wine (*vin de sable*) like those of the Landes. Irouléguy is the best-known name among Basque wines. There are both red and white Irouléguys, with a slight flinty taste. There is a widely known liqueur, Izarra, made from wild flowers. Finally the apple trees of the region provide a cider called *pittara*. To the unaccustomed taste, it is likely to appear rather tart.

Béarn and the County of Foix

E ast of the Basque country, occupying the other two
thirds of the Basses-Pyrénées, and thus twice as large
as all three Basque provinces put together—for that matter,
it was the largest of all the Pyrenean states—lies Béarn. It
presents many superficial resemblances to the Basque
country, but its people are not Basques. Lying deeper in
the mountains, the Béarnais displayed even more strongly
than the Basques the characteristic independence of hill
peoples. Like the Basques, they had their own bill of rights,
to which even their own sovereigns had to subscribe, and
when they found themselves under the tutelage of some
overlord, whether the king of England, the king of France,

the count of Foix, or anyone else, they saw to it that within their own borders they still retained a large autonomy. Even after the territory entered definitely into the group of those united under the French crown, it enjoyed a separate regime, with its own legislature, and, what was most important of all, the right to determine through its own administrations how much taxes it would accord, as a "voluntary contribution" to the treasury of the king. There was a separate Béarnais language, a dialect of the Gascon spoken in the territories to the north and east. As for the swashbuckling tradition, the Gascons were Caspar Milquetoasts compared with the Béarnais.

Certainly the most famous Béarnais, Henry IV, was the greatest swashbuckler in the history of French royalty. He was a *bon vivant* from birth—and expressly, for on the order of his grandfather, Henri d'Albret, King of Navarre, no sooner had he been born, on December 13, 1553, than his lips were rubbed with garlic and the local Jurançon wine —not any Jurançon, but that of the Clos de Gaye, which was considered the best.

The diet of Béarn was lusty rather than sophisticated, food for trenchermen, and despite the care exercised in the choice of wine with which the infant's lips were moistened, he was not brought up as a boy in a fashion calculated to turn him into a gourmet. During the first seven years of his life, indeed, he lived as though destined to become a peasant, not a king of France one of whose epithets was to be "the Great." He almost never wore shoes before he was eight, when he had to put them on to go to school. He knew no French, speaking only the local dialect. He lived on eggs, cheese, garlic, and coarse country bread. This healthy but rather unrelieved menu may have had something to do with his later preoccupation with food, not for himself alone, though he could wolf it down with the best eaters of his day, but for everybody. It was

Henry IV, you will remember, who first expressed the objective taken up in our time by lesser swashbucklers, of "a chicken in every pot"—his wish for the Sunday dinner of his peasants.

He was capable also of taking thought for the feeding of others on occasions when it might have been expected that for personal reasons he would have shown less magnanimity. There is a characteristic incident told of a call he made without warning on his mistress, Gabrielle d'Estrées, at her Paris house at 12, rue Gît le Cœur. Gabrielle was not alone when Henry entered the building. Her companion barely had time to scramble under the bed when the King entered. Henry seated himself affably, ordered an enormous meal sent up, and when it came handed a partridge to the quaking Gabrielle, helped himself to another, and then tossed a third under the bed. "Can't let the poor devil starve," he said.

Henry IV accords perfectly with the background of the Béarn, a rugged country of hearty, not to say roistering, good living, the source of many dishes that conquered the surrounding territory with the ease with which Béarnais fighters conquered their enemies. The most complete of those conquests was that made by the Béarnais *garbure*, which spread from the peaks and valleys of Béarn to the Bigorre to the east, the Basque country to the west, and the whole of Gascony to the north.

Garbure is one of those soups which is more than a soup, providing a full meal. Everything goes into one pot—soup, vegetable, meat—which should be so crowded with good things to eat that a ladle pushed into it will stand straight up, prevented by the contents of the *garbure* from sliding to the side. There is some argument about what the name means. Arguing that the soul of *garbure* is provided by the many aromatic herbs that perfume the dish, which is indisputable, one group of theorists derives its name from *gerbe* (sprig), referring to the little bunch of mixed herbs which goes into the soup. They point out that the Béarnais word *gaburatye* means a mixture of fresh green vegetables like those which enter the soup—but this word may just as well have come from *garbure* as the other way around. The case not being proved, there is still room for the second theory, that the origin of the name is the Spanish *garbías*, stew. It could be, of course, that the word crossed the Pyrenees in the other direction. The dish itself appears to be of local creation, though the Spanish *cocida* belongs to the same general family; but then every rural district has developed something along this line, nothing being more natural in food-raising territory than to keep tossing all sorts of farm produce into a pot on the back of the stove. Whether the result becomes remarkable or not in any one version depends upon the amount of art which goes into the combination and cooking of the diverse ingredients.

The result is certainly remarkable enough in the Béarnais *garbure*, owing to the meticulous attention which is given to getting it just right. It begins with the choice of the cooking dish, which must be, Béarnais cooks insist, of earthenware with an interior glaze. There is a special name for it in the local dialect, the *toupi*. Iron or metal pots are held to spoil the taste.

There are other tricks to getting the *garbure* just right. One is to let the water boil violently before anything else is put in. Thereafter it must never be allowed to stop boiling. If the cook is afraid that the quantity of cold additions going into the soup will momentarily drop the temperature of the liquid below the boiling point, he warms the ingredients before dropping them in.

Another fine point is the order in which the different constituents go into the pot. All of them require different periods of boiling to be done to a turn, and the art of making them all reach that point simultaneously is a subtle one.

It is not safe, for instance, to assume that a potato always requires a certain length of time to cook. That can vary with the size or the hardness of the potato, and perhaps also with the number and kind of other foods in the pot. It can also vary with altitude, which is something a cook in mountainous country cannot neglect. The success of a *garbure* may often depend on the cook's instinct for balancing various imponderables against one another and coming up with the correct answer.

Generally speaking, making *garbure* begins with putting peeled potatoes, cut up into pieces, into the boiling water first. Next come other fresh vegetables—usually fava beans, string beans, and peas, but this varies with the season, the locality, and the habits of different cooks. Sometimes beans are forced through a colander to make a thicker liquid. One of the most unexpected additions, favored by some cooks in the autumn, is chestnuts, which are roasted before being put in the soup.

The seasoning usually comes after the vegetables— thyme, parsley and marjolaine, garlic, and salt and pepper —sometimes red pimento instead of the last. This is allowed to cook lengthily, an hour or so, and then cabbage leaves without the ribs, chopped fine or cut into thin lengthwise strips, are added, the pot is covered, the boiling is continued until about half an hour before the cabbage would be cooked. Now comes the moment to add the *trébuc*—the meat. If it is an ordinary day, this might be a piece of ham or bacon, a sausage, or even nothing but a ham bone, added for flavor. But if it is a festive occasion, the *trébuc* is preserved goose or pork (the latter usually anointed with a little goose fat to make the effect somewhat finer). In the Basque country, the goose or pork, or perhaps duck, is practically invariable, and even in Béarn the richer version is the only one you are likely to find in restaurants catering to tourists. The other is for home consumption, or is served in inexpensive restaurants catering to the local trade.

When the *garbure* is served, it is poured over slices of thin stale bread placed in the bottom of the soup plates. Usually bouillon and vegetables go together into this, and the meat is served separately. Sometimes, especially in summer, the meat is allowed to cool off while the soup is kept warm, so that the hot bouillon is followed by cold meat. Connoisseurs like to *faire chabrot* with *garbure*, in the Bordelais fashion—that is, pour some red wine into the last few spoonfuls of the soup. Here the word is not *chabrot* but *goudale*.

Garbure is by no means the only important soup in the Béarn cuisine—soups are the classic peasant food everywhere, especially in mountainous territory. A rather luxurious one, from the peasant point of view, is the soup made famous by Henry IV's remark—*poule au pot*, which since his time has become known as *poule au pot* "*lou nouste Henric*," or "our Henry's chicken in a pot." This is a chicken stuffed with a mixture of its own chopped liver, Bayonne ham, bread without crust, and beaten eggs, seasoned with salt, pepper, nutmeg, herbs, and a little garlic, and dampened with Armagnac and perhaps, if it is quite dry, with a little lukewarm bouillon as well. The stuffed chicken, carefully sewed up, is then boiled for an hour in the classic bouillon known as *petite marmite*, itself made by boiling down beef, marrow bones, chicken livers, hearts and giblets, turnips, leeks, celery, onions, and carrots. Twenty minutes before the chicken is done, some of the stuffing, which has been saved for the purpose, is wrapped in cabbage leaves, sausage fashion, and cooked with the chicken. This dish is sometimes called *poulet à la ficelle*, the approved way of removing the chicken from the bouillon in which it has been cooked being to fish it out by means of a string tied to its foot.

Another Béarn soup is the *ouliat*, an onion soup, served with or without a touch of vinegar. When garlic and tomatoes are added to it, it becomes *tourin*. With leeks and cheese in addition, it is known as *soupe du berger*, shepherd's soup. *Cousinette* is a sort of salad soup—that is, it is made entirely from greens: Swiss chard, chicory, sorrel, and *mauve*, the last, so named from the color of its flowers, having perhaps no equivalent in English, though it belongs to the same family as the herbs known as mallows in England.

The hams that go to market as *jambons de Bayonne* come mostly from Béarn, as has already been mentioned. The raising of pigs here is not done on a large scale, but every farmer has a few. Poultry is raised in the same manner, and preserves of pork, goose, duck, and turkey are characteristic products of the peasants. There is a *confit d'oie béarnaise* resembling the Basque dish. In this case, a quarter of preserved goose is cooked in its own fat, served with sliced potatoes also cooked in goose fat, and a seasoning of chopped parsley with a crushed clove of garlic is added at the end. This plentiful use of goose fat is characteristic of the Béarn. A heavy percentage of fats is normal in mountain diets—the rigorous climates of high altitudes demand it—but the Béarnais are particularly given to it. When you eat a meal in the Béarn, according to one French saying, you plunge in grease up to the elbows.

If poultry and hogs are raised a few together by individual peasants, sheep, on the contrary, occur in large herds. Béarn and the Basque country together raise more sheep than any other part of France except the Rouergue. Unusually enough, the first concern of the Béarn sheep-breeders, like that of some of the Basques, is neither wool nor mutton, but milk—which goes to the Rouergue to be made into Roquefort cheese. Nevertheless, there are good meat animals in the Béarn (a sheep bred especially for milk is more likely to turn out to be a good mutton-producer as well than is one bred especially for wool), and the lambs of the Ossau valley are particularly prized by gourmets. Their meat is often so tender that it can be cut with the edge of a spoon.

Cattle-raising is less extensive in the Béarn (it was commoner in the days when the province received its arms, which show two belled cows), but not so rare as to have prevented one of the favorite local dishes from being made from beef—*estoufat*, otherwise *daube de bœuf à la béarnaise*. The Béarnais method of making this dish begins by cutting the beef into large cubes, through each of which is threaded a rolled-up strip of bacon containing chopped parsley and garlic, crushed thyme and laurel, and Cognac. This is marinated for two hours before cooking in a liquid composed of red wine and Cognac into which have been cut up bits of carrots, onions, parsley, thyme, and laurel. When the meat has been well soaked, each piece is rolled in flour, and the beef is built up in layers in the cooking pot, with alternating tiers of Bayonne ham and of carrots and sliced onions previously browned in goose or pork fat. A bunch of strongly aromatic herbs goes in the center. The meat is then covered with the juice in which it has been marinated, including the vegetables that were in it, plus crushed garlic and some bouillon. This is allowed to boil for about half an hour, after which the cover is sealed on the pot and it is placed in a slow even oven to cook for four hours. It is served with *broyo*, made of corn meal cooked in vegetable bouillon until it has become a very thick mush. It can be eaten hot in this form, but if allowed to cool it becomes firm and may be cut into slices. It is in this form that it usually appears with the *daube de bœuf*, whose gravy is ladled over it copiously, making it a delicious accompaniment to the main dish.

If the traveler in the Béarn is lucky, he may have a

chance to sample *isard*, the gamy Pyrenean chamois, but the animal is becoming rare and does not appear often on menus. It is usually eaten either in the form of a *civet* in a thick wine sauce, or in a *pâté*. Trout remain plentiful, and the mountain mushrooms are particularly luscious. Roquefort does not get all the Béarn sheep's milk, so some local cheeses made from it are to be found in the region. The best known is perhaps Oleron, alias Ossau Valley cheese. Amou is also excellent. Both are best from October to May.

Before leaving the subject of Béarnais food, we should perhaps note that the tag *à la béarnaise* on a menu does not necessarily denote Béarn cooking. Unless you happen to know that a specific dish of the region is involved, you are likely to discover that the dish so described is simply one accompanied by Béarnaise sauce—which you will remember was not invented in Béarn, but in the Ile-de-France.

The story of the newborn Henry IV and Jurançon wine attests to the fact that this is wine country. The Béarnais like their wines sweet, a taste that seems to accompany a cuisine rich in fat; both preferences are typical of mountainous regions. In the matter of wines, there are a number of similarities between the Jura mountains and those of Béarn, so it is only natural to find here a grape whose relationship to Jura growths is indicated by its name. But oddly enough no Jurançon grapes are used in making red Jurançon wine, though it is a blended wine composed of juice from a number of different types of grape—all except the one from which it takes its name. It is sometimes referred to as *bouchy*, which gets rid of the misnomer.

This red wine, drinkable enough as a table wine on the spot, is not nearly as highly esteemed as is the white Jurançon, which does use the Jurançon grape, and, as the dominant wine of the region, has passed on its name to the recessive red that happens to be grown near it, in the area just south of Pau, between the Pau and Oleron torrents.

Its color varies from gold to amber. It is heavy, full-bodied, syrupy, and highly perfumed—or at least these are the qualities usually associated with it. There are also some dry white Jurançons, but they are usually thought of as exceptions. The maderization of wine, strictly speaking a disease, which is what gives it a liqueur-like quality, is much appreciated by the Béarnais, who treat their wines with the deliberate object of producing this effect. There is a danger that excess sugar will drown all fragrance except mere sweetness in these wines, but in most years the flavor is strong enough to hold its own in spite of the high sugar content.

On the northern border of Béarn, just below Armagnac, is the region known as the Pacherenc du Vic-Bilh (the lands of the old villages). Here two wines much liked in the region are grown, Madiran and Portet, which, after a decline, are now returning to favor. Madiran is a very heavy-bodied red, and like most heavy wines is both slow to mature and long-lasting. It spends five or six years in the barrel before it is ready to bottle, and then should be allowed another ten in glass. Fifty years is not too old for a Madiran, so the great vintages of 1904 and 1916 should still be drinkable. It is reputed to have tonic qualities, and is a great aid to the digestion of the heavy food of the area.

Portet provides another link with the Jura. It is a white wine which is allowed to begin to spoil on the vines, like Sauternes, but as it is not harvested until nearly Christmas, which is after the frosts in this part of the world, it more nearly resembles the frost wine of the Jura. The effect is the same as for the Sauternes and Jura frost wines—a heavy, sweet, syrupy drink.

For everyday drinking, the visitor to the region will perhaps prefer the light *rosé du Béarn,* grown at Bellocq and Salies de Béarn, in the extreme northwest corner of the region. Without the overpowering personality of the other

Béarn wines, this is an agreeable, retiring sort of beverage, which for some reason was particularly popular in Holland and northern Germany in the seventeenth century and was exported there in considerable quantity.

The County of Bigorre, today the department of the Hautes-Pyrénées, is set among the highest peaks of this range. The wall which separates it from Spain is almost impenetrable. The few passes are almost as high as the summits. It is not so inaccessible from the French side, and despite the difficulty of the terrain, is probably better known to tourists than the larger and once much more important Béarn because within its restricted territory it includes a number of places of considerable interest. The capital of Béarn, Pau, draws more visitors than Tarbes, the capital of Bigorre, but this is about the only advantage the more western territory has. In the Bigorre is one of the most remarkable natural wonders of the region, the Cirque de Gavarnie, with its Grand Cascade; here, too, are winter sports centers, like Barèges; the most important spa of the Pyrenees, Luchon (strictly speaking, in the Comminges, but though this region has been a separate country also, it is being included here with Bigorre, having no particularly individual features of its own); and most famous of all, Lourdes, one of the two greatest shrines of France.

Long before Lourdes found its religious vocation, it had a history as warlike as the other strongholds of the Pyrenees. The castle perched upon its rock was an enviable position, and the Saracens got there first when Charlemagne was fighting them. The Emperor laid siege to the castle, cutting off the enemy's supplies, and the Saracens, reduced to starvation, were about to surrender when an eagle, flying overhead with a fat trout in its talons, let the fish fall to the rock. The Saracen leader, thinking to discourage the besiegers by giving them a false idea of the food situation inside the castle, sent the fish to Charlemagne as a present.

Up to this point, the story follows faithfully the lines of that told about Carcassonne, and about a good many other European strongholds, but this one presents a refreshing difference from all the others. The ruse did not work, and the Saracens surrendered. Possibly Charlemagne had learned something from experience. If this particular confidence game had been played anywhere near as often as the legends claim, it was inevitable that sooner or later it would fail.

It might be expected that the higher mountains of the Bigorre would discourage the raising of large animals to an even greater extent than in the Béarn. But though this is also important sheep country, it goes in for larger animals, too. It is not particularly surprising that mules should be raised here extensively, for their surefootedness makes them valuable beasts of burden in high mountains, but it may seem more curious that thoroughbred horses should also be bred here. Tarbes has a famous stud, a century and a half old, where a cross between Arab and English horses is bred. This is not the only place where horse-breeding is carried on in the Pyrenees, an activity that results from the importation of Arab steeds by the Saracens, an opportunity not to be missed simply because of unfavorable terrain. Actually the land between Tarbes and Lourdes is not unfavorable. Here, to the north of the high mountains, the ground has flattened out into a plateau, and high flat land has always been pasturage country. Thus one also finds in this region a variety of cow known as the Lourdaise, while the Aure Valley among the peaks has produced a mountain breed, small and well adapted to its environment, known as the Central Pyrenean cow. The presence of these animals has the effect of increasing the amount of butter used in the cooking of Bigorre.

Nevertheless, that cooking follows very closely the example of Béarn, and goose fat is by no means disdained here. The onion soup of Béarn is also popular in the Bigorre; the chief difference is that instead of being called *ouliat* it is now *toulia*. Bigorre adds a few preparations of its own to the Béarn menu. *Omelette à la bigourdane* mixes the eggs with diced truffles and laces them with Madeira sauce. Luchon has a specialty called *pétéran*, a stew of mutton, veal, and potatoes. The Barèges region is noted for its mutton cutlets. The chief cheese of the region is Vic-en-Bigorre, best from October to May.

There is small reason for realizing today that the County of Foix was once an important realm and that in the thirteenth and fourteenth centuries its rulers were accustomed to think of themselves as being virtually on equal terms with the kings of France. This small territory, now only the eastern part of the department of the Ariège, was administered by a succession of brilliant rulers who frequently held power simultaneously over other states that dwarfed their own, but the name of Foix means little today except to historians. Even the most resplendent of the long line of the counts of Foix has sunk into obscurity—Gaston Phœbus, so called for his beauty, one of whose features was a bright shock of golden hair which may have first suggested the comparison to Apollo. Froissart wrote of him: "I never saw none like him of personage, nor of so fair form, nor so well made," an estimate that may have been exact. But it is rather more difficult to follow him when he adds: "In everything he was so perfect that he cannot be praised too much." As he killed his own son and had his brother murdered, this statement seems somewhat strong, though it is true that he may have believed the first to be about to poison him at the suggestion of the second. The County of Foix was absorbed into France, becoming one of its thirty-three "countries," in 1589 or 1607, depending on which date you care to accept as definitive. Its political absorption was accompanied by the decline of its chief profitable industries. One was bear-training. Bears caught in the Pyrenees were taught to dance and paraded about France. But the bears became fewer, though there are still some in the Aston Valley, where an occasional brown bear is seen. You are not likely, however, to be offered a steak from one. Bear is occasionally for sale in the Paris markets, but it is imported.

Among the most prized products of Foix are its ham and its sausages. This is also the part of the country which still makes the old version of the rich wine sauce (*saupiquet*) mentioned in an earlier chapter; it is applied especially to hare. In this region, however, when you see *saupiquet ariégeois* on a menu without any other addition, it is probably served on beans, whose chief function is to give you a chance to taste the sauce.

Poitrine de mouton farcie à l'ariégeoise is a more substantial dish. The breast of mutton is stuffed with bread soaked in bouillon, hashed raw ham, chopped garlic and parsley, eggs, and high seasoning. The stuffing is sewed up inside the meat, which then goes into a buttered pan along with pork cracklings, carrots, and onions. This is allowed to warm ("sweat" is the way the French recipe puts it) very gently for about fifteen minutes, and then white wine, tomato essence, and brown gravy go into it. The pan is then covered and placed in the oven for forty-five minutes to an hour. The *poitrine de mouton* is surrounded with stuffed cabbage and potatoes cooked in bouillon and butter, and the whole is liberally doused with the cooking juices.

Poulet farci à l'ariégeoise is a hearty version of the Béarn's *poule au pot*. A large pullet is stuffed with bread soaked in bouillon (sometimes milk), chopped ham, the chicken's liver, also chopped, and the giblets, previously cooked in boullion, chopped too, garlic, onion, eggs, and the blood of the chicken. The seasoning is salt, pepper, nutmeg, and parsley. This is cooked in beef *pot-au-feu* bouillon with some backmeat of salt pork. When the chicken has been cooked, it is taken out, rice or vermicelli is added to the bouillon, and this is served as the first course. It is followed by the chicken, accompanied by the salt pork and garnished with stuffed cabbage and potatoes that have also been cooked in *pot-au-feu* bouillon. Tomato sauce with garlic is provided, but not put on the chicken, individual taste deciding whether to use it or not.

The County of Foix is another place where you may have a chance to taste *isard*. You should in any case be able to find *coq au bruyère*, a sort of grouse. There are salmon trout in the streams. One of the best local vegetables is asparagus, and there is a cheese which, though called Cierp de Luchon, which would seem to attribute it to the Comminges, is nevertheless produced in the Ariège.

The Roussillon

Ｅast of the County of Foix, for the rest of the distance to the Mediterranean, we encounter a mosaic of small but more or less distinct territories, each partitioned off from its neighbors by the mountains that box it in. Most of them will demand little attention. Their cooking, and for that matter many of their local customs, differ only in detail from those of their neighbors. The exception, and it is an important one, is the territory along the Spanish frontier. This is Catalan country, the second appearance in this region of a non-French culture straddling the Pyrenees between France and Spain. The Basques appeared at the west like the opening of a parenthesis; the Catalans stand at the east like its close.

Before we look at this territory, which will demand attention in detail, we can dispose quickly of what lies to the north. In the upper tier of territories, the Pays de Sault lies against the County of Foix. It is a high plateau at the edge of the Pyrenees, heavily wooded, of harsh climate, severe, and little visited. It eats the food of Foix, but not richly; it is poor country. Of local specialties, there is nothing notable except ham and sausages.

Next east is the Corbières, the last mountainous rampart of the Pyrenees, savage and difficult country, whose nature makes it easy to understand why, until the time of Louis XIV, this constituted the frontier between France and Spain. A chain of five strong fortresses, now all in ruins, defended the border, lying just south of Carcassonne, which constituted the main defensive position once French (or Languedocian) territory had been entered. Corbières also follows the cooking of the County of Foix, and its own contributions to the menu have dwindled of late years as sheepherding has declined. Like its neighbor, it produces ham and sausages. As for growing things, the soil is poor, and there has never been much agriculture in this region. However, Corbières has one asset that requires mention—its wines. They are not very well known outside of their own region, though as it happens the first time I ever tasted Corbières was in Paris, and I found it excellent, even so far from home. It has the qualities that enable a wine to travel well, and has begun to be advertised in Paris as a table wine. It is full-bodied, dark-red in color, and has a rich perfume, perhaps because of the same factors that on this soil and in this mountain air make herbs so piquant. Some of the Corbières wines are likely to be rather coarse; but Pitou, from a region that enjoys exceptionally favorable conditions, is a subtle wine deserving to be more widely known than it is.

The second tier of territories begins with the High Val-

XVIII · *The Roussillon*

ley of the Aude, through which some devotees of winter sports may have passed, as Mont Louis lies at its head, though by the time it is reached you are in the Cerdagne, which you enter even more deeply if you move on to the more famous winter resort of Font Romeu, not far away. The High Valley of the Aude shares the independent attitude of the Pyrenean states to the west; as late as 1848, it tried to set itself up as an independent republic. It also shares their diet, but here a difference begins to set in. While the chief specialty of the area is sausages, the ones made here are of the Catalan type. The influence of the cuisine to the south is beginning to make itself felt.

East of the Aude region is Le Fenouillet, another neglected area, though music-lovers who have found their way to Prades for the festivals of Pablo Casals may have passed through it. Prades, itself in Catalan country, lies on the main road that passes through Le Fenouillet. Again we have little to consider in the way of gastronomic contributions. The only one that needs to be mentioned is the wine of Maury, a *grenache*—an extremely sweet wine that sets my teeth on edge, but seems to have less unfortunate effects on admirers of syrupy drinks. Some of the Maury wine goes into a trademarked *apéritif*, Byrrh, whose cellars here are open to the public.

This brings us to the third and last tier of regions, the fascinating group along the Spanish frontier. Although it has its subdivisions, this whole territory is often lumped together under the name of the Roussillon, which more strictly should be applied only to the eastern end of it, lying along the Mediterranean. However, it all came into France in one piece and under that one name when Louis XIV signed the Treaty of the Pyrenees with Spain in 1659. It has all remained in one piece since also, for it is virtually congruent with the modern department of the Pyrénées-Orientales.

The whole of this territory had been included within a single political unit at one time before it was ceded to France. It was in the thirteenth century part of a curiously constituted and now forgotten state, the Kingdom of Mallorca, which combined the Balearic Islands, the Languedocian city of Montpellier, and all the territory later ceded to France as the Roussillon. Its capital was the now French city of Perpignan, and its life was short—the time for three kings to reign briefly, after which Aragon took it over and it became part of Catalonia, an autonomous region inside the government of Aragon. Today, on the French side of the border as well as on the Spanish, the local language remains Catalan. The buildings recall Spain, as do the customs—Perpignan has an Easter procession of penitents which resembles that of Seville. With the approach to the Mediterranean, the olive reappears in force. The cooking of the Catalans, like the cooking of Spain and the cooking of Provence, is based on olive oil.

Farthest west of the Roussillon territories is the Cerdagne, a high plateau that lies across the French-Spanish border, *meytat de França, meytat d'Espagna* (half in France, half in Spain) in the Catalan phrase. It has its own history of independent existence apart from the rest of the Roussillon, and its own type of cooking. This last was almost inevitable, for there is no resemblance between the local food resources of the Roussillon plain (and, of course, its products of the sea) and those of the high Cerdagne plateau. The latter naturally goes in for mountain food, but because of its comparative flatness in the midst of the surrounding mountains (it is believed to occupy the basin of a vanished prehistoric lake), produces some foods not typical of mountains. This level land lies at a high altitude, but the climatic effects of height are partly counteracted by plenty of southern sun, which permits the growing of grain. The Cerdagne is also able, like Foix on another plateau, to raise cattle, and has a special hardy variety of the Gascon cow, known as the Carolaise (from the village of La Tour de Carol, which means The Tower of Charlemagne).

Cerdagne cooking is a complex amalgam achieved by a fusion of a good many different elements. The base is the Catalan cuisine, as it exists across the frontier, which has many characteristics in common with that of Provence. Its favorite cooking method is frying. Its favorite ingredients are tomatoes, eggplant, and beans, its favorite flavorings garlic, saffron, and hot seasonings like red pimentos and cayenne pepper. Its favorite fat is olive oil. In France this Spanish cuisine was exposed to the influence of the cooking of Languedoc and altered by it. It remained nevertheless basically the cuisine of a warm country of comparatively low altitude. The high Cerdagne had to modify it, and in so doing added elements borrowed from the similarly mountainous County of Foix to the northwest.

In the soup category, the Cerdagne has its own variety of *potée*, the *braou bouffat* (literally, good eating). This is good game country, making a specialty of partridge cooked with *morilles* mushrooms. This is also one of the regions where finding a *civet d'isard* is not entirely out of the question. For the rest, virtually all the Catalan dishes except sea food, which will be mentioned shortly, are available in the Cerdagne as well. One Catalan eating habit, that of using a great deal of fruit, is not very well served in the Cerdagne, for the altitude limits its fruit production to apples, pears, and a few grapes. The pears, however, are of particularly good quality.

The territory separating the Cerdagne from the coastal Roussillon is, on the contrary, particularly noted for fruit. This is the Vallespir. The High Vallespir, which lies just next to the Cerdagne, and is the southernmost extension of the mainland of France, is not the place to look for it: here the altitude permits orchards and vegetable gardens to be located only in the bottoms of the deepest valleys, though there are chestnut forests, and pasturage is practical. But as one moves toward the sea, into Lower Vallespir, the effect of the warm Mediterranean begins to make itself felt, and at Céret the heart of the fruit-growing region of the Catalan country is reached.

Céret has another claim to fame. A little town of five thousand inhabitants apparently lost in the valley of the Tech among the now dwindling Pyrenees, it possesses in its local museum works by Picasso, Dufy, Chagall, and other modern artists which much larger institutions would be proud to hang. Its monument to the dead, a form of sculpture which in France as elsewhere seems to evoke the worst examples of official statuary, was executed here by no less an artist than Maillol. (There is also a statue by Manolo.) The explanation for this unexampled richness in a little town is that about 1910 its rural charm was discovered by a group of young and then rather generally despised artists. Picasso, Braque, and Manolo met here for the first time. Juan Gris, Kisling, Max Jacob, and others soon joined them. Céret became known as the Barbizon of Cubism. The artists who gave it this temporary fame have now abandoned it, or have died, but their works remain; and Céret, undisturbed by the Cubist example, produces now as before orthodox symmetrical cherries. The first cherries of France come from here, ripening even before those of the Riviera, in April. Cherries are the chief product of Céret, though not the only one (spring peas are another specialty), but in the surrounding country all sorts of fruits and vegetables are grown—Ille-sur-Têt, for instance, is famous for its peaches, and produces early spring vegetables as well.

The descent from the mountains to the coast brings the visitor into a new world. In the western Pyrenees the influence of the blustery Atlantic, and in the central Pyrenees the altitude, have made it possible to forget that this is the most southerly part of France. But on the coastal plain of the Roussillon, on the warm shores of the Mediterranean, the south comes into its own.

In this region, the Catalan cuisine is met in its full expansion. It can draw on the products of a more fertile soil and the riches of the Inland Sea. All about Perpignan, fruits and vegetables grow in profusion—melons, peaches, apricots, cherries, strawberries, and, on the higher levels, apples and pears. Anchovies, sardines, *rouget*, and lobster are the principal catches in this part of the Mediterranean. The cooking is dominated by garlic and olive oil. It is a Catalan habit to start the day with a tribute to these two savors by breakfasting on *el pa y all*—a slice of bread rubbed with garlic and moistened by a few drops of olive oil. The description *à la catalane*, applied to a dish whose special character you do not happen to know, will probably mean that it is sautéed in oil and accompanied with diced eggplant and a pilaf of rice soaked in tomato sauce.

The most famous of Catalan dishes is *ouillade*, the Catalan *potée*. It takes its name from the dish, or rather the dishes, in which it is made, the *ouilles*. Two are required, for the main part of this soup or stew is made in one vessel and the beans that are to go into it, as in so many other Catalan dishes, are cooked separately and added to the rest only at the last moment. The *ouilles* should never be allowed to grow cold and should never be washed. As they are presumably always kept filled with simmering *ouillade*, they never have the opportunity, in a sense, to become dirty. Washing would be superfluous.

As in the case of most *potées*, there is wide latitude on what can go into the Catalan soup. Whatever else may be included, beans in one pot must be balanced by cabbage in the other. The beans, except for seasoning—herbs and garlic—cook alone. The cabbage is accompanied by whatever else the cook sees fit to put into the pot—assorted vegetables, perhaps some pork, and of course the herbs and garlic. The name of *ouillade* is sometimes applied also, though this seems to be a misattribution, to a garlic-and-egg soup of the region. Some cooks cut the Gordian knot of this puzzle of nomenclature by combining the two soups, adding egg and a little more garlic to the cabbage department of the classic *ouillade*.

Because it possesses a coast, the Roussillon naturally has also its own version of *bouillabaisse*, sometimes referred to as *bouillabaisse catalane*. It does not resemble the Marseilles dish, using neither the same fish nor so rich a variety of them, and its seasoning is less subtle. It is called locally *bouillinade des pêcheurs*.

Catalan sausages run to the salami type—dry, highly spiced, and fragrant with garlic. An hors d'œuvre ascribed to the most enchanting of the fishing villages along the shore is an anchovy or two cooked into a bun—*pâté aux anchois de Collioure*. Snails are often eaten here to start a meal. They are called *cargolades*, are served grilled, and are not recommended in the summer. As the Catalan proverb puts it, "in July, neither snails nor women."

One might expect, in a part of the country that derives some of its inspiration from Spain, to meet here that most famous of Spanish dishes, *paella*. But Spanish rice has not crossed the border. This is no doubt because even in Spain *paella* is not a Catalan dish. It is commonly served in Barcelona, the Catalan capital, but it is a foreigner there, imported from Valencia. So it has not moved into French Catalonia. But another great Spanish favorite, the omelette in a bewildering number of combinations is popular everywhere. There is nothing non-French about omelettes, of course, but the importance they assume in the menu, and the tendency to combine the eggs with southern vegetables, is highly reminiscent of Spain. They are made with tomato (a particular favorite in Spain), pimento, wild asparagus tips, red peppers, eggplant, mushrooms, ham, and all sorts of combinations of these ingredients. Fried eggs *à la catalane* are presented on a bed of half tomatoes and slices of eggplant, separately fried in oil, hotly peppered, and flavored with chopped parsley and garlic.

Among the many individual dishes described as Catalan is *saucisses à la catalan*—which is not made with the type of Catalan sausage described above, but with the long soft variety bought by length, curled up like a garden hose. The chief characteristic of the Catalan way of cooking it is the overpowering amount of garlic used (no rarity in Catalan cooking)—twenty-four cloves of it for a kilogram (2.2 pounds) of sausage. The sausage is first browned in pork fat. Then it is taken out of the dish, and to the remaining juice flour, white wine, consommé, and tomato extract are added and cooked together for about fifteen minutes. This sauce is then removed from the cooking dish and strained. The sausage goes back in, accompanied with the two dozen pieces of garlic and a bunch of assorted herbs into the middle of which has been thrust a bit of bitter orange peel (a seasoning frequently encountered in Catalan cooking). The sauce is now poured over the sausage, the dish is covered, and it is allowed to simmer gently for half an hour.

The bitter orange appears again, this time complete, not just in the form of peel, in the Catalan fashion of cooking partridge. *Perdreau à la catalane* surrounds the bird with the little bitter oranges, cooking them together. The result is even more mouth-watering than the Rouennais combination of duck with oranges. Other wild birds found frequently here are *ortolans* and *étourneaux,* the latter looking like lark-sized blackbirds. Both of these small birds are hunted from small stone blinds.

You may meet in Catalonia the dish known as *épaule de mouton à la catalane*, which also appears as *pistache de mouton*, but it seems probable that this dish originated in Languedoc just to the north, and was so named because of two resemblances to Catalan dishes—it uses a great deal of garlic (fifty cloves for a shoulder of mutton) and it tucks bitter orange peel into the bunch of herbs which goes into the cooking. One reason for doubting its authentically Catalan nature is that it is cooked in goose fat, while the Catalans would presumably use oil. It is not strange if it has worked itself back into the region for which it was named even if it did not start there, for a good many creations of the neighboring province of Languedoc have done just that (and may, as we have already seen, have shared Spanish inspiration with Catalan cooking anyway). Doubt as to its origin need deter no one from trying it. It is a boned shoulder of mutton tied up into a roll, cooked in a casserole along with raw unsmoked ham, onions, and carrots, and flavored with a wine-bouillon sauce, and, of course, all that garlic. You may run into the word *pistache* in the same sense in which it is applied to this dish elsewhere in southwest France in which case you should be warned that it does not mean that pistachio has been used in the dish, but that its sole accompaniment is garlic, and lots of it. The usage is most frequent with mutton, but you may find it applied to partridge and pigeon also. *Perdreau* (or *pigeon*) *aux pistaches* is with pistachio nuts; *en pistache* is with garlic. If either of these two birds is described on the menu as *à la catalane*, expect the same treatment as if it read *en pistache*.

A favorite vegetable dish is *aubergines au gratin à la catalane*. This is stuffed eggplant, the stuffing being made with the pulp of the vegetable itself chopped up with a hard-boiled egg, onion cooked into near nothingness in olive oil, bread, parsley, and garlic. To get the *gratin* (crust) effect, the half eggplants thus stuffed are sprinkled with bread crumbs, dampened with olive oil, and cooked in the oven.

On the coast, the most characteristic sea food dish is probably *civet de langouste*. This lobster stew is basically the same dish as the much-disputed *homard* (in this case, *langouste*) *à l'américaine*. The tail of the animal is cut into chunks following its natural folds and is browned in olive oil. It is then taken out, and chopped onions, shallots, parsley, tarragon, plenty of tomatoes, and a great deal of garlic go in. (The chief difference between the Catalan dish and *langouste à l'américain* is that the former increases the percentage of tomato and garlic.) The lobster then goes back in and is enriched with white wine, fish bouillon, a little Cognac, and a dash of cayenne pepper. It becomes even more Catalan when it is described as *civet de langouste au Banyuls,* for the wine used in this case is local—a dry Banyuls the recipes specify, though I have never tasted a Banyuls that struck me as really dry. I suppose it is a relative description.

The two fish most eaten on the Roussillon coast are sardines and anchovies. The *rouget* exists here, but does not seem to be as popular as on the coast of Provence. It does not seem to be as good either, perhaps because the Catalans cook it differently, perhaps because a different type of sea bottom and different feeding habits have affected the taste. There are special Catalan treatments for the Mediterranean tuna, eels, and even mussels, though, as has already been noted, the last are less good in the Mediterranean than the Atlantic. But none of these rival the sardine and the anchovy. With cold fish, a good accompaniment is Collioure sauce. This is mayonnaise plus anchovy paste, chopped parsley, and grated garlic—except for the anchovy, much the same as the noted *aïoli* of Provence.

The Catalans have a sweet tooth, their pastries suggesting a borrowing from the desserts the Moors introduced into Spain. Nougat is a specialty of the region. *Touron* is a cake, usually ring-shaped, made with crushed almonds, white of egg, ordinary and confectioner's sugar, and ground pistachios. Almonds are also used in the cakes known as *rosquillas*. *Bunyetes* is simply the Catalan form of the French word *beignets*—fritters.

The Catalan sweet tooth extends also to wines. The effect, even when they are natural, is that of "cooked" wines. They are often drunk as *apéritifs*, if not as dessert wines. Banyuls in particular is considered an inexpensive domestic substitute for port. It does not have the richness of port; however, the popes found it pleasing when they were at Avignon, and a good deal of Banyuls was sent there.

Most of the other wines of this region—Rincio de Roussillon, Muscat, Malvoisie, Grenache—are also sweet. They are so close to being natural *apéritifs* or liqueurs that it was an obvious step to process them slightly and offer them as such. Perpignan is the center of this industry.

There are some wines in the region which will be a relief to those who do not appreciate the syrupy varieties. Salces produces a pleasant *rosé* called Sainte-Colombe. Collioures does not seem to be credited with a wine of its own in any of the listings, and its position just next to Banyuls should indicate sweet wines here also, but I recall drinking a rather dry, pleasant table wine there once which I was told was locally grown. Perpignan, which treasures a legend of its origin crediting the river Têt with having directed the city's founder, Father Pinya (Père Pinya) to a propitious spot to establish his vineyard, offers a wine called Père Pigne, apparently to recall the story. It seems to have no other claim to fame.

A NOTE ON
RESTAURANTS

The original edition of this book contained two lists of restaurants, one of establishments in Paris which offered worthy versions of provincial cooking, the other of restaurants throughout France which specialized in the cuisine of their regions. These lists have disappeared from this edition, and no one regrets it more than the author; for the reason is, alas, the present instability of French restaurants. The lists given in this book in 1958 would have to be almost completely revised for 1977; and as change is faster now, any new list would certainly be outdated, and consequently misleading, within the lifetime of this book.

I have therefore been obliged, reluctantly, to forgo listing recommended restaurants. I can only suggest to the traveler in France that he acquire the red Michelin guide, which is revised yearly and is thus able to keep up, more or less, with the frequent changes. It is not infallible—as it happens, the only two completely inedible meals I have ever had in France were both in restaurants to which Michelin had given a star—but it is the best there is. This is the guide to whose accolade one refers in speaking of one-star, two-star or three-star restaurants in France. Do not confuse this with the stars of the Tourist Hotels, awarded by the governmental tourist bureau, which have more to do with the general standard of the hotel than with its cooking.

In Paris, the Julliard Guide, a newcomer in the field, is highly reliable, and for those interested in regional cooking, it prints a listing of the Parisian restaurants which specialize in provincial dishes.

Except for these recommendations, I fear I must leave you on your own. Here is one tip, however: French restaurants ordinarily post their menus outside, and you can tell a great deal about the character of a restaurant from its menu. A sloppily presented menu is likely to indicate a sloppily run kitchen. A menu which contains nothing except run-of-the-mill dishes probably means that no one in the place is making much of an effort to set an interesting table. In the provinces, the listing of regional dishes is a good sign. The presence of specialties, especially unusual specialties, is another. So is a reasonably diverse choice of honest wines, for an establishment too modest to have a separate wine card. In general, a restaurant which takes pains about its food takes pains also to produce an attractive menu to go with it. Beware, however, of too much quaintness in a menu. When a restaurant starts describing its dishes in elaborate self-conscious terms or by employing a quaint medieval vocabulary, you are likely to find yourself confronted with a purely verbal exercise. Coyness in the menu is being used to distract attention from the shortcomings of the food. This is the French equivalent of our Olde English Tea Shoppes in the United States, a disease which France has not entirely escaped. There is, for instance, in the otherwise admirable town of Vézelay, an Olde Crusaders' Snack Bar.

I might add here one observation made, after a tour of France's noted restaurants, by the publisher of this book, Alfred A. Knopf, a trencherman of quality. He remarked that nowadays it is more rewarding to explore among two-star restaurants (Michelin stars, of course) than among the rare three-star establishments. It is a fact that three-star restaurants have become inordinately expensive—more expensive, that is, than the quality of the food, the pleasantness of the location, and the skill of the service justifies—and not a few of them have tended to become snobbish and to look down their noses at customers who may have ideas of their own about what they would like to order. I would still put at the head of French restaurants, from my own personal experiences in recent years, the three-star Père Bise at Talloires, on the lake of Annecy, though I must confess that I have not had occasion to try the three latest restaurants to receive three stars. But in Paris, where there are five three-star restaurants, I would cross at least three of them off the list. They seem to me to be coasting on past reputations.

GENERAL INDEX

This is not a guidebook; but with the help of this index it can serve as one. To save time, consult references given in **boldface type**; these are the most important. Cross references may refer to either of the two indexes. The following abbreviations are used: cath. = cathedral(s); ch. = cheese(s); chât. = château(x); edv. = eau-de-vie; liq. = liqueur; mt. = mountain(s); mus. = museum(s); R or rest. = restaurant(s); riv. = river; val. = valley; w. = wine(s).

Abbeville, 102
Abelard, 105, 181
absinthe, 207, 392
acacia flowers, 377
Adour riv., 404, 415, 424
Agde, 292, 293, 298
Agen, 52, 153, 162, 283
agneau: au lait, 337; *de Pauillac*, 159
Aiguesmortes, 290, 293, 302
Ain riv., 206, 208
airelle, 17; *see also* cranberry
Aise w., 232, 274
Aix-en-Provence, 318, 341, 343
Alaric II, 22
Albi, 37, 296–7, 300, 303, 309, 310
Alès, 288
Alesia, 177, 260
Alicante, 341
aligot ch., 286
aligoté: grape, 199; w., 194
Alise-Sainte-Reine, 177
Allier: riv., 183, 268; val., 258
almond, 340, 392; cake, 341, 420, 448; cookie, 309; Jordan, 195, 253, 309, 342
Alps, 224–34, 385; ch., 229–31

Alsace, 138, 237–8, 244; climate, 245; cooking, **244–5**, 254; language, 241–2; map, 239; wine, 244, **253–5**
Alsace-Lorraine, 10–11, 203, **239–56**
Amadour, St., 283
Amboise, 31, 35, 44; chât., 22, 40, 134
Ambonnay w., 110, 111
Amiens, 100, 103; cath., 63
Aminea vines, 284
Amou ch., 430
anchovy, 370, 371, 375, 376, 388, 444, 447
Andorra, 397, 398
Anet chât., 64
Angers, 26, 92, 94, 95
Anglet w., 421
Angoulême, 30, **163R**; cath., 114, 163
Angoumois, 93, 152, 162–7; map, 151; rest.; w., 163
anis, 195, 253, 392
Anjou, 21, 39, 60, 91–6; cooking, 94; cheese, 94–5; counts of, 92, 113; map, 23; w., 95–6

i

General Index

General Index

INDEX OF FOODS AND DISHES

This is not a cookbook; but a good natural cook may be able to reproduce some of the dishes here named, even though exact proportions and cooking techniques are not ordinarily given. The creations described in sufficient detail to make this possible are marked below with an asterisk (*).

Index of Foods and Dishes

fricassée, 279
fricassée à la périgourdine, 93–4*
fricassée de cèpes à la quercynoise, 283
fricassée de choux verts, 93*
fritter, 372, 377, 448; corn, 282;
oyster, 129
friture de la Loire, 47
friture de poissons, 373
frog: legs, 90; soup, 217

galantine, 50, 349, 277
galimafrée, 68
galinette, 354
ganses, 377
garbure, 161, 404, 412, 417, 424–7*
gâteau: de Compiègne, d'Etampes,
80
gaudes, 209
German-fried potatoes, 197
gigot de mouton à la bretonne,
141
gigot de mouton de Sologne à
l'eau, 86
gigorit, 90, 162
gimblettes, 309
gingerbread, 188, 194, 251
gnocchis à la niçoise, 375
gogues, 94
goose, roast, 247
gougère, 107, 193; de l'Aube, 107
gounerre, 195
graisse normande, 120
grape-pickers' soup, 157–8
gras double, 288; à la lyonnaise,
197
gratin, 446–7, 229–30
gratin de queues d'écrevisses, 215
gratin languedocien, 229–30
gratinée (onion soup), 279
grenouilles à la luçonnaise, 90
grives, 268, 288
guillaret, 94

halicot (haricot) de mouton, 80
hochepot, 104–5
homard à l'américaine (armoricaine), 77, 447; à la provençale,
77

hure, de porc à la parisienne, 80
hutspot, 104

jambon à l'alsacienne, 249
jambon à la bayonnaise, 417–18*
jambon de Bayonne, 415, 417, 419,
428
jambon de gibier, 45
jambon de volaille, 44–5
jambon glacé de Paris, 80
janots, 309
jau, 193
julienne, 250, 418

Kaffee krantz, 251
kokeboterom, 104
Kugelhopf, 251

lamb and beans, 88
lamb, leg of, 267–8
lamproies au vin rouge, 158–9
langouste à la calvaise, 388
lapereau à la solognote, 85
lapin de garenne aux pruneaux,
104
lièvre à la périgourdine, 272–3*
lièvre à la royale, 272–3*
lièvre en terrine, 85
lièvre étoffé à la périgourdine,
280–1*
lièvre farci en cabessal, 273
limousine, à la, 272
lochois, 53
lonzo, 389
lou fassum, 368
lou pastis en pott, 156–7*
loup de mer, 354, 362–3, 373

macaroni, 230, 390
macaroons, 53, 128, 160, 253, 274
madeleines, 253, 274
massepain, 274
matafan, 87
matefaim, 87
matelote, 69, 76, 78, 194, 250
matelote à la normande, 129–30
matelote d'anguille, 47, 93, 101
matelote de Beauvais, 80
menon, 376

About the Author

WAVERLEY ROOT has been eating in Europe and writing about it for over 40 years. A veteran foreign correspondent, he has represented the *Chicago Tribune, Washington Post,* United Press, *Time* and the Mutual Broadcasting System, and has been Paris correspondent for the Danish *Politiken.* He also contributes frequently to *The New York Times Magazine, The International Herald Tribune,* and *Gourmet.* Mr. Root is an officer in the French Legion of Honor and a leading authority on French and Italian restaurants. His published books include *The Food of Italy, Contemporary French Cooking, The Paris Dining Guide, The Best of Italian Cooking* and *Eating In America* (with Richard de Rochemont). He lives abroad.